The Power of Maps and the Politics of Borders

The Power of Maps and the Politics of Borders

Papers from the conference held at the American Philosophical Society

October 2019

Edited by
American Philosophical Society

American Philosophical Society Press

Philadelphia

Transactions of the
American Philosophical Society
Held at Philadelphia
for Promoting Useful Knowledge
Volume 110, Part 4

ISBN: 978-1-60618-104-1
Ebook ISBN: 978-1-60618-109-6
U.S. ISSN: 0065-9746

Library of Congress Control Number: 2021906609

Contents

Contributor List

George Gallwey, Harvard University

Nicholas Gliserman, Independent Scholar

Penelope K. Hardy, University of Wisconsin–La Crosse

Lucas P. Kelley, University of North Carolina–Chapel Hill

Katie McKinney, Colonial Williamsburg Foundation

Derek O'Leary, Bard High School Early College, Washington, DC

Julie L. Reed, Pennsylvania State University

Jackson Pearson, Texas Christian University

David I. Spanagel, Worcester Polytechnic Institute

Billy G. Smith, Montana State University

Austin Stewart, Lehigh University

Agnès Trouillet, Université Paris Nanterre

Introduction

Unpacking the Meaning of Maps, Power, and Boundaries

Nicholas Gliserman

THE DECADES FOLLOWING THE American Revolution were a period of enormous contingency for the newly minted United States of America. Anybody who has studied the drafting and ratification of the U.S. Constitution, for example, understands the very real possibility that the government today we take quite for granted came very close at many points to never existing. Many of the important, open-ended questions of the day were of a spatial nature, for example: What would the *shape* of the nation be, or What was America's *place* in the world? These spatial questions were closely related to other contemporary questions, such as: Who was to be included in the nation/citizenry? Where might power rest in the seesaw of state and national governments? Would land, trade, or industry define the national economy? Scholars looking to investigate these spatial questions might consult many kinds of sources, but maps should be at the top of their list.[1]

This volume takes up the role of maps and mapping in the early American republic. It grows out of an exhibit and conference at the American Philosophical Society. Why might such a volume be useful and necessary now? After all, it's already been a few decades since an international coalition of geographers, literary critics, historians, art historians, and post-structuralist theoreticians invigorated the study of historical maps! First, the field has changed since then, gradually shifting away from a view that maps held a kind of monolithic, almost disembodied kind of power. This present volume exemplifies the emerging consensus that if maps had power, it's largely because people gave them that power. Second, the history of cartography has unevenly penetrated the broader study of history. Many historians might use old maps as book covers or illustrations but remained perplexed by them as historical evidence. I hope this brief introduction can help demystify maps while, at the same time, showing their value in understanding history, particularly of the early United States.

The first thing to understand is just how prominently maps figured into the cultural, social, and political life of the young nation. Perhaps nothing illustrates this better than the facts that the first president began his adult life as a professional surveyor and that the third was the son of a surveyor. Or that land speculation was a major cause of the American Revolution and helped to fund the national government afterward. Dozens of trained military engineers, surveyors, and draftsmen had come to North America during the Seven Years War, many of whom remained in America to conduct geographical surveys of the British colonies. These surveys ended abruptly with the coming of the Revolutionary War, but the knowledge gained would fuel map printing during and after that war. Maps helped Americans to understand the world around them during the war and afterward, as domestic map printing emerged in the Early Republic, they helped to shape an emerging national consciousness. In this volume, for example, Katie McKinney explores how Major Sebastian Bauman used his 1782 map of the Battle of Yorktown to frame the battlefield as the birthplace of a new nation. After the war, maps also shaped how prominent political figures thought about political economy, infrastructure, westward expansion, and natural history—as George Gallwey illustrates in his piece on Albert Gallatin. To fully appreciate the implications of maps and mapping in this period, though, more context is helpful.[2]

Defining "Maps"

What is a map, anyway? We might extend that question by asking how our historical subjects might have answered it. We could say "maps *are* . . ." followed by a list of characteristics. Some scholars have even rejected the utility of the word "map" because it assumes a particular mindset or ideal. There's nothing wrong with these approaches or objections. Yet, to arrive at an all-encompassing definition, I like to start with what maps *do*: They diagram or represent relationships—often, but not necessarily, spatial relationships, occurring at or near the surface of the Earth. Maps help humans understand nonlinear relationships. Anybody who has read the text of a land deed, which linearly narrates the twists and turns of a plot of land, appreciates why it's so much easier to see those same boundary lines represented visually. You can now follow the boundary in either direction, grasp the overall shape of the parcel, and intuit spatial relationships not explicitly defined by the text (such as the distance between nonadjacent vertices). This verb-oriented definition also reminds us that, while maps might be static objects, they grow out of practices such as navigating an environment or visually representing information. So the map as artifact can help historians reconstruct mental and physical mapping processes.[3]

"Diagram" and "represent" are not the only verbs we might use to understand maps. "Misrepresent" is another good one. You see, maps of the geospatial variety inevitably fail at the thing they try to do. You could be forgiven for thinking that we might want to carve out an exception for ourselves in the present—we have better tools, after all, right? And it's true that a sophisticated GPS device, receiving signals from an array of satellites under ideal conditions, can with proper methods locate its own position on Earth within centimeters. Yet while the precision of our tools has increased, basic issues remain. First, a map can't show everything. Mapmakers must decide to include *this* kind of geographic phenomenon but not *that* one. Second, it's mathematically impossible to derive a flat surface from a sphere— and as the Earth bulges along the equator (this now-accepted theory was first tested in the eighteenth century) and has an uneven surface, this task is even more impossible. So any attempt to represent what's happening along the Earth's surface on a flat plane will inevitably distort that space in some way. Really, these are actually quite high-level concerns. Some mapmakers worked with bad information. Others just plain made things up as they went along. And everybody who has ever made a map is biased in some way. Mapmakers used and continue using their maps for their own purposes.[4]

"Ontology" is no verb, but it merits mention here: If maps represent something, they must draw upon an existing framework of meaning to do that representing. How does a society understand truth? How does the interaction of people with their environment shape what they want to map? How do they define and represent the phenomena in the map? How do they understand and measure space? When we start considering these questions, we begin to circle back to the first approach I briefly floated for defining "map"—i.e., asking how our historical subjects might have defined the term. Many of the papers in this volume concern indigenous mapping. Julie Reed, for example, helps us see the rich world of foods, scents, plants, animals, and myths that underpinned vertical maps made by Cherokee artists on the walls of sacred cave sites. In British America and the early United States, Euro-Americans often dismissed these kinds of maps because they did not conform to their own ontology. In their contributions to this volume, Austin Stewart and Lucas Kelley examine how Chickasaw and Cherokee negotiators sometimes adopted the ontological framework of these colonizing powers in attempts to preserve their territorial claims. These case studies illustrate that Native peoples were not simply victims of European maps but could and did use their geographical knowledge to their advantage.[5]

Time matters with regard to ontology. First, systems of meaning can and do change over time. Second, the culturally specific meaning, experience, and knowledge of time is a critical dimension of an ontology. On this point, we may consider the mapping of the ocean floor, which evolved from aiding navigation to later answering scientific questions about geological conditions or the circumstances (e.g., temperature, pressure, depth) in which different species lived—the focus of Penelope Hardy's article. These new lines of inquiry reflected a growing scientific consensus, which cast doubt on the Biblical timeline of the Earth. New questions about geological and evolutionary time frames animated this cartographic project and raised the stakes of locating rocks and fossils on the ocean's floor. Simply put, what these things meant in a broader regime of truth had shifted dramatically. It's a helpful reminder that if our own ideas of truth are informed by the satellites in the sky pinging the phones in our pockets, as we write history, we need to be careful to distinguish our ways of knowing in the present from those of our forebears in the past.

Maps and Power

In considering the "power of maps," we should avoid thinking of "power" in monolithic terms: Maps exerted many kinds of power and sometimes none at all. In a few cases, specific maps shaped worldviews, changed minds, and had dramatic consequences. In other cases, power rested in the cumulative effects of many maps. One stamp with the image of the nation-state might not accomplish much except for the fact it was one of millions in circulation; that critical mass may have helped fan the flames of nationalism. Some maps were used infrequently but proved immensely valuable when needed, such as cadastral maps used in land management or legal proceedings.[6]

Yet if some maps exerted concrete influence, others possessed little direct power in and of themselves, receding into the background. Hence, the question of maps and power is filled with paradox and contradiction. In my own research into mapping colonial America, for example, I have seen countless examples where a colonial governor or a military engineer sent a manuscript map to an imperial authority who thanked them for the great map but didn't quite know what else to say. They felt that the map mattered but lacked a specific understanding of why. These maps might slumber for centuries in imperial archives without guiding a single policy decision or diplomatic victory. Yet people continued to produce, send, and request maps, believing they could help advance their careers or illustrate their arguments. These individuals believed that their maps held power because others would find them powerful—a kind of self-fulfilling prophecy. And here, I think, is the core of this volume, something we see throughout its contributions: If maps had power, it's largely because people gave them that power through a series of conscious and unconscious decisions. This was a slow, winding process of accretion over centuries, negotiated by individuals who were unsure of the implication or outcomes.[7]

We might trace this inchoate European perception of maps as embodying power to new ideas about truth and vision, which began emerging as early as the fifteenth century, when Italian artists developed geometric principles to imitate on flat surfaces, the depth seen by a stationary human eye. They called this "perspective" and described it as a *truth* that would allow humans to order and control not just images on the canvas but also the physical world itself. Those in power came to increasingly believe that they could control the physical environment and the people within it by acts of *seeing* and *representing*. Not surprisingly, maps were a part of this story, too, as humanists and printers revived the dormant writing of Claudius Ptolemy. It wasn't just that European mapmakers were striving to proportionally represent space on a Euclidean plane but that elites began to believe that their ability to read a map well rendered them effective at the work of remaking and controlling a given landscape. To this effect, maps acquired symbolic value in portraiture, highlighting the cartographic literacy and/or territorial possession of lords, generals, and monarchs.[8]

In this light, we might consider one focal point of the APS exhibition: a reproduction of Edward Savage's life-sized portrait of the Washington family, begun in 1789, completed in 1795–1796, and weighted with symbolism (Figure 1). At the center of the painting, we see George, Martha, and Martha's granddaughter Eleanor Parke Custis sitting around a table, collectively holding open a map of the future city of Washington, D.C. The President wears a military uniform but pointedly rests his hat and sword on the table, showing that he has set aside the instruments of war. Instead, he rests his left hand by papers, which Savage intended to represent his Presidential powers. In the background of the portrait is the Potomac River, giving us a different vantage point of the environment to be remade. Here in a nutshell is the continuity of the European landscape ideology into and beyond the Age of Revolutions: The visual message is that the right leader (i.e., George Washington) can use maps to remake the environment that they oversee.

The dimensions and scope of the work suggest that Savage conceived it as a "history painting" but the portrait conjures an unusually strong sense of future, too. Washington

Figure 1. Edward Savage, *The Washington Family* (1789–1796), National Gallery of Art (Washington, D.C.), Accession Number: 1940.1.2.

rests his arm on his grandson George Washington Custis, who himself leans on a globe holding a compass. Here we might point to Tamara Thornton's presentation at the APS conference, where she argued that globes in this period were primarily a pedagogical tool, used to solve problems of mathematical geography and helpful for cultivating a particular kind of spatial thinking. Savage's painting suggests that more than the transformed landscape, the birthright of the post-revolutionary generation of Americans would be knowledge of how to wield tools that would impart mastery over world affairs. In other words, Savage weaves the old landscape ideology into an emerging national mythology that links past and present with destiny.

Savage likely held a limited view of which Americans were to be included in this vision but in *this* volume, thankfully, we see a diverse set of historical people who brought many kinds of knowledge to maps and mapping. Often, the imperialistic desire to see the power of the map realized meant that actors outside of the government could play on those fantasies to their own advantage—in this ever-evolving dance, the state and its partners found new ways for maps to embody and execute state power. This model applies in part to Savage himself, who emerged from obscurity only after Washington sat for him. Savage may not have been a mapmaker but nevertheless harnessed a map and a globe in evoking an optimistic narrative of future national greatness where George Washington was both the sitter and an important audience member.[9]

Maps and Borders

Usually, when we talk about borders, we mean the geographical boundaries separating one political entity from another. But within that definition, we can find a great deal of variation in what borders have meant and how they were created and upheld. For example, constructing a wall by conscripting peasants is very different than diplomatic squabbling over an imagined line that has absolutely no physical manifestation in the real world.

Where do maps enter into the picture? In the European tradition, maps started depicting abstract political borders a little over 500 years ago. But these were often fanciful rather than universally accepted by all parties. Take, for example, the 1494 Treaty of Tordesillas where Spanish and Portuguese diplomats divided the world along a North–South line "three hundred and seventy leagues west from the Cape Verde Islands." In theory, the Portuguese claimed the (non-Christian) world to the east of this line, and the Spanish everything to the west. The problem came in determining where exactly that line continued on the other side of the world. After it dawned on the Spanish that they could get in on the lucrative spice trade by sailing west beyond the Americas, they began claiming that the Moluccas (known as the Spice Islands) fell into their allotted half of the world. Spanish and Portuguese diplomats met once again to sort out the dispute. Negotiations faltered as each side quickly flashed maps at the other to prove their claims but then hid them away just as fast, fearful that they were giving proprietary knowledge to their rival. At a later meeting, diplomatic horse trading did far more than any map to settle the dispute, yet ironically, the episode made maps necessary tools of state. Even if they might not help resolve territorial claims, showing up without them was like coming to negotiate without clothes.[10]

In no time at all, within just a century, political borders were increasingly ubiquitous on regional, continental, and world maps. It wasn't simply that the proportion of maps depicting these borders had increased but that the overall number of maps had grown, too. Technologies for reproducing maps generally lagged a few decades behind other printing innovations but, in aggregate, the number of maps in circulation grew exponentially so that thousands of maps in Europe in 1400 would become millions by 1600. It bears noting, however, that the representations of borders in these maps had a limited relationship to the actual on-the-ground reach of political authority. Mapmakers were using borders as a convenient shorthand to show general rather than precise relationships.[11]

But you might ask: If these boundaries meant nothing in practice, then why do they matter to this story? Earlier, I described the concept of "ontology" and that comes to bear here. Maps do not simply reflect human systems of meaning but also help to shape them—another way in which maps are powerful. In this case, the proliferation of borders on maps slowly normalized the assumption that political space *should be* tightly defined and delineated. This coincided with a general trend in Europe toward the centralization of states with increasing resources for mapping projects, ambitious by the standards of the day. We could point to a smattering of such projects focused on borders in the seventeenth century such as the land survey of France begun in the 1660s under Giovanni Domenico Cassini. The number of these projects gradually increased in the eighteenth century, especially in colonial contexts, so that the idea of locating an abstract line over large swaths of space seemed increasingly plausible. As states (and the rulers and bureaucrats within them) became invested in the idea of maps being tools of governance, they became invested in the people who could make or furnish those maps.[12]

The American colonies figure into this story of borders. Imperial officials understood the continent as an empty space, ready to be divided up (in spite of the Native peoples who already lived there). When royals issued abstract decrees about where one colony's border was to fall, they often created overlapping jurisdictions with other colonies. Further confusing matters: A colony's claim to territory derived not just from royal charters but also from other sources such as Native land deeds, while the locations of important geographic markers could vary significantly from one printed map to the next. In this volume, for example, Agnès Trouillet shows how the protracted boundary dispute between Pennsylvania and Maryland hinged on the uncertain location of a place, sometimes called Cape Henlopen. Border disputes between colonies could provoke violence, but the intra-imperial nature of the conflict eventually created incentive to seek resolution. In the case of Maryland and Pennsylvania, for example, the proprietors eventually agreed in the 1760s to carry out a survey, resulting in the famous Mason–Dixon line.[13]

By the late eighteenth century, the ideal of territorial exclusivity defined vis-à-vis abstract borders was revealed in peace negotiations, such as the one in 1783 that concluded the American Revolutionary War. While diplomats might not have been able to locate these borders when they negotiated them, they were more committed to finding them than the Spanish and Portuguese centuries earlier at Tordesillas. For example, papers in this volume by Derek O'Leary and David Spanagel examine the process of locating boundaries in the wake of the Treaties of Paris (1783) and Ghent (1814). In these case studies, we watch historians and scientists, respectively, using maps and mapping to vindicate their expertise to the state. These papers remind us that the United States emerged at roughly the same time as the territorially sovereign nation-state was taking, and they subsequently evolved together. This had far-reaching social implications. For example, a national identity paperwork regime developed to deal with problems that arose in spaces that eluded territorial exclusivity, such as oceans. Whether at a given moment you were physically located inside or beyond national borders, your identity was increasingly bound up with a space imagined through those borders on a map.[14]

So maps may depict geopolitical borders but, as discussed above, they can also create or reinforce social boundaries. Sometimes this has everything to do with the actual borders depicted—think of redlining as one example. In other cases, it's precisely a lack of borders that marginalizes. When imperial maps indicate the general location of Indigenous people with floating labels but no actual boundaries, the subtext is: "These are nomads who don't have a specific claim to the land." Often, the social separation involves a map's decorative or rhetorical elements. Here we might point to exoticized bodies in cartouches that scream to European viewers: "This is the kind of body that lives in this kind of landscape . . . and it's different than yours!"[15]

To end this introduction on a more optimistic note: If maps have often acted as agents of social inequality, they can also help us today to retrospectively see and analyze that inequality. This is precisely what Billy Smith does in his article, using a geographic information system (GIS) to collate historical maps with demographic data. Smith has overlaid his own mappings onto these historical maps, helping us to see Philadelphia through the eyes of both Martha Washington and her slave Ona Judge, who would escape from bondage in 1796. The power of a map can extend far beyond the moment of its inception—it's the people along the way that make that happen and, in this case, flip that power on its head.

Notes

1. Woody Holton, *Unruly Americans and the Origins of the Constitution* (New York: Hill and Wang, 2007); Pauline Maier, *Ratification: The People Debate the Constitution, 1787–1788* (New York: Simon & Schuster, 2010); Joseph J. Ellis, *The Quartet: Orchestrating the Second American Revolution, 1783–1789* (New York: Alfred A. Knopf, 2015).

2. Douglas W. Marshall, "The British Military Engineers 1741–1783: A Study of Organization, Social Origin, and Cartography" (Ph.D. Dissertation, University of Michigan, 1976); J. B. Harley, Barbara Bartz Petchenik, and Lawrence W. Towner, *Mapping the American Revolutionary War* (Chicago: University of Chicago Press, 1978); Barnet Schecter, *George Washington's America: A Biography Through His Maps* (New York: Walker & Co., 2010); Stephen Hornsby, *Surveyors of Empire: Samuel Holland, J. W. F. Des Barres, and the Making of the Atlantic Neptune* (Montreal: McGill Queens University Press, 2011); Marcus Gallo, "Imaginary Lines, Real Power: Surveyors and Land Speculation in the Mid-Atlantic Borderlands, 1681–1800" (Dissertation, University of California, Davis, 2012); Susan Schulten, *Mapping the Nation: History and Cartography in Nineteenth-Century America* (Chicago: University of Chicago Press, 2012); Joel Kovarsky, *The True Geography of Our Country: Jefferson's Cartographic Vision* (Charlottesville: University of Virginia Press, 2014); Michael Albert Blaakman, "Speculation Nation: Land and Mania in the Revolutionary American Republic, 1776–1803" (Dissertation, Yale University, 2016); S. Max Edelson, *The New Map of Empire: How Britain Imagined America Before Independence* (Cambridge, MA: Harvard University Press, 2017); Alexander James Cook Johnson, *First Mapping of America: The General Survey of British North America* (London: I. B. Tauris, 2017).

3. For conceptual and critical works on cartography generally, see J. B. Harley, "Deconstructing the Map", *Cartographica: The International Journal for Geographic Information and Geovisualization* 26, no. 2 (June 1989): 1–20; Denis Wood, *The Power of Maps* (New York: Guilford Press, 1992); Wood, John Fels, and John Krygier, *Rethinking the Power of Maps* (New York: Guilford Press, 2010); John Pickles, *A History of Spaces: Cartographic Reason, Mapping, and the Geo-Coded World* (London, New York: Routledge, 2004); Christian Jacob, *The Sovereign Map: Theoretical Approaches in Cartography Throughout History*, Translated by Tom Conley (Chicago: University of Chicago Press, 2006); Denis Wood and John Fels, *The Natures of Maps: Cartographic Constructions of the Natural World* (Chicago: University of Chicago Press, 2008); Martin Dodge, Rob Kitchin, and Chris Perkins, eds., *Rethinking Maps: New Frontiers in Cartographic Theory* (London: Routledge, 2009); Matthew H. Edney, *Cartography: The Ideal and its History* (Chicago: University of Chicago Press, 2019).

4. Mark S. Monmonier, *How to Lie with Maps* (Chicago: University of Chicago Press, 1991); Wood, *The Power of Maps*; Jerry Brotton, *A History of the World in 12 Maps* (New York: Viking Adult, 2013), see pp. 405–436 for a striking example of how maps continue to serve the interests of those who made them. On Global Positioning Systems (GPS) and the shape of the world, see Paul Bolstad, *GIS Fundamentals: A First Text on Geographic Information Systems*. Sixth Edition (White Bear Lake, MN: Eider Press, 2019), 201–217.

On the expedition to test the bulge hypothesis, see Neil Safier, *Measuring the New World: Enlightenment Science and South America* (Chicago: University of Chicago Press, 2012).

5. On ontology in geography, see Gary J. Hunter, "Understanding Semantics and Ontologies: They're Quite Simple Really—If You Know What I Mean!" *Transactions in GIS* 6, no. 2 (2002): 83–87; D. M. Mark and A. G. Turk, "Landscape Categories in Yindjibarndi: Ontology, Environment, and Language" in *Spatial Information Theory: Foundations of Geographic Information Science*, edited by W. Kuhn, M. Worboys, and S. Timpf (Berlin: Springer, 2003), 28–45. On Indigenous mapmaking generally, see G. Malcolm Lewis, "Maps, Mapmaking, and Map Use by Native North Americans" in *Cartography in the Traditional African, American, Arctic, Australian, and Pacific Societies*, edited by David Woodward and G. Malcolm Lewis, The History of Cartography, vol. 2, book 3 (Chicago: University of Chicago Press, 1998), 51–182; Juliana Barr, "Geographies of Power: Mapping Indian Borders in the 'Borderlands' of the Early Southwest", *William and Mary Quarterly* 68, no. 1 (January 2011): 5–46. In the early years of encounter, Europeans often embraced Amerindian geographic knowledge as the best way to learn about the continental interior. See, for example, G. Malcolm Lewis, "Indicators of Unacknowledged Assimilations from Amerindian 'Maps' on Euro-American Maps of North America: Some General Principles Arising from a Study of La Vérendrye's Composite Map, 1728–29", *Imago Mundi* 38 (January 1, 1986): 9–34, and Lewis, ed. *Cartographic Encounters: Perspectives on Native American Mapmaking and Map Use* (Chicago: University of Chicago Press, 1998). However, "enlightenment" thinking degraded the value to Europeans of this indigenous knowledge in the eighteenth century. See Neil Safier, *Measuring the New World: Enlightenment Science and South America* (Chicago, London: University of Chicago Press, 2012).

6. For a few examples of very influential maps, see Brotton, *A History of the World in 12*. On maps and nationalism, see Benedict Anderson, *Imagined Communities: Reflections on the Origin and Spread of Nationalism*, Revised Edition (London: Verso, 2006). On cadastral maps, see Roger J. P. Kain, "Maps and Rural Land Management in Early Modern Europe" in *Cartography in the European Renaissance*, edited by David Woodward, The History of Cartography, vol. 3 (Chicago: University of Chicago Press, 2007), 705–18.

7. Nicholas Gliserman, "Landscapes of Conflict: Cartography and Empire in Northeastern America, 1680–1713" (Ph.D. Dissertation, University of Southern California, 2016) and "Assessing the Reliability of the 1760 British Geographical Survey of the St. Lawrence River Valley" (M.S. Thesis, University of Southern California, 2018).

8. Denis E. Cosgrove, *Social Formation and Symbolic Landscape* (London: Croom Helm, 1984); Patrick Gautier Dalché, "The Reception of Ptolemy's Geography (End of the Fourteenth to Beginning of the Sixteenth Century)" in *Cartography in the European Renaissance*, edited by David Woodward, The History of Cartography, vol. 3 (Chicago: University of Chicago Press, 2007), 285–364; Zur Shalev and Charles Burnett, eds., *Ptolemy's Geography in the Renaissance* (London: The Warburg Institute, 2011); Sean E. Roberts, *Printing a Mediterranean World: Florence, Constantinople, and the Renaissance of Geography* (Cambridge: Harvard University Press, 2013).

9. In considering the question of who was to be included in the nation vis-à-vis who was in the painting, we might consider the Black man standing behind the two women whose identity is unknown to us. An infrared reflectogram done of this figure in the portrait suggests that Savage may have actually had two different men in mind. The man's clothes match the wall and chair so much that he blends into the background. Savage omitted his name from the caption in the widely distributed engraved version, unlike the other four sitters. Ellen Gross Miles with Patricia Burda, Cynthia J. Mills, and Leslie Kaye Reinhardt, *American Paintings of the Eighteenth Century* (Washington, D.C.: National Gallery of Art, 1995), 146–158.

10. As quoted in Henry Harrisse, *The Diplomatic History of America: Its First Chapter 1452–1493–1494* (London: B.F. Stevens, 1897), 78; Jerry Brotton, *Trading Territories: Mapping the Early Modern World,* 2nd Edition (London: Reaktion Books, 2019).

11. David Woodward, ed., *Five Centuries of Map Printing* (Chicago: University of Chicago Press, 1975); James R. Akerman, "The Structuring of Political Territory in Early Printed Atlases", *Imago Mundi* 47 (1995): 138–54; Jordan Branch, *The Cartographic State: Maps, Territory and the Origins of Sovereignty* (Cambridge, United Kingdom: Cambridge University Press, 2015), 54–5, 77–88.

12. Marshall, "The British Military Engineers"; Josef W. Konvitz, *Cartography in France, 1660–1848: Science, Engineering, and Statecraft* (Chicago: University of Chicago Press, 1987); Hendrik Spruyt, *The Sovereign State and its Competitors: An Analysis of Systems Change* (Princeton, NJ: Princeton University Press, 1994); Ted McCormick, *William Petty and the Ambitions of Political Arithmetic* (Oxford: Oxford University Press, 2009); Jacob Soll, *The Information Master: Jean-Baptiste Colbert's Secret State Intelligence System* (Ann Arbor: University of Michigan Press, 2011); Branch, *The Cartographic State*, 55–99; Edelson, *The New Map of Empire*; Johnson, *First Mapping of America*.

13. Branch, *The Cartographic State*, 100–119; Patrick Spero, *Frontier Country: The Politics of War in Early Pennsylvania* (Philadelphia: University of Pennsylvania Press, 2018).

14. Branch, *The Cartographic State*, 120–141; Nathan Perl-Rosenthal, *Citizen Sailors: Becoming American in the Age of Revolution* (Cambridge, MA: Belknap Press of Harvard University Press, 2015).

15. J. B. Harley, "Silences and Secrecy: The Hidden Agenda of Cartography in Early Modern Europe", *Imago Mundi* 40 (January 1988): 57–76; Branch, *Cartographic State*, 100–119; Amy E. Hillier, "Residential Security Maps and Neighborhood Appraisals: The Home Owners' Loan Corporation and the Case of Philadelphia", *Social Science History* 29 (Summer 2005): 207–233; Benjamin Schmidt, "Collecting Global Icons: The Case of the Exotic Parasol" in *Collecting Across Cultures: Material Exchanges in the Early Atlantic World,* edited by Daniela Bleichmar and Peter C. Mancall (Philadelphia: University of Pennsylvania Press, 2011), 31–57 and *Inventing Exoticism: Geography, Globalism, and Europe's Early Modern World* (Philadelphia: University of Pennsylvania Press, 2015); Robert K. Nelson, LaDale Winling, Richard Marciano, Nathan Connolly, et al., "Mapping Inequality," in *American Panorama*, edited by Robert K. Nelson and Edward L. Ayers, accessed April 21, 2020, at https://dsl.richmond.edu/panorama/redlining.

"Suitable for the Parlor of an American"

The Legacy of Major Sebastian Bauman's
Map of the Siege of Yorktown

Katie McKinney

WHEN HIS MAP, *PLAN of the Investment of Gloucester and York*, was made available to subscribers in July 1782, Major Sebastian Bauman thanked them for their support, not only of his map but also in supporting the importance of mapmaking and engraving in the new United States.[1] He wrote, "And, indeed what is the history of a country without maps? A history of war without plans?"[2] Familiar with the idea that defining and maintaining boundaries were essential to legitimate statehood, Bauman was initiating the field of American cartography, which he felt should play a significant role in the definition of nationhood. The victory at Yorktown was an obvious place to start (Figure 1). Its inclusion of a dedication to George Washington, its publication a newly forming nation, its featuring a statement-making decorative cartouche by engraver Robert Scot, and the poignant text marking "The Field where the British laid down their Arms" at the center of the map all speak to its significance as a relic of victory rather than a purely functional cartographic object. Published in Philadelphia only months after the surrender, Bauman's map of Yorktown was, on a deeper level, the United States' first national map. That it was copied multiple times through the early national period, solidifying its importance as a vessel for national pride and iconic imagery, reinforces its status as a premier map.

Just as it was before the Revolution, most general maps and battle maps depicting the war, with a few exceptions, were published in London.[3] The publication of Bauman's ornate siege map within the United States was a patriotic act in itself. Both symbolically and materially, this map was a departure from previous forms of mapmaking in that it marked an economic separation with Britain's craftsmen, artists, engravers, and publishers and took advantage of the general desire for the economic independence to buy goods made in America.[4] By looking at the material histories of Bauman's map of Yorktown and later copies, ranging from a small woodcut version to a large-scale nearly duplicate copy published nearly forty years later by Benjamin Tanner after John Francis Renault, this chapter analyzes the influential role of Bauman's iconic plan of the siege at Yorktown on the formation of a new cartographic tradition in the early United States (Figure 2). Through an examination of how this map was subsequently copied in manuscript and engraved forms, this paper aims to

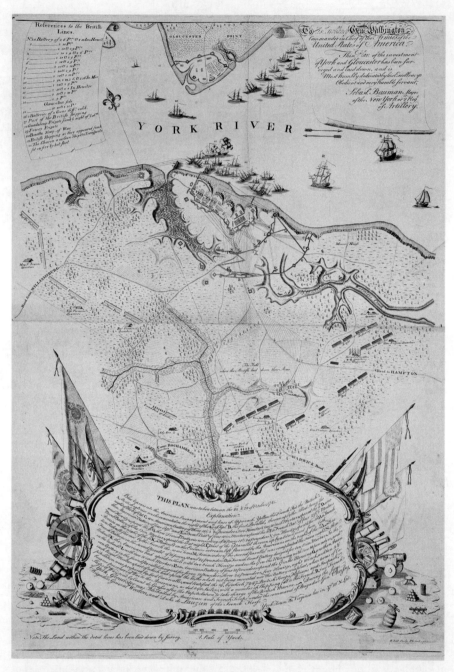

Figure 1. *This Plan of the investment of York and Gloucester has been surveyed and laid down...*; after Major Sebastian Bauman; engraved by Robert Scot; Philadelphia, 1782; Gift of Mr. and Mrs. Richard F. Barry, III, Mr. and Mrs. Macon F. Brock, Mr. and Mrs. David R. Goode, Mr. and Mrs. Conrad M. Hall, Mr. and Mrs. Thomas G. Johnson, Jr., Mr. and Mrs. Charles W. Moorman, IV, and Mr. and Mrs. Richard D. Roberts; Colonial Williamsburg Foundation (CWF), 2017–238.

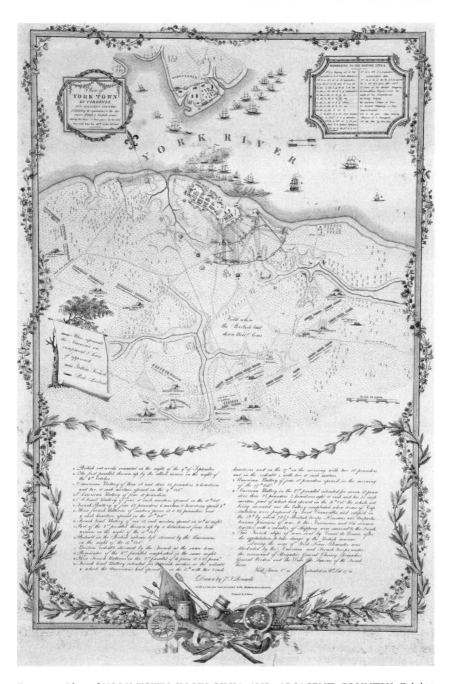

Figure 2. *Plan of YORK TOWN IN VIRGINIA AND ADJACENT COUNTRY, Exhibiting the operations of the American French & English armies during the Siege of that place in Oct. 1781*; after John Francis Renault; engraved and published by Benjamin Tanner; after Sebastian Bauman; Philadelphia, 1823, Gift of Mr. and Mrs. Richard F. Barry, III, Mr. and Mrs. Macon F. Brock, Mr. and Mrs. David R. Goode, Mr. and Mrs. Conrad M. Hall, Mr. and Mrs. Thomas G. Johnson, Jr., Mr. and Mrs. Charles W. Moorman, IV, and Mr. and Mrs. Richard D. Roberts, CWF, 2017–242.

better understand the power that maps can have as commemorative objects within the Early Republic and why their production in America held such significance. Using the map copied several decades later by John Francis Renault as a case study, this paper more specifically aims to address how the Bauman map became a symbolic commemorative object and how it was used by its maker as a legitimizing force of a distinct American identity.

American mapmaking up to the point of Bauman's publication was scarce and primarily the result of necessity or symbolic production, largely due to the superiority and availability of expertly produced English maps and the lack of adequate materials, equipment, makers, and infrastructure.[5] In his "material biography" of Lewis Evans' 1755 publication of *A General Map of the Middle British Colonies*, which was the "first large-sheet map made from start to finish in the colonies," Martin Brückner identifies considerable obstacles encountered by American mapmakers in the eighteenth century, particularly within the period he refers to as "artisanal map production."[6] Without the foundation necessary for large-scale or efficient production, American mapmakers were reduced to a precarious process of soliciting enough subscribers for funding, securing qualified engravers, and affording and locating materials, qualified pressmen, and equipment. If those feats were accomplished in the American colonies, they then needed to make good on their promises and deliver their final product or find a way to produce the map in England.[7] Prior to Bauman's map, Bernard Romans had capitalized on American optimism following the battle of Breed's Hill in 1775. He hastily produced a map of the middle colonies, with small insets referring to the current events in *This Map of the Seat of Civil War in America*, which was published by the end of that year, along with an accompanying print of the Battle at Charlestown.[8] Romans, who claimed to be "on the spot" during the battles of Lexington and Bunker Hill, was not present at either.[9]

The American Revolution both stymied and emphasized the necessity of the then-presumptive nation to establish a cartographic industry. Though he served as an artillerist in America, Bauman was also an engineer trained in surveying and keenly aware of the deficiency of current and accurate cartographic information that plagued American military leaders throughout the war.[10] This lack of resources and official government patronage would continue to hinder American mapmakers, who were reliant on individual subscribers garnered by word-of-mouth, newspaper advertisements, and commercial personal entreaties through the first decades of the nineteenth century.

Like most early American mapmakers, Bauman would not have claimed mapmaking as a sole profession.[11] Born in Frankfurt-am-Main in 1739, he was educated as a military engineer and artillerist at Heidelberg University and served in the Austrian Army.[12] He immigrated to America, settling in New York before or around the time of the French and Indian War, in which he served.[13] After the war, in 1766, he married Anna Wetzell in New York City, where he operated a successful business selling dry goods.[14] At the start of the American Revolution, he served as a captain and commanded an artillery company of the New York Militia, which was redesignated in January 1777 to the main army in General John Lamb's Second Continental Artillery.[15] Bauman served in the northern campaigns of 1776 and 1777 and was elevated to the rank of Major. During his time as artillery commander at West Point, Captain John André was captured carrying maps of American fortifications prepared by Bauman for General George Washington.[16]

The Siege of Yorktown began in early October 1781 and continued for nearly two weeks. Bauman was present as Continental and French artillery batteries relentlessly bombarded the besieged town of Yorktown, where Lieutenant General Charles, Lord Cornwallis, and 8,000 troops were holed up.[17] On October 19, trapped by land and water, Cornwallis surrendered. In the days after the surrender, between October 22 and 28, Bauman drew upon his training as an engineer and set to work surveying the Yorktown battlefield at the request of General Washington, resulting in a printed map published in Philadelphia in July 1782.[18] The area included in his survey, which is indicated by dotted lines on the map, focused on the land siege of Yorktown and not on the naval engagement between the British Navy and the French fleet in Chesapeake Bay that helped clinch victory for the Americans. On the map, each important location or moment is indicated by a letter and referenced in a key below. He noted encampments, roadways, fortifications, and naval ships and highlighted important landmarks such as Washington's tent and the Moore House, where the terms of surrender were negotiated. The wide rendering of the battlefield serves as a canvas for the map's most important detail. In sprawling letters, the map proclaims: "The Field where the British laid down their Arms."[19]

The financial costs behind publishing a map or print in this period were considerable and reliant on the patronage of subscribers. In January 1782, Bauman began advertising his intentions to create "a MAP of the Investment of York and Gloucester" in Philadelphia newspapers. He used military connections to garner support. In an advertisement in the *New Jersey Journal*, subscribers could apply to fellow veteran Captain Jacob Arnold, who ran a tavern in Morristown, New Jersey.[20] By July, the map was available for subscribers, with some extra copies available to be sold.[21] The print run was limited, and there is only one state known. Bauman wrote, "Although this Map bears a military appearance, yet the explanations render it intelligible to those who are not conversant in military structure."[22] It was designed to encapsulate the battle for a particular, educated audience, the military personal and public figures to whom he personally sent copies, while remaining artistic enough to hold a broader appeal as well.[23]

Finding skilled engravers and materials to produce such a map was difficult in America before the Revolution. Robert Scot, a Scottish engraver trained in Edinburgh, had emigrated to Virginia in the early 1770s before moving to Philadelphia around 1782.[24] There, he engraved currency under the supervision of Robert Morris, who served as the Superintendent of the Office of Finance. These notes would finance the Siege of Yorktown. Appropriately, Bauman selected him to engrave his map. Bauman wrote to a friend after the map was published that ". . . the Engraver who cut the plate, this being the first he ever did of the kind; yet the Public have expressed their intense approbation with respect to the artist; and the army, American, French, and British of the accuracy of the design . . .."[25] Scot's ornate rococo cartouche is laden with military equipage, weapons, and flags that surround text detailing the events of the battle. The style of cartouche provides the map with artistic qualities that render the map a decorative object suitable for display as a furnishing in one's home.[26] These decorative elements, combined with the narrow scope of geographic information and a descriptive key that outlined the significant actors, events, and locations of the siege, made it less a useful cartographic object and more a commemorative image and document.

Ultimately, this was not a map that held wide public or commercial appeal in the sense that it was broadly accessible to the public. Instead, its audience would be confined to a more specific, educated audience interested in such commemorative items. It saw only one run of publication between January and July 1782 and was advertised only in Philadelphia for subscription.[27] When the map was finally printed in July, Bauman wrote that once copies were delivered to subscribers, he would have a few remaining for any "Gentleman" who "wish to refresh their memories with a lively representation of the fate of lord Cornwallis and his army."[28] In October, David Claypoole, who retailed map, the reminded readers to "call for their Copies before it is too late." His entreaty around the year anniversary of the map reminded the gentlemen of Philadelphia why this map mattered: ". . . it is easy to presume, every curious Person in these States would wish to be possessed of, and leave to his posterity, as a lively Representations of one of the most material Events which contributed to the Establishment of the Liberty and Independence of his Country."[29] In October, overburdened with engagements and responsibilities (he was still in charge of his New York Artillery regiment), Bauman left Philadelphia to return to New York. Although he made this trip with some copies of the map in hand, in his haste he left behind the copper plate from which the map was engraved.[30]

Despite the optimism felt by those invested in the burgeoning ideas of the nation, it was also a moment of great uncertainty and caution. Bauman struggled with the physical, financial, and familial costs of war, wondering in a letter to Governor George Clinton of New York in 1783 what it had all been for.[31] When he agreed to raise a company of artillery at the start of the war, he left behind "prosperous & lucrative business & a helpless family to protect & assist themselves."[32] In his eyes, New York had failed to adequately support him and his troops, leaving him insecure about his future in the new nation. Now in debt, after almost a decade of fighting and hardship placed on his family, he wrote to the Governor, "I am grown old and debilitated in the War. I have spent my time and money & even my moveables and wearing appearalls [sic] to maintain me in public service. I have nothing but some paper certificates left."[33] His ambiguous position left him fearful:

If I should be discharged before what is owe me or part of it is paid, my family would be in a miserable condition indeed—we should become objects of division not only to those who Luxuriously Enjoy the riches I fought for at a Turble [sic] risk of my life, but so those ingrates who have forfeit them, they would rejoice to see an American officer with dejected countenance reduced to the necessity of begging alms, instead of possessing an ample reward, for securing to America unbounded freedom and Empire.[34]

Like his map, this letter was a way of reminding those in power and his fellow citizens of his service and personal sacrifices, that he might not be forgotten in the narrative of nation-building. By the end of 1783, Bauman was back in New York City and still employed, having assisted with the expulsion of British troops.[35] The following year, he was inducted as an original member of the Society of Cincinnati, solidifying his position among the elite veterans of the Revolution.[36] He would go on to command New York Artillery, putting on patriotic musters and fireworks and reviews. Hoping to move to a more comfortable position, he served as the first Federal postmaster of the city of New York until his death in 1803.[37]

When the map was published, less than a year after the Revolution, it was unclear what form the new nation would take and how the country would live up to its revolutionary ideas.[38] Scholars have argued that no single American identity existed during the Early National period. Rather, there existed a multiplicity of conflicting and intermingling backgrounds, political ideologies, and motivations running concurrently between the different groups of people that would make up the future country.[39] Just as he expressed optimism in the future of American cartography, Bauman's map was published during a moment of expectation and optimism for this new nation in which the promises of the Revolution were yet to be fulfilled, in which possibilities seemed endless.[40]

If Bauman's map was to be a significant representation of American victory, it is necessary to examine what he included as essential to this vision of American nationhood and what is left obscured or not included. The map is dedicated to Washington, who was canonized as the nation's first national hero and a man to whom Bauman owed a great deal personally, having served under the General for much of the war. Washington's tent is highlighted and enlarged, tucked at the lower left corner of the battlefield, standing in for the General himself. What were in reality steep ravines, heavily shelled buildings, burnt fields, and muddy swamps are delineated as orderly landscapes—as was consistent with military mapmaking—sparsely populated with military headquarters. The burning, sinking, and scuttled British ships in the York River are the only indicators of the destruction wrought during the bloody drawn-out siege. Bauman's scope was the battlefield only. Bauman, writing as a military engineer, stated, "but I hope you will pardon Both, for I had but little time in the survey. The only object then to me was the lines."[41] The map that resulted was a celebratory and sanitized portrayal of a bloody siege, characteristic of military maps published following battles using maps and surveys drawn up by military engineers and cartographers.

This view of a national beginning also leaves out a substantial portion of the population who were also present at the siege who would not reap the benefits proclaimed by the map. Yorktown was not only disastrous for the British Army but also devastating to the hundreds of starving and diseased formerly enslaved Black Virginians who had fled to the British lines either to fight with the army or for protection with the promise of freedom under Dunmore's Proclamation of 1778.[42] When supplies ran low during the siege in October 1781, Cornwallis expelled from the battlefield Blacks whose labor or military service was not deemed necessary—the sick, women, and children.[43] They were ejected into a hostile country, which viewed their time with the British as theft.[44] To those who survived the siege and smallpox epidemic, Yorktown was an event that represented broken promises and closed the door on their hopes for freedom.[45] Advertised to "gentlemen" in Philadelphia, the seat of the Continental Congress in 1782, the map was intended for a specific white audience who had the ability and power to envision a new nation, one that celebrated the acts of military leaders, such as Washington, and Bauman (himself a slaveholder), but more importantly claimed victory to define a new country in their own image.[46]

Americans struggled to linguistically and culturally separate and define their Republic away from the imperial legacies of Britain and the past.[47] As maps were an important component of the effort of symbolic nation-building, this break was not an easy one cartographically speaking, and old structures were recycled.[48] The genre of published maps commemorating and summarizing military victories was centuries old by the time of the Revolution, and these cartographic representations were a prime tool of empire- and nation-building.[49] For example, after the battle of Portobello (present-day Panama), copies of Lieutenant Philip Durrell's *Plan of the Harbour Town and Forts of Portobello* were sold in the American colonies, where they would have kept colonists appraised and connected with the Empire.[50] The map provides the general facts of the British victory over the Spanish in 1739: the key components of the battle, noting that Vernon was able to take the fortified port city and force the Spanish Colonial Governor to surrender with a force of only six Men of War. The victory was also celebrated in other commemorative commodities, like Staffordshire tea wares, medals, and accessories like a fan depicting a bird's-eye view that summarized the events of the battle of Portobello, featuring a Spanish soldier waving a white flag of surrender while the colonial governor kneels prostrate at Vice-Admiral Vernon's feet (Figure 3). The dissemination of maps and imagery of victory had the power to bind and control, in ways that text alone could not, through the act of informing and unifying the victor.[51] This had an impact on Colonial Americans—the battle inspired the names of several Virginia houses. John Murray, 4th Earl of Dunmore, the last royal governor of Virginia, named his hunting lodge outside of Williamsburg Porto Bello. Lawrence Washington, half-brother of George Washington, memorialized the Admiral by naming his home on the Potomac River: Mount Vernon.

Figure 3. Fan, made by M. Gamble, ca. 1740, London, Museum Purchase, CWF, 1981-195.

The language Bauman used in advertisements to promote the map reveals not only that he had particular ambitions to foster the production of maps in the United States, but also that he was making an appeal for the creation of an American textual history more broadly. In short, he was seeking to establish, shape, and capitalize on an origin story. He continued this cartographic and literary beginning to show the world what exactly the United States was. He wrote:

> What idea can a person form, who shall happen to read in a remote corner of the earth, or even in the America, the history of this war, the different situations of Saratoga and York-Town, routs, marches, and innumerable scenes of action throughout this extensive continent, without plans are intermixed there the interesting pages of it?[52]

Bauman sought to commemorate the conflict that created the United States of America and to begin to fill in the pages of the history of a new nation. In her discussion of historical maps and atlases, Susan Schulten describes the necessity of mapping for historical purposes:

> Historical maps and atlases were not used to explain geographical problems, but rather to cultivate a shared identity by offering tangible evidence of a nation's evolution over time. The purpose was not to explore the nuances of geography, but to document the evolution of as a sovereign territory.[53]

In this sense, Bauman sought to create the nation anew through the geographic rendering of what was depicted as not only the place where the British laid down their arms but also the place where the victors of Yorktown established the foundations for a new nation.

Bauman's map, though often disassociated with its maker, went on to become a popular image in the American mapmaking. The map was copied for the first time only months after it was published. In October 1782, Hartford printers Nathaniel Patten and Bavil Webster advertised the publication of *The United States Almanack*, which featured a crude woodcut of *A Plan of the Investment of York-Town and Gloucester by the American and Allied Armies* (Figure 5). At 6 ¼" × 4", an explanation of the map on the second page of the diminutive reproduction lists the phrase, "The place where the British Laid Down their arms," making it the first imitation of the map. During the Revolution, almanacs and newspapers were leading sources of news and played an important role in the process of canonizing which events would be seen as significant within the history of the young nation.[54] Patten advertised that, "Those who buy to sell again shall be supplied on a reasonable term as at any place in America," suggesting that the publishers hoped that their patriotic publication might find a larger market.[55]

Copied versions Bauman's map of Yorktown became the standard in publications of the period as the representation of the victory. In 1785, David Ramsey, the first American to pen a history of the United States, published a book that was interspersed with maps, including a miniaturized copy of Bauman's by Scottish American engraver Thomas Abernethie.[56] In 1796, twenty-one-year-old Benjamin Tanner adapted the map to accompany Charles Smith's "The Monthly Military Repository" (1796–1797) or the compilation of the American material from the series entitled "The American War from 1775 to 1783: with Plans."[57] Engraved copies, however, were not the only replicas made of the Bauman map. Some individuals who had access to the map made their own copies, which is a testament to the map's significance in the period and confirmation of Claypoole and Bauman's claim that, "every curious Person in these States would wish to be possessed of" such a map and that they might wish to ". . . leave [the map] to his posterity."[58] Surviving copies of this map in manuscript form speak to the scarcity of the printed version but also to the monumental victory that this map represented. A map in the Clements Library collection at the University of Michigan was composed in ink and watercolor by Christian Waldschmidt, a Pennsylvania veteran of the Revolutionary War who later moved to Ohio and opened a paper mill.[59] Several manuscript maps that copy parts of the Bauman map were presented to the American Philosophical Society in 1831 by Richard Randolph of Virginia.[60] The meeting notes indicated that they were "An original Plan of the Siege of Yorktown, made by Major Bauman, New York Artillery," though the watermarks on the paper indicate that the maps were drawn after 1803, the year Bauman died.[61]

The most significant reconfiguration of the Bauman map was published in 1823 by Benjamin Tanner in Philadelphia. The story of its production began many years before and within vastly different, yet similar, conditions to the relatively smooth production of its inspiration. In November 1823, Tanner announced that he was publishing a

Figure 4. Copper plate and engraving: *British Surrendering their Arms to Gen: Washington after their defeat at York Town*; after John Francis Renault; engraved by Tanner, Vallance, Kearny, and Co.; published by Benjamin Tanner, Philadelphia, plate finished 1819, engraving published 1823; Museum Purchase, CWF, 1976–63,1 (plate); 1986–122 (print).

historical print of the surrender of Yorktown and an accompanying plan of the Yorktown battlefield after the work of a man named J. F. Renault: "In commemoration of that most Important and Interesting Event of the American Revolution: The British Surrendering their Arms to General Washington, after their defeat at Yorktown"[62] (Figure 4). His print, which Renault had referred to as "a child fostered in his bosom, cultivated, and suckled by patriotism,"[63] was to be accompanied by a "correct and handsomely ornamented PLAN of YORKTOWN and the adjacent country . . .."[64] That "plan of Yorktown" was an exact copy of the Bauman map's cartography with altered decoration.

By 1823, commercial American mapmaking was coming into its own in terms of a more integrated production that shifted emphasis from the production of single maps to individual mapmaker with the ability to produce a unified and expansive catalogue of material that was recognizably part of their "brand."[65] The material and financial difficulties that plagued Renault's efforts to embark on an ambitious engraving and map project are reflective of the struggles of publishing graphic materials in America during the early Republic outside of that model of mapmaking.[66]

Renault came to the United States as part of the mass exile of refugees—white, Black, and enslaved individuals from Saint Domingue—during the summer of 1793 following the battle of Cap Français.[67] Capitalizing on recent events, he drew on his skills in drawing and possibly skills gleaned from a career as an engineer in the French Navy; he completed a map of Cap Français that was engraved by Cornelius Tiebout and published by James Harrison in September 1793.[68] An advertisement described the map of "CAPE FRANCOIS, in its present state which shews not only the ruins of the town, but points out every building that still remain [sic] standing."[69] Freshly arrived from Saint Domingue, Renault would have been able to discuss the battle in detail with individuals interested in the bloody conflict, including what buildings remained. However, it is more than likely he copied this map from another source.

Though his early history is unclear, Renault claimed to have served in various capacities in the French Navy in the Caribbean and with the François Joseph Paul, Comte de Grasse at Yorktown. Research on his service, however, is incomplete and has yet to be substantiated.[70] If true, he might have sailed with the Comte de Grasse's fleet based out of Saint Domingue which held off the British fleet, sent to rescue Cornwallis, at the Battle of the Capes in September 1781.[71] In 1783, Renault advertised his intention to start a school in Cap Français, where he would teach penmanship, among other skills. The school was in operation until the late 1780s, at which point Renault appeared in New York City. The influx of refugees from Saint Domingue comprised a population of white, free people of color, and the enslaved, who flooded port cities of New Orleans, Philadelphia, Norfolk, Baltimore, and New York, presenting the new republic with its first refugee crisis.[72]

Renault ingratiated himself in 1796 by publishing a print entitled the *Triumph of Liberty* that was "dedicated to the Americans" and meant to serve as a "monument to immortalize the memories to those Victorious men who have employed their time, their virtues, and their talents in founding the liberties of their country, as well as those generous heroes who fell gloriously in the defence of them."[73] The print combines symbols of the French Revolution (Rousseau and the Marseilles Hymn) with names of the "American Heros" (such as Franklin and Hancock), all set against a landscape that greatly resembles the mountainous terrain of Cap Français. In this portrayal, the "heroes" of the new American nation were not presented in isolation but as part of a larger narrative of revolutionary movements and notables of the Enlightenment. In an effusive advertisement to thank the subscribers, Renault remembered his fellow refugees. He wrote: "Neither do we forget those French Gentlemen, who thou not rich, have greatly encouraged our work, and made great efforts in assisting us to give the public satisfaction."[74] This early work demonstrates the formula he would apply to his later works, in which he negotiated his layered identities as he tried to make a living in the New Republic.

The arrival of refugees from Saint Domingue presented a challenge to the young United States regarding how to handle this influx of francophone exiles expelled by a conflict its elites feared the most: a slave resurrection.[75] Historian Gary Nash has calculated that "about 15,000 islanders, roughly two-thirds white and one-third black, reached American seaports."[76] These refugees gravitated toward places with large populations of their countrymen, but as they attempted to gain a foothold, they grappled with their identity in their new homeland by asserting their San Dominguan origins while also playing up their cosmopolitan French roots.[77] By the end of the decade, tensions ran high between France and America, and sympathies toward those of French extraction withered. In 1798, a Federalist congress passed the Alien Enemies Act, which enabled the governors to expel foreigners who did not demonstrate the correct values or were viewed as radical and therefore dangerous to the state.[78] The suspicion Renault and his fellow refugees experienced when they first arrived in North America remained with him for the rest of his life. He was to repeatedly face accusations of being "dirty looking," and the authenticity of his French heritage was debated, his perceived otherness rendering him always an outsider.[79] Renault left New York, which had turned hostile toward foreigners around the same time the Alien Enemies Act was passed, and reappeared in Blandford, Virginia, a town outside of the inner-coastal port city of Petersburg, which had a community of refugees from Saint Domingue.[80]

Relying on the established formula of European royal or government patronage, American artists, printmakers, mapmakers, inventors, and makers translated this tradition into soliciting wealthy individuals and government officials, particularly the President, to aid with promoting or underwriting their projects. In November 1803, Renault wrote to President Thomas Jefferson from Blandford that he had spent the past three years laboring over a graphite drawing entitled *The British Surrendering their Arms to General Washington, after their defeat at Yorktown*.[81] He praised Jefferson as a "Father of the Arts and Science" and reminded him that all great men, from Augustus to Charles the V and Peter the Great, had protected the arts and sciences.[82] On March 19, 1804, Jefferson paid the full subscription price of $12 to "Renaut" for his engraving.[83]

Just as other refugees and immigrants found connection and security in enclave communities, Renault bounced between metropolitan centers with French populations. Twelve years after soliciting this subscription, Renault had advertised a drawing school in Norfolk, held patriotic fireworks displays in Washington, D.C., and painted portraits in Richmond, but he had yet to produce a single copy of the print.[84] The total cost of the print was to be the sum of $12, with $1 due at the time of subscription, and "eleven on delivery of the Engraving without framing."[85] Typically, subscribers expected to see results in a timely fashion, which caused alarm as Renault moved from place to place without producing a print. On June 16, 1815, the editor of the *Raleigh Star* warned his readership to be weary of, "A dirty looking Frenchman whose name is not recollected and whose dialect would hardly convict him of his country, has subsisted a dozen years by obtaining subscriptions for an engraving of the Surrender of Cornwallis at York Town."[86] In addition to calling him "dirty looking," the editor accused him of not actually being French, possibly a reference to his roots in Saint Domingue, and an implication that he might be of mixed race.[87]

When these accusations reached Renault, he issued a furious defense of his character that was published in North Carolina, Virginia, and Maryland newspapers. Renault defended his efforts to produce the print, placing the blame on the lack of quality in American printmaking. He wrote: "None of his subscribers would have been satisfied to have paid 12 dollars for a sheet of paper fitted to grace a Stable or a Barber's Shop, rather than the parlor of an American."[88] He claimed to have lost property in "Saint Domingo" in the Revolution; there were debts incurred from his traveling expenses and the cost of pencils—which he noted were the "dearest of paint." His total losses, he claimed, were to the tune of $6,500.[89] To offset these costs, he sold his extensive print collection, tried to pull off some fireworks displays, and painted portraits. He complained that, "the profit realized by him and ready to be deposited in the bank is Hope, and the title of 'an imposter of the first grade.'"[90]

The attacks emboldened Renault, and a year later, in 1816, he proudly announced that he had signed a contract with engraver Benjamin Tanner of Philadelphia. After threats and tales thwarted his attempts to take the drawing to France for publication, Renault effused that he was proud to have an American artist working on his American print.[91] He deposited the pencil drawing and the subscription book with Benjamin Tanner, who had recently entered into a partnership with his brother Henry Schenck Tanner and skilled engravers John Vallance and Francis Kearny.[92] The partnership engraved the copper plate and deposited a proof with the Library of Congress in January 1819.[93] The copper plate for the print was finally complete, but financial difficulties caused by the ambitious nature of their project to publish the *New American Atlas* resulted in the partnership officially dissolving the following year.[94] On the 12th day of June 1823, Julia Renault filed probate in Philadelphia for her husband, portrait painter, John Francis Renault.[95]

With the partnership between Tanner, Vallance, and Kearny dissolved, the stakeholders went their separate ways. Henry S. Tanner went on to complete the *New American Atlas* and would become one of the most prolific and successful map publishers of the next twenty years.[96] Five months after Renault's death, Henry's brother, Benjamin Tanner, who was in possession of the copperplates and had struck out on his own, finally advertised the publication of Renault's print with an accompanying map of Yorktown. The reception of the prints and whether or not the original subscribers ever saw their copies is unclear. The publishers of Jefferson's memorandum book note that though Renault claimed he would dedicate the print to the president, there is no record that Jefferson ever received or owned a copy.[97] This advertisement is the first mention of Renault's map, yet the map is attributed to him. The map, which copied the geography and much of the text from Bauman's map, was entitled *Plan of YORK TOWN IN VIRGINIA AND ADJACENT COUNTRY . . . .*[98] The lack of attribution to Bauman is not unusual, but increasingly, mapmakers had started to make a practice of acknowledging the source material for their productions.[99] The engraver, Tanner, was aware of the original source material for the map, having engraved a miniature copy for Charles Smith's *The Monthly Military Repository* a decade prior; however, Bauman's name appears on neither version.

The geographic core of the map can be attributed to Bauman, the main differences being in matters of format and decoration. An architectural border surrounds the body of the map, entwined with alternating swags of laurels and flowers. Scot's rococo cartouche is simplified by gathering the ordnance and flags into a neat central motive tied neatly with a bow. Just above this motif is the inscription, but the published map is signed at the bottom: "Drawn by J.ⁿ F. Renault./ with a Crow-pen and presented to the MARQUIS DE LA FAYETTE . . .." Renault, who referred to himself as a "Historical Drawer" or "Historical Designer," might have claimed authorship over the map due to his artistic re-rendering of the map's design, updating the visual motifs for a contemporary audience using what he describes as a "crow-pen" or quill.[100] He frequently emphasized his skill as a draftsman, apparently working with a lead pencil or in ink. Forty years later, due to the Bauman map's limited print run, and the repeated reproduction of his cartographic imagery without attribution, the original map likely lost the association with its original author.[101]

By conjuring up Lafayette (who was about to embark on his farewell tour of the United States) and resurrecting Bauman's map, Tanner and Renault reinvented the map for a new generation, one for which the American Revolution was a distant memory.[102] Several factors can account for the timing of the actual publication of the print in 1823, particularly: Renault's death just a few months earlier and the announcement of the farewell tour of the Revolution's great French hero, the Marquis de Lafayette. Text on the map claims that a copy was "presented to the MARQUIS DE LAFAYETTE." Renault died before Lafayette ever arrived in the United States; therefore, it seems unlikely that he ever presented him personally with a copy. One advertisement for the engraving published in 1823 claimed Lafayette as a selling point for the print, noting that he was one of the most "conspicuous of the officers represented."[103]

Perhaps before his death Renault sent Layfette a copy of his drawing of Bauman's map, or had he been alive at the time of the French war hero's tour, the presentation of this commemorative object might have been one of many gifts given to Lafayette. The aging French military leader was presented with a number of ceremonial objects during his tour, such as an inscribed silver map-case given to him by the Governor of South Carolina in March 1825.[104] The case was signed and possibly made by Charleston silversmith Louis Boudo, a refugee from Saint Domingue who arrived in Charleston as a young boy.[105] Kevin D. Murphy likens the presentation of such objects as monuments in their own right, inscribed with meaning that commemorates the receiver, but reaffirms the present-day memory of the American Revolution. He refers to the performative nature of commemorating through Lafayette's return tour through dedications of monuments, extensive press coverage, souvenirs, and presentation gifts as "ways of inscribing the American Revolution in space and of using history to create unity in the present."[106]

The excitement of Lafayette's 1824–1825 farewell tour stirred up memories of the Revolution and nostalgic warm feelings for the French, feelings that Renault tried to

Figure 5. Detail (left) John Francis Renault, *The British Surrendering Their Arms to General Washington after Their Defeat at Yorktown in Virginia, October, 1781*, c. 1800–1815, Graphite on wove paper, Dimensions: Drawing is in two sections; Top portion: 21 1/2 × 33 3/4 in. (54.6 × 85.7 cm), Bottom portion: 1 1/4 × 33 3/4 in. (3.2 × 85.7 cm), Credit Line: The Museum of Fine Arts, Houston, The Bayou Bend Collection, museum purchase funded by Robert H. Allen, Jerry E. Finger, Jonathan S. Finger, Marvy A. Finger, Richard B. Finger, Walter G. Finger, Downey Bridgwater and Stuart Yudofsky in honor of Jerry E. Finger and Robert H. Allen at "One Great Night in November, 2002", B.2002.27; (right) Detail of figure 4.

elicit in his drawing of the surrender, which placed Lafayette in a prominent position and where he proclaimed his alleged military connection to the Comte de Grasse. Just as he set his print *The Triumph of Liberty* against a biographical backdrop, Renault insinuated himself onto the map, both by signing the print as his own creation (or adaptation) and by inserting his self-portrait into both the engraving of the surrender and the map. In the print, each character in the main group, made up of notable officers who were and were not present at the surrender, is identified, though there is one character that is not named and does not wear military dress. The prospectus describes this figure as "an old farmer eager to contemplate the scene."[107] In Renault's original pencil drawing, this man's features—a balding head and large nose—are more distinctive than they appear in the printed version (Figure 5). It is possible that Renault fashioned this contemplative farmer after his own image, based on another likeness that appears in the map. The back of one of the cannons in the decorative element at the bottom of the map is inscribed with the profile of a similar face (Figure 6). In his exile on the losing side of Revolution in Saint Domingue, Renault clung to the tenants and identity of the American Revolution, while inserting his own story as a leitmotif. Such subjects of national pride were, after all, profitable and defined Renault's work. His use of Bauman's map as a template, due to the image's iconic status, further legitimize his connection to the American Revolution and young Republic, by negotiating his identities between Frenchman, American, and "other."

In both cases, it was their military service—one well substantiated and rewarded with acclaim and positions after the war, the other met with suspicion by his contemporaries

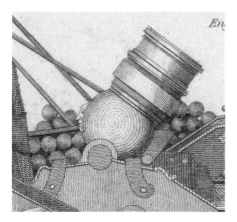

Figure 6. Detail *Plan of YORK TOWN/ IN VIRGINIA AND ADJACENT COUNTRY*, John Francis Renault, CWF, 2017–242. Detail of figure 2.

and unsubstantiated by scholars today—through which they gained entrée into the world of mapmaking. Bauman's participation in the battle and personal relationship with many of the key players gave his map an aura of authenticity that Renault spent years trying to achieve. When his reputation was challenged in 1815, Renault wrote that "I have lived in Richmond for three years, and as the Editor of the Virginia Patriot pretends to be ignorant of my character."[108] He then rattled off an extensive list of military appointments he had held and claimed that he had shown these commissions to the (conveniently) late Governor Barbour. Ever the promoter, he wrote that "Every printer who giving the above insertion will be entitled to an engraving, and many thanks from the author."[109]

Bauman's military record and affiliations were considerably more verifiable, and he used them to his advantage. In October 1782, just before the year anniversary of the surrender, Bauman returned to West Point to resume military duties, and sent out at least two copies of the map as gifts to General William Heath of Massachusetts and Major General Alexander McDougall of New York.[110] In his letter to McDougall, Bauman is apologetic for what he considered the haphazard nature in which the map was produced. He wrote, ". . . the map might have been more minutely and afterwards better executed."[111] This anxiety about the talents and scarcity of accomplished engravers in America resonated with Renault two decades later. Before securing Tanner, who had already demonstrated skill and experience in executing large-scale and sophisticated prints, Renault contemplated going to France to publish his print claiming that "there has yet to appeared [sic] in this country an artist who could undertake the engraving of a picture of this consequence in the manner required by the proposals."[112] Renault was finally able to deposit the drawing and his rendition of Bauman's map with Tanner. He was pleased to announce that the print, which he called a ". . . particular production of America," would ". . . be engraved and executed by an able artist of renown, and finally finished in his native country without the help of stranger talents."[113] Rejecting the notion that he was viewed by many as a "stranger," he was counting on Americans, who had only recently survived a second contest with Great Britain, to celebrate their "native" talents and reject reliance on England and Europe. The print, and ostensibly his copy of the Bauman map, would finally be "suitable for . . . the parlor of an American."[114]

Rather than attempting to publish a map of the new United States, which would have been much outside of his skillset and purview, Bauman created a map that isolated Yorktown as the birthplace of the American nation and designated his map as a starting point for American cartography. Military maps of this kind, designed to bring the public under a common cause, are performative in nature and allow the viewer to participate within the space the object presents.[115] As David Waldstreicher points out, American Nationalism was "a set of practices that empowered Americans to fight over the legacy of their national Revolution and to protest their exclusion from the Revolution's fruits."[116] If Bauman helped lay the bedrock of that dispute, Renault was decades later fashioning his own contribution. While Renault spent much of his life entertaining the public with fireworks displays and supplying artwork that supported celebration of the American Revolution, critics always regarded him with suspicion as a foreigner and outsider. Bauman, also not native-born, similarly put on patriotic fireworks displays and entreated the young country to support the industry of mapmaking, in hopes of ingratiating himself into the history of the new nation. This map, for both men, became a vehicle through which to legitimize their places in the United States.

Notes

1. "To the Public," *The Pennsylvania Packet*, July 18, 1782.

2. *Ibid.*

3. For more on the history of American maps before the Revolution, see Martin Brückner, *Social Life of Maps in America, 1750–1860* (Williamsburg, Va.: Omohundro Institute of Early American History and Culture and the University of North Carolina Press, 2018), 25–39; Margaret Beck Pritchard and Henry G. Taliaferro, *Degrees of Latitude: Mapping Colonial America* (Williamsburg, Va.: Colonial Williamsburg Foundation, in association with H. N. Abrams, 2002); Walter William Ristow, *American Maps and Mapmakers: Commercial Cartography in the Nineteenth Century* (Detroit: Wayne State University Press, 1986), chapter 1; James Clements Wheat and Christian F. Brun, *Maps and Charts Published in America Before 1800: A Bibliography* (New Haven, Conn.: Yale University Press, 1969).

4. Kariann Akemi Yokota, *Unbecoming British: How Revolutionary America Became a Postcolonial Nation* (New York: Oxford University Press, 2014), 26–32.

5. "Private Properties: Ornamental Maps and The Decorum of Interiority," chapter 5 in *Social Life of Maps in America, 1750–1860* (Williamsburg, Va.: Omohundro Institute of Early American History and Culture and the University of North Carolina Press, 2018), 28.

6. Brückner, *Social Life of Maps in America, 28,* Chapter 1.

7. *Ibid.*

8. Pritchard and Taliaferro, *Degrees of Latitude,* 245–246.

9. *Pennsylvania Gazette,* August 23, 1775.

10. Brückner, *Social Life of Maps in America,* 42.

11. *Ibid.,* 45.

12. A.O.V., "The Bauman Map of the Siege of Yorktown," *The Yale University Library Gazette,* vol. 21, no. 2, October 1946, 15.

13. Walter W. Ristow, *American Maps and Mapmakers: Commercial Cartography in the Nineteenth Century* (Detroit: Wayne University Press, 1985), 44.

14. Mary Christina (Doll) Fairchild and Eliza Susan (Morton) Quincy, *Memoirs of Colonel Sebastian Bauman and His Descendants* (Franklin, Ohio: Editor pub. co., 1900), 36.

15. Robert K. Wright, Jr., *The Continental Army: Army Lineage Series* (Washington, DC: Center of Military History, United States Army, 2006), 337.

16. Pritchard and Taliaferro, *Degrees of Latitude,* 292.

17. Alan Taylor, *American Revolutions: A Continental History, 1750–1804* (New York: W.W. Norton, 2017), 293.

18. French manuscript maps made by the Comte de Rochambeau's mapmakers, such as maps in Library of Congress, feature plans similar to those of Bauman's focusing on French and American fortifications and their vantage point during the land battle.

19. British maps of the siege, like this manuscript map by John Hills and later engraved by William Faden, featured areas of British fortified by the British Yorktown and Gloucester and understandably focus less on the infrastructure of their enemies. These go as far as the mill pond off of Wormley's creek, cutting Bauman's surveyed area in half. They omit the surrender field. A manuscript map at the British Library has been identified by Richard Brown and Paul Cohen as being by Bauman's hand. It does indeed depict only the areas shown on the engraved map. See Brown and Cohen, *Revolution: Mapping the Road to American independence 1755–1783.* New York: W.W. Norton, 2015, fig. 68, 135.

20. January 30, 1782, quoted in A.O.V., "The Bauman Map of the Siege of Yorktown," *The Yale University Library Gazette,* vol. 21, no. 2, October 1946, 16.

21. "Advertisement," *Pennsylvania Packet,* Philadelphia, January 8, 1782.

22. "Advertisement," *Pennsylvania Packet,* July 20, 1782.

23. In October 1782, Bauman sent copies to General William Heath and Major General Alexander McDougall. Many thanks to Matthew Skic for sharing the letter. During the Revolution, he served as a major general in the Continental Army. William Heath, Papers, 1774–1872.46 reels, correspondence, orderly books, diaries, Massachusetts Historical Society; and Bauman to McDougall, October 24, 1782, West Point, New York Historical Society (NYHS).

24. Robert Scot was born in England and came to Virginia in the 1770s, where he worked as a watchmaker and engraver. He moved to Philadelphia in 1781, and shortly thereafter he engraved this map. Scot would go on to have a significant career, engraving

maps, book illustrations, and currency. He served as the first Chief Engraver of the United States Mint from 1793 until his death in 1824. See George Barton Cutten, *The Silversmiths of Virginia, Together with Watchmakers and Jewelers, from 1694 to 1850* (Richmond, Va.: Dietz Press, 1952), 41; see footnote on Scot in "Robert Scot's Invoice for Executing an Indian Medal, with Jefferson's Memoranda [13–21 October 1780]," *Founders Online,* National Archives, https://founders.archives.gov/documents/ Jefferson/01-04-02-0038. [Original source: The Papers of Thomas Jefferson, vol. 4, 1 October 1780–24 February 1781, ed. Julian P. Boyd. Princeton, N.J.: Princeton University Press, 1951, pp. 35–37.]

25. Bauman to McDougall, October 24, 1782, NYHS.

26. For more on ornamental maps and maps in the home, see Brückner, "Private Properties: Ornamental Maps and the Decorum of Interiority," chapter 5 in *Social Life of Maps in America*), 161.

27. *Ibid.,* 33.

28. "To the Public," *Pennsylvania Packet,* July 18, 1782.

29. "Advertisement," *Pennsylvania Packet,* October 22, 1782.

30. Bauman to McDougall, October 24, 1782, NYHS.

31. Bauman to Governor George Clinton, June 6, 1783, Sebastian, Bauman Correspondence, 1775–1795, West Point, NYHS. He appears to have retrieved the plate at some point as his 1803 probate inventory lists "1 Engraving on Copper" appraised at $2.00. "Inventory of the Goods Chattles [sic] & Credits of the Estate of Sebastian Bauman deceased taken by the Administrators, 22 Nov. 1803," 1803, New York, NYHS.

32. In 1774, Bauman advertised in the *New York Gazette* that he was selling imported wines from Rhineland and Strasburg "In BROADWAY, at the sign of the LAMB," implying that he dealt in liquors or dry goods; Sebastian Bauman, "TO BE SOLD," *New York Gazette and Weekly Mercury,* April 25, 1774.

33. According to a family history published in 1900, Bauman "pawned his plate, and silver of all kinds, to buy provisions for his famishing troops, paying a very large percentage from his own private funds." See Mary Christina (Doll) Fairchild and Eliza Susan (Morton) Quincy, *Memoirs of Colonel Sebastian Beauman and His Descendants* (Franklin, Ohio: Editor pub. co., 1900), 6.

34. Bauman to Clinton, June 6, 1783, NYHS.

35. After the war, he would continue to serve as an officer in the New York Artillery until he resigned in 1797. In 1789, he became the postmaster of New York, holding that position until his death in 1803. "To Thomas Jefferson from Sebastian Bauman, 29 May 1797," *Founders Online,* National Archives, accessed September 29, 2019, https:// founders.archives.gov/documents/Jefferson/01-29-02-0319. [Original source: *The Papers of Thomas Jefferson,* vol. 29, 1 March 1796–31 December 1797, ed. Barbara B. Oberg. Princeton, N.J.: Princeton University Press, 2002, pp. 403–404.]

36. "From George Washington to the Society of the Cincinnati, 4 July 1789," *Founders Online,* National Archives, accessed September 29, 2019, https://

founders.archives.gov/documents/Washington/05-03-02-0055. [Original source: *The Papers of George Washington*, Presidential Series, vol. 3, *15 June 1789–5 September 1789*, ed. Dorothy Twohig. Charlottesville: University Press of Virginia, 1989, pp. 114–116.]

37. A.O.V., "The Bauman Map of the Siege of Yorktown," 17.

38. Gordon S. Wood, "Experiment in Republicanism," chapter 1 in *Empire of Liberty: A History of the Early Republic, 1789–1815* (Oxford, United Kingdom: Oxford University Press, 2009).

39. Waldstreicher, *In the Midst of Perpetual Fêtes*, 45–46.

40. For more on American post-revolutionary cultural identity and the discourse surrounding it Joseph Ellis, "Paradoxes: Culture and Capitalism," chapter 2 in *After the Revolution: Profiles of Early American Culture* (New York: W.W. Norton, 1979).

41. Bauman to McDougall, October 24, 1782, NYHS.

42. Edward Countryman, *Enjoy the Same Liberty: Black Americans and the Revolutionary Era: Black Americans and the Revolutionary Era* (Lanham, Md.: Rowman & Littlefield, 2014), 47.

43. See Philip Ranlet, "The British, Slaves, and Smallpox in Revolutionary Virginia," *The Journal of Negro History* 84, no. 3 (1999): 217–26. doi:10.2307/2649002.

44. Throughout the war, smallpox ravaged these formerly enslaved soldiers and civilians because they were not inoculated like the British soldiers; see *Ibid*.

45. For a discussion of the fates of Black Americans who fought with the British, see Countryman, *Enjoy the Same Liberty*, 48–49.

46. At the time of his death in 1803, Bauman's inventory listed four enslaved individuals described as "servant." Their names were June, Harry, Jenny, and Silvya. "Inventory of the Goods Chattles [sic] & Credits of the Estate of Sebastian Bauman deceased taken by the Administrators, 22 Nov. 1803," NYHS.

47. Brückner, "Maps, Spellers, and the Semiotics of Nationalism in the Early Republic," chapter 3 in *The Geographic Revolution in Early America: Maps, Literacy, and National Identity* (Chapel Hill: University of North Carolina Press, 2012).

48. See Yokota, "A New Nation on the Margins of the Global Map," chapter 1 in *Unbecoming British*; and Brückner, "The Continent Speaks: Geography, Oratory, and the Figuration of Identity in Revolutionary America," chapter 2 in *The Geographic Revolution*.

49. John Brian Harley, Paul Laxton, and J. H. Andrews, *The New Nature of Maps: Essays in the History of Cartography* (Baltimore: Johns Hopkins University Press, 2002), 61.

50. For an advertisement for this map in October 16, 1740, see Pritchard and Taliaferro, *Degrees of Latitude*, 143.

51. Harley writes, "In the articulation of power the symbolic level is often paramount in cartographic communication and it is in this mode that maps are at their most rhetorical and persuasive." See *Ibid.*, 71.

52. "Advertisement," *Pennsylvania Packet*, July 18, 1782.

53. Susan Schulten, *Mapping the Nation: History and Cartography in Nineteenth-Century America* (Chicago: University of Chicago Press, 2012), 12.

54. Waldstreicher, *In the Midst of Perpetual Fêtes,* 45–46.

55. "Advertisement," *Connecticut Courant* October 1, 1782.

56. Thomas Abernethie from David Ramsay's *History of the Revolution of South Carolina. America, New Jersey, Trenton,* 1785; Two volumes; CWF, 2017–140, 1 & 2.

57. William C. Wooldridge, *Mapping Virginia: From the Age of Exploration to the Civil War* (Charlottesville: University of Virginia Press, 2012), #167, pp. 181–183.

58. "Advertisement," *Pennsylvania Packet*, October 22, 1782.

59. Indian Hill Historical Society, "Christian Waldschmidt," last modified in 2015, https://www.indianhill.org/history/people-indian-hill-history/christian-waldschmidt/; Clements Library, University of Michigan, *To his e[xcellency] G. Washington commander in chief of the armies of the United States of America this plan of the investment of York and Gloucester [sic]* Christian Waldeschimdt (Waldsmith, Waltsmit), 1785, http://mirlyn.lib.umich.edu/Record/004672529.

60. *Plan of Yorktown, Virginia depicting the armies when Cornwallis Surrendered,* 3 pieces, Presented by Richard Randolph, 7 October 1831, American Philosophical Society, 54: 1781: B321ytv.

61. The American Philosophical Society, *Early Proceedings of the American Philosophical Society for the Promotion of Useful Knowledge; Compiled by One of the Secretaries; From the Manuscript Minutes of its Meetings from 1744 to 1838* (Philadelphia: Press of McCalla & Staveley, 237–9, Dock Street, 1884), 619.

62. John Francis Renault deposited either a copy or his intention to publish "A Historical and Allegorical Picture, Entitled The Siege of York or the British surrendering their arms to General Washington after their defeat at York Town in Virginia in the month of October 1781" with the circuit court in Washington, D.C., Uriah Forest, *National Intelligencer, and Washington Advertiser*, Washington, D.C., April 11, 1804.

63. Renault, "Siege of York," *Baltimore Patriot*, Baltimore, December 20, 1816.

64. "Prospectus of an Elegant Large Historical & Allegorical Print," *Independent Chronicle & Boston Patriot*, Boston, November 22, 1823.

65. Brückner, *Social Life of Maps in America,* 51–52.

66. See Brückner's arguments about the "Artisanal" versus "Manufactured Map": "The Artisanal Map, 1750–1815: Workshops and Shopkeepers from Lewis Evans to Samuel Lewis," chapter 1, "The Manufactured Map, 1790–1830: Centralization and Integration from Matthew Carey to John Melish," chapter 2 in *Ibid.*

67. Ashli White, *Encountering Revolution: Haiti and the Making of the Early Republic* (Baltimore: Johns Hopkins University Press, 2010), 5.

68. *Plan de la ville du Cap Français ou est marque en feu ce qui et incendie pour copie conforme a l'original... Renault delin. Gravé par C. Tiebout,* after work by John Francis

Renault, engraved by Cornelius Tiebout, published by James Harrison, New York, no. 38, Maiden Lane, 1793, American Antiquarian Society.

69. "Advertisement," *Daily Advertiser*, New York, October 16, 1793.

70. The author owes an enormous debt of gratitude to William Wooldridge for his generosity and research on Renault. He and Marianne McKee published the first article exclusively on Renault entitled "Trouble in Mapland: The Absconder, the Debtor, and the Affabulateur (Frederick Bossler, Samuel Lewis, and John Francis Renault)," *The Portolan*, Winter, 2013.

71. Taylor, *American Revolutions*, 293.

72. For more on the refugees of the Haitian Revolution in America, see White, *Encountering Revolution*, White, *'A Flood of Impure Lava': Saint Dominguan Refugees in the United States, 1791–1820,* PhD dissertation, Columbia University, 2003, ProQuest (AAT 3088451); and Garvey F. Lundy, "Early Saint Dominguan Migration to America and the Attraction of Philadelphia," *Journal of Haitian Studies*, vol. 12, no. 1 (Spring 2006), pp. 76–94; and for Philadelphia's patterns of settlement Furstenberg, "Settling in America: Philadelphia Speaks French," chapter 2 in *When the United States Spoke French.*

73. Renault, "Triumph of Liberty," *Argus, Greenleaf's New Daily Advertiser*, New York, December 1796.

74. "Advertisement," *New York Journal*, January 18, 1797; *Triumph of Liberty*, after work by John Francis Renault, engraved by Cornelius Tiebout, New York, 1796, CWF, 1964–310, 1–2.

75. White, "The Politics of 'French negros' in the United States," *Historical Reflections/Réflections Historiques*, vol. 29. no. 1, Slavery and Citizenship in the Age of the Atlantic Revolutions (Spring 2003), pp. 103–121.

76. Gary Nash, "Reverberations of Haiti in the American North: Black Saint Dominguans in Philadelphia," *Explorations in Early American Culture: A Special Supplemental Issue of Pennsylvania History*, 65 (1998), 45.

77. White, *Encountering Revolution*, 35; François Furstenberg, *When the United States Spoke French* (New York: Penguin Books, 2014), 103–110; and Nash, "Reverberations of Haiti," 46–47.

78. *Ibid.*, 121.

79. "Editorial," *The Star*, Raleigh, North Carolina, June 16, 1815.

80. Amrita Chakrabarti Myers, *Forging Freedom: Black Women and the Pursuit of Liberty in Antebellum Charleston* (Chapel Hill: University of North Carolina Press, 2018), chapter 2, n. 22 (endnote is on page 217); "To Thomas Jefferson from John Francis Renault, 20 November 1803," Founders Online, National Archives, accessed April 11, 2019, https://founders.archives.gov/documents/Jefferson/01-42-02-0016. [Original source: *The Papers of Thomas Jefferson*, vol. 42, 16 November 1803–10 March 1804, ed. James P. McClure. Princeton, N.J.: Princeton University Press, 2016, pp. 19–22.]

81. *The British surrendering their Arms to Gen: Washington after their defeat at York Town in Virginia October 1781*; drawn by John Francis Renault, graphite on laid paper, 1800–1803, Blandford, Virginia, Museum of Fine Arts Houston.

82. Renault was in Washington in the beginning of 1804, obtaining a copyright and subscriptions for his print. Uriah Forest, "Advertisement," *National Intelligencer* Washington, D.C., April 11, 1804. The prospectus that promised that the print would never be sold in stores and that subscription price was 12.00, $1 at the time of subscription and $11 on delivery. See Renault, "Prospectus of an historical and allegorical picture, entitled, the Siege of York. . ." "Philadelphia,1804, accessed Readex, Early American Imprints, Series 2, no. 7168 (filmed).

83. The publishers of Jefferson's Memorandum book note that there is no record that Jefferson ever received or owned a copy—also, the print was not dedicated to him, as Renault promised in his letter; see "To Thomas Jefferson from John Francis Renault, 20 November 1803," Founders Online, National Archives, accessed April 11, 2019, https://founders.archives.gov/documents/Jefferson/01-42-02-0016. [Original source: *The Papers of Thomas Jefferson*, vol. 42, 16 November 1803–10 March 1804, ed. James P. McClure. Princeton: Princeton University Press, 2016, pp. 19–22.]

84. Renault, "Historical Drawer," *Norfolk Gazette and Publick Ledger*, January 4, 1808; "Grand Fire Works," *National Intelligencer*, June 4, 1810; and "To the Public," *Baltimore Patriot and Evening Advertiser*, December 26, 1816 (originally written on July 22, 1815 in Richmond, Va., and later syndicated in Baltimore).

85. Renault, "Prospectus of an Historical and Allegorical Picture Entitled the Siege of York Town," David M. Rubenstien Rare Book & Manuscript Library, Duke University.

86. "Editorial," *The Star*, Raleigh, N.C. June 16, 1815.

87. For more on race, slavery, and the perception of Black and white Saint Dominguan refugees, see White, "The Limits of Fear: The Saint Dominguan Challenge to Slave Trade Abolition in the United States," *Early American Studies*, vol. 2, no. 2 (Fall 2004), pp. 362–397; and Gary Nash, "Reverberations of Haiti in the American North: Black Saint Dominguans in Philadelphia," *Explorations in Early American Culture: A Special Supplemental Issue of Pennsylvania History*, 65 (1998), 45.

88. Renault, "To the Public," *Baltimore Patriot and Evening Advertiser*, December 26, 1816.

89. Renault, "To the Public," *Richmond Argus*, July 22, 1815.

90. *Ibid.*

91. Renault wrote twice, in his self defense, that he intended to take his drawing and subscription book to France in order to publish the print of Yorktown. He claimed to have been thwarted by the War of 1812 and the Napoleonic Wars.

92. Ristow, *American Maps and Mapmakers*, 191.

93. See imprint on the print of *The British Surrendering their Arms,* which reads, "Enter;d according to Act of Congress, the 28th day of January, 1819."

94. "Advertisement," Franklin Gazette, Philadelphia, January 27, 1820.

95. Renault, Administration Files, No. 121–185, 1823, Pennsylvania, Wills and Probate Records, 1683–1993 [database on-line], Provo, Utah, Ancestry.com Operations, Inc., 2016s, Original Data: Pennsylvania County, District and Probate Courts.

96. Ristow, *American Maps and Mapmakers*, 191.

97. "To Thomas Jefferson from Renault, 20 November 1803," Founders Online, National Archives, accessed April 11, 2019, https://founders.archives.gov/documents/Jefferson/01-42-02-0016. [Original source: *The Papers of Thomas Jefferson*, vol. 42, 16 November 1803–10 March 1804, ed. James P. McClure. Princeton, N.J.: Princeton University Press, 2016, pp. 19–22.]

98. Both copperplates for *The British Surrendering their Arms* are in the collections of Colonial Williamsburg. The copperplate for the print is much larger and made of thicker copper imported from London. Tanner is solely responsible for the copperplate for the map, which is made of thinner copper that is marked Philadelphia. See CWF 1976–63, 1 & 2.

99. Brückner, *Social Life of Maps in America,* 90.

100. Renault, "Historical Drawer," *Norfolk Gazette and Publick Ledger*, January 4, 1808.

101. This is also suggested by the number of manuscript copies already mentioned.

102. Whether or not Lafayette received copies of Renault's engraved map is unknown. Renault died before Lafayette ever arrived in the United States; therefore, it seems difficult he ever presented him personally with a copy. One advertisement for the engraving from a Rhode Island newspaper used Lafayette as a selling point for the print, noting that he was one of the most "conspicuous of the officers represented." "Advertisement," *Chronicle & Boston Patriot*, November 22, 1823.

103. Ibid.

104. Kevin D. Murphy, "A Presentation Map Case for the Marquis de Lafayette: Memory and Geography in the Early Republic," *West 86th: A Journal of Decorative Arts, Design History, and Material Culture*, vol. 20, no. 1 (Spring–Summer 2013), 94–95.

105. *Ibid.*

106. *Ibid.*

107. "Prospectus of an Historical and Allegorical Picture Entitled The Siege of York Town," Duke University.

108. Renault, "To the Public," *Richmond Argus*, July 22, 1815.

109. *Ibid.*

110. Bauman to McDougall, October 24, 1782, NYHS.

111. *Ibid.*

112. Renault, "To the Public," *Baltimore Patriot and Evening Advertiser*, December 26, 1816.

113. Ibid., December 20, 1816.

114. Ibid, December 26, 1816.

115. Harley likens maps that "proclaim victory" to "military parades, songs, and poems"; see Harley et al, The New Nature of Maps, 61.

116. Waldstreicher, *In the Midst of Perpetual Fêtes,* 3.

Albert Gallatin, Mapping Old and New Empires in the Early United States

George Gallwey

ALBERT GALLATIN'S GENEVAN ORIGINS and his career in American politics, public finance, and diplomacy provide remarkably clear illustrations of two conceptions of empire. His policies and writings belonged to an early modern understanding of constitutions and also to a modern sensibility of changing commercial and political norms. Both facets are essential to our understanding of the politics of borders in the early United States. Here, I explore how Gallatin's biography was redolent of the politics and economics of borders—from his personal and practical experience of surveying and his approach to central banking and the circulation of money in the federal union to the disputed claims of diplomatic and jurisdictional authority under the law of nations. His approaches to questions of sovereignty, commercial improvement, and territorial expansion were examples of the application of a changing conception of the politics of republican states. The United States, a federal union of states, conceived itself as a large republic, whose boundaries were to be extended through territorial expansion in North America. Even as he acknowledged in his later life the impact such ambitions had had on Native Americans, Gallatin understood the settlement of land by white Anglo-Saxon peoples to be the destiny of the new American nation, belonging to a stadial history of progress and civilization in the Americas.

For Gallatin, maps were an essential means by which economic interests and claims of natural right or justice could be represented figuratively. Accomplished in different aspects of natural philosophy, including cartography and philology, his political and natural philosophical interests relied upon policing, recording, and instrumentalizing the circulation of knowledge and value in monetary mediums, geographic data, and native languages. In this way, Gallatin's interests were closely related to the intellectual interests advanced in learned societies and universities by natural philosophers. As a preoccupation of early modern thought, the process of understanding and analogizing circulation in natural and artificial bodies was key to the formation of political and economic thought.[1] Gallatin's Genevan heritage and his contributions to the history of the early republic illustrate the importance of cartographical representation as a powerful tool of republican empire.

Born in 1761, Gallatin was a citizen of the small European republic of Geneva, and these origins have helped situate his biography within the romantic history of European enthusiasts for the cause of American independence.[2] However, recent scholarship on the political and intellectual history of Geneva has shown the importance of its geography, political institutions, and eighteenth-century history to the generation of revolutionaries, known as the *representants*, who took part in the 1782 uprising. This event helped shape the European debate on democracy and modern republicanism, less than a decade before the seismic events of the French Revolution would transform domestic and foreign politics in the Atlantic world.[3] The cosmopolitan sensibility of many of Gallatin's Genevan generation was expressed in their aspirations for the transformation of domestic and international politics through the spread of peaceful commerce and a reformed law of nations.[4] Although Gallatin did not take part in the uprising against the city's oligarchic and aristocratic republican government, his personal and intellectual connections with members of that circle provide some important geopolitical context for the development of his own attachment to the United States and for his conception of borders within a modern conception of republican empire.[5]

The Geneva of Gallatin's youth was a small republic existing within a Europe of hundreds of small states and principalities, which themselves belonged to composite monarchies, feudal dependencies, confederacies, and alliances.[6] The boundaries of states within this heterogeneous mix of political communities had invariably shifted over time. Since free cities and small republics were often under the threat of subjugation by larger states, it was the custom to form defensive alliances, or, as was the case with the Swiss or the Netherlands, to incorporate smaller states within a federal union. With its famous city walls, Geneva had a long history of negotiating and defending itself against external aggression through the fortification of its borders. Its proud history of independence was nurtured by its combination of Calvinist constitutionalism, civic virtue, and commercial innovation, providing a leading example of the survival and prosperity of small republic into the eighteenth century.[7]

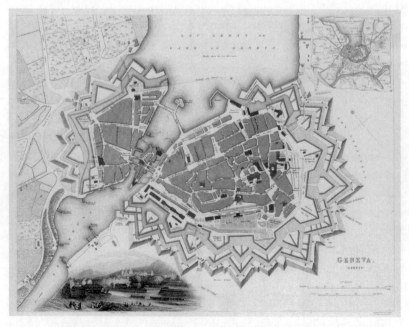

Figure 1. Map of Geneva and its fortifications in 1841. National Public Domain Archive.

The eighteenth century had witnessed fundamental changes in the capacity of large states to fight wars and to draw upon the resources of large public debts to support imperial wars and ambitions.[8] The growth in overseas trade and markets for the sale of goods and people also meant that commerce had come to define state power, supporting and emboldening the expansion of fiscal powers. There was much debate over whether or not smaller states could survive the combination of military and commercial consolidation that occurred over the course of the eighteenth century.[9] At the same time, the generation of revolutionary thinkers who went on to lead the uprising in 1782 agitated against Geneva's oligarchic system of representation, supporting instead the expansion of democratic representation. Significantly, for Gallatin's American experience, the tenor of this debate focused on how the mechanism of survival centered on shrinking the power of monarchies and transforming republics into larger political entities.[10] It was this idea of an expanded republic that provided clear intellectual and political linkages between Geneva, France, and the United States in the late eighteenth century. In this sense, the approach to questions of political union and economy in America's republics grew out of an experience deeply informed by the problem of warring European states, where peace was understood to lie in the balance of power, or the aspiration toward perpetual peace in a great continental republic.[11] European observers saw the union of the North American colonies, united as states under the Articles and later the Constitution, as "indebted to the structures and defensive strategies of the Swiss cantons and Dutch federation."[12] Like these small states, the colonists resisted the imposition of taxes and political control by a large ambitious empire and in doing so organized for their own defense in ways which self-consciously mimicked the strategies of small republics.

In a letter written toward the end of his life, Gallatin made mention of the closeness in morals, manners, and doctrines between the Genevese and the Pilgrims of New England, with their shared culture of Calvinist belief, supporting a Protestant conception of republican government. However, the difference was a matter of scale and space; where young male Genevan citizens found themselves confined to a narrow territory, able to distinguish themselves only through abstract learning or crafts, for the Pilgrims, "Their mission was to conquer the wilderness, to multiply indefinitely, to settle and inhabit a whole continent, and to carry their institutions and civilization from the Atlantic to the Pacific Ocean".[13] It was the same romantic sentiment that prompted Gallatin at the age of nineteen to leave for France, where he crossed the Atlantic to Boston in the spring of 1780. Like many young Europeans, he hoped to make a fortune in the new world and admired the ambitious spirit of the colonies in revolt against the British empire. Writing to his friend John Badollet in Geneva in 1780, he set out a plan for an agricultural settlement, transporting indentured European peasants to work on land owned by proprietors, supported by an aristocratic conception of politics. However, having come to identify with the politics of Geneva's representants, by 1783 he saw the newly independent polities of the United States as a new experiment in republican government. Their attachment to political equality, commercial liberty, and representative institutions, reserved, of course, for white male citizens, combined with the resources and climate of North America, made it a perfect setting for new model constitutions.[14]

For several decades, Gallatin invested time and money in schemes aimed at founding a republican community on the model of a new Geneva. His efforts to transport Genevans to America blended together the search for profitable investment and industry with the preservation of its intellectual and religious culture.[15] Actively pursuing the commercial prospects of speculating in frontier lands, he entered into partnership to buy land claims in Virginia. Learning to survey, he laid out lines, followed the course of streams, and produced detailed maps. His diary entries describe the intense enjoyment he gained from this work. So carefully did he execute his surveys that subsequent generations of Native Americans and settlers continued to refer to boundaries as Gallatin lines.[16]

Benjamin Franklin famously wrote a pamphlet based on the speculation in land documents, or platts.[17] His belief in the efficacy of provincial land banks and paper money as a means of improving and growing white settler populations was eventually channeled into an imperial scheme for a form of currency union. Gallatin was to be a particularly vocal opponent of circulating paper currency not backed by specie. However, both men used local knowledge of mechanisms for claiming and surveying land in their infrastructural vision underlying republican expansion. Although not as accomplished as Franklin, Gallatin was a savant and a polymath, skills he brought to his management of state and federal finances. After being elected to Pennsylvania's House of Representatives in 1790, he quickly established a leading role in plans for refinancing the public debts, while advocating for a state bank, land sales, and internal improvements.[18] Gallatin was staunchly opposed to the expansion of public debts but championed banking and credit as essential machines for commerce in a republican democracy. Such views were not incompatible with his skepticism of the powers granted by the constitution of 1787 to the federal government and his defense of small state republican freedoms, including opposition to the imposition of taxes. Gallatin associated the system of public debt advocated by Hamilton with fiscal-militarism and British aspirations for universal monarchy, or global dominion over land and sea.

Thomas Jefferson considered Gallatin to be the only candidate capable of running the Treasury after the election of 1800. Like Jefferson, Gallatin's political economy stressed the virtues of frugality in national finance, derived in part from the conceptual origins of the term *oeconomy*, as household management. Here again, we could point to the Genevan context of Gallatin's ideas, since the honest and industrious stewardship of resources was a civic virtue and Calvinist tenet. The prudent management of the finances of the American republic would be secured through steadily scaling down public debt and the burdens of taxation.[19] Habits of frugality had to be continually inculcated and reinforced in the practices of government, necessitating studious accounting of its expenses and costs. A permanent national debt was inimical to this end. His personal model was the Genevan-born Jacques Necker, French finance minister under Louis XVI, whose financial morality exhorted governments to live within their means, including the reduction and prompt payment of public debts, equitable taxation, and regular statements of public accounts.[20]

However, Necker's conception of fiscal stewardship extended to the laying out of capital to support infrastructure for the union, an objective Gallatin carefully crafted in systematic detail in the *Report of the Secretary of the Treasury; on the Subject of Public Roads and Canals* (1808). The report grew out of a congressional bill in 1807 for a federal survey of the eastern coastline intended as a measure of public welfare for mariners, passenger ships, and cargoes. Gallatin's Treasury Department oversaw the survey, appointing another Swiss immigrant and natural philosopher, Ferdinand Hassler.[21] Gallatin's proposals for improvements, investing government surpluses gained from economies made on reducing the public debt, were highly ambitious. They recognized the need for government to be the mobilizer of capital, in a country where money and property were insecure to allow private investment to lead the course of improvement.[22] Commercial improvement was married to the need for defense in a large republican state, or, as he put it, to "the dangers, which may result from a vast extent of territory, can no otherwise be radically removed, or prevented, than by opening speedy and easy communications through all its parts. Good roads and canals, will shorten distances, facilitate commercial and personal intercourse, and unite by a still more intimate community of interests, the most remote quarters of the United States."[23]

The public utility of internal improvements and their place in an enlarged republican empire was rooted in the conception of commercial sociability. Here, in conditions of "natural liberty" outlined by Adam Smith in *The Wealth of Nations* (1776), unimpeded by governmental force or corruption, free white male citizens would improve their farms and trade their goods, joining together America's enlarged union.[24] This imperial project, Jefferson's famous "empire of liberty," was based on the capacity of the federal government to sell land it had acquired after 1783 in the western territories, in small plots, with the aim of mapping onto a grid system, a policy which required a massive exercise in surveying.[25] A speculator experienced in clearing and settling land in western Pennsylvania, Gallatin would have well understood the necessity of roads and transportation in the process of commercial improvement. Without transportation land could not be opened up or the products of agriculture made profitable for settlers. Jeffersonian political economy sought to promote the industry of small farms producing food for export in foreign markets, ensuring a middle path of development for the United States, in which plentiful lands for white settlers protected republican equality and liberties.[26]

Gallatin's national plan called for roads and canals along the Atlantic coast. Canals would provide intercoastal trade with quicker access to markets, while a turnpike would run from Maine to Georgia. The more ambitious aspect of the plan proposed hybrid road canal systems to cross the Allegheny mountains. His report outlined the connecting of eastern waterways or Atlantic streams with western ones through canal systems, including New York along the Hudson to Lake Ontario.[27] New York would eventually complete an even more ambitious canal system than Gallatin's, completing the Erie Canal, stretching from Albany to Buffalo, in 1825. Joseph Louis Etienne Cordier, who led the corps of engineers under Napoleon, later produced one of the first maps of the canal in the 1820s, as part of his attempt to persuade his government of the necessity of similar water communication in France.[28] In the early United States, Americans often looked toward European sources for empirical and theoretical knowledge on commerce, navigation, and political economy.[29] However, the flow of knowledge could just as easily move in the opposite direction. Cordier's mapping of the Canal was simultaneous with his correspondence with Gallatin on America's infrastructure. The *Report* of 1808 was published alongside documents on the Erie Canal as part of Cordier's work *Histoire de la navigation intérieure* (1820).

The institutional means by which improvement could be designed and instituted was through the use of public and private corporations and agreements between state and federal governments. The boundaries between state and federal, private and public authorities, were quite fluid in his thinking on this issue—much more so than in Jefferson's. He imagined financial agreements between different levels or jurisdictions of authority and the role of private corporations in establishing commercial contracts for engineering roads and waterways.[30] The published version of Gallatin's *Report* included a letter written by the commercial steamboat engineer Robert Fulton. The letter described the process by which the commercial monarchies of Europe had "bound" their constituent parts together through "turnpike roads, canals, and reciprocal interests." When the United States was itself "bound together by canals, by cheap and easy access to market in all directions," it would no longer be possible to "split them into independent and separate governments, each lining its frontiers with fortifications and troops, to shackle their own exports and imports to and from the neighboring states."[31]

The practical application of natural philosophical knowledge in surveying, astronomy, navigation, natural history, and cartography was essential to the expansion of the claims of the United States to lands in the Trans-Missouri West. The possibility that the westward course of the Missouri would provide a passage to the East Indies was an idea Jefferson had known since childhood. His vision of the Missouri country imagined a waterway navigable to the source with only a single portage. By the early nineteenth century, he possessed an unrivaled collection of materials, in books and maps, on western lands, much of it written on Louisiana by French writers. In planning an exploration of the West beyond the Mississippi, both men relied upon networks of specialized knowledge among philosophers and mechanics, as well as published natural histories, cartography, and speculations on theoretical geography.[32] Gallatin's contribution to the expedition included commissioning a "blank map" from the Philadelphia cartographer Nicholas King. Drawing and weighing evidence from the best available sources on western North America, Gallatin instructed King to consult, among others, the maps of Arrowsmith, Mackenzie, Mitchell, and Vancouver.[33] Gallatin urged Jefferson that their exchanges be made confidential, since it entailed a movement "outside of our own territory" into land claimed by Spain and Britain.[34] Territorial ambitions as state secrets recalled the republican traditions of reason of state, or *arcani imperri*, while the practical mechanics of natural philosophical method drew upon a tradition of trade secrets, where valuable knowledge was strictly policed.[35] Although conjectural geographies of the West relied upon specialized knowledge and available printed sources, they were also heavily dependent upon Indian knowledge, a fact represented in King's map, with the distance recorded in days of travel between mountains and coast. Jefferson approached Congress with the proposal for a discovery corps, which aimed to establish trade posts and traffic with Indians along the Missouri all the way to the Pacific.[36]

Robert Fulton's enthusiasm for the technology of American infrastructure in Gallatin's *Report* was manifested in his launching the first steamboat on the Mississippi River in 1811, something he anticipated would transform the "civilized world."[37] Steamboat technology was essential to the growth in markets for land, cotton, and slaves. An area of long-standing Spanish and French imperial ambition, the commodification of the Mississippi Valley, acquired by the United States after the Louisiana Purchase in 1803, saw a mass forced migration of enslaved African Americans, transported to work on land taken from Native Americans. The Mississippi River would be a key conduit for the agricultural goods produced by farmers in the Trans-Appalachian West.[38] When Spain ceded Louisiana to France in 1801, the danger of a rising French empire in North America blocking westward expansion was made more apparent when a year later the French-controlled port at New Orleans began to impose limitations on American shipping. Taking advantage of the collapse of French Saint Domingue in 1803 and Napoleon's military weakness in the Caribbean, Congress gave Jefferson backing to negotiate the purchase of Louisiana.

Despite the contingencies of imperial politics and entanglements in the Gulf of Mexico and Caribbean, the inevitability of the United States expanding into a new continental entity was an ideological constant.[39] The idea of the demographic inevitability of Anglo-American continental expansion had been argued by various writers before the Revolution.[40] Gallatin had written in 1794 that the benefits of the American Union, including the "free navigation of the Mississippi" and the "full enjoyment of those advantages . . . nature has entitled," outweighed the risks posed by a powerful federal government.[41] In letters to Jefferson in 1803 Gallatin described the inevitable settling of the people of the United States on the Louisiana territory and calculated the revenues gained and lost from the alteration of its borders. He explained his reasons for supporting the right of the United States to acquire territory, in the face of Jefferson's concerns that the exercise of such power required a constitutional amendment. Attorney General Levi Lincoln had suggested that the only solution lay in allowing existing states to extend their boundaries to incorporate the territory. Lincoln was relying upon a theory of acquisition leading to sovereignty through occupation and the employment of land and labor, a Lockean understanding of property rights that was regularly cited before the Revolution.[42]

Gallatin's rationale dismissed Lincoln's constitutional objections, basing his case on the kind of argument put forward by the Swiss jurist Emer de Vattel, in which only existing nations could establish sovereignty over a new territory. Gallatin described the power or "inherent rights" of the United States as a state, nation, or sovereign power to "acquire territory" through the making of treaties, a reference to the capacity for states to act outside of their existing borders according to the law of nations.[43] He remained committed to the union as a federal republic with decentralized power for individual states. However, in the Vattelian sense, "nation" or "state" was a term used to describe external powers, without regard to its internal structure as a kingdom, republic, or empire.[44] Gallatin was using this argument at a time when Republicans made regular resort to the right of neutrality, itself part of the law of nations, in defending American maritime commerce.[45] His later explication of the law of nations suggests the way in which he also applied the ideas of seventeenth-century Dutch jurist Hugo Grotius, citing the principle by which "in case of a river" the "rights derived from it" "extended to the whole country drained by that river and its tributaries."[46] Here again he disagreed with Lincoln's contentions that individual states could define their expansion according to the natural borders of land and rivers. In Gallatin's mind, the acquisition of the Mississippi and the charting of the Missouri were key to establishing this international sovereignty over the continent.

Gallatin's central role in financing the massive territorial increase of the United States illustrates the connections between finance, borders, and empire in the early Republic. France sought payment in the form of federal bonds, and in doing so, sold them at a large discount to the Baring family on the London and Amsterdam markets. This adversely affected the credit of the United States, a fact that caused Gallatin considerable annoyance.[47] During the Revolutionary War the American confederacy had struggled to raise loans in Europe, lacking the credibility that came with recognized sovereignty.[48] Gallatin, at this time, defended the Bank of the United States as an essential institution for securing American public credit at home and abroad. This was against Jefferson's desire to abolish the institution and distribute government monies to republican banks. For Jefferson, the Bank of the United States posed a threat to the republic's security in large part because its stock was "held in so great a proportion by foreigners."[49] Such concerns were not shared by Gallatin, since he conceived of the role, authority, and reach of the Bank as circumscribed by a wise and cautious management.[50] In this way, his conception of the national bank was informed by the Swiss financial experience, where the powerful merchant banking families of Geneva maintained "few links with the domestic economy" and largely served an "international clientele."[51] Gallatin's "Genevan fiscal conscience" understood the role of the Bank of the United States as a prudent depository for the government's funds.[52] Allowing the "government's money to circulate within the banking system" meant that merchants were able to pay import duties, which aided the government and its approach to regulating foreign trade. It was in the context of "securing an instantaneous transmission of such monies from any one part of the continent to another" and allowing merchants to make their payments of import duties to the government that he favored the establishment of a branch of the United States in New Orleans after the acquisition of the Mississippi. Its establishment would help extend the authority of the United States in a vast territory, circulating specie and bank notes, just as roads and canals trafficked goods and people.[53]

Along with the frugal stewardship of resources, *oeconomy* was also a term in natural philosophy, implying a complex structure in nature and often compared with artificial bodies or machines.[54] Understanding natural laws of motion were the theoretical and experimental tasks of philosophers. However, in the early financial history of the United States, public figures such as astronomer David Rittenhouse, who was appointed as director of the U.S. Mint in 1792, were employed by the federal government to enforce standards of value and uniformity in commercial exchange.[55] The complexity of the coinage circulating in the United States, the absence of a real currency union, was a problem Gallatin acknowledged before the election of 1800.[56] In the seventeenth and eighteenth centuries, North American colonies' money, as a unit of account, was measured in pounds, but money as the medium of exchange appeared as foreign specie coins, most commonly the Spanish dollar, with their value in metal being usually fixed by a colony's legislature. These foreign specie coins continued to be used well into the nineteenth century as legal tender, adding to the eclectic mix of currencies circulating in the early Republic. The circulation of coin, especially Spanish reales, reflected the geopolitics of empire. John Quincy Adams remarked in 1822 that though "nearly thirty years since our new monies of account" had been "established . . . we have English denominations most absurdly and diversely applied to Spanish coins; while our own lawfully established dime and mille remain, to the great mass of the people, among the hidden mysteries of political economy—state secrets."[57]

The broad ideological spectrum on questions of political economy in the Republican party meant that Gallatin found himself in the company of those who stood opposed to his own approach of careful fiscal management through national institutions.[58] In congressional debate over abolishing the U.S. Mint in 1797 and 1803, Gallatin had joined in criticisms of the institution, citing its lack of utility in a country where foreign coins circulated at a higher value than U.S. coins, deterring people from taking the former out of circulation. However, his criticisms were far less strident than some of his Republican colleagues, who saw the mint as a monopoly institution again. One member saw the relationship between the circulation of a uniform coin within the borders of the United States as a relic of the practices of small states, continuing in the "small states of Germany" but hardly indicative of their "independence."[59] Instead Gallatin carefully calibrated the benefits of a mint producing a common currency for the circulation of goods.

The problem of the distribution of land and the circulation of money had been closely tied together for white settler populations since the seventeenth century.[60] Franklin had spent much of his political career in colonial politics thinking about this question. As a consequence he provided much reflection on the capacities of paper credit, given a wide circulation, to solve scarcity of coin, increase trade, population, and expand the boundaries of white settlement.[61] Gallatin instead took a staunchly hard-money approach that closely resembled the claims made by Calvinist Minister and president of Princeton John Witherspoon in the late 1780s.[62] The approach to federal lands sale by the Treasury under Gallatin was premised on a democratic distribution of land for the benefit of the "poor man" against speculators.[63] Having previously supported credit sales for land purchases, his experience of overseeing the terms of land sales had shown him how credit undoubtedly increased their volume, yet at the same time led to the increasing indebtedness of poorer settlers.[64] Credit was necessary for landed expansion, yet the growth in privately chartered banks had led to the proliferation of bank notes from state companies. Gallatin was particularly opposed to the conflation of paper money, issued by government or chartered banks, even if backed by specie, with the properties of a metallic currency. Specie was a natural property that circulated across borders, its quantity within a territory being determined by the level of industry or product exchanged in foreign trade. In other words, the demand for specie in exchange for goods was the determinant of its quantity.

Gallatin's contribution to American monetary theory continued after he left his position as Treasury Secretary, but his interventions were regarded by many as narrowly focused on his support for the Bank of the United States. "Want of credit" was too often "mistaken for a want of currency." National and state banks were "of great commercial utility, by bringing into circulation monies otherwise . . . inactive . . . and by increasing the rapidity of circulation." The size of the United States lent itself to a system of banks with a central authority managing the currency. Gallatin made this point in an attempt to put down those arguments for an expansion in the money supply, by a cheaper use of paper currency, as a means of stimulating trade and investment, and insulating the United States from the external demand for specie.[65]

Ironically, there was little distance between Jacksonian hard metallists and Gallatin on the basic theory of monetary value. He staunchly defended "gold and silver" as the "only substances which have been . . . the universal currency of civilized nations." There is no doubt that *Considerations on the Currency and Banking System of the United States* (1830) was an attempt to persuade Jacksonian opponents of the national Bank that without its management of the money supply, the problem of inflationary paper currency would continue to pose risks to the security of specie deposits and credit networks on which planters relied for liquidity. Gallatin contrasted the value of a planter's property, its capacity to be valued in a currency with inherent value, with the purely representative or sign-based qualities of artificial currency. The basic problem of the money supply expanding too rapidly in relation to the quantity of specie in the country was only exacerbated by the vulnerability of the United States, with trade deficits, to the "shock" of external market downturns. In this instance, as he put it, the "internal" and the "external" causes of currency fluctuations had to be distinguished, since it was only in the latter case that an "exportation of coins" to pay foreign debts met with the problem of literal scarcity.[66]

In this respect, Gallatin described the suspension of specie payments in 1814 as "the catastrophe" which "first disclosed the insecurity of the American banking system."[67] The suspension of specie had also been employed in Britain during the Napoleonic Wars. The specie standard, a register of natural justice, was the mechanism for "regulating currency and credit" in both the internal and the external relations of states. The loss of confidence in the capacity of specie to find a natural circulation between states coincided with the changing status of the balance of power as its own mechanism for regulating the exercise of sovereign power in international politics. Gallatin was connected to efforts in Britain and America to establish a revised basis for the law of nations, which for Jeremy Bentham entailed a program of codification designed to help secure "property and markets" against the "recurrence of ruinous conflict amongst the commercial classes of rival nations." [68] The unacknowledged truth, however, was that both the territorial expansion of the United States and the expansion of slavery in the United States were facilitated by the massive extension of private and public credit. Slavery was at the very center of financial panics and speculation in the early Republic with slaves providing the security upon which settlers bought land and attempted improvement.[68]

Gallatin's diplomatic career followed on from his experiences in the Treasury, where he used personal connections forged during that time to the advantage of the United States. Gallatin had met Barring when the latter came to collect the sale of American bonds and the two struck up a friendship. Barring had secured loans for Gallatin when the United States acquired Louisiana, but not before consulting the British government on the American purchase, receiving the go-ahead from Prime Minister Addington that Louisiana in the hands of the Americans would provide additional markets for the "vent" of British manufacturers "in preference to France."[69] The use of his personal connection with Barring to help resolve a credit crisis for the United States in 1814 and ongoing border disputes with Britain expressed the importance of codes of honor, reputation, and credit in the early nineteenth-century worlds of finance and diplomacy.[70] That the condition of a state's public credit, its capacity to raise loans, was reliant on the personal standing of its diplomats had been the key experience of the diplomacy of the American Revolution. In raising loans among Dutch investors, Adams had been engaged in the debate over the decline of the Dutch Republic, a union of small states, and the likelihood of its surviving domestic and international pressures.[71]

Barring's assistance also featured in Gallatin's involvement in negotiations for the Treaty of Ghent with Britain (1813–1814) and in the resolution of the Northeast boundary controversy in the 1830s. Both episodes were connected to the ongoing process of the United States extricating itself from the imperial ambitions of Britain in North America.[72] In attempting to break apart British hegemony in maritime disputes over impressment and shipping rights, the United States had drawn upon various arguments for neutrality under the doctrine of just war, an area of the law of nations that had undergone considerable change since the French and Indian War.[73] In the negotiations for peace with Britain that year, Gallatin aimed to secure Russian mediation as a neutral power, following on from the success of the League of Armed Neutrality under Catherine the Great. However, British refusal to recognize Russian mediation was derived, according to Barring, from its characterizing the conflict as a "family quarrel" between "cousins" rather than an international quarrel between sovereigns. The aim of resolving the problems of embargo and neutral rights to shipping were objectives that Britain shunned, instead pressing for the agreement on Indian boundaries in the disputed territories of the Northeast. The larger objective was to impede the continental expansion of the United States and to secure British navigation rights on the Mississippi.[74]

Gallatin's response to these British terms was to dismiss the possibility of Americans waiving "the rights of sovereignty and of soil over one third of the territorial dominions of the United States to a number of Indians." The British proposals for peace had been "dishonorable to the United States" in challenging "their natural rights on their own shores and on their own waters."[75] In his diplomatic career, he made frequent use of the language of natural justice in the resolution of border disputes. This use of natural law was consistent with the eighteenth-century understanding of the law of nations, whereby "man could, by acting in accordance with his natural capacity for reason, deduce certain universal laws binding upon all mankind."[76]

In his role as a leading American diplomat in Europe in the late 1810s and 1820s, Gallatin was engaged in boundary disputes which according to the customs of the law of nations involved third-party arbitration for dispute settlement. This convention included an agreement over the choice of maps to be used for representing claims and in negotiations over the Northeastern boundary with Britain in 1826—Mitchell's map was used.[77] Gallatin's attention to the cartography of the Northeastern dispute came to illustrate the manipulation of maps to support the claims of rival powers and authentic borders. As Gallatin recorded it, his duty in the negotiations of 1826 had been to assert the "legitimate rights" of the United States, acknowledging the extent to which the process of claiming a right to territory involved the imperfect process of "compromise" or negotiation between legitimate sovereign powers. However, between the 1820s and the early 1840s, a prolonged dispute over the boundary included the recovery and concealment of maps dating to the treaty negotiations between Britain and the United States in 1782.[78] Copies of Mitchell's map bearing red lines of agreed-upon borders were recovered from European archives and personal collections and used to support rival claims to British and American accuracy. In the early 1840s, Gallatin delivered an address before the New York Historical Society where, with forensic detail, he traced the history of diplomatic communications, treaty stipulations, and border lines. Producing a recently discovered map originally belonging to John Jay, Gallatin explained how its lines indicated support favorable to the American claim.[79] As artifacts, even if only to support what Gallatin acknowledged were otherwise purely abstract arguments of no import, maps provided the opportunity to assert greater intellectual authority between rival states.

Even as the United States continued to settle lands outside of its own borders, pressing toward the outermost edges of the continent, Gallatin thought it possible to establish a conception of the natural justice in the acquisition of lands through. As part of the background to the Webster–Ashburton Treaty (1842) with Britain, the now elderly Gallatin wrote publicly on what he saw as the *illegitimate* claims of the United States to move beyond its continentalist conception of republican empire, into lands "outside" of the Southwest, initiating war with Mexico and the reoccupation of Oregon. The pamphlet *Peace with Mexico* (1840) made clear that the further progress of the United States as a "civilized" and "Christian" nation entailed a gulf in access to credit and the resources for waging war. Mexico's inferior position in terms of development did not mean the United States was justified in waging a war outside of the parameters of "honor" and "justice" found in defensive wars as stipulated by the law of nations. Gallatin's argument was part of his attempt to express opposition to the changing conception of international law based on positive right where "might" prevailed.[80]

Just as he regarded the circulation of specie as a natural property of all civilized nations engaged in trade, he regarded the protection of the rights of property as a sacrosanct duty between states. It was in this light that Gallatin had successfully pressed for compensating American citizens whose slaves had fled over the Canadian border during the Revolutionary War.[81] The relationship between natural rights to property and territorial claims in the Americas was a defining feature of the law of nations in the seventeenth-century writings of Grotius. In his negotiations with Britain over Oregon in 1818 and 1826, the dispute over a vast area of territory understood to be void of sovereignty involved competing ideological claims to legitimate ownership. As Gallatin argued in *The Oregon Question* (1846), a pamphlet published close to his death in 1849, "In the nature of things it seems almost impossible that a complete and absolute right to any portion of America can exist, unless it be by prescriptive and undisputed *actual* possession and settlements, or by virtue of a treaty."[82] He described his opposition to the racialized claims of the United States to expand its empire according to the "destiny of the Anglo-Saxon race . . . for universal monarchy over the whole of North America." Such arguments were profoundly antagonistic to democratic principles and reminiscent of the old world empires.[83]

Gallatin understood the natural justice of the United States to settle and improve lands, including those occupied by the native peoples of North America, as the consequence of its expanding population. Discarding Vattel's conception of acquisition through sovereign right, individuals made claims to occupation through legitimate need and employment of labor.[84] Citing the Roman law of occupation as an authority upon which legitimate possession or acquisition of land could be established, he described the "natural" claims to possession through the migration and settlement of Americans as "cultivators of the soil." With an allusion to the Roman empire's failures to establish durable colonies, Britain's artificial means of claiming possession through sending out a colony would not provide a lasting settlement of the area. His reference to universal monarchy was made with a recognition that the old empires of Spain, France, and Britain had in previous centuries been the scourge of peace, progress, and enlightenment, through their claims to absolute dominion over the earth and its peoples.[85]

It was in keeping with enlightenment theories of stadial or civilizational progress that he viewed the history of Native American peoples. Gallatin had developed a close friendship with the German naturalist Alexander von Humboldt during his French mission (1816–1823). An earlier meeting between the two had occurred after Humboldt's arrival in the United States from Mexico. Gallatin had angered Humboldt after he secretly copied a map of New Spain without permission. Carrying with him maps and statistical reports on its economy that had been lying in imperial archives, Humboldt had provided unprecedented and secret information to Jefferson's government just as the acquisition of Louisiana was reconfiguring the borders of the United States with New Spain. Gallatin and Humboldt discussed topics of mutual interest, including the mines of Spain and the mineral deposits of North America. Their mutual fascination with Native American ethnography was the catalyst for Gallatin's writing that became *A Synopsis of the Indian Tribes* (1836), which included a map based on his study of Indian languages and their geographic distribution.[86] The *Synopsis* was shortly followed by a study of Indian modes of subsistence. Here, the history of the human stewardship of resources was the means by which Indian populations could be traced, compared, and fixed within boundaries of development.[87]

Since Aristotle, language had been associated with civilization and the differentiation of humans from animals. Gallatin's *Map of the Indian Tribes of North America* (1836) represented the continental distribution of tribes across two centuries, with the Atlantic coast depicted in 1600 and the Pacific in 1800. Although he drew upon Lewis and Clark's cartography for western lands beyond the Rockies, he also incorporated new detail on the source areas of western rivers and the geographic findings of Jedediah Smith's explorations in 1826. Its lack of apocryphal features has been taken as a departure in cartography at the time, just as his philologic study is thought to have established American ethnography.[88] However, the *Map of the Indian Tribes* also belonged to a changing context for geography and cartography, where maps expressed more than descriptive detail, but analyzed the interaction between natural and human environments. It was Humboldt's climatic studies and his representation of data which pioneered the "conceptual power of thematic mapping," offering a new illustration of the concerns of oeconomy. In this sense Gallatin's 1836 map bore something in common with the more elaborately embellished *Map of the Inhabited World* (1821) by William Channing Woodbridge, which was meant to represent complexities of information on population, religion, and government across natural and artificial borders.[89]

Figure 2. Gallatin, "Map of the Indian Tribes of North America about 1600 A.D. along the Atlantic, & about 1800 A.D. westwardly," American Antiquarian Society, Transactions and Collections, Vol. 2, 1836, fol. p. 264.

Gallatin's map, which depicted Indian tribes within the borders of a rapidly changing continent across two centuries, spoke to his contrary impulses and ironies. A fascination and appreciation for Indian languages was a common point of connection among natural philosophers also engaged in the study of commerce in the new science of political economy. The circulation of money within and across national boundaries was increasingly understood as a measure of time and uniformity of recorded values. Gallatin was among those American polymaths who looked to fill the dearth of information on an ancient America that they understood to lie hidden within Indian cultures. Attempts to preserve and uncover knowledge that might otherwise be lost was another register by which modern American history seemed to suggest an acceleration of time. Also preoccupied with ancient and modern American history, the polymath Constantine Rafinesque, an immigrant from the Ottoman Empire, set down in 1825, in an unpublished manuscript, an analysis of modes of life in which "Selfishness and Individual . . . competition, accumulation, buying and selling" were contrasted with their opposites.[90] Gallatin, too, shared ambivalence about the benefits of progress and civilization. A point borne out by his most famous contribution to American cartography; a historical statement that elided white settler's conscious pursuit of republican expansion with a bounded conception of rights and liberties, enforced through the politics of borders and racial injustice.

Notes

1. *Empires of Knowledge: Scientific Networks in the Early Modern World*, ed. Paula Findlen (Abingdon: Routledge, 2019); Joyce E. Chaplin, *The First Scientific American, Benjamin Franklin and the Pursuit of Genius* (New York: Basic Books, 2006), pp. 73–115; *Oeconomies in the Age of Newton*, eds. Margaret Schabas and Neil De Marchi (Durham: Duke University Press, 2003); Schabas, *The Natural Origins of Economics* (Chicago: University of Chicago Press, 2006).

2. Raymond Walters, Jr., *Albert Gallatin, Jeffersonian Financier and Diplomat* (New York: Macmillan, 1957).

3. Richard Whatmore, *Against War and Empire: Geneva, Britain, and France in the Eighteenth Century* (New Haven, Conn.: Yale University Press, 2012).

4. Whatmore, *Against War and Empire*.

5. Gallatin's school friends, Pierre Dumont and Etienne Claviere were key members of this group, who on the violent suppression of the revolution by France fled the city. Dumont became the editor of the papers of the philosopher Jeremy Bentham, while Claviere became Minister of Finance during the French Revolution.

6. J. H. Elliot, "A Europe of Composite Monarchies," *Past & Present, No. 137, The Cultural and Political Construction of Europe*, Nov., 1992, pp. 48–71.

7. Whatmore, *Against War and Empire*.

8. John Brewer, *The Sinews of Power: War, Money, and the English State, 1688–1783* (Oxford: Oxford University Press, 1990).

9. Koen Stapelbroek, "Neutrality and Trade in the Dutch Republic (1775–1783): Preludes to a Piecemeal Revolution," in Manuela Albertone and Antonino De Fracesco, eds., *Rethinking the Atlantic World: Europe and America in the Age of Democratic Revolutions* (London, 2009), p. 111.

10. Whatmore, *Against War and Empire*.

11. Peter Onuf and Nicholas Onuf, *Federal Union, Modern World, The Law of Nations in an Age of Revolutions, 1776–1814* (Madison: Madison House, 1993), David C. Hendrickson, *Peace Pact: The Lost World of the American Founding* (Kansas, 2003), Eliga H. Gould, *Among the Powers of the Earth: The American Revolution and the Making*

of a New World Empire (Cambridge, 2012), *Empire and Nation: The American Revolution in the Atlantic World*, eds. Eliga H. Gould and Peter S. Onuf (Baltimore: John Hopkins University Press, 2015).

12. Whatmore, "The French and North American Revolutions in Comparative Context," in *Rethinking the Atlantic World: Europe and America in the Age of Democratic Revolutions*, eds. Manuela Albertone and Antonino De Fracesco (London, 2009), p. 223.

13. Gallatin to Eben Dodge, New York, January 21, 1847, *The Writings of Albert Gallatin*, vol. 2, ed. Henry Adams (Philadelphia, 1879), p. 648.

14. Gallatin to Badollet, Philadelphie ce ler octobre 1783, *The Life of Albert Gallatin*, pp. 47–53.

15. Jennifer Powell Mcnutt and Richard Whatmore, "The Attempts to Transfer the Genevan Academy to Ireland and to America, 1782–1795," *The Historical Journal*, vol. 56, no. 2 (June 2013), pp. 345–368. On the intellectual context of these attempts for European politics, see Whatmore, *Terrorists, Anarchists, and Republicans: The Genevans and the Irish in Time of Revolution* (Princeton, N.J.: Princeton University Press, 2019).

16. Henry M. Dater, "Albert Gallatin—Land Speculator," *The Mississippi Valley Historical Review*, vol. 26, no. 1 (June, 1939), p. 33.

17. Benjamin Franklin, "The Nature and Necessity of a Paper-Currency, 1729," *PBF*, vol. 1, pp. 139–157; Martin Bruckner, *The Geographic Revolution in Early America: Maps, Literacy, and National Identity* (Chapel Hill: University of North Carolina Press, 2012), p. 25.

18. May, *Jefferson's Treasure*, pp. 30–34.

19. May, *Jefferson's Treasure*, p. 31.

20. Walters, *Albert Gallatin*, p. 8. Hamilton, however, also cited Necker as an inspiration. Donald F. Swanson and Andrew P. Trout, "Alexander Hamilton, 'The Celebrated Mr. Neckar,' and Public Credit," *The William and Mary Quarterly*, vol. 47, no. 3 (Jul., 1990), pp. 422–430.

21. Hassler would later collaborate with Gallatin as head of the Bureau of Weights and Measures in the late 1820s. Morris M. Thompson, *Maps for America, Cartographic Products of the US Geological Survey and Others* (U.S. Department of the Interior, Geological Survey, 1981), pp. 1–2.

22. Gallatin, *Report of the Secretary of the Treasury; on the Subject of Public Roads and Canals* (Washington, 1808), p. 6.

23. Albert Gallatin, *Report*.

24. Drew McCoy, *The Elusive Republic: Political Economy in Jeffersonian America* (New York: Norton, 1980), p. 41.

25. Gordon Wood, *The Empire of Liberty, A History of the Early Republic, 1789–1815* (Oxford: Oxford University Press, 2009), pp. 8–10; Walter Johnson, *River of Dark Dreams, Slavery and Empire in the Cotton Kingdom* (Cambridge, Mass.: Belknap Press of Harvard University, 2013), p. 24; Michael J. Lacey, "Federalism and National Planning: The Nineteenth Century Legacy," in *The American Planning Tradition: Culture and Policy*, ed. Robert Fishman (Baltimore: Johns Hopkins, 2000), pp. 89–146.

26. McCoy, *The Elusive Republic*.

27. For a contemporary map of Gallatin's plan and their proximity to later infrastructural development see D. W. Meinig, *The Shaping of America: A Geographical Perspective on 500 Years of History, Vol. 2: Continental America, 1800–1867* (New Haven, Conn.: Yale University Press, 1995), p. 314.

28. https://mappingmovement.newberry.org/selection/plan-and-profile-erie-canal-1820; Richard Haw, *Engineering America: The Life and Times of John A. Roebling* (Oxford: Oxford University Press, 2020), p. 35.

29. See the review of Benjamin Smith Barton's *A Dissertation on the Freedom of Navigation* (1802), Benjamin Smith Barton Papers, Series II, *American Philosophical Society*. Peter Stephen Du Ponceau, a French immigrant and American trained lawyer who settled in Philadelphia after the Revolution, translated works on international maritime into English across multiple languages, "List of books on the law of nations, Philadelphia," Peter Stephen Du Ponceau Collection, American Philosophical Society.

30. May, *Jefferson's Treasure*, pp. 133–137.

31. Gallatin, *Report of the Secretary of the Treasury*, p. 122.

32. John Logan Allen, *Lewis and Clark and the Image of the American Northwest* (New York: Dover Books, 1975), pp. 154–167.

33. The full list was Ellicott, Cook, Vancouver, Arrowsmith, Mackenzie, Thompson, Mitchell, d'Anville, and Delisle. "To Thomas Jefferson from Albert Gallatin, 14 March 1803," *PTJ*, vol. 40, pp. 59–61.

34. "III. Gallatin's Remarks on the Draft, 21 November 1802," *The Papers of Thomas Jefferson*, vol. 39, ed. Barbara B. Oberg (Princeton, N.J.: Princeton University Press, 2012), pp. 18–25.

35. Chaplin, *The First Scientific American*, p. 12.

36. Allen, *Lewis and Clark and the Image of the American Northwest*, p. 102.

37. Johnson, *River of Dark Dreams*, p. 73.

38. *Ibid.*

39. Eliga H. Gould, "Entangled Histories, Entangled Worlds: The English-Speaking Atlantic as a Spanish Periphery," *The American Historical Review*, vol. 112, no. 3 (June, 2007), pp. 764–786; Peter J. Kastor, "'What Are the Advantages of the Acquisition?': Inventing Expansion in the Early American Republic," *American Quarterly*, vol. 60, no. 4 (Dec., 2008), pp. 1003–1035; Jonathan Israel, *The Expanding Blaze, How the American Revolution Ignited the World, 1775–1848* (Princeton, N.J.: Princeton University Press, 2017), pp. 400–404; Deborah J. Allen, "Acquiring 'Knowledge of Our Own Continent': Geopolitics, Science, and Jeffersonian Geography, 1783–1803," *Journal of American Studies*, vol. 40, no. 2 (Aug., 2006), pp. 205–232.

40. Alison Bashford and Chaplin, *The New Worlds of Thomas Robert Malthus, Rereading the Principle of Population* (Princeton, N.J.: Princeton University Press, 2016).

41. Gallatin, "Declaration of the Committees of Fayette County, September 1794," in *Selected Writings of Albert Gallatin*, ed. E. James Ferguson (Indianapolis: Bobbs-Merrill, 1967), p. 25.

42. "To Thomas Jefferson from Levi Lincoln, 10 January 1803," *PTJ*, vol. 39, pp. 302–305; Andrew Fitzmaurice, *Sovereignty, Property, and Empire* (Cambridge, United Kingdom: Cambridge University Press, 2014), pp. 198–220.

43. "To Thomas Jefferson from Albert Gallatin, 13 January 1803," *PTJ*, vol. 39, pp. 324–327.

44. Daniel J. Hulsebosch, "Being Seen Like a State: How Americans (and Britons) Built the Constitutional Infrastructure of a Developing Nation," *William & Mary Law Review*, vol. 59, issue 4, article 3, p. 1245.

45. Onuf and Onuf, *Federal Union, Modern World.*

46. Gallatin, *WAG*, vol. 3, p. 532.

47. "Gallatin to Jefferson New York, 31st August, 1803," *WAG*, vol. 1, p. 149; "Gallatin to Baring 15th and 29th November, 2nd December 1814," *WAG*, vol. 2, p. 643.

48. E. James Ferguson, *The Power of the Purse, A History of American Public Finance, 1776–1790* (Chapel Hill, 1961).

49. Jefferson to Gallatin, October 7, 1802, *The Thomas Jefferson Papers at the Library of Congress*: Series 1: General Correspondence. 1651 to 1827 (25,884).

50. "Gallatin to Jefferson," *PTJ*, vol. 37, pp. 616–617.

51. *Handbook of the History of European Banks*, ed. Manfred Pohl (Aldershot, United Kingdom: Edward Elgar, 1994), p. 1015.

52. Walters, *Albert Gallatin*, p. 156.

53. "Memorandum from Albert Gallatin, 18 June 1802," *PTJ*, vol. 37, pp. 616–617.

54. Schabas, *Oeconomies in the Age of Newton*; Lisbet Rausing, "Underwriting the Oeconomy: Linnaeus on Nature and Mind," *History of Political Economy*, vol. 35, Annual Supplement, 2003, pp. 173–203.

55. William Huntting Howell, "A More Perfect Copy: David Rittenhouse and the Reproduction of Republican Virtue," *The William and Mary Quarterly*, Third Series, vol. 64, no. 4 (Oct., 2007), pp. 757–790; Dustin Gish and Daniel Klinghard, *Thomas Jefferson and the Science of Republican Government: A Political Biography of Notes on the State of Virginia* (Cambridge: Cambridge University Press, 2017), p. 163.

56. *Annals of Congress,* House of Representatives, 5th Congress, 2nd Session, pp. 733–734.

57. John Quincy Adams, "Report Upon Weights and Measures," *The North American Review*, vol. 14, p. 206.

58. Andrew Shankman, *Crucible of American Democracy* (Lawrence: University of Kansas, 2004).

59. *Annals of Congress,* House of Representatives, 5th Congress, 2nd Session, pp. 733–734; *The Debates and Proceedings in the Congress of the United States*, vol. 11, p. 486.

60. Jeffrey Sklansky, *Sovereign of the Market: Money in Early America* (Chicago: University of Chicago Press 2017).

61. Franklin, "Modest Enquiry into the Nature and Necessity of a Paper-Currency," p. 139.

62. John Witherspoon, *Essay on Money as a Medium of Commerce; with Remarks on the Advantages and Disadvantages of Paper Admitted into General Circulation. By a Citizen of the United States* (Philadelphia, 1786).

63. *The Debates and Proceedings in the Congress of the United States* (Washington, 1849), pp. 411–412.

64. May, *Jefferson's Treasure*, p. 127.

65. Gallatin, *Considerations on the Currency and Banking System of the United States* (Philadelphia, 1830), pp. 19–27.

66. *Ibid.*, pp. 19–35.

67. *Ibid.*, p. 6.

68. Edward E. Baptist, "Toxic Debt, Liar Loans, and Securitized Human Beings: The Panic of 1837 and the Fate of Slavery," in *Capitalism Takes Command: The Social Transformation of Nineteenth Century America*, eds. Michael Zakim and Gary J. Kornblith (Chicago, 2013).

69. Sven Beckert, *Empire of Cotton, A Global History* (New York: Vintage Books, 2014), p. 107.

70. So as to avoid the problem spreading to its European creditors, Gallatin had asked Barring to extend credit to the United States as it defaulted on the interest of its public debt in 1814. Barring was loaning money to an enemy of his government, but he also stood to lose if the American debt collapsed in value, since his Bank had sold bonds to its own customers. "Gallatin to Monroe, Ghent, 26th October, 1814," *WAG*, vol. 1, p. 642; May, *Jefferson's Treasure*, p. 246.

71. Koen Stapelbroek, "Neutrality and Trade in the Dutch Republic (1775–1783): Preludes to a Piecemeal Revolution," in Manuela Albertone and Antonino De Fracesco, eds., *Rethinking the Atlantic World: Europe and America in the Age of Democratic Revolutions* (London, 2009); Friedrich Edler, *The Dutch Republic and the American Revolution* (Baltimore, 1911).

72. Walters, *Albert Gallatin*, p. 268.

73. Tara Helfman, "Neutrality, the Law of Nations, and the Natural Law Tradition: A Study of the Seven Years' War," 30 Yale J. Int'l L. (2005).

74. Walters, *Albert Gallatin*, pp. 268–274.

75. *Ibid.*, p. 279.

76. Tara Helfman, "Neutrality, the Law of Nations," p. 551.

77. John P. D. Dunbabin, "The 1831 Dutch Arbitration of the Canadian–American Boundary Dispute: Another View," *The New England Quarterly*, vol. 75, no. 4 (Dec., 2002), p. 628.

78. Francis M. Carroll, *A Good and Wise Measure: The Search for the Canadian–American Boundary, 1783–1842* (Toronto: University of Toronto Press, 2001), p. 301.

79. Gallatin, *A Memoir on the North-Eastern Boundary: In Connexion with Mr. Jay's Map* (New York, 1843), p. 7.

80. Gallatin, *Peace with Mexico* (New York, 1847), pp. 2–10; May, *Jefferson's Treasure*, p. 305.

81. Walters, *Albert Gallatin*, p. 332.

82. Gallatin, *The Oregon Question* (New York, 1846), p. 14.

83. Gallatin to Garrett Davis, New York, February 16, 1848, *WAG*, vol. 2, p. 661; Gallatin, *Oregon Question*.

84. Fitzmaurice, *Sovereignty, Property, and Empire*, pp. 208–211.

85. Gallatin, *The Oregon Question*, pp. 14, 70.

86. Gallatin, *A Synopsis of the Indian Tribes*, in *American Antiquarian Society's Archaeologia Americana*, vol. 2 (1836), pp. 1–422 (4); Helmut de Terra, "Alexander von Humboldt's Correspondence with Jefferson, Madison, and Gallatin," *Proceedings of the American Philosophical Society*, vol. 103, no. 6, *Studies of Historical Documents in the Library of the American Philosophical Society* (Dec. 15, 1959), pp. 783–806; William A. Koelsch, "Thomas Jefferson, American Geographers, and the Uses of Geography," *Geographical Review*, vol. 98, no. 2 (April, 2008), p. 270.

87. Gallatin, "On the Geographical Distribution and Means of Subsistence of the North American Indians at the Time of the Discovery of America," *Proceedings of the Antiquarian Society*, vols. 11–12, October 1849.

88. Allen, *North American Exploration: A Continent Explored* (Lincoln and London: University of Nebraska Press, 1997), p. 166; James Turner, *Philology: The Forgotten Origins of the Modern Humanities* (Princeton, N.J.: Princeton University Press, 2014), p. 139.

89. Susan Shulten, *Mapping the Nation: History and Cartography in Nineteenth-Century America* (Chicago: University of Chicago Press, 2012), pp. 80–85.

90. C. S. Rafinesque, "[Outline for a] lecture on American history, undated"; "A view of the contrast between the 3 systems or modes of social life & dealings, 1825," C. S. (Constantine Samuel) Rafinesque Papers, 1808–1840, American Philosophical Society.

Thinking Multidimensionally

Cherokee Boundaries Above, Below, and Beyond

Julie L. Reed

"For wherever one journeys in the country of the past, *instructive [people and] places abound.*"[1] (My extra words and italics)

As OTHER CHAPTERS IN this volume point out, by the late eighteenth and early nineteenth centuries, Five "Civilized" Tribes political leaders showed sophistication in their interactions with U.S. officials as they used maps and boundaries to shore up not only claims to their homelands but also their legal rights and national sovereignty. These assertions often complicated claims to common hunting grounds and shared border spaces between tribal communities, as Lucas Kelley's chapter in this volume discusses, but nonetheless these same actions slowed the bureaucratic machinations of the young United States eager to lay claims to Indigenous homelands and assert its own nascent sovereignty as Gallwey's chapter in this volume delves into. My chapter asks us to consider a span of time leading up to and overlapping with the periods covered by Kelley, Pearson, and Gallwey in this volume. From the moment Europeans arrived in the Native South and running through the early nineteenth centuries, Indigenous peoples conceptualized the world around them and mapped its dimensions in different ways than Europeans eager to map the geography in order to open trade, exploit its resources, and displace Native peoples for Euro-American settlement. The earliest maps produced by or with the aid of Indigenous wayfinders and informants hint at the inadequacy of two-dimensional tools like maps to express the knowledge Indigenous peoples possessed. The maps produced also reflect the inability of European students, hamstrung by "romantic hyperbole, heavy Eurocentric bias, and egocentric exaggeration," to grapple with the epistemologies Native peoples likely introduced.[2] Paired with the smaller archive of maps and pictographs produced by Native peoples that demonstrate the relationships between peoples residing throughout the Native South, a richer more textured world emerges. If we are willing to imagine how other living "silent witnesses" might have (re) mapped their worlds, it drives home the limitations of maps to offer us a full rendering of the world Indigenous people had studied, lived in, and mapped for centuries prior to the arrival of Europeans.[3]

The interdisciplinary work in caves that I have been involved in for the past five years drives home the point Keith Basso, author of *Wisdom Sits in Places,* quoted at the onset of this piece, offered readers in terms of how to make sense of Indigenous place-making in the past and in the present. He alludes to the educational component imbedded in and on Indigenous homelands. Basso's book highlights his collaborative mapmaking process with the Apache guided by Indigenous informants. Unfortunately, unlike Basso's project, the maps handed down to us from Euro-Americans obscure the contributions of Indigenous people and fail to depict the world Indigenous people occupied. There is no doubt that Indigenous peoples acted as wayfinders and cartographers to the earliest Europeans arriving on their lands.[4] Maps may serve as inanimate "silent witnesses" to the past, but Indigenous southerners and the environment itself served as the earliest teachers.[5] One key difference between Basso's process and the process carried out by the earliest mapmakers in the Native South is not the absence of Indigenous teachers, it is the failure of the non-Native students to master the cumulative curriculum. Because of this, those same students failed to appreciate the larger world of the southeast that may have been described or could have been described to them if they had considered other informants. In many ways, this chapter asks readers to consider women, children, and nonhuman actors as a "shadow presence" at the time early Euro-American maps were produced, the maps we lack as a result, and the inadequacy of those maps to consider how Indigenous peoples continued to rely on multidimensional renderings of the world to meet future demands. What Euro-American mapmakers likely would have learned from "silent witnesses" would not have been adequately depicted in two-dimensional formats.

As maps of North America began circulating, European cartographers increasingly relied on the general contours of older maps to create new versions. They often added additional details, clarified questions, or focused on other purposes. These maps created a two-dimensional understanding of the world that failed to fully record the multidimensional spaces Cherokees resided in and knew surrounded them above and below. Maps denoted boundaries and borders and offered a first look into Native communities for those who might follow the paths provided. Cartographers grew more sophisticated in their craft, becoming more attuned to the importance of scale and creating more consistent keys, yet their maps and their understandings of Native people often remained flat or receded. As European powers vied over land claims in Native North America, maps often served as a symbolic battleground over there, to use Jackson Pearson's phrase from his chapter, "anticipatory empires."[6] Cartographers grew more silent on the contributions of Indigenous informants and muted Indigenous worldviews.

DeSoto, one of the first Europeans to attempt to map the Indigenous south, failed to comprehend the lessons imparted to him as his team attempted to map the river systems and trails. They recorded rivers and streams as continuously connected in curvilinear paths, instead of dendritic tentacles of streams and rivers as they naturally occurred.[7] They did this based on what they thought Indian informants were drawing or describing. For Native Americans, "the overall transport or communication network was of principal concern—not whether one segment was on land and had to be walked, while another was a waterway that required a canoe for passage."[8] In an Indigenous cartographer's maps, land and water were linked, and one need not break that connection to represent pathways and boundaries, a lesson DeSoto failed to comprehend.

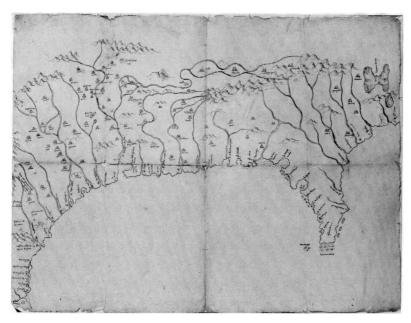

Figure 1. "Mapa del Golfo y costa de la Nueva España: desde el Río de Panuco hasta el cabo de Santa Elena," often referred to as the De Soto Map. Alonso de Santa Cruz, ca. 1572, Library of Congress.

The earliest maps created by explorers, surveyors, and traders marked off the political landscapes and borders of the Native South. In what archaeologists deploying GIS today might term an "econometric approach" centering human resources and their uses, John Smith titled the tract that accompanied his map of Virginia "A Map of Virginia with a Description of the Country, the Commodities, People, Government and Religion." He focused his attention on the economic resources (established towns, waterways, and hunting areas). These were the objects Smith chose to record likely based on his community's decision making, with only a smidge of culture mixed in (people, government, and religion), another subset of what today's archaeologists term an interpretive approach.[9]

Nevertheless, maps provide a jumping-off point to better understand the simultaneously micro- and macro-landscape that existed below, above, and beyond what cartographers highlighted on the maps and the boundaries they seemed incapable of considering. Native informants would have attempted to convey the vastness and interconnectivity of the world in which they lived and the boundaries they crossed and avoided crossing. As Martin Brückner argued, for early Euro-Americans, geographic literacy was infused with national identity. Unfortunately, despite the fact Indigenous informants were the earliest teachers, their cultural expertise and geographic literacy were likely lost on their students or in some instances blatantly ignored.[10] Even if John Smith consistently acknowledged the role of Indian informants in his early cartographic endeavors, those who immediately followed erased and silenced those contributions.[11] Additionally, as Juliana Barr points out, "Euro-American maps functioned as geopolitical 'statements of territorial appropriation' that erased Indian geography by replacing Indian domains with blank spaces of pristine wilderness awaiting colonial development."[12]

Cartographers' focus on economic and political interests relative to southern tribes and territorial claims to those lands often inhibited their ability to learn other lessons about the landscape and its relationships with its long-term residents. Cartographers' early maps note the significant without full recognition of the deep meaning of a place being marked. They could see and were blind at the same time, as we will see with the references to the ancient city of Kituhwa. In a series of towns running northeast along a river in the mountains, George Hunter's 1730 map, based on an earlier map created by Colonel John Herbert, lists "Kattewa" as just another Cherokee town.[13] John Mitchell's 1755 map based off of Colonel John Barnwell's earlier map "A Map of the British and French Dominions in North America" notes the presence of "Kittowa."[14] John Stuart's 1775 "A Map of the Southern Indian District" also includes "Kittua."[15] The continued presence of Kituhwa on various maps over time indicates its long-standing and continued importance to Cherokee people, but the maps fail to reflect that. Kituhwa has been continually occupied for the past 10,000 years. Even archaeologists agree that Cherokees have occupied Kituhwa for at least the past 800 years.

Kituhwa served as a Mother Town, an ancient town with an elevated status among all Cherokee communities. Mother Towns often had mounds that swelled like pregnant bellies from the surface. Cherokee people often built and rebuilt town houses on the tops of the mounds.[16] The people who called (and continue to call) themselves Ani Kituhwa, the people of Kituhwa, believed that their origin story begins at that place.[17] The earth gave birth to them there. Maps and their makers lacked the most basic understanding of the centrality of Mother Towns, and Kituhwa specifically, to Cherokee people. If maps acknowledge the place yet erase the most basic curriculums for Cherokee people, what else did these early primary documents fail to capture about the geography that Cherokees knew so well?

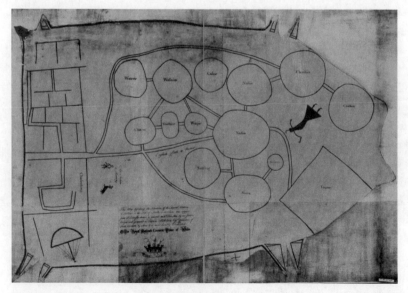

Figure 2. "Map of the several nations of Indians to the Northwest of South Carolina," Francis Nicholson (Contributor), c. 1721. Geography and Map Division, Library of Congress.

One of the few maps produced by a Native cartographer underscores the reconceptualization necessary to map the Native South. "A Map Describing the Situation of the Several Nations of Indians between South Carolina and the Massissipi River," also referred to as the Catawba Deerskin Map, breaks with the standards of European cartographers. The Indian cartographer, speculated to be Catawba or Cherokee, chooses to depict Native nations as circles linked to one another through paths.[18] Non-Native Charleston is depicted through straight lines and grids. The circles hearkened back to ways Indian informants described the pathways that connected them to the larger world, misrepresented by the DeSoto map as only waterways.

These Indigenous mapmaking conventions connect to a larger pattern of representation and means of place-making and marking throughout the southeast. Early explorers and naturalists noted that Native peoples used pictographs, sometimes humans, sometimes animals, carved into bark to indicate boundaries and mark paths. Others cited the ability of Native peoples to recognize North based on where mosses grew. They navigated fog-encased waters with invisible shores by watching how sticks and wood broke on the water.[19] Navigating the world happened in relation to who and what was above, below, and all around.

The particular cartographer responsible for the Catawba Deerskin map also drew a world that acknowledged gendered power. The Indigenous mapmaker drew a deer close to a hunter and a prominent woman drawn in red on the far side of the map closest to the Cherokees' location. In his article arguing for a Cherokee creator of the Catawba Deerskin Map, Ian Chambers uses Cherokee oral tradition to describe Selu the Corn Mother's relationship with her children. This symbolically strengthens his evidence for the map's Cherokee origins.

> They also saw how their mother entered a small cabin, placed a basket on the ground and, standing over it, jumped up and down until large ears of corn began to fall into it. Furthermore, what has hitherto been interpreted as a tail emerging from Selu's skirt can now be recognized as representing the corn she produced by jumping over her basket. We see too, from the single feather protruding from her head and the fluidity of the lines representing her arms, that she is dancing. The mother's proximity to the Cherokee's circular homeland has a double significance. In the first place, it refers to the next episode in the story, according to which, when the children observed Selu producing corn from her stomach, they decided that she must be a witch and plotted to kill her. Instantly aware of their intention, Selu tells them that after they have killed her, they were to clear a large piece of ground in front of the house and drag her body seven times around the circle. In the second place, her position on the map acknowledges her role as the person who remained in the village at all times and who controlled Cherokee domestic life.[20]

Gendered and age-based knowledge and power are absent from European-produced maps and are often unclear even in early ethnographic accounts of the Southeast. It is frustratingly difficult to track demographics because sometimes only warriors were counted and other times only the number of villages or towns. (How to define a warrior by age is never discussed.) And yet, there is no doubt that women and girls served as other "silent witnesses" and likely behind-the-scenes arbiters of cartographic information exchange. This acknowledgment of the prominent place women occupied in matrilineal worlds prompts the intellectual question, what would female cartographers who remained close to their villages have mapped?

My thirteen-year-old has been to Kituhwa less than a dozen times. She knows that the name connects to "the People," although she is less clear on Kituhwa's meaning, which is not surprising, since its original meaning can only be speculated. She knows a mound is there and a river runs along the site. She is always eager to swim there, even though she has never been allowed to do it. She knows there is a farm on the property and that it is close to Cherokee, North Carolina, the capital of the Eastern Band of Cherokee Indians. She knows it's important to Cherokee people, but she has never taken a class there or gone for official reasons. She knows these details about Kituhwa because as her mother I have shared them with her or because she has engaged in what historian of education Milton Gaither refers to as landscape learning.[21] She paid attention to her environment. My daughter, an enrolled citizen of the Cherokee Nation, has never lived in a Cherokee community, despite the fact that we lived in the Cherokee homelands in Knoxville for seven years. What she knows and how she knows it is not completely dissimilar to some of the ways her thirteen-year-old counterparts who resided at Kituhwa when cartographers began charting and surveying the region would have learned about the place they lived. And yet, her counterparts' geographic knowledge of that place would have been far deeper and richer and more essential to their existence than my Cherokee daughter's understandings today. A thirteen-year-old informant likely could have sketched out a rich and detailed world for an outsider seeking to better understand the region.

Even if a girl, *ageyutsa*, never ventured beyond a ten-square-mile boundary of Kituhwa, she lived and learned in one of the most biodiverse ecosystems in the world. When *ageyutsa* looked up, a blanket of 60- to 100-foot-tall mature yellow poplar, white oak, and American chestnut trees protected her from harsh sun and rain.[22] The mythical "giants" and now nearly extinct American chestnut surrounded her. American chestnut trees stretched from Massachusetts to Northern Georgia and resided on both sides of the Appalachian Mountains. The Gentleman of Elvas who accompanied DeSoto's expedition remarked in his 1557 account, "Wherever there are mountains, there are chestnuts."[23] Even though she may have lived only in her 10 square miles, *ageyutsa*'s Iroquoian kin to the north, separated by time and geography, played, explored, and learned under American chestnuts, too. In fact, one key difference between an oral history shared by both Cherokee and Iroquois people is the presence of a chestnut tree in the Iroquois version rather than the tobacco weed in the Cherokee version.[24] What would the trees have looked like on maps *ageyutsa* chose to create?

Smell likely played another role in *ageyutsa*'s relationship with chestnuts. During the late summer, especially in the mornings and evenings, a distinct odor from the long spindly male creamy white flowers wafted throughout the woods. If a child smelled it once, it would be recognizable to her year after year. My daughter and I memorized a similar smell after a single season in Knoxville as a result of the Chinese chestnuts that grew in our backyard. These Chinese chestnuts, American chestnut cousins, were planted there as a result of an earlier Knoxville master gardener's attempt to repopulate the region with chestnuts after the chestnut blight that began in 1904 and swept from New York to Alabama at a pace of 19 miles per year.[25] Through the late summer and early autumn, the American chestnuts grew nut-filled burrs that would begin to fall from above around the first frost. During the fall harvest, Cherokees burned the forests where chestnuts grew in order to harvest them more easily.[26] During this time, *ageyutsa* needed only to listen to hear the burrs raining from their branches to the ground. If she spent much time in the woods, she certainly had one of these burrs hit her head. With only two trees in my yard, the necessary number for pollination, and only five years in my house, the number of times a burr struck me while walking or mowing the yard are too numerous to count. An area of 10 square miles before the chestnut blight would have contained 750,000 trees, around 10% of them American chestnuts.[27] *Ageyutsa* certainly wafted the smoke in the air at harvest and faced far more shellings than me when she gathered those nuts.

Ageyutsa wasn't the only living thing to rely on the American chestnut and reckon with its height. When those burrs dropped, they provided food not only for *ageyutsa* and her community but also for a variety of critters who ranged and resided in those 10 square miles. *Ageyutsa* competed with the 250 white-tailed deer inhabiting the area and the 40,000 gray and flying squirrels scurrying from tree to tree above and on the ground.[28] She may have watched the now-extinct American parakeet pass through the region to the swampier areas. Blue jays; red-bellied, hairy, and downy woodpeckers; owls; hawks; and eagles all lived year-round among the trees. After the blight, fewer Canada warblers, wood thrushes, or black-throated blue warblers entered the region.[29]

The nutrients provided by American chestnuts seeped into the soil and nourished more than just the creatures who walked the land. When the chestnut blight occurred, the trees that took their place never provided the same combination or level of nutrients that American chestnuts had.[30] This affected the diets of animals and humans who relied on the soil and the chestnuts themselves to produce a bounty, but it also impacted the invertebrates that many other creatures relied on for food. After the chestnut blight, far fewer crane flies existed in the region.[31] Despite the continued diversity and significance of salamanders to the region, a shift in the presence of invertebrates likely would have impacted their food supply as well. White-tailed deer, wild turkeys, now extinct passenger pigeons, wapiti, and black bears also relied on the American chestnut's canopy and the nourishment provided by the nuts.[32]

The relationship between bears, humans, and the chestnut points to "the spiraling patterns of feedback intrinsic to all coevolutionary processes" that early Native cartographers and writer-artists attempted to convey in their graphic circular relationships with other Native peoples, their nonhuman neighbors, and the natural world.[33] Bears moved between and semiannually resided in powerful spaces that often never made it onto maps, but nonetheless permeated how Cherokee people mapped the world. Bears, like the first Cherokee man Kanati, relied on caves for their well-being. Kanati rolled a stone away from a cave to release game for Cherokee people to eat, until his mischievous sons accidentally released all the game and forced Cherokee people to take up hunting. Bears relied on caves for torpor, but according to Cherokee oral tradition, bears used caves to commune with one another, store food, and occasionally interact with humans.

My daughter has frog-walked into caves in the Cherokee homelands, similar to those described in the story of the "Bear Man" recorded by ethnographer James Mooney. In it, a bear took a human hunter into a cave to attend a bear council. The space the man traversed linked a smaller entry hole and passage to a room that resembled a Cherokee council house. There, the bears discussed food shortages. The solution to those shortages was the announcement by two bears in attendance that they had explored, discovered, and mapped another mountainous area filled with chestnuts and acorns.[34] The bears celebrated—as might *ageyutsa*, when she recalled this story and felt the power of her own experience of exploration. Like their human and nonhuman counterparts, bears relied on chestnuts and adjusted their exploration and future living patterns to the prevalence of those trees.

Cherokee clans reinforce the close relationships between humans and their animal counterparts who made places together. When the bear council ended, the bear and the man who accompanied him left and traveled to another cave, where they dwelled together. The longer they lived together, the more the man became like the bear. This corresponds to another oral traditional recorded by Mooney documenting the relationship between bears and humans. Cherokees believed that a clan of Cherokee people, known as the Anitsâgûhĭ, went into the mountains and turned into bears. The Anitsâgûhĭ moved to the mountains because a boy who had also communed with bears suggested it as a solution to overcome the food shortages and the trials they faced. The Cherokee Blue Clan is thought to be made up of remnant members of the Anitsâgûhĭ.

Clans reinforced the permeable boundaries that existed between humans and animals. As Mooney puts it, "there is no essential difference between men and animals."[35] Cherokee clans traced their matrilineal origins to a single ancestor, and often those ancestral origins tied to "trees, plants, animals, birds, and the elements."[36] Given the prevalence of deer as a source of food, a direct clan lineage, and a neighbor in the woods, it is not surprising to find their likeness on a map potentially created by a Cherokee cartographer who understood these relationships.[37] The relationship between bears, deer, and humans then was not simply one of shared geography, but also of shared kinship.

And yet, that geography, including those spaces below where bears and Cherokee hunters palavered, which never showed up on maps, also figured significantly into Cherokee geographic instruction. Cherokee cosmology charted the world as a space that included an upper realm, a middle realm, and a lower realm. My own daughter worried about getting trapped in the first cave she entered; *ageyutsa* might have worried about what powerful forces entered the middle realm, where she resided, from the cave. Caves, waterways, and the sky opened gateways to other realms and what moved between those realms could produce positive or negative consequences. It is within caves where the lower realm and the middle realm meet and where temperatures maintain a constant balance. The limestone-rich region that most Cherokees called home prior to forced removal is filled with caves. The state of Tennessee, which completely housed the Overhill Towns, one of the three subdivisions of Cherokee settlements in the Southeast prior to removal, contains over 10,000 documented caves. Ethnographer James Mooney recorded numerous oral accounts that linked Cherokee people to caves. He recorded that the Seneca called Cherokee people the "cave people." Caves also provided shelter for Cherokee people during both storms and war. Predators including Tla' Nuwa, giant hawks, lived on the north bank of the Little Tennessee river below the mouth of Citico creek, not far from where I lived in Knoxville. Cherokee people respected caves as a space where other inhabitants of the world resided, but those caves also mapped on to a geography European cartographers sought to document. By the late eighteenth century, Euro-Americans began documenting caves in the region in order to mine saltpeter for bullet manufacturing. The hashmarks marking the resource extraction still cover many of those cave walls.[38]

Throughout the southeast, iconography within caves maps the presence of serpent-like creatures. Mud Glyph Cave contains a serpent with horns, 12th Unnamed Cave has an antlered rattlesnake, and 1st Unnamed Cave located in eastern Tennessee has a snake 5 meters in length. Mooney met a Shawnee man in the 1890s who lived among the Cherokees who claimed to possess a crystal from the uktena, a powerful serpent-like creature that lived in the waterways and valleys in the Appalachians. However, because of the crystal's power and the care necessary for its maintenance, the man kept it in a cave and conducted ceremonies there every seven days to keep the uktena at bay. Places below existed on Cherokee people's maps. They also represented boundaries one should approach cautiously. *Ageyutsa* would have likely climbed back out of the cave after her brief exploration, breathless in her knowledge that she had tempted fate.

The world below remained an important part of at least some Cherokee people's relationship with their world even after they grasped the cartographic conventions of Euro-Americans and added to their literacy, geographic and otherwise. It is easy to overstate, as many early scholars of Cherokee history did, that by the early nineteenth century Cherokees had "assimilated" to Euro-American practices. There is little doubt that after 100 years of cartographic exposure, Cherokee people understood the Euro-American aims of surveying and mapmaking. As both Lucas Kelley's and Austin Stewart's chapters in this book discuss, by the 1790s and beyond, Cherokee leaders used surveys and mapped boundaries to assert sovereign rights to ancestral lands and craft legal arguments. Yet, as Kelley's chapter makes clear, Cherokee diplomatic tactics merged Indigenous understandings of communal land use with newer understandings of maps as both weapons and fantasies of empires. Even across tribes (as in the case of the Cherokees and Chickasaws) and within communities (as in the case of the Cherokees, who continued to resist removal in the east and those who after numerous depredations and pressures had chosen to remove west of the Mississippi) contests over control of land and boundaries came into sharp relief.

However, other technological adaptations during the same moment reinforced how a subset of Cherokees continued to relate to the geographic and cosmological world around them. In two caves in the former homelands of the Cherokee Nation, Cherokee writers of the syllabary, a writing system invented by Sequoyah by 1821 and rapidly disseminated and adopted by Cherokee people after his daughter aided him in demonstrating its efficacy to the Cherokee National Council in 1825, entered caves to use the new technology. Even though some of it can be translated and dated and its meaning understood, its placement within the caves suggests at least some attempt by at least one Cherokee writer to map a multidimensional world that could never be confined or adequately represented on a paper or globe.[39]

In 2015, I joined an interdisciplinary team of researchers to document what appeared to be syllabary in two caves in the southern Chickamauga region of the former Cherokee homelands.[40] In one of the caves, the writing spread throughout the deeper parts of the cave as single syllables that all led to a huge chamber. In that chamber, Cherokee writers had written on the walls and ceilings. Regardless of the translations, the questions of placement baffled me and left me awestruck. I kept asking myself how I was supposed to read a multidimensional document? Since that time, members of the team have translated the larger portions of text, but my original question remains. Is there something more mapped here that simply reading the words does not satisfactorily answer?

Even when Cherokee people had other techniques available to them, some people continued to map space and boundaries in multidimensional ways that European maps fell woefully short of depicting. As DeVorsey points out in his treatment of Bernard Roman's 1775 Choctaw pictograph (Figure 3) and his overall diagnostics of key differences between mapping conventions of Europeans and Native Americans reinforced in Chamber's analysis of the Catawba map, circles and enclosures often denoted "us."[41] Even when Cherokees had the syllabary available to them, they chose to write cosmological messages and their kinship positioning within a circle on the ceiling of a cave (Figure 4).[42] They went into spaces ignored by European maps, but key to a map of the world where Cherokees resided, to communicate their location to beings and kin who resided in the upper realm.

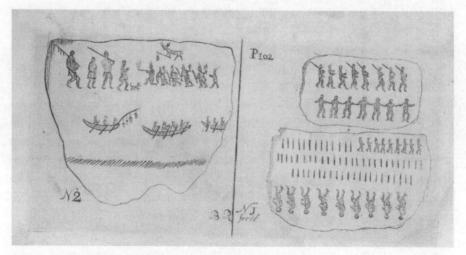

Figure 3. Indian [Choctaw] Pictographs as shown in Bernard Roman Concise Natural History of East and West Florida (1775).

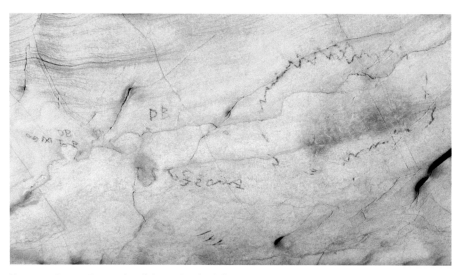

Figure 4. Cave ceiling with syllabary. On the left text is written in circle. First someone smoked the ceiling, and then they etched writing within it. Credit Alan Cressler.

If we aspire as scholars to employ geographical methods successfully, as Jamie Carson points out, "Native American history, culture, land, and people must intersect in a cohesive whole."[43] That whole can and should include the use of two-dimensional maps created by early European immigrants, but we can stop there. We must consider what the informants' knowledge conveys about the world they might have chosen to map with a different set of tools. Additionally, we must consider the degree to which a narrow range of informants limits our abilities to expand our understanding of the mapped world of Indigenous people. If we take seriously the interconnectivity of pathways and peoples described by Native informants, we must also consider the microcosmic mapping that Native people might have offered. To adequately map the Native South, Indian Country broadly, or the world we live in today, we must be prepared to consider the realms above, below, and all around us where Native informants and their nonhuman kin resided.

Notes

1. Keith H. Basso, *Wisdom Sits in Places: Landscape and Language Among the Western Apache* (University of New Mexico Press, 1996).

2. William Patterson Cumming and Louis DeVorsey, *The Southeast in Early Maps* (Chapel Hill: University of North Carolina Press, 1998), 75–78; Waselkov analyzes in depth six maps of the southeast created by Indian cartographers, five of which survive. He also makes the point that "only rarely . . . did European explorers express any interest in Indian cosmography." Gregory A. Waselkov, "Indian Maps of the Colonial Southeast," in *Powhatan's Mantle: Indians in the Colonial Southeast* (Lincoln: University of Nebraska Press, 2006).

3. Mishuana Goeman, *Mark My Words: Native Women Mapping Our Nations* (Minneapolis: University of Minnesota Press, 2013), 2–5.

4. Cumming and DeVorsey, *The Southeast in Early Maps*, 65–66.

5. Louis De Vorsey, "Silent Witnesses: Native American Maps," *The Georgia Review* 46, no. 4 (1992): 709–26.

6. This is a point Paulett makes in his work, but the phraseology of Pearson's chapter succinctly expresses a similar idea. Robert Paulett, *An Empire of Small Places: Mapping the Southeastern Anglo-Indian Trade, 1732–1795* (Athens: University of Georgia Press, 2012), 15.

7. Plate 5. DeSoto. Mapa del Grofo y Costa de la Neuva España. Ca. 1544 MS [Map 1] William Patterson Cumming and Louis DeVorsey, *The Southeast in Early Maps* (Chapel Hill: University of North Carolina Press, 1998).

8. Cumming and DeVorsey, 71.

9. Steve Kosiba and Andrew M. Bauer, "Mapping the Political Landscape: Toward a GIS Analysis of Environmental and Social Difference," *Journal of Archaeological Method and Theory* 20, no. 1 (March 2013): 61–101, https://doi.org/10.1007/s10816-011-9126-z.

10. Cumming and DeVorsey, *The Southeast in Early Maps*, 73.

11. Cumming and DeVorsey, 77.

12. Juliana Barr, "Geographies of Power: Mapping Indian Borders in the 'Borderlands' of the Early Southwest," *The William and Mary Quarterly* 68, no. 1 (2011): 5–46, https://doi.org/10.5309/willmaryquar.68.1.0005.

13. George Hunter and A.S. (Alexander Samuel) Salley, "George Hunter's Map of the Cherokee Country and the Path Thereto in 1730," 1917, https://dc.statelibrary.sc.gov/handle/10827/7842.

14. "A Map of the British and French Dominions in North America, with the Roads, Distances, Limits, and Extent of the Settlements, Humbly Inscribed to the Right Honourable the Earl of Halifax, and the Other Right Honourable the Lords Commissioners for Trade & Plantations," image, Library of Congress, Washington, D.C. 20540, USA, accessed February 3, 2020, https://www.loc.gov/resource/g3300.np000009/.

15. Louis De Vorsey, "The Colonial Southeast on 'An Accurate General Map,'" *Southeastern Geographer* 6 (1966): 20–32.

16. Christopher Bernard Rodning, *Center Places and Cherokee Towns: Archaeological Perspectives on Native American Architecture and Landscape in the Southern Appalachians* (Tuscaloosa: University of Alabama Press, 2015).

17. James Mooney, *Myths of the Cherokee* (Washington, 1902), 396, http://hdl.handle.net/2027/coo1.ark:/13960/t2891smow.

18. Chambers makes a strong case that rather than a Catawba cartographer as put forth by Waselkov and Warhaus, a Cherokee created "A Map Describing the Situation of the Several Nations of Indians between South Carolina and the Massissipi River," commonly referred to as the Catawba Deerskin Map. Ian Chambers, "A Cherokee Origin for the 'Catawba' Deerskin Map (c.1721)," *Imago Mundi* 65, no. 2 (June 2013): 207–16, https://doi.org/10.1080/03085694.2013.784564.

19. Cumming and DeVorsey, *The Southeast in Early Maps*, 88–90.

20. Chambers, "A Cherokee Origin for the 'Catawba' Deerskin Map (c .1721)."

21. Milton Gaither, "The History of North American Education, 15,000 BCE to 1491," *History of Education Quarterly* 54, no. 3 (August 2014): 330, https://doi.org/10.1111/hoeq.12070.

22. Rachel J. Collins, et al., "American Chestnut: Re-Examining the Historical Attributes of a Lost Tree," *Journal of Forestry*, 2017, https://doi.org/10.5849/JOF-2016-014.

23. "A Gentleman of Elvas with DeSoto—Part 4 of 5," accessed September 14, 2019, http://floridahistory.com/elvas-5.html.

24. Mooney, *Myths of the Cherokee*.

25. Collins et al., 68.

26. Mooney, *Myths of the Cherokee*.

27. Bennie C. Keel, *Cherokee Archaeology: A Study of the Appalachian Summit* (Knoxville: University of Tennessee Press, 1987); Collins et al., "American Chestnut."

28. Victor E. Shelford, *The Ecology of North America* (Urbana, Ill.: University of Illinois Press, 1965).

29. Shelford, 42.

30. Collins et al., "American Chestnut."

31. Shelford, *The Ecology of North America*, 42.

32. The wapiti was a large deer misnamed an elk by early European settlers. Shelford, *The Ecology of North America*.

33. Andrew Shryock, Daniel Lord Smail, and Timothy Earle, *Deep History: The Architecture of Past and Present* (Berkeley: University of California Press, 2011), xi.

34. Mooney, *Myths of the Cherokee*, 262, 327–29.

35. Mooney, *Myths of the Cherokee*.

36. Christopher B. Teuton and America Meredith, *Cherokee Stories of the Turtle Island Liars' Club*, 2016, 77, http://www.vlebooks.com/vleweb/product/openreader?id=none&isbn=9781469601526.

37. Tanya M. Peres and Heidi Altman, "The Magic of Improbable Appendages: Deer Antler Objects in the Archaeological Record of the American South," *Journal of Archaeological Science: Reports* 20 (August 2018): 888–95, https://doi.org/10.1016/j.jasrep.2017.10.028; Chambers, "A Cherokee Origin for the 'Catawba' Deerskin Map (c .1721)."

38. H.C. Hovey, "American Saltpeter Caves," *Scientific American* 65, no. 1 (July 4, 1891): 2; David A. Hubbard, "Saltpetre Mining," in *Encyclopedia of Caves* (Elsevier, 2012), 676–79, https://doi.org/10.1016/B978-0-12-383832-2.00099-2.

39. Beau Duke Carroll, et al., "Talking Stones: Cherokee Syllabary in Manitou Cave, Alabama," *Antiquity* 93, no. 368 (April 2019): 519–36, https://doi.org/10.15184/aqy.2019.15.

40. The Chickamaugas, a subset of Cherokee warriors, continued fighting well after other most Cherokees declared peace with the infant United States at the time of

the American Revolution. They fortified themselves in the southernmost towns of the Cherokee Nation and established new towns in what had been Creek territory. For a more thorough discussion of their origins and relationship with the larger body of Cherokees, see Tyler Boulware, *Deconstructing the Cherokee Nation: Town, Region, and Nation among Eighteenth-Century Cherokees* (Gainesville: University Press of Florida, 2011).

41. Cumming and DeVorsey, *The Southeast in Early Maps*, 94–95.

42. Carroll et al., "Talking Stones."

43. J.T. Carson, "Ethnogeography and the Native American Past," *Ethnohistory* 49, no. 4 (October 1, 2002): 769–88, https://doi.org/10.1215/00141801-49-4-769.

Wielding the Power of Mapping

Cherokee Territoriality, Anglo-American Surveying, and the Creation of Borders in the Early Nineteenth-Century West

Austin Stewart

On July 8, 1817, Cherokee leaders signed the Treaty of Hiawassee, which assigned Cherokees then living in the trans-Mississippi West and Cherokees who enrolled in a relocation plan common ownership of a tract of land in the Arkansas River Valley. Beginning on June 20, two Arkansas Cherokee delegates met with the American treaty commissioners and national Cherokee leaders at Hiawassee to attempt to hammer out the details of the treaty. At the conference, the Arkansas delegates proposed to cede a portion of Cherokee lands that were east of the Mississippi River in exchange for legal rights to territory where many Cherokees lived in the trans-Mississippi West. Some national Cherokee headmen vehemently protested the proposed agreement because it promised to award the Arkansas Cherokees, not the entire nation, a portion of land equal to the amount ceded by the Cherokee nation, and divested the Westerners of all land claims east of the Mississippi in proportion to their population. Nevertheless, the two Arkansas delegates, four other minor chiefs from Arkansas, and seven chiefs willing to migrate west expressed an urgent desire for the United States to consent to the agreement because of the precarious nature of their Western land claims against other Native peoples and the potential claims of white colonizers and land speculators. For the Arkansas Cherokee party, the treaty would establish permanent territorial borders and quell their fears of future Anglo-American attempts to dispossess them of their land. "We have found this Country—we love it," the Arkansas Cherokee chiefs exclaimed, "and we now ask our father the President, to lay off and mark out for us our land on the Arkansas." Among other provisions, the treaty sanctioned the Arkansas Cherokees' right to a diamond-shaped tract of land separating American and Cherokee property lines within a territory that Cherokee emigrants had already colonized and claimed between the Arkansas and White Rivers.[1]

The main purpose of the treaty, the exchange of territory, should not overshadow the significance of the Arkansas Cherokees' request to have their new country marked and measured by American surveyors. This essay traces the history of why the Arkansas Cherokees, alternatively identified here as Western Cherokees or Cherokee emigrants, wanted scientific measurements of their new territory and how these demands helped shape the practice of geopolitical border-making in the early nineteenth-century West. As scholar

David Bernstein notes, the mapping of the early nineteenth-century trans-Mississippi West was not a "zero-sum process," and attempts to construct a binary between colonial and Indigenous geographies led scholars to "discount Native participation in the cartographic construction of the region." Indeed, a monolithic understanding of Indigenous geographies ignores how Natives "had complicated political, social, economic, and personal reasons for their actions," and "excludes Native people from one of the fundamental aspects of nation building."[2] Cherokee emigrant leaders incorporated surveying and mapping as a colonizing tool, which made them instrumental to the drawing of boundary lines and the expansion of American state power in the trans-Mississippi West. They parlayed their knowledge of Anglo-American surveying practices to advance their own colonizing agenda, and viewed mapping as the optimal means to support and legitimize their land claims within Western American spaces. Western Cherokee leaders consciously adhered to Euro-American border-making practices in the effort to eliminate contested and overlapping spaces of sovereignty in the Arkansas Valley. For the Cherokee emigrants, Anglo-American mapping and surveying represented a discrete form of cultural borrowing that justified their colonization of the Arkansas River Valley and their displacement of local tribes, most prominently the Arkansas Osages. By wielding the power of mapping, early nineteenth-century Cherokee colonizers helped turn geographic fictions of territorial control into tangible, legal geopolitical borders, which also facilitated the expansion of American state power and settler colonialism onto the periphery of an emerging American territorial empire.

The first part of this study analyzes how eighteenth-century Cherokees went through a process of intercultural learning about Eurocentric mapping and Anglo-American surveying practices. As mapping and surveying emerged as one of the most prominent Euro-American colonizing strategies, Cherokee leaders integrated the language of mapping and surveying into cross-cultural negotiations, especially when land became central to these diplomatic encounters. Two different types of eighteenth-century Indigenous mapping, the Catawba deerskin map of 1721 and a map drawn by the Cherokee Chief Old Tassel at the Treaty of Hopewell in 1785, reveal how Anglo-American understandings of geography and cartography gradually infiltrated eighteenth-century Cherokee understandings of how territory was defined and controlled. During the period between the construction of the Catawba map and Old Tassel's Hopewell map, European mapping permeated Cherokee–Anglo cross-cultural diplomacy, which resulted in a veritable transformation of Cherokee territoriality.[3] Anglo-Americans communicated their own ideas and practices of territoriality through maps and surveyors' plats and the negotiation of treaties that divided the land into controllable units. Cherokee leaders responded to this form of cross-cultural communication by embracing certain aspects of the European-descended logic of territoriality, most significantly Anglo-American surveying practices, thus altering previously established ways of claiming land, establishing possession of territory, and enforcing control over specific geographic areas. As Lucas Kelley's essay in this volume deftly demonstrates, Cherokee leaders sought to establish clear boundaries between their sovereign territory and that of other southeastern Indian nations and the United States well into the nineteenth century. Southeastern Indian nations frequently united Eurocentric notions of legal possession of territory and their own conceptions of territoriality to resist American colonization during the same period Cherokee emigrants began relocating to the trans-Mississippi West.

The second part investigates how the broader shift in Cherokee modes of territoriality resonated among early nineteenth-century Cherokee emigrant leaders. While adjusting to the specter of Anglo-American surveying and mapping was essential in defending against colonialism in the East, Cherokee headmen wielded mapping as a colonizing tool of power in the early nineteenth-century West. As Kathleen DuVal has shown, the Cherokee emigrants emerged as the first colonizers to successfully penetrate the "native ground" in the Arkansas River Valley. Indeed, if territoriality is an essential element of settler colonialism, then early nineteenth-century Cherokee emigrants acted like settler-colonists when negotiating their own access to land and resources via Euro-American border-making practices.[4] As they transitioned from a colonial past—in which they were colonized and dispossessed of some of their land—the Cherokee emigrants wielded the language and logic of Anglo-American practices of territoriality to justify dispossessing the Osages in the Arkansas Valley. By the time a new wave of Cherokees migrated west during the early 1810s, the trans-Mississippi West remained relatively unmapped space in the eyes of Euro-Americans, and land claims were both abundant and ambiguous on paper and in practice. Because Americans administrators viewed these Western spaces as "empty" or "vacant" landscapes, Anglo-American surveying practices, among other colonizing activities, allowed the Western Cherokees to appropriate the land as settler space through the conceptual displacement of Indigenous peoples that were native to the Arkansas Valley.[5] Moreover, when Anglo-American surveying practices threatened to injure or even erase their own land claims, Chief Taluntuskee and other headmen made certain that surveyors also demarcated the linear, geometric borders of their territory. Western Cherokee leaders, simply put, saw scientific mapping as a means to maximize the legitimization of their land claims in the Arkansas River Valley quite literally in the eyes of American officials, which resulted in the erasure of the Arkansas Osages' alternative claim to land and sovereignty.

The Western Cherokees' adoption of particular aspects of the Euro-American language and logic of territoriality also invited the expansion of American state power and federal sovereignty into and beyond the Arkansas River Valley. When Western Cherokee leaders wielded Anglo-American surveying practices to negotiate the creation of exclusive territorial borders—which were conceptualized and communicated through geometric boundaries that theoretically divided Cherokee, Osage, and American territories—they also enlisted the federal government's support for their claims to land and sovereignty. The Cherokees' colonizing activities amplified state power because they selectively chose to sanction and bolster federal authority by demanding that surveyors demarcate the bounded limits of their sovereign territory. Some American administrators, mainly Indian agents and federal officials, eagerly collaborated with Western Cherokee leaders to create fixed, exclusive political borders in the effort to establish federal/imperial authority and a sense of order within their Western territories. Once the Western Cherokees' colonizing agenda diverged from the broader geopolitical agenda advocated by local white settlers, federal officials became the ultimate adjudicators of how territory was divided among the Western

Cherokees, other Indigenous peoples, and American settlers in the early nineteenth-century West. In short, the Western Cherokees contributed to the institutionalization of new political-legal ways of organizing territories in the trans-Mississippi West.

Cherokee Territoriality

In the early 1720s, Francis Nicholson, the royal governor of South Carolina, collected two deerskin maps from southeastern Indian cartographers and produced copies of the Catawba deerskin map of 1721 (Figure 1) and the Chickasaw deerskin map of 1723. Scholars generally agree that the two maps are useful representations of the broader cartographic knowledge and spatial understandings of colonial southeastern Indian groups. Additionally, scholar Ian Chambers has suggested that the Catawba map may actually have Cherokee origins. The Catawba map articulated an ethnocentric worldview where geographic constructions of spatial domains and political boundaries did not correlate with the linear lines of territorial jurisdiction found on contemporary European maps. Instead, the Native cartographer emphasized the existence of particular political, social, and economic relationships between occupied sites by linking together disparate geographic spaces occupied by different sociopolitical groups and leaving unoccupied spaces in between them. The network map recorded the connectivity or nonconnectivity that existed between sociopolitical groups along trading paths, thus indicating specific relationships; a broken or nonexistent path indicated that enmity probably existed because a political or economic relationship was not in place.[6]

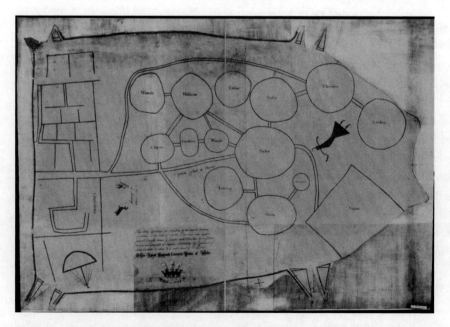

Figure 1. The Catawba Deerskin Map of 1721. (Copy of) [Map of the several nations of Indians to the Northwest of South Carolina] or [Catawba Deerskin Map] (1929; orig. [1724?]). Francis Nicholson (contributor). Geography and Map Division, Library of Congress, Washington, DC. https://www.loc.gov/item/2005625337/.

The Catawba map reveals important aspects of early eighteenth-century Cherokee ideas and practices of territoriality. European officials such as Nicholson coveted Native cartographic and geographic knowledge of the American landscape, but did not attempt to fully comprehend how Cherokee peoples and their Indigenous neighbors structured human space. The map portrayed social and political relationships rather than territorial borders and placed importance on controlling the pathways and routes between occupied territory rather than demonstrating occupation of the land itself. Thus, Cherokee peoples understood that the southeastern landscape existed as a series of commercial and social spaces, linked together by pathways and rivers, which moved from occupied site to occupied site. This understanding of human geography meant that within the early eighteenth-century Cherokee logic of territoriality, they valued mobility, or their ability to move between various geographic spaces, and did not consider the construction of fixed political borders as essential in controlling the flow of human and material resources. Cherokees and their Indigenous neighbors traveled along and sought to establish control over pathways, rivers, and streams connecting the interior spaces of eastern North America to sustain access to material resources and political, social, and economic relationships within these geographic spaces: They traded, hunted, created alliances, conducted warfare, communicated, and spread information through their knowledge, use, and control of the well-traveled trade routes and pathways of the American interior.[7]

Early eighteenth-century Cherokee ideas and practices of territoriality would have seemed impractical to Europeans precisely because these foreigners aspired to create order and extend their control over territory by producing maps containing fixed, linear political boundaries separating empires, colonies, and Indian nations. By the time Francis Nicholson collected the Catawba and Chickasaw maps, Europeans had grown accustomed to devising maps that contained legal, political, and ideological messages of territorial appropriation, a projected image of power and possession that diminished non-European constructions of territoriality.[8] Within the eighteenth-century British American context, land surveying exploded as a scientific practice and profession because mapping out geometrical boundaries or "running the line" served the purpose of legitimizing claims to territorial sovereignty or securing land rights, and many of these concrete boundaries eventually found their way onto British maps. Throughout the 1740s and 1750s, the British Board of Trade tightened control over colonial defense, administration, and settlement in light of the perceived French geopolitical threat and commanded colonial governors to resurvey the geometric boundaries of their colonies to more accurately portray Britain's colonial possessions. Surveyor's artificial marks, such as stones put on the ground or cuts in a tree, accompanied surveying maps in crafting clear, often straight lines that delineated the territorial boundaries separating British colonies from one another and separating British and Indian territory. For British colonial leaders, fixed territorial boundaries also created a better sense of jurisdiction and sociopolitical order—the borders of authority. The scientific practice of land surveying helped etch out geometric boundaries throughout the colonial British American landscape as a counter to French mapmakers in addition to diminishing the ways in which Indigenous peoples organized territory.[9]

The Seven Years' War (1754–1763) ushered in a new era of cross-cultural communication that accelerated the evolution of Cherokee notions of territoriality. The Anglo–Cherokee conflict (1759–1761) emerged, in part, as a result of South Carolinian encroachment upon Cherokee hunting grounds near Long Canes Creek close to the Cherokee Lower town of Keowee. The war within a war ravished the Cherokee–South Carolina frontier and a firm peace was not established before many Cherokee towns went up in flames. During peace talks in 1761, the disputed boundary between Cherokee country and South Carolina emerged as a central talking point between Cherokee and British leaders. Lower-town Cherokees rejected a proposed boundary clause that would have set the Cherokee–South Carolinian border at Twenty-Six Miles River (26 miles for Keowee) and forced them to essentially relinquish control of their shrinking hunting grounds, a geographic space they considered to be a part of their territory. After the removal of the original boundary clause from the preliminary treaty, South Carolinians compelled British negotiators to reinsert a Cherokee territorial concession within the final treaty, but this time the border was fixed at the Forty Mile River. Cherokee headmen accepted the boundary set in the Treaty of Charlestown, signed December 18, 1761, yet their motives for signing the treaty reflected a new emphasis on balancing older Cherokee notions of territoriality and the British practice of creating fixed political borders. On one hand, Cherokee leaders saw the treaty as a means to keep open some trading and diplomatic paths between themselves and Carolina. On the other hand, the final boundary agreement highlighted the closing of some older paths, the former in-between spaces near Long Canes Creek that had been overrun by white colonists, and at least created a temporary obstacle in the form of a fixed border separating their towns and an intruding white population.[10]

After the Seven Years' War, British imperialists presented Cherokee leaders with a foundational reference point for the cross-cultural negotiation of political borders: the Proclamation Line of 1763. Using the Appalachian Mountains as an abstract boundary, the Proclamation Line created a contiguous borderline separating the British colonies from New York to the Carolinas from an Indian reservation in the West that was under British "Sovereignty, Protection, and Dominion, for the Use of the said *Indians*."[11] At the Treaty of Augusta in early November 1763, John Stuart, Britain's Southern Superintendent of Indians Affairs, and Southern colonial governors actively informed Cherokee and other southeastern Indian attendees about key details of the Proclamation, and even issued copies of the document. British overtures included promises of the protection of Native hunting grounds and the retention of rights to all lands beyond the Proclamation Line. The promise of a definitive concrete boundary line between Cherokee country and the British colonies was very appealing to Cherokee attendees; they made sure their talks mentioned the recently established boundary set at the Treaty of Charlestown in 1761 as a reminder of this fact. Chief Attakullakulla, for example, certainly wanted the "path kept straight" between the Cherokees and Britain, but demanded that the "White People . . .

settled beyond the long Canes . . . may stay there but must proceed no farther." Some paths still flowed between the Cherokees and the British, while others were now fixed in space.[12]

As the negotiation of political borders became an essential function of Cherokee–British diplomacy, Cherokee leaders embraced a particular aspect of the Anglo-American logic of territoriality: surveying. During the mid-1760s, for example, Cherokee leaders negotiated the establishment of linear boundary lines separating Cherokee country and the two Carolina colonies, and readily assisted Anglo-American surveyors in demarcating these geometric lines using British surveying techniques. After establishing a more favorable Cherokee–South Carolina boundary for their people in 1766, Cherokee headmen met with British officials to discuss the Cherokee–North Carolina boundary in the summer of 1767. While giving his talk, Chief Ostenaco placed a string of white wampum beads "on the course the line was to run," which was a "straight course" from the South Carolina boundary line. On June 4, Ostenaco and a few other Cherokee warriors proceeded to help Anglo-American surveyors "run the line" and marked trees "with the Initial Letters of the Commissioners names and several other Trees with the names and marks" of the participating Cherokee surveyors. When the boundary line reached Tryon Mountain, the surveying party went to its peak, marked a tree, and plotted "a direct Line to Chiswell's Mines in Virginia," thus completing the "Boundary line between the said Frontiers of North Carolina and the Cherokee Hunting Grounds."[13]

Even as Cherokee leaders were forced to cede various pieces of their hunting grounds to settle geopolitical disputes and trade debts, they made sure that proper surveys were conducted to guarantee that dubious land titles could not be produced by land-hungry white colonists. Disputes over the Cherokee–Virginia boundary led to the Treaty of Hard Labour in 1768, where Cherokee and British leaders, including John Stuart, ratified the Carolina boundaries and reissued competing proposals for establishing a new permanent territorial boundary separating Virginia from Cherokee country. Virginians contested the Hard Labour boundary line, especially due to speculation and settler activity beyond the line, and two new lines, the Lochaber Line following the Treaty of Lochaber in 1770 and the Donelson Line (1771), were eventually surveyed prior to the American Revolution. In these agreements, the Cherokees renounced their claims to eastern Kentucky hunting grounds and again aided British surveyors in demarcating the extended boundary, which theoretically opened up lands below the Ohio River for British settlement.[14] In 1772, Oconostata, the principal chief of the Cherokee nation, also agreed to sell some land within the theoretical boundaries of Georgia colony to settle a large Cherokee debt to the Indian trader Edward Wilkinson. The Cherokee headman asked John Stuart to inform King George of his people's desire to confirm the agreement, which granted Wilkinson title to Cherokee lands between the Cherokee boundary line and the Saluda River. Oconostata admitted that the Saluda River formed "a much better boundary line" because that land was of "no great service" with the "Deer being mostly killed off it." He appointed Attakullakulla and Terrapin to "attend, and direct a Surveyor to mark out the Land," and "to send a Plat" to Stuart. Overseeing the mapping of the land agreements brought some insurance that British Americans were not marking out falsified boundaries that served their own territorial ambitions.[15]

After the American Revolution, Cherokee headmen used Anglo-American mapping and surveying practices, which were now deeply entrenched within the Cherokee logic of territoriality, to assert their own sovereignty. In November 1785, Cherokee headmen and diplomats met with U.S. commissioners to discuss a new peace treaty following the American victory in their war for independence at Hopewell, South Carolina. During his initial talk to the commissioners on November 23, Cherokee headman Old Tassel (*Utsi'dsata*), the principal chief of the Overhill Cherokees, recalled previous treaties and boundary lines that marked the territorial limits of Virginia and North Carolina. He informed the commissioners that Virginians and North Carolinians paid little attention to these boundaries "and encroached on our lands expressly against our inclination." The American commissioners, seeking a peaceful resolution, asked the Cherokee leader to inform them of the territorial boundaries separating the United States from Cherokee country so they may redress the situation. After two days of talks and internal discussions, Cherokee headmen "requested the commissioners to give them some paper and a pencil, and leave them to themselves, and they would draw the map of their country." On November 26, Old Tassel produced a map of Cherokee country that marked Cherokee territorial claims and a fixed boundary between Cherokee and U.S. land. Cherokee leaders not only replicated the European practice of mapping out geometrical lines of jurisdiction but also told the American commissioners that they would physically "mark a line for the white people" by surveying the territorial boundaries delineated on Old Tassel's map.[16]

The hand-drawn map (Figure 2) was both representative of a Cherokee perspective of the contested nature of territorial boundaries in the late-eighteenth-century American South and a symbolic visualization of the evolution of Cherokee territoriality between 1721 and 1785. The 1783 Treaty of Paris, which ended the American Revolution, left the southern and western boundaries of the U.S. jurisdiction in dispute. Indians, empires, and American states all claimed sovereignty over interior lands extending to the Mississippi River beyond the boundaries of the original thirteen American colonies. Old Tassel's map, directly centering on Cherokee country, embodied one alternative vision of territorial sovereignty over land in the late-eighteenth-century American South.[17] Using the language of mapping, Cherokee leaders communicated their cartographic knowledge of and claims to sovereignty over American interior spaces to the American commissioners, which included a single, dotted boundary line separating Cherokee country from American territories. In short, Old Tassel's map epitomized the substantial break from the Catawba and Chickasaw maps of the 1720s: Social relationships were no longer defined by connectivity between occupied sites; the "in-between" geographic spaces were no longer unclaimed.

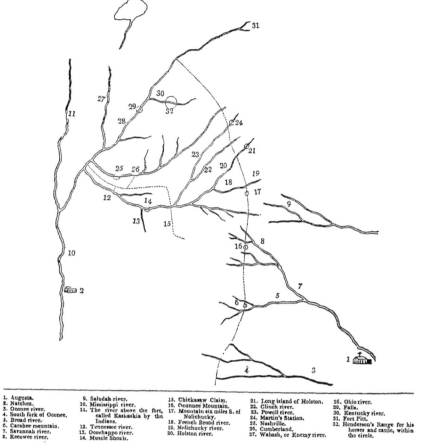

1. Augusta.	9. Saludah river.	15. Chickasaw Claim.	21. Long island of Holston.	28. Ohio river.
2. Natchez.	10. Mississippi river.	16. Ocunnee Mountain.	22. Clinch river.	29. Falls.
3. Oconee river.	11. The river above the fort,	17. Mountain six miles S. of	23. Powell river.	30. Kentucky river.
4. South fork of Oconee.	called Kaskaskia by the	Nolichucky.	24. Martin's Station.	31. Fort Pitt.
5. Broad river.	Indians.	18. French Broad river.	25. Nashville.	32. Henderson's Range for his
6. Carahee mountain.	12. Tennessee river.	19. Nolichucky river.	26. Cumberland.	horses and cattle, within
7. Savannah river.	13. Ocochappo river.	20. Holston river.	27. Wabash, or Enemy river.	the circle.
8. Keeowee river.	14. Muscle Shoals.			

Figure 2. Onitositah (Old Tassel), Map of the Cherokee Nation, November 1785 in *American State Papers: Documents, Legislative and Executive, of the United States*, Class II: Indian Affairs, eds. Walter Lowrie and Walter S. Franklin (Washington: Gales and Seaton, 1834), 1: 40.

Mapping Borders in the West

Mapping eventually played an important role in shaping the colonizing strategies of early nineteenth-century Cherokee emigrants in the trans-Mississippi West. Despite the substantial presence of Indians and emigrants, including Cherokees who migrated during the late eighteenth century, American officials began visualizing the trans-Mississippi West as a blank canvas, "vacant" space or *terra nullius*, and encouraged Cherokees to relocate west under this same premise. After the United States purchased the Louisiana Territory in 1803, President Thomas Jefferson, U.S. Indian agents, and Secretary of War Henry Dearborn viewed Arkansas as the ideal place for the Eastern tribes to exchange their lands and relocate their peoples because it contained an abundance of game, many Eastern woodland Indians hunted and even lived on its periphery, and Osage and Quapaw Indians, who claimed Arkansas lands and hunting grounds, sparsely populated that territory.[18] After Missouri Governor William Clark negotiated a treaty with Osage Chief Pawhuska that ceded some

50,000 square miles of Osage land between the Arkansas and Missouri Rivers in November 1808, Jefferson firmly believed Cherokee migrants could relocate relatively unimpeded into the trans-Mississippi West[19] (Figure 3). On January 9, 1809, President Jefferson delivered a talk to a Cherokee delegation in Washington where he offered Cherokees who desired to retain "their attachment to the hunter's life" the opportunity to "remove across the Mississippi, to some of the vacant lands of the United States, where game is abundant." For Jefferson, "those who wish to remove are permitted to send an exploring party to reconnoitre the country on the waters of the Arkansas and White rivers" for the purpose of finding "a tract of country suiting the emigrants, and not claimed by other Indians."[20]

Figure 3. Treaty of Fort Clark, November 10, 1808 (Denotated in green on the map). A portion of the geographic region known as Lovely's Purchase is denotated in yellow. Indian land cessions in the United States. 1899. *Smithsonian Institution. Bureau of American Ethnology. Eighteenth Annual Report of the Bureau of American Ethnology, 1896-'97. pt. 2*, comp. Charles C. Royce (Washington: Government Printing Office, 1899), 521-997.

Among Cherokee emigrants, Chief Taluntuskee most adeptly manipulated the American point of view that unmapped Western lands essentially equaled "vacant" territory. In 1810–1811, many new emigrants joined a well-established Cherokee community along the St. Francis River in present-day southeast Missouri.[21] Because American officials gave no guidelines to where and how much territory the Cherokee emigrants could actually claim, however, Taluntuskee immediately began scouting for an ideal location to establish new settlements. Writing from the St. Francis River in the summer of 1811, the exiled Cherokee chief informed Cherokee agent Return Meigs that he had "found a Country" for his people, which was substantially further west in the Arkansas River Valley. The New Madrid Earthquakes, which occurred throughout the winter of 1811–12, essentially flooded and destroyed the Cherokee communities on the St. Francis River, and inadvertently gave Taluntuskee the justification he needed to stake a claim to land within the Arkansas

Valley.[22] Taluntuskee's party found a new place to live near Dardanelle Rock, which is located on the south side of the Arkansas River and north of the Ouachita Mountains in northeast Arkansas. By early 1813, Taluntuskee suggested that the United States hastily permit Cherokee emigrants to take possession of land located at the Illinois Bayou and the base the Ozark Plateau because "for two years" he had been standing patiently "in water" until his "feet got cold." The Cherokee leader informed Return Meigs that the Cherokees had chosen "a good water Country" after leaving "the ponds and reachd the dry land and settled among the Mountains," which was "a good place to build my houses."[23]

In addition to building new homes, Taluntuskee and other Cherokee leaders sought to build geopolitical borders as well. After Cherokee headmen clamored for an American agent, officials sent Major William Lovely, a sub-agent and Taluntuskee's confidant, to their aid. With Lovely's assistance, Western Cherokees accommodated Euro-American border-making practices to win American assent for a new homeland amidst Native peoples who were less familiar with Eurocentric methods of creating borders. Shortly after arriving in Arkansas, Lovely "called a Council of Indians, and established certain temporary boundaries with them." As part of these new boundaries, the Cherokee sub-agent also included an abstract, geometric boundary between "the Cherokees and the White people in order to keep peace and harmony between Them." The temporary boundaries essentially awarded the Cherokees exclusive possession of a very large tract of land between the White and Arkansas Rivers following the line "that was agreed on between General Clarke and the Osage Nation" in 1808, and included territory along the Petit Jean River on the south side of the Arkansas River and extending "to a point Claimd by Other Tribes that is to say the line between the Terrytory of Misouri and State of Louisiana, thence a westerly Course till it intercepts the affore said Osage boundariy." While Lovely's paper boundary lines initially meant little to local tribes such as the Osages, white settlers were horrified by the creation of these geographic fictions of territorial control, especially because they appeared to be partisan in favor of the Cherokee emigrants.[24]

Lovely's temporary boundaries permitted the Cherokee emigrants to conceptualize a fixed territory that they needed to legally defend from outsiders, both Native peoples and white Americans. By 1815, white population growth in the Missouri Territory spurred the creation of new counties and the first survey of lands within the Louisiana Territory, which threatened to supersede the tenuous borders Lovely had created in an ad hoc fashion in 1813. The Missouri Territory was also a land of promise for veterans of the recently ended War of 1812. An Act of Congress in 1812 tentatively set aside 2,000,000 acres of bounty land for war veterans between the St. Francis and Arkansas Rivers. American lawmakers planned to survey and divide the public land into townships, and subdivide the townships in sections and quarter sections (which equaled to 160-acre tracts). Congress also created the U.S. General Land Office (GLO), which was to oversee the surveying of the territory gained in the Louisiana Purchase. In late 1815, William Rector, later named surveyor general of Illinois, Missouri, and Arkansas, hired surveyors Prospect K. Robbins and Joseph C. Brown to run the Five Principal Meridian, a standard north–south line that began at the mouth of the Arkansas River, and the east–west baseline, which began at the mouth of the

St. Francis River and intersected with the Fifth Principal Meridian at what became known as initial point, a geographic/cartographic reference for future surveys in the American West. Beginning their work in October 1815, Robbins and Brown completed their task of locating the initial point by the end of the year. In the aftermath of the Louisiana Purchase Survey, President James Madison appointed Rector surveyor general, and Rector undertook an ambitious plan to identify and survey the Arkansas bounty lands in early 1816.[25]

As Anglo-American surveyors closed in around the Cherokee emigrants, the boundaries set by William Lovely eventually provoked land disputes between the Cherokees and local Indigenous peoples, the Osages and Quapaws. Cherokee attempts to simply erase the ways in which these Indigenous groups organized space did not sit well with either tribe. In 1816, the Indian commissioners assigned to adjudicate the disputes questioned whether or not the Cherokee emigrants were living illegally on Osage territory. They took seriously Osage complaints that the Arkansas Cherokees "have settled upon their lands," which the commissioners suggested was the "principal cause of hostility between" the Cherokees and Osages. According to the commissioners, "any published Map" would confirm this fact, but they were willing to wait until surveyors ran the boundary line of the Osage purchase of 1808 "from Missouri to the Arkansaw" to make any necessary adjudications to the intertribal boundary dispute. The commissioners were not opposed to removing them from the land claimed by the Osages as well as the Quapaws on the "south side of the Arkansas" if American surveys found Cherokee settlements to be existing within either tribe's territory.[26]

Western Cherokee leaders responded to the threat to their land claims posed by the Missouri Territory, the GLO, and local Indigenous groups by requesting that American federal administrators also have surveyors mark out the borders of their territory. On May 23, 1815, for example, Chief Taluntuskee sent a letter to Governor William Clark of the Missouri Territory arguing for the legitimization of the Western Cherokees' claim to possession of Western lands through the demarcation of territorial boundaries. The Cherokee headman told Clark that many Cherokees, including himself, migrated to Arkansas "with the consent of the president of United States" for the purpose of taking possession of vacant lands. Although the Western Cherokees wanted "to be friendly with our Brothers the whites," they also wanted to know that their people walked "upon our ground." For Taluntuskee, his people had been "industrious," had "cleared nine miles On Each side" of the Arkansas River, and he wished to have "our Boundaries Run according to our agreement." At a council meeting in April 1816, Chief Takatoka expressed a similar sentiment. He reminded the Americans that President Jefferson had granted Cherokee emigrants the right to find and settle upon "a tract of land not owned by any other tribe." After erecting settlements on lands located on the north side and south side of the Arkansas River, Cherokee emigrants had become "much distressed at hearing that it is to be given to the Whites." Takatoka did not object to having "White neighbors; but it will not suit well for White and Indians to live in the same neighborhood unless they know their limits and live each on their own ground." If the Cherokee emigrants were to agree to exchange Eastern lands for Western lands, then

Anglo-American surveyors needed to mark out the limits of their new territory so that their boundaries were "clearly known."[27]

The Western Cherokees' pursuit of geopolitical borders culminated in the 1817 Treaty of Hiawassee. Western Cherokee headmen quickly ended any impasse over the validity of their territorial claims by negotiating the treaty with Andrew Jackson and Tennessee Governor Joseph McMinn in which they ceded some Eastern territory in exchange for Arkansas territory where no other Indians had "any just claim." Cherokees living in Arkansas and those who enrolled to relocate were now entitled to common ownership of the tract of land that included most of the geographic area encompassing the temporary geopolitical borders created by William Lovely in 1813. Only those Cherokees who had established farms on the south side of the Arkansas River were required to give up their improvements and move to the north side of the river.[28] Although Cherokee leaders complained about the delay, American surveyors eventually marked out the eastern or lower boundary of the Western Cherokee land grant by August 1819. The new geopolitical borders placed the Cherokee emigrants within the newly created Arkansas Territory, which separated from Missouri on March 2, 1819.[29]

Despite their adoption of Euro-American border-making practices to secure land rights in the Arkansas Valley, the Western Cherokees maintained a dynamic conceptualization of territoriality. They also desired permanent access to western Arkansas hunting grounds, where most of the hunting resources resided after Cherokee and white colonists erected settlements in central Arkansas. Leaders such as Taluntuskee often spoke about the progress of Cherokee civilization—their transition from hunters to farmers—yet these same leaders recognized that many Cherokee emigrants still relied on hunting for sustenance and to participate in the exchange economy. During the 1810s, Cherokee emigrants frequently fought against Osage bands over hunting rights on Lovely's Purchase, a geographic area spanning from present-day northeastern Oklahoma to northwestern Arkansas. As a result, their broader colonizing agenda involved establishing new rules of access to Lovely's Purchase and erasing Osage sovereign claims to the same territory.[30]

Western Cherokees framed their campaign to drive the Arkansas Osages from the Western hunting grounds as a defensive war, yet clearly viewed Lovely's Purchase as claimable territory. During the summer of 1816, William Lovely arranged a meeting between Cherokee and Osages leaders to ease the tension between the two Indigenous groups soon after Indian commissioners alleged that a war between the Osages and the Cherokees was inevitable "without the interposition of the American Government." While the main objective was obtaining peace, Lovely induced the Osages to cede a 7-million-acre tract of land known as "Lovely's Purchase" located from the Verdigris River to the older boundary line negotiated in Clark's Osage treaty in 1808 and down to the Western Cherokee settlements between the White and Arkansas Rivers. On September 25, 1818, Great and Little Osage leaders officially ceded Lovely's Purchase to the United States, who, in turn, promised the Western Cherokees that they would have unimpeded hunting access to Lovely's Purchase, which would essentially remain an

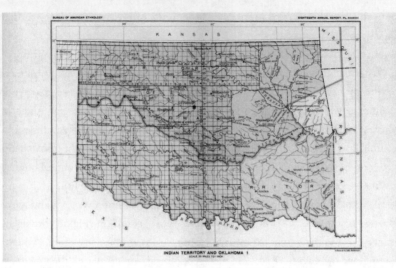

Figure 4. Treaty of St. Louis, September 25, 1818 (Lovely's Purchase, the territory ceded by the Osages, is denotated in yellow.) Indian land cessions in the United States. 1899. *Smithsonian Institution. Bureau of American Ethnology. Eighteenth Annual Report of the Bureau of American Ethnology, 1896-'97. pt. 2*, comp. Charles C. Royce (Washington: Government Printing Office, 1899), 521-997.

unmapped space and a "neutral" site used by Cherokee and Osage hunters (Figure 4). To the frustration of the Osages, the treaty emboldened Cherokee leaders to claim the ceded hunting grounds as part of their sovereign territory. Arkansas Osage headman Clermont II complained that his people did not cede the right to hunt on Lovely's Purchase.[31]

During the early 1820s, Western Cherokees and the white citizens of the Arkansas Territory became interlocked in a quasi-legal conflict over the rights to Lovely's Purchase, and the Osages' claims were ostensibly cast aside. Cherokee headmen again demanded that U.S. officials survey or resurvey the linear, geometric territorial borders separating their territory from Osage and American lands. Around early October in 1822, they sent delegates to Washington to discuss "the limits of the land they are to hold" north of the Arkansas River, which included the surveying of the unmapped western or upper boundary of their territory. In Washington, Cherokee representatives disagreed with both the quantity of land allotted to the Western Cherokees (3,285,710 acres) and the proposed limits of their western boundary, which they believed should be run further west, maybe even to the Osage boundary. Otherwise, Cherokee leaders claimed, white settlers would certainly move into Lovely's Purchase and deprive the Cherokees "of that outlet to the west which our great father has promised."[32] Federal officials indefinitely banned white settlement within the contested territory in the attempt to keep their promise to Cherokee and Osage leaders that the area would remain strictly a hunting outlet. Nevertheless, local American officials and white settlers feared the Western Cherokees were scheming to outright acquire the right to parts of or all of the territory encompassing Lovely's Purchase. Robert Crittenden, the acting governor of the Arkansas Territory, reassured local American citizens that the Cherokees' western boundary would be much further east than the Osage boundary. Soon after, Congress intervened in the land dispute. Missouri

Senator Thomas Hart Benton and other congressmen proposed and passed a bill that fixed the geometric western boundary of the Arkansas Territory 40 miles west of the proposed Cherokee boundary line. The creation of the new western boundary, which President James Monroe signed into law on May 26, 1824, meant that most of Lovely's Purchase was theoretically included within the jurisdictional boundaries of the Arkansas Territory.[33]

Much like their eighteenth-century Cherokee predecessors, Western Cherokee headmen used the language of mapping to support their claims to sovereignty over American interior spaces. In 1823, the Anglo-American surveyor, Captain Benjamin Shattuck, ran the original western boundary in accordance with the instructions given by Crittenden rather than the boundary line Cherokee leaders expected to be fixed, which gave the Cherokees only a 36-mile front on the Arkansas River. In early 1824, Cherokee headmen notified American officials that they disagreed with the placement of the recently surveyed western boundary line and presented a rough sketch of the eastern and western boundaries, which exhibited "a more easy and perspicuous view of them than words alone could furnish." Although the map did not show the correct meanders of the Arkansas and White Rivers or topography of the country, it was designed to show the relative position of Cherokee territory in relation to lands held by the United States and the Osages. Unfortunately, this map is lost, but Cherokee leaders, once again, employed mapping as a tool to support their land claims. Cherokee leaders argued that "these lines and circumstances are inconsistent with a just and fair interpretation of the Treaty," and sought to correct the mistakes made by American surveyors. They demanded that the upper boundary line be moved further west past Skin Bayou, giving them some extra eighty to one hundred riverfront miles along the Arkansas River, and have the line run parallel to the lower boundary.[34]

By January 1825, the revised boundaries of the Western Cherokees' sovereign territory became a temporary reality and even appeared relatively quickly on American atlases. American surveyor Allen Martin established a new eastern boundary that began at its base at Point Remove Creek and ran northeast toward Harden's Bluff on the White River and a revised western boundary that started at a point less than 2 miles above Skin Bayou and continued northeast around 12 miles above Fort Smith and some 134 miles toward the White River. Martin's survey increased the Cherokees' riverfront on the Arkansas by 114 miles and reduced their front on the White River from about 208 to 134 miles.[35] The new geopolitical borders also gave the Western Cherokees a small portion of Lovely's Purchase. David Vance's *Map of the United States of North America* (1825) was the first map to visually depict both the eastern and the western boundaries, but the latter boundary erroneously begins near the Illinois River in present-day Oklahoma. Vance's pocket map entitled *Map of the State of Missouri and Territory of Arkansas* (1826) more accurately portrays the revised western boundary, which commences just west of Fort Smith and travels at a northeast angle that is parallel to the eastern boundary (Figures 5 and 6).

While having Anglo-American surveyors mark out their territory supported the Western Cherokees' colonizing agenda for over a decade, these border-making activities also had strengthened state power and federal sovereignty. By 1828, Cherokee headmen felt that their

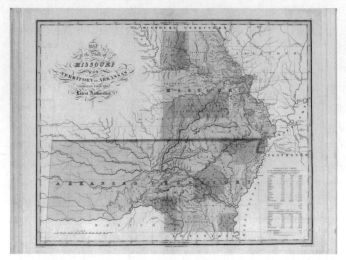

Figure 5. Map of the State of Missouri and Territory of Arkansas, 1826. Map of the State of Missouri And Territory of Arkansas Compiled From The Latest Authorities. Drawn by D.H. Vance. Engraved by J.H. Young. Published by A. Finley Philadelphia 1826. David Rumsey Map Collection, David Rumsey Map Center, Stanford Libraries.

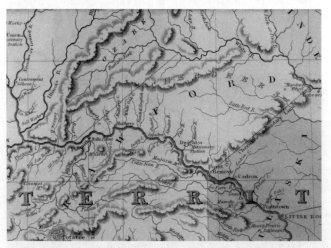

Figure 6. Western Cherokee Boundary Lines, 1826. Map of the State of Missouri And Territory of Arkansas Compiled From The Latest Authorities. Drawn by D.H. Vance. Engraved by J.H. Young. Published by A. Finley Philadelphia 1826. David Rumsey Map Collection, David Rumsey Map Center, Stanford Libraries.

only recourse toward settling their increasingly contentious dispute with white Arkansans over the rights to Lovely's Purchase was to solicit support from American federal officials. On April 5, 1826, Congress authorized the survey and sale of any unassigned land within Lovely's Purchase. After Cherokee leaders learned that the Americans planned to survey the remaining land laying between the Cherokee and Osage boundaries, they literally intercepted René Paul, the surveyor instructed to extensively map out Lovely's Purchase, in December 1826, asked Paul for a copy of his instructions, and pleaded with the surveyor to postpone his mission until the Cherokees could negotiate with the U.S. government for the annexation of more land within Lovely's Purchase. Although federal officials eventually suspended the survey, Arkansas territorial leaders aimed to cut off Western Cherokee peoples' access to the Western hunting grounds by surrounding them with white settlers on Lovely's Purchase. On October 13, 1827, territorial assemblymen passed *An act for the division of Crawford County*, which created Lovely County out of "all that portion of the county of Crawford called and known by the name of Lovely's Purchase" as well as any adjacent territories that remained unincorporated into another county within the borders of the Arkansas Territory. Alarmed by this act, Western Cherokee leaders sent a delegation to Washington in the winter of 1827–2188 to meet with federal officials and address their claims to Lovely's Purchase.[36]

In Washington, the Adams administration made it known to the Western Cherokee delegation that they would have to choose between maintaining a culturally hybrid form of territoriality outside of the Arkansas River Valley and adhering to the Euro-centric borders they helped create. President John Quincy Adams, who remained peripheral to the closed-doors negotiations, privately told his secretary of war, James Barbour, that the "collision" between the government's pledge made to the Western Cherokees and the "just and reasonable demands of our own people" could be resolved only if the Indians accepted "a right of peaceful way" to Lovely's Purchase, which would be colonized by white settlers. Adams implied that the Cherokee emigrants could either have a path to their hunting outlet or permanently relocate to Lovely's Purchase. Federal officials were no longer as amenable to the Western Cherokees' logic of having some boundaries fixed in space while also maintaining an ambiguous geographic space "in-between" the emerging borders of property and sovereignty in the early nineteenth-century West.[37]

Feeling pressured to make an undesirable choice between maintaining their current boundaries and relocating to Lovely's Purchase, Western Cherokee representatives signed the Treaty of Washington on May 6, 1828, which extinguished the Western Cherokees' right to land and sovereignty within the borders of the Arkansas Territory. The diplomatic agreement required the Cherokee emigrants to abandon their homes and improvements in the Arkansas River Valley and move outside of the current western boundary of Arkansas. In return, the treaty relocated Arkansas's western border to its original position 40 miles east, and the Western Cherokee nation procured 7 million acres beyond the western boundary of the Arkansas Territory, which included millions of acres within Lovely's Purchase. The land ceded to the Western Cherokees formed the basis for the sovereign territory of the present-day Cherokee nation.[38]

Conclusion

The late-eighteenth-century Cherokee adaptation of particular aspects of a Eurocentric logic of territoriality, most prominently Anglo-American surveying culture, influenced how Cherokee emigrant leaders defended their territory and enforced control over specific geographic areas in the trans-Mississippi West. During the early nineteenth century, Western Cherokee headmen selectively used the language and logic of Euro-American border-making practices to advance a broader colonizing agenda, which included dispossessing and replacing Indigenous populations in the Arkansas River Valley and pushing white settlers to the edges of their territory. They consistently pestered the United States to mark out and run the boundary lines of their land reserve to avoid further disputes over the legitimacy of their territorial claims even after securing land rights by treaty. Nevertheless, the Cherokees' desire to maintain a hunting outlet in the geographic area known as Lovely's Purchase ran counter to the highly political and legal act of surveying and mapping out American spaces and creating fixed territorial borders separating American states and territories, and Indian nations. Once the Western Cherokees' colonizing agenda diverged from the broader geopolitical agenda advocated by local white settlers and federal officials, some Cherokee headmen begrudgingly negotiated a new treaty agreement and accepted a new borderline that forced Western Cherokee peoples to relocate west of the Arkansas River Valley. In the end, if American surveying helped build a nation, then the Western Cherokees' participation in the cartographic construction of the early nineteenth-century West, which shaped the contours of geographic boundaries and state power within an emerging American continental empire, should not be overlooked.

Notes

Austin is currently a doctoral candidate in the Department of History at Lehigh University. He would like to thank Michelle LeMaster and Jay Donis for their critique of this essay.

1. Arkansas Cherokee to Andrew Jackson, April 18, 1817, Andrew Jackson Papers, MSS 27532, vol. 44, Library of Congress, Washington, D.C.; Cherokees of the Arkansas to Indian Commissioners, June 28, 1817, Andrew Jackson Papers, MSS 27532, vol. 45, Library of Congress, Washington, D.C.; Cherokee nation to Indian Commissioners, July 2, 1817, in *American State Papers, Indian Affairs* (hereafter *ASPIA*) (Washington, D.C.: Gales and Seaton, 1832), 2: 142–43; William G. McLoughlin, *Cherokee Renascence in the New Republic* (Princeton, N.J.: Princeton University Press, 1986), 220–31; Treaty with the Cherokee, July 8, 1817, in *Indian Affairs. Laws and Treaties*, ed. Charles J. Kappler (United States Government Printing Office, 1904), 2: 140–44; Derek R. Everett, "On The Extreme Frontier: Crafting the Western Arkansas Boundary," *Arkansas Historical Quarterly*, 67, no. 1 (Spring, 2008): 4.

2. David Bernstein, *How the West Was Drawn: Mapping, Indians, and the Construction of the Trans-Mississippi West* (Lincoln: University of Nebraska Press, 2018), 10.

3. Territoriality is defined here as a human social construct of a geographical strategy attempting to affect, influence, or control actions and interactions (of people, things, and relationships) by communicating and/or attempting to enforce control over a geographic area. See Robert D. Sack, "Human Territoriality: A Theory," *Annals of the Association of American Geographers*, 73, no. 1 (Mar., 1983): 55; Robert D. Sack, *Human Territoriality: Its Theory and History* (Cambridge, United Kingdom: Cambridge University Press, 1986), 19–31.

4. Patrick Wolfe, "Settler colonialism and the elimination of the native," *Journal of Genocide Research*, 8, no. 4 (December 2006): 387–88; Kathleen Duval, *The Native Ground: Indians and Colonists in the Heart of the Continent* (Philadelphia: University of Pennsylvania Press, 2006), 196–226.

5. Lorenzo Veracini, *Settler Colonialism: A Theoretical Overview* (London: Palgrave Macmillan, 2010), 35–7.

6. Juliana Barr and Edward Countryman, "Maps and Spaces, Paths to Connect, and Lines to Divide," in *Contested Spaces of Early America*, eds. Julianna Barr and Edward Countryman (Philadelphia: University of Pennsylvania Press, 2014), 11; Pekka Hämäläinen, "The Shapes of Power: Indians, Europeans, and North American Worlds from the Seventeenth to the Nineteenth Century," in *Ibid.*, 36–7; Gregory A. Waselkov, "Indian Maps of the Colonial Southeast," in *Powhatan's Mantle: Indians in the Colonial Southeast*, eds. Peter H. Wood, Gregory A. Waselkov, and M. Thomas Hatley (Lincoln, 1989), 292–303; Gregory H. Nobles, "Straight Lines and Stability: Mapping the Political Order of the Anglo-American Frontier," *Journal of American History*, 80, no. 1 (June, 1993): 26–7; Ian David Chambers, "Space: The Final Frontier?: Spatial Understandings in the 18th-Century American Southeast" (PhD dissertation, University of California–Riverside, 2006), 159–65; John Rennie Short, *Cartographic Encounters: Indigenous Peoples and the Exploration of the New World* (London: Reaktion Books, 2009), 28–9; S. Max Edelson, *The New Map of Empire: How Britain Imagined America Before Independence* (Cambridge, Mass.: Harvard University Press, 2017), 145–47; James H. Merrell, *The Indians' New World: Catawbas and Their Neighbors from European Contact through the Era of Removal* (Chapel Hill: University of North Carolina Press, 1989), 92–5; Robin Beck, *Chiefdoms, Collapse, and Coalescence in the Early American South* (Cambridge, United Kingdom: Cambridge University Press, 2013), chapter 6; Ian Chambers, "A Cherokee Origin for the 'Catawba' Deerskin Map (c. 1721)," *Imago Mundi*, 65, no. 2 (June, 2013): 207–16.

7. Daniel H. Usner, Jr., *Indians, Settlers, and Slaves in a Frontier Exchange Economy: The Lower Mississippi Valley Before 1783* (Chapel Hill: University of North Carolina Press, 1992); Eric Hinderaker, *Elusive Empires: Constructing Colonialism in the Ohio Valley, 1673–1800* (Cambridge, United Kingdom: Cambridge University Press, 1997); Angela Pulley Hudson, *Creek Paths and Federal Roads: Indians, Settlers, and Slaves and the Making of the American South* (Chapel Hill: University of North Carolina Press, 2010), chapter 1; April Lee Hatfield, *Atlantic Virginia: Intercolonial Relations in the Seventeenth Century* (Philadelphia: University of Pennsylvania Press, 2004), 13–4; Robert Paulett, *An Empire of Small Places: Mapping the Southeastern Anglo-Indian Trade, 1732–1795* (Athens: University of Georgia Press, 2012); Jon Parmenter, *The Edge of the Woods: Iroquoia, 1534–1701* (East Lansing: Michigan State University Press, 2010); Sami Lakomaki, *Gathering Together: The Shawnee People Through Diaspora and Nationhood, 1600–1870* (New Haven, Conn.: Yale University Press, 2014); Michael A. McDonnell, *Masters of Empire: Great Lakes Indians and the Making of America* (New York: Hill and Wang, 2015); Alejandra Dubcovsky, *Informed Power: Communication in the Early South* (Cambridge, Mass.: Harvard University Press, 2016).

8. J.B. Harley and David Woodward, "Concluding Remarks," in J.B. Harley and David Woodward, eds., *History of Cartography, vol. I: Cartography in Prehistoric, Ancient, and Medieval Europe and the Mediterranean* (Chicago, 1987), 506; Walter D. Mignolo, *The Darker Side of the Renaissance: Literacy, Territoriality, and Colonization* (Ann Arbor: University of Michigan Press, 1995); Benjamin Schmidt, "Mapping an Empire: Cartographic and Colonial Rivalry in Seventeenth-Century Dutch and English North America," *The William*

and Mary Quarterly, 54, no. 3 (July, 1997): 551–52; John R. Short, *Representing the Republic: Mapping the United States, 1600–1900* (London: Reaktion Books, 2001), chapter 3; Ken MacMillan, *Sovereignty and Possession in the English New World: The Legal Foundations of Empire, 1576–1640* (Cambridge, Mass.: Cambridge University Press, 2006), chapter 5.

9. Martin Brückner, *The Geographic Revolution of Early America: Maps, Literacy, and National Identity* (Chapel Hill: University of North Carolina Press, 2006), 16–23; Allen Greer, *Property and Dispossession: Natives, Empires, and Land in Early Modern North America* (Cambridge, United Kingdom: Cambridge University Press, 2018), 317–20; Nancy Shoemaker, *A Strange Likeness: Becoming Red and White in Eighteenth-Century North America* (Oxford, United Kingdom: Oxford University Press, 2004), 20–31; Edelson, *The New Map of Empire*, chapter 1. See also Paul W. Mapp, *The Elusive West and the Contest for Empire, 1713–1763* (Chapel Hill: University of North Carolina Press, 2011).

10. Tom Hatley, *The Dividing Paths: Cherokees and South Carolinians Through the Revolutionary Era* (Oxford, United Kingdom: Oxford University Press, 1993), 204–7; John Oliphant, *Peace and War on the Anglo-Cherokee Frontier, 1756–63* (Baton Rouge: Louisiana State University Press, 2001), chapter 6.

11. Among the many places a copy of the Royal Proclamation can be found is Milton W. Hamilton, ed., *The Papers of Sir William Johnson*, vol. 10 (Albany: University of the State of New York, 1951), 977–85.

12. "Journal of the Proceedings of the Southern Congress at Augusta," in *The State Records of North Carolina*, ed. Walter Clark (Goldsboro, N.C.: Nash Brothers, 1895), 11: 179–207; John Richard Alden, *John Stuart and the Southern Colonial Frontier: A Study of Indian Relations, War, Trade, and Land Problems in the Southern Wilderness, 1754–1775* (Ann Arbor: University of Michigan Press, 1944), chapter 11.

13. Address by Ostenaco to William Tryon, June 2, 1767, in *The Colonial Records of North Carolina*, ed. William L. Saunders (Raleigh: P.M. Hale, 1890), 7: 464–66; Agreement between North Carolina and the Cherokee Nation concerning the boundary between North Carolina and Cherokee land, in *Ibid.*, 7: 469–71.

14. See Louis De Vorsey, Jr., *The Indian Boundary in the Southern Colonies, 1763–1775* (Chapel Hill: University of North Carolina Press, 1961).

15. Oconostata to Stuart, November 7, 1772, British Colonial Office Records, Class 5/74/43-4.

16. Journal of Commissioners at Treaty of Hopewell, 1785, *ASPIA*, 1: 40–3.

17. Adam Rothman, *Slave Country: American Expansion and the Origins of the Deep South* (Cambridge, Mass.: Harvard University Press, 2005), 9–10.

18. Anthony F.C. Wallace, *Jefferson and the Indians: The Tragic Fate of the First Americans* (Cambridge, Mass.: Belknap Press, 1999), chapter 8; Willard H. Rollings, "Living in a Graveyard: Native Americans in Colonial Arkansas," in *Cultural Encounters in the Early South: Indians and Europeans in Arkansas*, ed. Jeannie Whayne (Fayetteville: University of Arkansas Press, 1995), 60. See also Walter Johnson, *River of Dark Dreams: Slavery and Empire in the Cotton Kingdom* (Cambridge, Mass.: Harvard University Press, 2013), chapter 1.

19. Duval, *The Native Ground*, 195–209.

20. William Clark to William Eustis, February 20, 1810, *ASPIA*, 1: 765; Thomas Jefferson to Cherokee Deputation of the Upper and Lower Towns, January 9, 1809, *ASPIA*, 2:125.

21. McLoughlin, *Cherokee Renascence*, 159–60.

22. Robert A. Myers, "Cherokee Pioneers in Arkansas: The St. Francis Years, 1985–1813," *Arkansas Historical Quarterly*, 56, no. 2 (Summer, 1997): 153–54; Deposition of Henry Cassidy, January 23, 1813, in *The Territorial Paper of the United States* (hereafter, TP), ed. Clarence E. Carter (Washington, D.C.: United States Government Printing Office, 1948), 14: 623–25; W.D. Williams, ed., "Louis Bringier and His Description of Arkansas in 1812," *Arkansas Historical Quarterly*, 48, no. 2 (Summer, 1989): 123–24. See also Conevery Bolton Valencius, *The Lost History of the New Madrid Earthquakes* (Chicago: University of Chicago Press, 2013).

23. John D. Chisholm to Return Meigs, June 28, 1812, M208, Records of the Cherokee Indian Agency in Tennessee, 1801–1835, Record Group 75, National Archives, Washington, D.C. (hereafter, NARA); Toluntuskee to Return Meigs, March 14, 1813, M208, RG 75, NARA; George Sabo III, *Paths of Our Children: Historic Indians of Arkansas, Arkansas Archeological Survey Popular Series No. 3* (Fayetteville: Arkansas Archeological Survey, 1992), 98.

24. William Russell to Delegate Edward Hempstead, November 1, 1813, in *TP*, 14: 720–21; William L. Lovely to Governor Clark, May 27, 1815, in *TP*, 15: 56–7; Lovely to the Cherokees, July 20, 1813, in *TP*, 14:721–22. William Russell to Delegate Edward Hempstead, November 1, 1813, in *TP*, 14: 720–21; Clark to Lovely, September 29, 1813, in *TP*, 15: 50–1.

25. Resolution of the Territorial Assembly, January 15, 1815, in *TP*, 15: 38–9; William Rector to Josiah Meigs, April 17, 1815, in *TP*, 15: 26–32; William E. Foley, *The Genesis of Missouri: From Wilderness Outpost to Statehood* (Columbia: University of Missouri Press, 1989), 238–44; S. Charles Bolton, *Territorial Ambition: Land and Society in Arkansas, 1800–1840* (Fayetteville: University of Arkansas Press, 1993), 20–3; David A. Smith, "Preparing the Wilderness for Settlement: Public Land Survey Administration, 1803–1836," *Arkansas Historical Quarterly*, 71, no. 4 (Winter 2012): 381–406; J. Blake Perkins, "Women and American Settlement in Territorial Lawrence County," *Arkansas Historical Quarterly*, 75, no. 2 (Summer 2016): 111–13.

26. Indian Commissioners to the Secretary of War, June 30, 1816, in *TP*, 15: 151–53.

27. Chief Taluntuskee to Governor Clark, May 23, 1815, M208, RG 75, NARA; The Talk of Tee-kee-to-ka, April 26, 1816, Andrew Jackson Papers, MSS 27532, vol. 40, Library of Congress, Washington, D.C.; Robert A. Myers, "Cherokee Pioneers in Arkansas: The St. Francis Years, 1985–1813," *Arkansas Historical Quarterly*, 56, no. 2 (Summer, 1997): 127–57; Joseph Patrick Key, "Indians and Ecological Conflict in Territorial Arkansas," *Arkansas Historical Quarterly*, 59, no. 2 (Summer, 2000): 127–46.

28. McLoughlin, *Cherokee Renascence*, 230–31, 262; Treaty with the Cherokee, July 8, 1817, in *Indian Affairs. Laws and Treaties*, 2: 140–44.

29. John Calhoun to Reuben Lewis, August 2, 1819, in *TP*, 19: 90.

30. Lovely to Meigs, July 16, 1813, M208, RG 75, NARA; Return J. Meigs to William Crawford, February 17, 1816, *TP*, 15:121–23.

31. The Indian Commissioners to the Secretary of War, June 17, 1816, in *TP*, 17: 355; Brad Agnew, "The Cherokee Struggle for Lovely's Purchase," *American Indian Quarterly*, 2, no. 4 (Winter, 1975–76): 347; Lovely to Cleremont, and all the Chiefs of the Osage Nation, U.S. Congress, House, document no. 263, 20th Congress, 1st Session, 38; Treaty with the Osages, 1818, in *Indian Affairs. Laws and Treaties*, 2: 167–68; DuVal, *The Native Ground*, 210–11.

32. Matthew Arbuckle to C.J. Nourse, September 30, 1822, in *TP*, 19: 462–63; Chiefs of the Arkansas Cherokee to John C. Calhoun, June 24, 1823, in *TP*, 19: 525–27.

33. Governor Miller to John C. Calhoun, March 24, 1820, in *TP*, 19: 153–55; James Miller to John C. Calhoun, June 20, 1820, in *TP*, 19: 191–95; John C. Calhoun to William Bradford, April 30, 1821, in *TP*, 19: 286; Matthew Arbuckle to C. J. Nourse, September 30, 1822, in *TP*, 19: 463; *Arkansas Gazette*, June 17, 1823; Robert Crittenden to John C. Calhoun, September 28, 1823, in *TP*, 19: 548; Henry Conway to John C. Calhoun, June 3, 1824, in *TP*, 19: 670–71; Memorial to the President by the Territorial Assembly, October 18, 1823, in TP, 19: 671–72; John C. Calhoun to Robert Crittenden, July 8, 1824, in *TP*, 19: 686; Agnew, "The Cherokee Struggle for Lovely's Purchase," 351; Everett, "On the Extreme Frontier," 13–4; An act to fix the western boundary line of the territory of Arkansas, and for other purposes, May 26, 1824, in *Public Statues at Large of the United States of America*, ed. Richard Peters (Boston: Little and Brown, 1846), 4: 40–1.

34. Governor Miller to John C. Calhoun, August 12, 1821, in *TP*, 19: 310–11; John C. Calhoun to Governor Miller, March 4, 1823, in *TP*, 19: 498–99; Matthew Arbuckle to C. J. Nourse, February 20, 1824, in *TP*, 19: 610–11; Edward W. DuVal to John C. Calhoun, March 1, 1824, in *TP*, 19: 613–16; John C. Calhoun to Acting Governor Crittenden, April 28, 1824, in *TP*, 19: 653–57; Thomas McKenney to Governor Crittenden, July 8, 1824, in TP, 19: 686–87; Agnew, "The Cherokee Struggle for Lovely's Purchase," 351; *Arkansas Gazette*, February 22, 1825; Matthew Arbuckle to Edward W. DuVal, January 14, 1825, in *TP*, 19: 747; Thomas McKenney to John C. Calhoun, December 15, 1825, in *TP*, 20: 166–67.

35. *Arkansas Gazette*, February 22, 1825.

36. Memorial of the Arkansas Cherokee to Edward W. DuVal, July 24, 1826, in *TP*, 20: 331–32; René Paul to William McCree, January 26, 1827, in *TP*, 20: 423–24; Cherokee Chiefs to René Paul, December 13, 1826, in *TP*, 20: 424; René Paul to Cherokee Chiefs, December 13, 1826, in *TP*, 20: 424–25; Agnew, "The Cherokee Struggle for Lovely's Purchase," 353–58; Thomas L. McKenney to the Secretary of War, March 26, 1827, in *TP*, 20: 430–32; *Arkansas Gazette*, November 20, 1827; Ina Gabler, "Lovely's Purchase and Lovely County," *Arkansas Historical Quarterly*, 19, no. 1 (Spring, 1960): 31–9.

37. Charles Francis Adams, ed., *Memoirs of John Quincy Adams: Comprising Portions of His Diary from 1795 to 1848* (Philadelphia: J.B. Lippincott and Co., 1875), 7: 499, 502–3.

38. Agnew, "The Cherokee Struggle for Lovely's Purchase," 355–56; Thomas L. McKenney to the Arkansas Cherokee Delegation, April 3, 1828, in *TP*, 20: 637–39; Thomas L. McKenney to the Secretary of War, April 12, 1828, in *TP*, 20: 647–50; Treaty with the Western Cherokee, 1828, in *Indian Affairs. Laws and Treaties*, 2: 288–92.

Clear Boundaries or Shared Territory

Chickasaw and Cherokee Resistance to American Colonization, 1785–1816

Lucas P. Kelley

IN THE LATE SUMMER of 1807, Cherokee leaders Enola (Black Fox), Atawgwatihih (The Glass), Selukuki Wohellengh (Turtle-at-Home), Richard Brown, and Totowiltoto met U.S. boundary commissioners Return J. Meigs and James Robertson at the Chickasaw Old Fields on the south side of the Tennessee River.[1] Cherokees were there to supervise the final survey of a new international border negotiated in 1806, specifically the section that would stretch from the Tennessee River northeast to the headwaters of the Duck River in what would become Middle Tennessee.[2] Yet once on the ground, Meigs and Robertson instead convinced the Cherokee leaders to alter the boundary line to locate 200 American families—currently settled illegally on Native land—within the limits of the United States. In exchange, Meigs canceled the Cherokee Nation's debt to the United States and issued $1,000 and two rifles to the Native diplomats in attendance.[3] Surveyor Thomas Freeman's map of the new boundaries revealed the proximity of Cherokee and Chickasaw borders[4].

This cession of Indigenous land infuriated Chickasaw leaders. They argued that the territory ceded by Cherokees actually belonged to the Chickasaw Nation. "If the [U.S.] government has purchased" the new land, protested Chinubbee and other leading Chickasaw officials, "it has not been of the right owners, but of people who had no right to sell."[5] Only days after the Cherokee diplomats negotiated the new border at the Muscle Shoals, Chickasaws attempted to settle their boundary dispute at a summit in the Creek Nation. Despite Cherokees' attendance, leaders of the two nations failed to come to an agreement.[6] Yet Chickasaws remained committed to their national territory. Chickasaw officials subsequently demanded that the United States "have the white people removed off our land, that the Cherokees have sold," or Chickasaws would "move them off by force."[7] If Americans continued to disregard their national boundaries without fear of punishment, Chickasaws could "no more be a nation."[8] This controversy over the new international border was only one flashpoint in the decades-long struggle between the Cherokee and Chickasaw Nations over their overlapping territorial boundaries in the Tennessee Valley.

In the late eighteenth century, Cherokees and Chickasaws began to support clear borders to challenge American expansion. Native peoples had always known their national

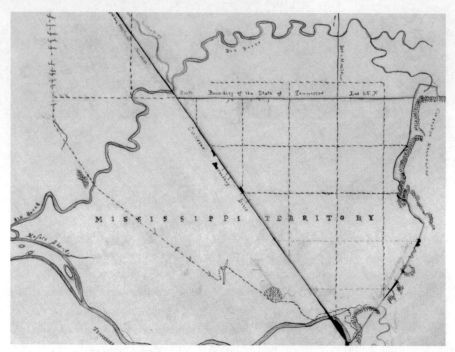

Figure 1. A Map of Indian Boundary Lines and the Southern Boundary of the State of Tennessee (detail), Thomas Freeman, September 1807, Map 1407, Tennessee Virtual Archive, Tennessee State Library and Archives, Nashville, TN. The Chickasaws' boundary line stretched northwest from the Tennessee River, where it intersected the Cherokee border. The surveyed territory would be organized a year later as Madison County under the jurisdiction of the Mississippi Territory.

limits, but by bounding their land, Indians could identify when white Americans settled illegally in their territory and prevent other Indigenous nations from ceding their land to the federal government. Yet surveying these borders forced Cherokees and Chickasaws to argue for their particular nation's exclusive right to specific territory, including valuable land in the Tennessee and Cumberland Valleys that Indigenous nations had long shared as "the middle ground."[9] To support their conflicting territorial claims, Native leaders crafted intricate legal arguments based on a variety of evidence, including Indigenous notions of historical occupation and creation stories, conquest theory, and even U.S. treaty law. Their compelling arguments in treaty negotiations and conversations with U.S. and Native diplomats made it more difficult for American officials to wrest land away from the Chickasaws and Cherokees by requiring the cash-strapped United States to fund numerous treaty councils with representatives of both nations, even if this strategy did perpetuate conflict between the two nations for over thirty years.

Recovering Chickasaws' and Cherokees' arguments in support of their national territory overturns the "inevitability of the modern map" at the heart of the settler state.[10] As scholars of settler colonialism have emphasized, settler nations, like the United States, thrive though the "logic of elimination" of Indigenous peoples.[11] While especially evident in genocidal campaigns against Native nations and Indian Removal of the 1830s, settler colonialism is an ongoing project of erasure that relegates Indigenous peoples to the past.[12] This includes "the casting of early America as proto-nationalist spaces whose stories are the seedbed for modern nation-states," a teleological interpretation most obvious in projections of colonial empires and contemporary nations onto maps of North America with little acknowledgment of Native sovereignty.[13] Many scholars are rectifying this historiographical failure by recognizing the varying degrees in which many Native peoples successfully resisted European colonization, maintained power and sovereignty well into the nineteenth century, and continue to persist against the settler project in the present day.[14]

Yet Native borders and territoriality—the political control, social organization, and cultural significance of territory—rarely figure in this new scholarship.[15] As historian Juliana Barr argues, "the spatial dimension of Indian assertions of power has not yet been wholly realized" because scholars have overemphasized the permeability of territorial boundaries by "exploring the relations that developed along and across borders" rather than the existing geographical dimensions of Indian polities that Europeans encountered.[16] While scholars of the American Southwest have been the most receptive to the benefits of territoriality, it remains largely absent from most studies of the American Southeast.[17] Cherokees and Chickasaws, however, approached territoriality in ways that reflected their unique cultural, social, and political adaptations to colonization. A regional framework that compares their spatial responses with American expansion provides a more accurate representation of Indigenous territoriality than an analysis of one Native nation and its interaction with European colonizers.[18]

Cherokees and Chickasaws defended their conflicting territorial boundaries by crafting intricate legal arguments, providing a window into a complex legal conversation generated by American expansion but occurring within Native America. To wrest territory away from Cherokees and Chickasaws, U.S. officials employed Euro-centric understandings of nationhood, sovereignty, and property. Native leaders, however, defended their nations' land claims by combining colonizers' legal theories with their own Indigenous conceptions of law and territoriality. Indeed, law was much more accessible and diffuse in the early republic than many scholars have previously realized.[19] Native peoples not only had their own legal cultures but were also widely familiar with European legal regimes, and they used both to defend their territorial possessions.[20] "Colonization," argues historian Saliha Belmessous, "was opposed not only by force but also by ideas, often ideas that were easily translated into European discourse, ideas that drew from European discourse, or ideas that were generated precisely from cross-cultural contacts." She and other scholars have furthermore encouraged historians to recognize how "indigenous legal arguments" are not solely a "phenomenon of contemporary rights claims" but are based on "indigenous legal traditions that were used for the same purpose from the moment colonization began."[21] Most analyses of Native land claims, nevertheless, focus on the sixteenth and early seventeenth centuries, before the Proclamation of 1763 outlawed private land purchases from Indian nations and vested Europeans' property rights in distant colonial, state, and national governments.[22] Exploring how Cherokees and Chickasaws defended their national boundaries well into the nineteenth century reveals the persistence of Indians' legal traditions and accompanying territoriality in the face of American expansion.

The contest between Chickasaws and Cherokees over their national boundaries ended in 1816 only when leaders of both nations ceded their remaining conflicting territorial claims in the Tennessee Valley to the federal government. While their disagreements structured relationships among the two nations and the United States from the moment that white intruders began clearing land and claiming property in Cherokee and Chickasaw territory, this essay will focus primarily on three specific instances where the issue of the conflicting Native title was readily apparent. It begins by analyzing Cherokee and Chickasaw negotiations with U.S. officials in 1785, explores Native land cessions in 1805 and 1806 that further inflamed the dispute, and concludes with an analysis of how leaders of both nations combined Indigenous and European notions of sovereignty at the Treaty of Chickasaw Council House in 1816.

After the United States gained independence from Great Britain, Indians and white Americans confronted difficult choices about how their nations could best succeed in this new and unstable political environment. Many people, both white and Native, decided on continued warfare to either protect their existing national sovereignty or acquire more territory in a war of conquest.[23] Others hoped to create an orderly relationship between the infant United States and trans-Appalachian Native nations based on negotiated treaties and controlled American expansion.[24] As part of this latter effort, U.S. officials invited representatives of the Cherokee, Chickasaw, and Choctaw Nations to Hopewell Plantation in Upcountry South Carolina in the winter of 1785–1786 to negotiate for peace.[25]

Facing hordes of white intruders, Cherokees believed that a formal border, enforced by the United States, was the only way to end Americans' continuing invasion. They explained "how the white people have encroached on our lands, on every side of us," and, in the words of Cherokee delegate Chescoenwhee, hoped that the United States would "adjust and settle our limits, so that we may be secured in the possession of our own . . . lands."[26] Over the course of their weeklong meeting, Cherokee and U.S. officials agreed on an international border that arced from the confluence of the Duck and Tennessee Rivers northeast to the Kentucky country and then back southeast toward the headwaters of the Oconee River in what would become northern Georgia.[27] Speaking for the entire Cherokee delegation, Onitositah (Old Tassel) lectured American commissioners that they "must know the red people are the aborigines of this land," making it clear that Cherokees' claim to the land stemmed from their long occupation, as opposed to white Americans' recent migration.[28] Cherokee delegates considered their national boundaries so important that Onitositah drew a map for the U.S. commissioners, a powerful strategy to assert territorial control that would have been familiar to the American commissioners.[29]

The Chickasaw delegation similarly articulated their nation's boundaries in negotiations with the U.S. officials at Hopewell. Though some British loyalists had fled into the Chickasaw Nation during the Revolution, white Americans had only recently begun to infringe on their territory and in much smaller numbers than those faced by the Cherokees.[30] Piominko, the Chickasaw Nation's leading diplomat, did complain that

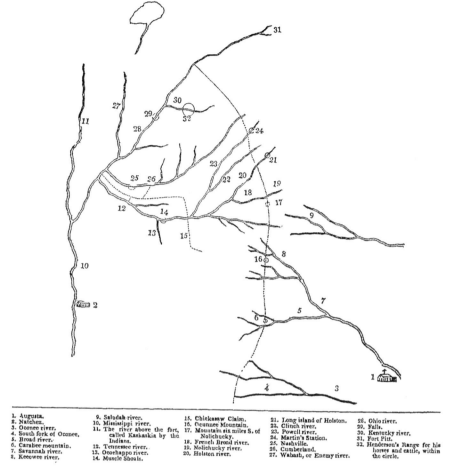

1. Augusta.	9. Saludah river.	15. Chickasaw Claim.	21. Long island of Holston.	28. Ohio river.
2. Natchez.	10. Mississippi river.	16. Oeunnee Mountain.	22. Clinch river.	29. Falls.
3. Oconee river.	11. The river above the fort,	17. Mountain six miles S. of	23. Powell river.	30. Kentucky river.
4. South fork of Oconee.	called Kaskaskia by the	Nolichucky.	24. Martin's Station.	31. Fort Pitt.
5. Broad river.	Indians.	18. French Broad river.	25. Nashville.	32. Henderson's Range for his
6. Carabee mountain.	12. Tennessee river.	19. Nolichucky river.	26. Cumberland.	horses and cattle, within
7. Savannah river.	13. Ocochappo river.	20. Holston river.	27. Wabash, or Enemy river.	the circle.
8. Keeowee river.	14. Muscle Shoals.			

Figure 2. *Map of the Cherokee Nation, Onitositah (Old Tassel), November 1785, in* American State Papers: Documents, Legislative and Executive, of the United States, Class II: Indian Affairs, *ed. Walter Lowrie and Walter S. Franklin (Washington: Gales and Seaton, 1834), 1: 40. Onitositah drew this map during the Hopewell negotiations. The line on the map's right is the Cherokee-U.S. border. Chickasaws' "Claim" is labeled no. 15, though it is noticeably ambiguous.*

whites were building houses and raising cattle on Chickasaw territory, but access to U.S. trade goods was Chickasaws' main priority at the negotiations.[31] Clear boundary lines were also important. When the U.S. commissioners produced Onitositah's map, Piominko was unsatisfied that it did not demarcate his nation's entire international border and "wished Congress would point out his lands to him; he wanted to know his own." But instead of allowing the Chickasaws to describe their national boundaries, the U.S. commissioners merely told the Chickasaw leaders that they "must agree with the neighboring tribes respecting their boundary," which could be determined at a later date.[32]

The federal commissioners cared little about the borders between Native nations. In negotiations with the Cherokees, for example, the U.S. diplomats admitted that they wanted to know "the boundary of [Cherokees'] country, particularly to the northward and eastward," where American settlers were most likely to invade Native land.[33] While the Cherokee and Chickasaw treaties outlined both nations' border with the United States, neither included a clear description of their shared boundary.[34] This lack of clarity would be the basis for conflict between the two nations. For even during the negotiations in 1785, Cherokee commissioners Onitositah and Tuskegatahee worried that Chickasaws were going to claim exclusive right to territory near the Cumberland River around Nashville, insisting that the region "is a kind of common right in all the Indians, and [the Chickasaws] had no right of themselves" to allow Americans to live on it.[35] Before leaving the treaty ground, the Cherokees did define a "Chickasaw claim" on their map of the region and admitted that the Chickasaws were sovereign over land south of a line drawn from "the mouth of the Duck River" to a point on "the ridge between the Tennessee and Cumberland."[36] Chickasaws never agreed to this arbitrary and ill-defined boundary, and the United States had little incentive to survey international borders between Native nations, as they had no bearing on Americans' access to Indian land in the mid-1780s. The Hopewell negotiations may have ended with clear boundaries between the United States and the southeastern Indian nations but set the stage for subsequent disagreements about where, and even if, the Cherokee–Chickasaw border existed.

Despite promising that the new treaties would result in a "permanent boundary" with the United States, American leaders did nothing to prevent white settlers' ongoing invasion of the Chickasaw and Cherokee Nations.[37] The Confederation Congress lacked clear authority and the necessary funds to remove white settlers from Indian land. Even after acquiring more centralized power under the U.S. Constitution, federal officials could do little to enforce treaty boundaries. North Carolina claimed sovereignty over much of the Tennessee and Cumberland Valleys, and its state legislators refused to ratify the Constitution until 1789. National leaders watched as speculators organized surveys and settlers cleared land across the negotiated borders of the Hopewell Treaties.[38]

Cherokees and Chickasaws continued to defend their right to their national land in the face of white encroachment, though with growing tension between the two Indigenous nations. Many Chickamauga Cherokees, those living in the Tennessee Valley south of the Hiwassee River, organized military resistance against trans-Appalachian whites.[39] Chickasaws, on the other hand, worked hard to differentiate themselves from the Cherokee Nation, combining arguments about their territorial sovereignty with references to Chickamaugas' violence. Meeting again with federal officials in Nashville in 1792, for example, Piominko explained that the Chickasaws wanted to outline their national boundaries in light of recent events. He knew that Cherokees "were always sharpening their knives" against American settlers, and he "feared the whites, in retaliation . . . might take my land, supposing it belonged to the Cherokees." Chickasaw leaders then provided a detailed outline of their borders, specifically mentioning that all of the Elk and Duck River Valleys and territory along the Tennessee River upstream from the Muscle Shoals to Flint Creek was within their nation.[40] President Washington later codified Piominko's description of the Chickasaw Nation's boundaries in a 1794 national proclamation and ordered U.S. citizens "not to commit any injury, trespass or molestation whatever on the persons, Lands, hunting Grounds or other rights or property of the Said Indians."[41] Even at the time, Cherokee leaders realized how the document endangered their access to valuable Tennessee and Cumberland Valley hunting land. They protested to their federal agent that "they did not see the propriety of the white people drawing boundary lines between the nations of red people."[42] Cherokees were right to be wary. Long after Washington issued his proclamation, Chickasaws continued to draw on the document as evidence of their sole legal title to land also claimed by the Cherokee Nation.

Despite Washington's promise, U.S. officials and local white settlers alike continued to covet the Tennessee Valley, particularly the rich land in the river's Great Bend in what would become northern Alabama and parts of Middle Tennessee. White Americans had speculated in, traveled through, fought on, and even organized a formal settlement venture at the Tennessee River's Muscle Shoals, but until the first decade of the 1800s, the United States had not formally attempted to negotiate with Indigenous peoples for the territory.[43] Though Cherokees refused to even consider a territorial cession in 1801, they faced increasing pressure from all fronts in the ensuing years. White settlers employed a strategy that had worked in the past: Invade Native land, resist removal, and petition for a territorial cession.[44] They were aided by state leaders. In his annual message to the General Assembly in 1803, Governor John Sevier of Tennessee lamented that "a great and valuable part of the state remains unsettled and uncultivated, very prejudicial and injurious to our revenue, the community at large, and the adventurers." Many Tennesseans claimed property rights within the Indian boundary line, and Sevier hoped that legislators would order Tennessee's congressional delegation "to make application for the purpose of extinguishing the Indian claim to the lands north of Tennessee river."[45]

Federal officials, too, favored a major land cession, hoping it could facilitate the "civilization" policy of the United States. Without large tracts of hunting land, Cherokees and Chickasaws would be forced to rely solely on commercial and subsistence agriculture, like their white neighbors.[46] Assistant U.S. Cherokee agent William S. Lovely lectured assembled Cherokee leaders at an 1804 conference near the Hiwassee River that their possession of so much hunting land harmed the nation because it was "the Seat of Idleness and horse Stealing." Excess territory, continued Lovely, "encourages all the lazy to hide themselves from cultivating their farms" and increased the risk of famine in the Cherokee Nation.[47]

Because of such widespread sentiment, Secretary of War Henry Dearborn appointed federal Cherokee agent Return J. Meigs and Daniel Smith, a former U.S. senator from Tennessee and longtime surveyor and land speculator, to negotiate for a Cherokee cession in 1804.[48] Though Meigs, Smith, and two Tennessee state commissioners convinced Cherokees to sell a small tract in the southeastern portion of their nation, they failed in their larger effort to acquire Cherokees' hunting land in the Tennessee Valley.[49] Before leaving the treaty ground, however, the American commissioners decided to take advantage of the divisions between the Cherokees and the Chickasaws. They falsely informed Chickasaw leaders that the Cherokee Nation might cede the disputed territory and that "it would be well for [the Chickasaw Nation] to get something for their lands, as to let the Cherokees have it all."[50] U.S. officials privately believed that the Chickasaw Nation possessed the best claim to the region but hoped to exaggerate the Cherokees' ownership to pressure Chickasaws to sell, fomenting division to facilitate dispossession.[51]

Yet Chickasaw leaders, including Tootemastubbe (George Colbert) and Chinubbee, refused to meet with U.S. officials. They were fully aware of the value of their hunting lands north of the Tennessee River and explained that if they ever were to sell the territory, the Chickasaw Nation would instead "have it surveyed and have so much an acre for it, the same as the white people does to one another with their lands."[52] Tootemastubbe and Chinubbee were using Americans' notions of property to oppose further colonization. The Chickasaws also took the opportunity to remind American leaders that the United States could not claim Chickasaw land based on prior conquest.[53] They recognized, and even celebrated, U.S. victory over the Creeks and Cherokees during the American Revolution, which caused these two Native nations "to lose the best part of their Country." The Chickasaws, however, narrated a history of peaceful relations with the United States, which had allowed them to maintain all of their ancestral territory. If anything, Chinubbee and the other leaders argued for their nation's own claim to conquest by driving the Shawnees out of the Tennessee Valley in the eighteenth century.[54] Familiar with U.S. officials' arguments in support of their nation's sovereignty over the interior of North America, Chickasaws repurposed these arguments for their own benefit.

Yet the Chickasaw Nation eventually did decide to cede much of their Tennessee Valley land to the United States in a treaty signed on July 23, 1805.[55] This decision, ironically, stemmed from their sovereignty claims. Chickasaws had known for years that the Cherokee Nation also claimed much of the Tennessee Valley and that the United States was attempting to negotiate cessions with the two nations concurrently. They also recognized the true value of their national territory, given the windfall that the federal government and white speculators hoped to gain from a cession, and resented the low price offered by the United States for their land.[56] Cherokees' conflicting claim, however, devalued Chickasaws' property, at least in the minds of white negotiators, who were accustomed to American speculators' overlapping land claims.[57] Chickasaw leaders could best maximize their profit by ceding first, when the government's demand for land was at its peak and before a possible Cherokee cession.

Even as Chickasaw leaders negotiated with American treaty commissioners in the spring and summer of 1805, Cherokees were working to support their own nation's exclusive claim to the Tennessee Valley by similarly combining European and Indigenous notions of sovereignty and property.[58] Chickasaws may have claimed conquest rights over the Great Bend because of their defeat over Shawnees, but Cherokees directed their conquest narrative at the Chickasaw Nation. Cherokee leaders admitted that Chickasaw troops defeated Shawnee soldiers but that the Cherokee Nation possessed "a prior right, & reconquered it by driving the Chickasaws" out of the region.[59] Additionally, Cherokee negotiators mentioned repeatedly that only their nation had Native settlers, including Chuquilatague (Doublehead) and Kalegiskee, living within the disputed territory at the

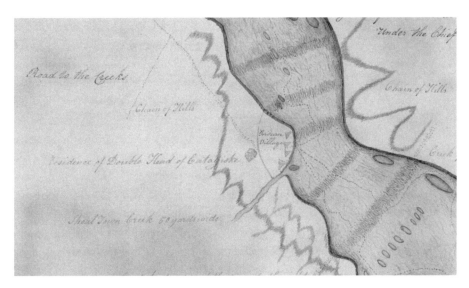

Figure 3. A Small Sketch of the Muscle Shoals (detail), James Wilkinson, 1801, Individually Catalogued Manuscript Maps, Map 66, Realms of Gold, American Philosophical Society, Philadelphia, PA. Wilkinson made sure to identify Chuquilatague's Settlement, located on the Tennessee River's south bank.

Muscle Shoals.[60] An American traveler down the Tennessee River in 1801 had noted Chuquilatague's settlement on the river's south bank, bolstering Cherokees' claim.[61] It was an important piece of evidence given white Americans' belief that occupation and "improvement" of vacant land constituted legitimate property ownership.[62] The Cherokee settlement was so significant that Chickasaw leader George Colbert countered that Cherokee settlers lived there only with his permission.[63]

Cherokees even hoped that Creek leaders could vouch for their land claims. In June 1805, thirty Cherokee delegates traveled south to Tukabatchee in the Creek Nation, where they complained to the Creeks about the pending Chickasaw–U.S. treaty.[64] Cherokees likely expected Creeks to support their nation's sovereignty and property rights or, at the very least, agree that the land was shared hunting ground and could not be the sole possession of one Indigenous nation. American leaders would have recognized Cherokees' formula to support their land claims. Cherokee defeat over the Chickasaws gave them right of conquest to the region; Cherokee settlers living within the disputed boundary legitimized their possession; and the recognition of their claims from a foreign power, like the Creek Nation, shared similarities with Americans' attempts to gain international recognition for U.S. possessions in North America.[65]

The Chickasaw treaty of July 1805 destroyed Cherokee opposition to a land cession. Chickasaws' conflicting land claims had insulated Cherokees' claims from the full force of federal negotiators. Upon learning that their valuable hunting land would soon be open to white settlement, however, many Cherokee leaders began advocating for a cession of their own.[66] Meeting with federal officials in October 1805, Cherokees ceded all their land between East Tennessee and white settlements around Nashville.[67] Had no further negotiations taken place, the 1805 treaty would have ended the Cherokee

Nation's decades-long conflict with the Chickasaws, as the Cherokee delegates ceded to the federal government only the land that had been previously sold by the Chickasaw Nation three months before. Instead, a subsequent Cherokee cession in January 1806 reinvigorated conflict between the two nations after Cherokee delegates turned the tables on the Chickasaws and ceded their nation's claims to the rich lands of the Duck and Elk River watersheds north of the Tennessee River.[68]

Chickasaw leaders responded with increased intensity that their nation still possessed sovereignty over much of the land ceded to the United States by the Cherokees' 1806 treaty. Upon learning of the cession, twenty-nine prominent Chickasaws, a cross-section of the nation, drafted a biting petition to Secretary of War Henry Dearborn. They claimed that Cherokees had sold "part of our Country, laying on the north side of Tennessee river . . . without leting [sic] us know any thing and without our approbation." Chickasaw leaders furthermore charged that federal Indian agents and local land speculators had actively obstructed the efforts of the Cherokees, Chickasaws, Creeks, and Choctaws to determine their shared international borders, arguing that unclear boundary lines facilitated Native dispossession.[69] The urgency of the Chickasaws' petition, issued nearly two years after the 1806 treaty, correlated with the federal government's survey of the cession boundaries and the growing white population at the Muscle Shoals. While federal officials began preparations to identify "the boundary line" among the Four Nations in the fall of 1811, war with Great Britain and the Red Stick Creeks interfered, perpetuating the conflict over Cherokee and Chickasaw land claims for several years.[70]

The War of 1812 was a war of conquest that accelerated American expansion.[71] In the South, this process began with the 1814 Treaty of Fort Jackson, a massive land grab designed to geographically isolate Southern Indians from one another.[72] Reflecting American enslavers' long demand for the region's rich agricultural territory, Andrew Jackson, the lead American negotiator, coerced Creek allies of the United States to cede 23 million acres in what would become southwestern Alabama and southern Georgia.[73] The few Cherokee leaders in attendance realized that unclear boundaries could threaten their nation and wanted the Creeks to "make a definitive statement" of the border between the two nations. Creek leaders insisted that "the present distressed state of their nation" made it impossible to definitively settle the boundaries, though they agreed to draft an informal outline of the border between the Creek and Cherokee Nations. Yet even this description, made by Native representatives, was unclear with regard to the northern boundary of the Creek cession. It hinged on the specific location of "the old corner boundary" between the Creeks, Cherokees, and Chickasaws, defined by Creek leaders as "the Flat rock" and "known to the Cherokees by the appellation of the long leafed pine."[74] Jackson intentionally left the Creek cession boundaries vague. White settlers and many federal officials chose to believe that the cession included territory south of the Tennessee River's Great Bend, land that Cherokees and Chickasaws claimed to be within their nations.[75]

Over the next two years, Cherokee and Chickasaw leaders worked tirelessly to invalidate the Creek cession by combining their Indigenous notions of territoriality with European concepts of international law. Their arguments often centered on land claims "derived from antiquity," defined by a federal commissioner as evidence "handed down by tradition & possession for a great number of years."[76] In a meeting with President Madison in early 1816, for example, Cherokee leaders presented oral histories from their nation's elderly residents, both white and Native. Interviewees' testimony revealed that all territory on the Tennessee "to its mouth on *both sides* including the lands on any of its waters" was within the Cherokee Nation.[77] Chickasaws, too, collected oral histories and combined them with previous U.S. treaties and the all-important 1794 proclamation of George Washington to support their national limits.[78]

Cherokees also relied on fictive kinship relations to prove their nation's superior status over both Creeks and Chickasaws. Atawgwatihih (The Glass), who was seventy-one and had occupied a prominent position in the nation for over thirty years, explained for federal officials that the Creeks recognized Cherokees as their "oldest Brothers and the Cherokees always called the Creeks their young[er B]rothers."[79] Other Cherokees later reported that the Chickasaws and Choctaws similarly considered Cherokees to be their "elder brothers" in numerous diplomatic negotiations. Cherokees, however, knew these peoples as "nephews," a significant metaphor given that maternal uncles held much of the responsibility for child-rearing in Cherokee society.[80] Kinship notions were essential components in diplomatic relationships throughout Native America, but in the context of the competing Indigenous land claims, they took on a meaning not dissimilar from European international law.[81] By arguing that they were elder brothers to the three other Native nations, Cherokee leaders believed that their national superiority would provide their nation with added credibility in negotiations with the federal government. They initially succeeded. On March 22, 1816, Cherokee delegates and federal officials signed a new treaty that "recognized a claim on the part of the Cherokee nation to the lands south of the Big Bend of the Tennessee river" and ordered federal commissioners to delay marking the Creek cession boundary.[82]

Southern whites erupted in anger upon learning that the federal government had accepted Cherokees' arguments.[83] Many, such as William Russell living along Bear Creek near the Muscle Shoals, were veterans of the Creek War and had occupied land in the Creek cession before the boundaries could be surveyed as their just right for their defeat of the Red Sticks.[84] Russell and white Southerners like him felt betrayed upon hearing that "the president and secretary at war have settled the southwestern boundary of the cherokee nation so as to leave our improvements within their Territory."[85] Petitioners and politicians barked at federal officials to open the land so that they could transform Indians' "pathless wilderness into peaceful habitations of freemen, yielding individual wealth and natural prosperity."[86] It took little time for U.S. leaders to succumb to public outcry. Secretary of War William Crawford quickly organized another round of treaty negotiations.[87] The success of Chickasaw and Cherokee leaders in challenging the limits of the Creek cession forced Americans to negotiate new treaties. By September 1816, Cherokees and Chickasaws were once again under pressure to cede land to the federal government.

Cherokees and Chickasaws hoped that the upcoming conference, held at the Chickasaw Council House, would settle the boundary dispute over their conflicting claims to the Tennessee River territory, though they certainly could not have anticipated the outcome. Once negotiations began on September 8, the American commission, led again by Andrew Jackson, invited the Native delegates to present evidence of their land claims.[88] Tishominko, speaker for the Chickasaws, began by introducing Washington's 1794 Proclamation alongside a packet of oral histories collected during the previous spring.[89] Yet negotiations soon took on the semblance of legal proceedings. Chickasaws called on witnesses to vouch for their interpretations of the boundary, and Cherokees and American commissioners cross-examined them. Chickasaw deponents focused much of their testimony on past military campaigns and negotiations, their memories reaching as far back as the 1780s.[90]

Several Chickasaw leaders challenged Cherokees' land claims based on Indigenous notions of "ancient times." Hullteropory (Major Glover) explained that he had been taught that Cherokees had originally lived along the Atlantic Coast before moving west.[91] Hulltewmarlatha (John Brown) likewise recounted "that the Cherokee nation came from between the Ocone[e] & Ogetchee [Ogeechee] Rivers & crossed the mountains." Chickasaws, by comparison, "have occupied the present lands long before either his recollection, or of that of any of the nations living."[92] Mattahameeko was even more specific in his testimony. After coming from the West, he explained that Chickasaws

> settled first at what is called the Chickasaw old Fields . . . to collect a great quantity of Flint on the Tennessee & then called the Tennessee the river where they gathered flint. That from the Chickasaw old Fields they removed to the field in this vicinity & there formed the land of life.[93]

Cherokees, according to such testimony, were relative newcomers, while Chickasaws had lived in the Tennessee Valley since before recorded memory. Chickasaw leaders believed their indigeneity proved their sovereignty.

Cherokees recognized the power of such arguments and were unable to counter them. Their speaker Toochelar freely admitted that Cherokee delegates "were not prepared, . . . that they had no witnesses with them, their old People & Traders having been left in the nation."[94] They did, once again, insist that Chuquilatague's settlement at the Muscle Shoals proved their claim to the region, but Chickasaws countered that Cherokees had settled there only with the permission of their nation.[95]

Jackson and the other federal commissioners were prepared, however, and matched Chickasaws' arguments with their own evidence. Their goal was to prove that the region south of the Tennessee River had been within the national boundaries of the Creek Nation until 1814, making it U.S. territory after the cession at Fort Jackson. Thus, Andrew Jackson, the very personification of American expansion, set about making the case for past Creek sovereignty based on oral histories, witness testimony, and reports from federal surveyors. Unlike the Chickasaws and Cherokees, who relied on the knowledge of their elderly leaders, every one of Jackson's witnesses was a former army officer under the general's command in the Red Stick War.[96] All six of the affidavits, too, included oral histories from white inhabitants of Tennessee and the Mississippi Territory, settlers with a vested interest in acquiring as much Native land as possible.[97] The only Indigenous knowledge offered by the American commissioners was a June 1816 written statement by Creek leaders that merely outlined their national boundaries. Even this document reeked of Jackson's interference, as it was delivered in the presence of his speculator ally John Coffee two years after the land cession, a time when Creek leaders had little incentive to oppose the wishes of U.S. officials.[98] The assembled Chickasaws and Cherokees must have been little surprised, therefore, when the commissioners declared that they found "the Creek claim the strongest," based almost exclusively, of course, on the evidence provided by American expansionists.[99]

Upon the conclusion of the farcical investigation, the U.S. commissioners then pressured leaders of both Native nations to cede land on the north and south sides of the Tennessee River. The Cherokees were first to relent, doing so only after hearing that the United States refused to remove any white intruders from the limits of the Creek cession.[100] On September 14, they agreed to a provisional cession, approved later by the national council, of all their claims south of the Tennessee River that had been included in the Creek cession, though they persisted in their refusal to sell any land north of the river.[101] Chickasaws held out for several more days, possibly while some of the leaders negotiated for guarantees that they could keep their personal plantations within the ceded territory.[102] Yet on September 20, Chickasaws agreed to a massive cession of their remaining land north of the Tennessee River and all of their territory south of the river that had overlapped the boundaries of the Creek cession.[103]

The two treaties crafted at the Chickasaw Council House ended the territorial dispute that had long divided Chickasaws and Cherokees, though not with the result that either nation had hoped for. Richard Brown, a Cherokee leader living near the Tennessee River, described the 1816 treaty as "one of the crookadist line that Ever was Run in this country" since white speculators had convinced Creek leaders "to say there is more land belonging to them."[104] It is tempting for historians to share Brown's sentiment and focus solely on Americans' deception in opening Indian land for white settlement. Yet such a narrow perspective overlooks the ways Native peoples resisted U.S. expansion by adapting their Indigenous notions of territoriality into complex and convincing legal arguments. These "hidden transcripts," as one historian calls them, were powerful diplomatic tools in negotiations with both American officials and leaders of other Indian Nations.[105]

The recent U.S. Supreme Court ruling in *McGirt v. Oklahoma* only adds to the significance of Native legal claims and national borders. In the landmark decision, the Court confirmed the Muscogee (Creek) Nation's territorial boundaries in cases of criminal law. The Court's opinion drew on the historical relationship between the United States and the Creeks and emphasized the continued operation of existing treaty agreements between the two parties.[106] Although the case dealt specifically with the Muscogee (Creek) Nation, the ruling was more than a legal victory. In the words of Jonodev O. Chaudhuri, ambassador of the Muscogee (Creek) Nation, it "affirmed Indian Country sovereignty" and will likely set important precedents for future Supreme Court rulings.[107] Cherokees and Chickasaws may have lost control over their Tennessee Valley land due to pressure from the settler state, but *McGirt* demonstrates that law remains a viable defense of Indigenous peoples' territorial sovereignty. Native boundaries continue to impact American settler colonialism in 2020, just as they did in the eighteenth and nineteenth centuries.

Notes

1. Entry for September 9, 1807, *Journal of Occurrences*, Meigs Family Papers, 1772–1862, Microfilm 17,052-1N-1P, Library of Congress, Washington, D.C.; Elucidation of a Convention with the Cherokee Nation, September 11, 1807, in *Indian Treaties, 1778–1883*, ed. Charles J. Kappler (1904; repr., Mattituck, N.Y.: Amereon House, 1972), 91–92.

2. Henry Dearborn to James Robertson, April 1, 1807, folder 10, box 4; Return J. Meigs to James Robertson, May 5, 1807, folder 8, box 3, both in James Robertson Papers, Tennessee State Library and Archives, Nashville, TN. Hereafter cited as TSLA.

3. Elucidation of a Convention with the Cherokee Nation, September 11, 1807, in Kappler, *Indian Treaties*, 91–92; Return J. Meigs to Henry Dearborn, September 28, 1807, in *American State Papers: Documents, Legislative and Executive, of the United States*, Class II: Indian Affairs, ed. Walter Lowrie and Walter S. Franklin (Washington: Gales and Seaton, 1834), 1: 249. Hereafter cited as *ASP: IA*.

4. A Map of Indian Boundary Lines and the Southern Boundary of the State of Tennessee, September 1807, Tennessee Virtual Archive, TSLA, https://teva.contentdm. oclc.org/digital/collection/p15138coll23/id/9064/rec/5.

5. Chinubbee Mingo [Chinubbee], et al. to James Robertson, April 19, 1809, folder 17, box 2, James Robertson Papers, TSLA.

6. Benjamin Hawkins to Henry Dearborn, September 16, 1807, in *Letters, Journals and Writings of Benjamin Hawkins*, ed. C.L. Grant (Savannah, GA: The Beehive Press, 1980), 2: 524–526.

7. Chinubbee King [Chinubbee], et al. to Henry Dearborn, August 25, 1808, Bureau of Indian Affairs, Records of the Cherokee Indian Agency in Tennessee, 1801–1835, Record Group 75, Microcopy 208, National Archives, Washington, D.C. (first quotation, hereafter cited as M-208); Thomas Freeman to Albert Gallatin, March 4, 1809, in *Territorial Papers of the United States*, vol. 5, *The Territory of Mississippi, 1798–1817*, ed. Clarence Edwin Carter (Washington, D.C.: GPO, 1937), 721 (second quotation).

8. Chinubbee King [Chinubbee], et al. to Henry Dearborn, August 25, 1808, M-208.

9. Ilepooenaatla (Shot in the Mouth), *ASP: IA*, 1: 285. On the region's significance as a crossroads for Native peoples, see Kristofer Ray, "Understanding the Tennessee Corridor," introduction to *Before the Volunteer State: New Thoughts on Early Tennessee, 1540–1800*, ed. Kristofer Ray (Knoxville: University of Tennessee Press, 2014): iv–xxii.

10. Benjamin H. Johnson and Andrew R. Graybill, "Borders and Their Historians in North America," introduction to *Bridging National Borders in North America: Transnational and Comparative Histories*, ed. Benjamin H. Johnson and Andrew Graybill (Durham, NC: Duke University Press, 2010), 2. This point is made powerfully by Juliana Barr and Edward Countryman in Barr and Countryman, "Maps and Spaces, Paths to Connect, and Lines to Divide," introduction to *Contested Spaces of Early America*, ed. Juliana Barr and Edward Countryman (Philadelphia: University of Pennsylvania Press, 2014), 22–23. See also, Michael Witgen, "A Nation of Settlers: The Early American Republic and the Colonization of the Northwest Territory," *William and Mary Quarterly* 76, no. 3 (July 2019): 391–398. On Native peoples' contribution to and appropriation of cartographic representations in the nineteenth century, see David Bernstein, *How the West Was Drawn: Mapping, Indians, and the Construction of the Trans-Mississippi West* (Lincoln: University of Nebraska Press, 2018); and Cane West, "'They Have Exercised Every Art': Ecological Rhetoric, a War of Maps, and Cherokee Sovereignty in the Arkansas Valley, 1812–1828," *Journal of the Early Republic* 40, no. 2 (Summer 2020): 297–327.

11. Patrick Wolfe, "Land Labor, and Difference: Elementary Structures of Race," *American Historical Review* 106, no. 3 (June 2001): 866–905 (quotation on 868); Lorenzo Veracini, *Settler Colonialism: A Theoretical Overview* (New York: Palgrave Macmillan, 2010); *Ibid.,* "'Settler Colonialism': Career of a Concept," *The Journal of Imperial and Commonwealth History* 41, no. 2 (2013): 313–333; Walter L. Hixson, *American Settler Colonialism: A History* (New York: Palgrave Macmillan, 2013). For two excellent applications of settler colonial theory to American expansion, see Margaret D. Jacobs, *White Mother to a Dark Race: Settler Colonialism, Maternalism, and the Removal of Indigenous Children in the American West and Australia, 1880–1940* (Lincoln: University of Nebraska Press, 2009); and Laurel Clark Shire, *The Threshold of Manifest Destiny: Gender and National Expansion in Florida* (Philadelphia: University of Pennsylvania Press, 2016).

12. Benjamin Madley, *An American Genocide: The United States and the California Indian Catastrophe, 1846–1873* (New Haven, Conn.: Yale University Press, 2016); Jeffery Ostler, *Surviving Genocide: Native Nations and the United States from the American Revolution to Bleeding Kansas* (New Haven, Conn.: Yale University Press, 2019); John P. Bowes, *Land Too Good for Indians: Northern Indian Removal* (Norman: University of Oklahoma Press, 2016); Claudio Saunt, *Unworthy Republic: The Dispossession of Native Americans and the Road to Indian Territory* (New York: Norton, 2020). For a discussion of the applicability of settler colonial theory to the history of early America, see the forum Settler Colonialism in Early American History, ed. Jeffrey Ostler and Nancy Shoemaker, *William and Mary Quarterly,* 76, no. 3 (July 2019). On the relegation of Indians to

the past, see Laurel Clark Shire and Joe Knetsch, "Ambivalence of the Settler Colonial Present: The Legacies of Jacksonian Expansion," *Tennessee Historical Quarterly* 76, no. 3 (Fall 2017): 258–275, esp. 269–272.

13. Barr and Countryman, "Maps and Spaces," 22 (quotation); Frederick E. Hoxie, "Retrieving the Red Continent: Settler Colonialism and the History of American Indians in the US," *Ethnic and Racial Studies* 31, no. 6 (Sep. 2008): 1153–1167.

14. For recent examples, see James H. Merrell, *The Indians New World: Catawbas and Their Neighbors from European Contact Through the Era of Removal* (1989; reprinted, New York: Norton, 1991); Richard White, *The Middle Ground: Indians, Empires, and Republics in the Great Lakes Region, 1650–1815* (New York: Cambridge University Press, 1991); Colin G. Calloway, *One Vast Winter Count: The Native American West Before Lewis and Clark* (Lincoln: University of Nebraska Press, 2003); Kathleen DuVal, *The Native Ground: Indians and Colonists in the Heart of the Continent* (Philadelphia: University of Pennsylvania Press, 2006); Alan Taylor, *The Divided Ground: Indians, Settlers, and the Northern Borderland of the American Revolution* (New York: Knopf, 2006); Juliana Barr, *Peace Came in the Form of a Woman: Indians and Spaniards in the Texas Borderlands* (Chapel Hill: University of North Carolina Press, 2007); Pekka Hämäläinen, *The Comanche Empire* (New Haven, Conn.: Yale University Press, 2008); Michael Witgen, *An Infinity of Nations: How the Native New World Shaped Early America* (Philadelphia: University of Pennsylvania Press, 2012); Sami Lakomäki, *Gathering Together: The Shawnee People Through Diaspora and Nationhood, 1600–1870* (New Haven, Conn.: Yale University Press, 2014); Elizabeth A. Fenn, *Encounters at the Heart of the World: A History of the Mandan People* (New York: Hill and Wang, 2014); Michael A. McDonnell, *Masters of Empire: Great Lakes Indians and the Making of America* (New York: Hill and Wang, 2015); Pekka Hämäläinen, *Lakota America: A New History of Indigenous Power* (New Haven, Conn.: Yale University Press, 2019). For a few works that focus on Native peoples' ongoing commitment to their sovereignty, see Jessica Cattelino, *High States: Florida Seminole Gaming and Sovereignty* (Durham, NC: Duke University Press, 2008); Malinda Maynor Lowery, *The Lumbee Indians: An American Struggle* (Chapel Hill: University of North Carolina Press, 2018); Mark Edwin Miller, *Forgotten Tribes: Unrecognized Indians and the Federal Acknowledgement Process* (Lincoln: University of Nebraska Press, 2004); Katherine M. B. Osburn, *Choctaw Resurgence in Mississippi: Race, Class, and Nation Building in the Jim Crow South, 1830–1977* (Lincoln: University of Nebraska Press, 2014).

15. On the definition of territoriality, see Robert David Sack, *Human Territoriality: Its Theory and History* (New York: Cambridge University Press, 1986); Walter D. Mignolo, "Colonial Situations, Geographical Discourses and Territorial Representations: Toward a Diatopical Understanding of Colonial Semiosis," *Dispositio* 14, no. 36–38 (1989), 128–132; Peter J. Usher, Frank J. Tough, and Robert M. Galois, "Reclaiming the Land: Aboriginal Title, Treaty Rights and Land Claims in Canada," *Applied Geography* 12 (1992): 112; Charles S. Maier, "Consigning the Twentieth Century to History: Alternative Narratives for the Modern Era," *The American Historical Review* 105, no. 3

(June 2000), 808; *Ibid., Once Within Borders: Territories of Power, Wealth, and Belonging* (Cambridge, Mass.: Harvard University Press, 2016), 8; Cecilia Sheridan, "Social Control and Native Territoriality in Northeastern New Spain," in *Choice, Persuasion, and Coercion: Social Control on Spain's North American Frontiers*, ed. Jesús F. de la Teja and Ross Frank (Albuquerque: University of New Mexico Press, 2005), 121–148; Matthew Babcock, "Territoriality and the Historiography of Early North America," *Journal of American Studies* 50 (2016), 518; and Angela Pulley Hudson, *Creek Paths and Federal Roads: Indians, Settlers, and Slaves and the Making of the American South* (Chapel Hill: University of North Carolina Press, 2010), 20.

   16. Juliana Barr, "Geographies of Power: Mapping Indian Borders in the 'Borderlands' of the Early Southwest," *William and Mary Quarterly* 68, no. 1 (Jan. 2011): 5–46 (quotation 8); *Ibid.*, "Borders and Borderlands," in *Why You Can't Teach United States History without American Indians*, ed. Susan Sleeper-Smith, et al. (Chapel Hill: University of North Carolina Press, 2015): 9–25.

   17. This is a point made by Matthew Babcock in his historiographical overview of Native territoriality; see Babcock, "Territoriality and the Historiography of Early North America," *Journal of American Studies* 50, no. 3 (Spring 2016): 515–536, esp. 533–534. For scholars who have looked at dimensions of territoriality in the American Southeast, see DuVal, *Native Ground*; Hudson, *Creek Paths and Federal Roads*; West, "Cherokee Sovereignty in the Arkansas Valley"; Merrell, *Indians' New World*; Tyler Boulware, *Deconstructing the Cherokee Nation: Town, Region, and Nation among Eighteenth-Century Cherokees* (Gainesville: University Press of Florida, 2011); *Ibid.*, "'It Seems Like Coming into Our Houses': Challenges to Cherokee Hunting Grounds, 1750–1775," in *Before the Volunteer State*, ed. Ray, 65–81; Joshua H. Haynes, *Patrolling the Border: Theft and Violence on the Creek–Georgia Frontier, 1770–1796* (Athens: University of Georgia Press, 2018); Malinda Maynor Lowery, *Lumbee Indians: An American Struggle* (Chapel Hill: University of North Carolina Press, 2018), esp. 42–58; and Bradley J. Dixon, "'His One Netev ples': The Chowans and the Politics of Native Petitions in the Colonial South," *William and Mary Quarterly* 26, no. 1 (Jan. 2019): 41–74. Austin Stewart also explores Cherokee territoriality in his essay included in this volume.

   18. Patricia Albers and Jeanne Kay, "Sharing the Land: A Study in American Indian Territoriality," in *American Indians: A Cultural Geography*, ed. Thomas E. Ross, Tyrel G. Moore, Laura R. King, 2nd ed. (Southern Pines, NC: Karo Hollow Press, 1995): 49–88; Babcock, "Territoriality and the Historiography of Early North America."

   19. Laura Edwards, "Sarah Allingham's Sheet and Other Lessons from Legal History," *Journal of the Early Republic* 38, no. 1 (Spring 2018): 121–147.

   20. Gregory Ablavsky, "Species of Sovereignty: Native Nationhood, the United States, and International Law, 1783–1795, *Journal of American History* 106, no. 3 (Dec. 2019): 591–613. Indians also had a significant impact on the formation of U.S. law. See Ablavsky, "The Savage Constitution," *Duke Law Journal* 63, no. 5 (Feb. 2014): 999–1090; and Maggie Blackhawk, "Federal Indian Law as Paradigm within Public Law," *Harvard Law Review* 132, no. 7 (May 2019): 1787–1877.

21. Saliha Belmessous, "The Problem of Indigenous Claim Making in Colonial History," introduction to *Native Claims: Indigenous Law against Empire, 1500–1920*, ed. Saliha Belmessous (Oxford, United Kingdom: Oxford University Press, 2012), 15 (quotation). For how recent scholars have emphasized the significance of Indigenous land claims in early modern North America, see Andrew Fitzmaurice, "Powhatan Legal Claims," in *Native Claims*, ed. Belmessous, 85–106; Nancy Shoemaker, *A Strange Likeness: Becoming Red and White in Eighteenth-Century North America* (Oxford, United Kingdom: Oxford University Press, 2004), 13–34; Pekka Hämäläinen, "The Shapes of Power: Indians, Europeans, and North American Worlds from the Seventeenth to the Nineteenth Century," in *Contested Spaces of Early America*, ed. Barr and Countryman, 31–68; Allan Greer, "Dispossession in a Commercial Idiom: From Indian Deeds to Land Cession Treaties," in *Contested Spaces*, ed. Barr and Countryman, 69–92; Allan Greer, *Property and Dispossession: Natives, Empires and Land in Early Modern North America* (Cambridge, United Kingdom: Cambridge University Press, 2018); Ian Saxine, *Properties of Empire: Indians, Colonists, and Land Speculators on the New England Frontier* (New York: New York University Press, 2019); and Barr, "Geographies of Power."

22. Prior to the Proclamation's centralization of imperial control over access to Indian land, British settlers and speculators negotiated directly with Native peoples for land sales, and often their successful land claims depended on proving that Indian sellers possessed legal title before making the sales. Alan Taylor, *Liberty Men and Great Proprietors: The Revolutionary Settlement on the Maine Frontier* (Chapel Hill: University of North Carolina Press, 1990), 12–14; Anthony Pagden, "Law, Colonization, Legitimation, and the European Background," in *Cambridge History of Law in America*, vol. 1, *Early America (1580–1815)*, ed. Michael Grossberg and Christopher Tomlins (Cambridge, United Kingdom: Cambridge University Press, 2008), 25; James Muldoon, "Discovery, Grant, Charter, Conquest, or Purchase: John Adams on the Legal Basis for English Possession of North America," in *The Many Legalities of Early America*, ed. Christopher Tomlins and Bruce H. Mann (Chapel Hill: University of North Carolina Press, 2001); Saxine, *Properties of Empire*. On the Proclamation's disastrous consequences for American Indians by reorienting settlers' and speculators' property rights, see Stuart Banner, *How the Indians Lost Their Land: Law and Power on the Frontier* (Cambridge, Mass.: Belknap Press of Harvard University Press, 2007), 93–95, 104–111; Michael Blaakman, "Speculation Nation: Land Mania in the Revolutionary American Republic, 1776–1803" (PhD dissertation, Yale University, 2016), 381–474; Saxine, *Properties of Empire*, 193; Greer, *Property and Dispossession*, 405–415; Pagden, "Law, Colonization, Legitimation, and the European Background," 26–27.

23. Kathleen DuVal, *Independence Lost: Lives on the Edge of the American Revolution* (New York: Random House, 2016), 292–304.

24. David Nichols, *Red Gentlemen and White Savages: Indians, Federalists, and the Search for Order on the American Frontier* (Charlottesville: University of Virginia Press, 2008). For how treaty negotiations reveal various dimensions of Native nationhood, see, for two examples, Shoemaker, *A Strange Likeness*; Heidi Kiiwetinepinesiik Stark, "Marked

by Fire: Anishinaabe Articulations of Nationhood in Treaty Making with the United States and Canada," *American Indian Quarterly* 36, no. 2 (Spring 2012): 119–149.

25. For the Hopewell Treaty Negotiations, see *ASP: IA*, 1: 41–44, 48–54; Nichols, *Red Gentlemen and White Savages*, 44–54; DuVal, *Independence Lost*, 305–307.

26. Hopewell Negotiations, *ASP: IA*: 1, 41, 42. Descriptions of treaty negotiations, including Indians' arguments against colonization, were most often made by European or American observers, leading some scholars to rightly question whether the Native ideas presented in these sources were actually their own or merely European ideas embedded in Indians' voices, a concept described by Andrew Fitzmaurice as "ethnological ventriloquism." Fitzmaurice agrees that scholars should approach such sources critically but insists that these arguments must be taken seriously or risk overlooking Native perspectives entirely. See Fitzmaurice, "Powhatan Legal Claims," 86–87.

27. Treaty with the Cherokee, November 28, 1785, in Kappler, *Indian Treaties*, 8–11.

28. Hopewell Negotiations, *ASP: IA*, 1: 41.

29. Hopewell Negotiations, *ASP: IA*, 1: 40. For more on how European powers used maps to project their right to geographic space, see S. Max Edelson, *The New Map of Empire: How Britain Imagined America before Independence* (Cambridge, Mass.: Harvard University Press, 2017).

30. DuVal, *Independence Lost*, 306.

31. *ASP: IA*, 1: 51–52. For how livestock facilitated European and American colonization, see Virginia DeJohn Anderson, *How Domestic Animals Transformed Early America* (New York: Oxford University Press, 2004). Historians have traditionally referred to Piominko as "Piomingo," but I have chosen to use Piominko in accordance with a recent decision of the Chickasaw Nation. Media Relations Office of the Chickasaw Nation, "Chickasaw Nation Corrects Names of Famed Leaders," October 7, 2014, https://www. chickasaw.net/News/Press-Releases/Release/Chickasaw-Nation-corrects-names-of-famed-leaders-1693.aspx.

32. Hopewell Negotiations, *ASP: IA*, 1: 51.

33. Hopewell Negotiations, *ASP: IA*, 1: 42.

34. Treaty with the Chickasaw, January 10, 1786, in Kappler, *Indian Treaties*, 14–16.

35. Hopewell Negotiations, *ASP: IA*, 1: 43.

36. Hopewell Negotiations, *ASP: IA*, 1: 43.

37. Hopewell Negotiations, *ASP: IA*, 1: 42.

38. Thomas Perkins Abernethy, *From Frontier to Plantation in Tennessee: A Study in Frontier Democracy* (Chapel Hill: University of North Carolina Press, 1932), 34–114; John R. Finger, *Tennessee's Frontiers: Three Regions in Transition* (Bloomington: Indiana University Press, 2001), 53–124.

39. For more on the Chickamauga Cherokees, see Tyler Boulware, *Deconstructing the Cherokee Nation: Town, Region, and Nation among Eighteenth-Century Cherokees* (Gainesville: University Press of Florida, 2011), 161–177; Colin G. Calloway, "Declaring Independence and Rebuilding a Nation: Dragging Canoe and the Chickamauga Revolution," in *Revolutionary Founders: Rebels, Radicals, and Reformers in the Making of a*

Nation, ed. Alfred F. Young, Gary B. Nash, and Ray Raphael (New York: Alfred A. Knopf, 2011): 185–198.

40. Nashville Conference, *ASP: IA*, 1: 286 (quotation); Daniel Smith to William Dickson [1804], Draper MSS (microfilm edition), State Historical Society of Wisconsin, 4XX59.

41. Proclamation of George Washington, July 21, 1794, folder 14, box 4, James Robertson Papers, TSLA.

42. Silas Dinsmore to Timothy Pickering, October 26, 1795, page 72, reel 20, Timothy Pickering Papers, Massachusetts Historical Society, Boston, MA.

43. Kevin Barksdale, *Lost State of Franklin: America's First Secession* (Lexington: University Press of Kentucky, 2009), 83–90; Thomas Perkins Abernethy, *The South in the New Nation, 1789–1819* (Baton Rouge: Louisiana State University Press, 1961), 74–101; A.P. Whitaker, "The Muscle Shoals Speculation, 1783–1789," *The Mississippi Valley Historical Review* 13, no. 3 (Dec. 1926): 365–386.

44. The Glass to Return Meigs, March 10, 1804, M-208; John Sevier to Inhabitants and People Said to be Settled on the Indian Lands, April 1, 1804, folder 1, box 1, GP—4, John Sevier Governor's Papers, TSLA; Return Meigs to John Ballinger, July 15, 1804, M-208.

45. John Sevier Legislative Message, October 7, 1803, in Robert H. White, *Messages of the Governors of Tennessee*, vol. 1: *1796–1821* (Nashville: Tennessee Historical Commission, 1952), 138.

46. Henry Dearborn to Return Meigs, April 23, 1804, M-208.

47. William S. Lovely to Chiefs of Hiwassee, June 1, 1804, M-208.

48. Henry Dearborn to Daniel Smith and Return Meigs, April 4, 1804; Henry Dearborn to Return Meigs, April 23, 1804, both in M-208.

49. William G. McLoughlin, *Cherokee Renascence in the New Republic* (Princeton, N.J.: Princeton University Press, 1986), 91.

50. John Sevier to James Robertson, November 7, 1804, folder 2, box 4, James Robertson Papers, TSLA.

51. Return Meigs to James Robertson, December 21, 1804, folder 8, box 3, James Robertson Papers, TSLA.

52. Chennebee [Chinubbee] et al. to James Robertson, January 25, 1805, M-208.

53. Conquest theory had long been a significant justification for European colonization of Indigenous nations, and Americans adeptly appropriated it for their own use after gaining independence. See Ken MacMillan, *Sovereignty and Possession in the English New World: The Legal Foundations of Empire, 1576–1640* (Cambridge, United Kingdom: Cambridge University Press, 2006), 7–10; *Ibid.*, *The Atlantic Imperial Constitution: Center and Periphery in the English Atlantic World* (New York: Palgrave Macmillan, 2011), 14–17; Banner, *How the Indians Lost Their Land*, 17–22.

54. Chennebee [Chinubbee] et al. to James Robertson, January 25, 1805, M-208. On earlier Chickasaw–Shawnee conflict, see Finger, *Tennessee Frontiers*, 75–76.

55. Treaty with the Chickasaw, July 23, 1805, in Kappler, *Indian Treaties*, 79–80.

56. James Robertson to Henry Dearborn, August 8, 1805, folder 20, box, 3, James Robertson Papers, TSLA.

57. For examples of how overlapping claims affected land prices in various locales, see Stephen Aron, *How the West Was Lost: The Transformation of Kentucky from Daniel Boone to Henry Clay* (Baltimore: Johns Hopkins University Press, 1996), 82–123; Gregory Ablavsky, "The Adjudicatory State: Sovereignty, Property, and Law in the U.S. Territories, 1783–1802" (PhD dissertation, University of Pennsylvania, 2016), 76–101.

58. Henry Dearborn to Silas Dinsmore and James Robertson, March 20, 1805, M-208.

59. Return Meigs to James Robertson, May 5, 1805, M-208. James R. Atkinson argues that this was a reference to a 1766 attack by Cherokees against Chickasaws living along the Tennessee River. See James R. Atkinson, *Splendid Land, Splendid People: The Chickasaw Indians to Removal* (Tuscaloosa: University of Alabama Press, 2004), 23, 86.

60. Return Meigs to Henry Dearborn, January 23, 1805; Return Meigs to Daniel Smith, February 1, 1805; James Robertson to James Vann, April 22, 1805, all in M-208; James Robertson to James Vann, August 26, 1805, folder 20, box 3, James Robertson Papers, TSLA.

61. James Wilkinson, A Small Sketch of the Muscle Shoals, 1801, Miscellaneous Manuscript Maps, American Philosophical Society, Philadelphia.

62. Belmessous points out that Indigenous and European arguments about sovereignty and their arguments about property rights frequently overlapped and are difficult to differentiate from one another. See Belmessous, "Indigenous Claim Making," 11–13. For more on how theories of occupation contributed to European colonization of Indigenous land, see Banner, *How the Indians Lost Their Land*, 150–190; MacMillan: *Sovereignty and Possession*; Andrew Fitzmaurice, *Sovereignty, Property and Empire, 1500–2000* (Cambridge, United Kingdom: Cambridge University Press, 2014); Allan Greer, "Commons and Enclosure in the Colonization of North America," *The American Historical Review* 117, no. 2 (April 2012): 365–386; Michael Witgen, "A Nation of Settlers: The Early Republic and the Colonization of the Northwest Territory," *William and Mary Quarterly* 76, no. 3 (July 2019): 391–398. Lauren Benton complicates scholars' emphasis on occupation as the driving force behind colonization by highlighting the significance of the legal concept of possession; see Lauren Benton, "Possessing Empire: Iberian Claims and Interpolity Law," in *Native Claims*, 19–40.

63. James Robertson to James Vann, April 22, 1805, M-208; James Robertson to James Vann, August 26, 1805, folder 20, box 3, James Robertson Papers, TSLA.

64. Return Meigs to James Robertson, May 27, 1805, M-208; Benjamin Hawkins to Return Meigs, June 12, 1805, M-208; Daniel Smith to James Robertson, box 4, folder 4, James Robertson Papers, TSLA; Benjamin Hawkins to Henry Dearborn, June 14, 1805, in *Letters, Journals and Writings of Benjamin Hawkins*, ed. Grant, 2: 493.

65. To see how Americans sought recognition from European powers, see Elijah Gould, *Among the Powers of the Earth: The American Revolution and the Making of a New World Empire* (Cambridge, Mass.: Harvard University Press, 2012).

66. Doublehead [Chuquilatague] Address to Daniel Smith and Return Meigs, July 17, 1805, Daniel Smith and Return Meigs to Henry Dearborn, July 27, 1805, Doublehead [Chuquilatague] et al. to Black Fox et al., August 9, 1805; Return Meigs to Daniel Smith, August 19, 1805, all in M-208.

67. Treaty with the Cherokee, October 25, 1805, in Kappler, *Indian Treaties*, 82–83. For more on the negotiations, see Return Meigs to Daniel Smith, August 19, 1805, and Doublehead [Chuquilatague] et al. to Black Fox et al., August 9, 1805, both in M-208.

68. Treaty with the Cherokee, January 7, 1806, in Kappler, *Indian Treaties*, 90–92.

69. Chinubbee King [Chinubbee], et al. to Henry Dearborn, August 25, 1808, M-208. Emphasis in original.

70. William Eustis to Return Meigs, May 8, 1811, M-208.

71. Michael D. Green, *The Politics of Indian Removal: Creek Government and Society in Crisis* (Lincoln: University of Nebraska Press, 1982), 43; Hudson, *Creek Paths and Federal Roads*, 118–120.

72. Andrew Jackson to William Crawford, August 10, 1814, *ASP: IA*, 1: 838 (quotation); Green, *Politics of Indian Removal*, 43.

73. Statistic from Adam Rothman, *Slave Country: American Expansion and the Origins of the Deep South* (Cambridge, Mass.: Harvard University Press), 168. For a description of the negotiations, see Benjamin Hawkins to George Graham, August 1, 1815, in *Letters of Benjamin Hawkins*, 2: 743–746. Tustunnugee Thlucco later explained that Jackson "threatened us and made us comply with his talk about a cession" (*Journal of Occurrences at the Convention of the Creeks at Tookaubatche [Tukabatchee]*, September 18, 1815, in *Letters of Benjamin Hawkins*, 2: 755).

74. Notes of a Convention between the Creeks and Cherokees, August 9, 1814 (quotations), Return Meigs to Andrew Jackson, August 8, 1815, both in M-208. For overviews of negotiations at the conference, see Thurman Wilkins, *Cherokee Tragedy: The Ridge Family and the Decimation of a People* (Norman: University of Oklahoma Press, 1989), 81–83; Claudio Saunt, *A New Order of Things: Property, Power, and the Transformation of the Creek Indians, 1733–1816* (Cambridge, United Kingdom: Cambridge University Press, 1999), 270–272; Hudson, *Creek Paths and Federal Roads*, 117–119.

75. Treaty with the Creeks, August 9, 1814, in Kappler, *Indian Treaties*, 108. Creek Agent Benjamin Hawkins repeated the vague description of the cession boundary in his reports after the negotiations ended; see Benjamin Hawkins to John Armstrong, August 16, 1814, in *Letters of Benjamin Hawkins*, 2: 693.

76. Return Meigs to Andrew Jackson, August 8, 1815, M-208.

77. Affidavit of The Glass, December 21, 1815 (quotation); Affidavit of John Rogers, December 22, 1815, both in M-208. Emphasis in original.

78. See enclosures in William Cocke to unknown, May 12, 1816, frame# 1001–1013, Reel 2, Bureau of Indian Affairs, Letters Received by the Secretary of War Relating to Indian Affairs, 1800–1823, Record Group 75, Microcopy 271, National Archives, Washington, D.C. Hereafter cited as M-271.

79. Affidavit of The Glass, December 21, 1815, M-208.

80. Charles Hicks to Return Meigs, July 4, 1816, M-208 (quotation). Theda Perdue, *Cherokee Women: Gender and Culture Change, 1700–1835* (Lincoln: University of Nebraska Press, 1998), 45–46.

81. For more on kinship diplomacy, see *Beyond the Covenant Chain: The Iroquois and Their Neighbors in Indian North America, 1600–1800*, ed. Daniel Richter and James H. Merrell (Syracuse, N.Y.: Syracuse University Press, 1987); Cynthia Cumfer, *Separate Peoples, One Land: The Minds of Cherokees, Blacks, and Whites on the Tennessee Frontier* (Chapel Hill: University of North Carolina Press, 2007), 23–49.

82. Treaty with the Cherokee, March 22, 1816, in Kappler, *Indian Treaties*, 125–126.

83. Andrew Jackson to William Crawford, June 10, 1816, *ASP: IA*, 2: 110–111; William Russell to John Coffee, May 8, 1816, folder 2, box 1, John Coffee Papers, Alabama Department of Archives and History, Montgomery, AL. Hereafter cited as ADAH.

84. Andrew Jackson to William Crawford, June 10, 1816, *ASP: IA*, 2: 110–111.

85. William Russell to John Coffee, May 8, 1816, folder 2, box 1, John Coffee Papers, ADAH.

86. Memorial to the President of the United States, Jenkin Whitesides et al., *The Nashville Whig*, July 16, 1816 (quotation); McLoughlin, *Cherokee Renascence*, 201–203.

87. William Crawford to Return Meigs, June 15, 1816, M-208; William Crawford to John McKee, May 20, 1816, *ASP: IA*, 2: 118.

88. For Crawford's instructions to the commissioners, see William Crawford to Andrew Jackson, David Meriwether, and Jesse Franklin, July 5 [3] 1816, *ASP: IA*, 2: 100–102.

89. Journal of the Proceedings of General Andrew Jackson, General David Meriwether, and Jesse Franklin Esq. Commissioners appointed by the President of the United States of America to Hold Conferences & Settle a Treaty with the Chickasaw & Cherokee Tribes or Nations of Indians, in the Jesse Franklin Indian Treaty Papers, #3656-z, Southern Historical Collection, The Wilson Library, University of North Carolina at Chapel Hill, Chapel Hill, NC, 9–13. Hereafter cited as Franklin Journal. Like Piominko, historians traditionally referred to Tishominko as "Tishomingo." Media Relations Office of the Chickasaw Nation, "Chickasaw Nation Corrects Names of Famed Leaders."

90. Franklin Journal, 13–18.

91. Franklin Journal, 18.

92. *Ibid.*, 19. For more on the significance of geography to Chickasaw origin stories, see Dustin J. Mack, "Chickasaws' Place-World: The Mississippi River in Chickasaw History and Geography," *Native South* 11 (2018): 1–28.

93. Franklin Journal, 20.

94. *Ibid.*, 21.

95. *Ibid.*, 18, 16.

96. Jackson's witnesses were Captain John Gordon; Colonel Newton Cannon; Captain John Hutchings, Jackson's nephew; and a Mr. Potter, who was Jackson's quartermaster. See *Ibid.*, 22–26.

97. *Ibid.*, 28–35.

98. *Ibid.*, 26–28.

99. *Ibid.*, 37.

100. *Ibid.*, 38–39; Andrew Jackson to John Coffee, September 19, 1816, in *The Papers of Andrew Jackson*, ed. Harold D. Moser, vol. 4, 1816–1820, ed. Harold D. Moser, David R. Hoth, and George H. Hoeman (Knoxville: University of Tennessee Press, 1994), 63.

101. Treaty with the Cherokee, September 14, 1816, in Kappler, *Indian Treaties*, 133–134; Andrew Jackson, David Meriwether, and Jesse Franklin to William Crawford, September 20, 1816, in *Papers of Andrew Jackson*, 4: 65–68.

102. Franklin Journal, 43–44; Andrew Jackson, David Meriwether, and Jesse Franklin to William Crawford, September 20, 1816, *Papers of Andrew Jackson*, 4: 65–68.

103. Treaty with the Chickasaw, September 20, 1816, in Kappler, *Indian Treaties*, 135–137.

104. Richard Brown to Charles Hicks, December 12, 1816, frame#915–916, M-271.

105. Duncan Ivison, "The Normative Force of the Past," afterword in *Native Claims*, ed. Belmessous, 249.

106. *McGirt v. Oklahoma*, 591 U.S. ____ (2020).

107. Jonodev O. Chaudhuri, comments during The Most Significant Indian Law Case of the Century: *McGirt v. Oklahoma* webinar, Indian Legal Program at the Sandra Day O'Connor College of Law, Arizona State University, July 23, 2020.

Finding the History of the World at the Bottom of the Ocean

Hydrography, Natural History, and the Sea in the Nineteenth Century

Penelope K. Hardy

IN EARLY 1873, NAVIGATING Sublieutenant Herbert Swire, at sea onboard the Royal Navy vessel HMS *Challenger*, recorded his thoughts about the trip thus far. Swire and the *Challenger* had left Britain a few months earlier in company with a handful of civilian "scientifics" on a three-and-a-half-year circumnavigation whose goal was to study the global ocean. The voyage would often be remembered as the origin of oceanography, but to Swire, tossing about in the Atlantic as the embarked naturalists lowered instruments and samplers into the deep, much of it seemed to be about mud. "We have been dredging ever since leaving Lisbon," he reported, "'drudging', the bluejackets call it, with their customary correctness and a dash of sarcasm [. . . . W]e never get anything in the dredge except a lot of mud, but then I don't know anything about the matter and possibly the mud may be worth its weight in gold to the 'philosophers.'"[1]

Swire was correct. To the naturalists onboard, the mud would prove quite valuable. The sediment recovered from the bottom of the sea via sounding lead and dredge allowed them to better understand both zoological and geological processes, to weigh in on scientific debates back home, and to postulate about the formation of the ancient earth. Ocean sediments thus became a tool for theorizing, as well as the material with which the naturalists painted a new and colorful mental map of a landscape they could never see or touch. Most scholarship on the *Challenger* expedition has concentrated on its zoological efforts—as did more than forty of the fifty results volumes published in the twenty years after the expedition's return—its role in understanding currents, or the novelty of conducting laboratory work onboard a vessel.[2] Yet they were working within a framework established in the decades before their trip and by their own preliminary work that explicitly linked marine zoology with ongoing debates in paleontology and geology. The *Challenger* naturalists used the sediments they collected with sounder and dredge to enter the fray in these debates, turning ocean sediment into a tool for making arguments about earth's geological past and about conditions in the unseeable depths of the modern ocean.[3]

Sailors had long used sounding lines and weights charged with tallow to sample the sea bottom for hydrographic purposes, and by the mid-eighteenth century individual investigators adopted the oysterman's dredge to investigate the distribution of benthic fauna. While other

117

naturalists echoed them in ones and twos, it wasn't until the nineteenth century that naturalists in larger numbers became interested in exploring the bottom of the sea. Especially in Britain, naturalists like Edward Forbes expanded the use of the dredge to organize systematic studies of local marine fauna before making forays into northern and Mediterranean waters.

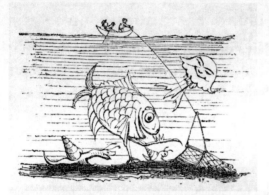

Figure 1. Frontispiece to Natural History of the European Seas by Edward Forbes, edited by Robert Godwin-Austen, c. 1855. Archival photo by Steve Nicklas, National Ocean Service (NOS). Image courtesy of NOAA Photo Library.

Forbes, like his predecessors, was largely interested in the fauna, though he paid attention to the depth and associated pressure, temperature, and darkness that marked the habitats of the animals he found. He often turned the results of his studies, though, to the purposes of geology. Geologists were struggling to explain the stratified layers they found in terrestrial rock, and particularly to explain the appearance of apparently marine fossils in various layers, often far from the ocean. When Forbes found similar animals still living in the depths, he realized that a thorough understanding of their distribution and the conditions of depth under which they lived could help explain the conditions under which the ancient fossil beds had formed.[4] He was here partly following the work of Charles Lyell, who had pointed to fossils as indicators of ancient environment.[5] Forbes and others thus acknowledged geology as a motivation for dredging by the 1840s (though as historian Philip Rehbock noted, geology enjoyed more popularity than zoology at the time, so Forbes was perhaps being strategic in hitching his research to the higher star).[6]

Forbes' work around Britain and then in the Aegean led him to delineate "regions" or depth zones, partly borrowing from earlier French work, in which specific varieties of animal lived.[7] Organisms were not distributed at random, but instead lived in certain zones corresponding with their preferred temperature, depth, and light levels. He also laid out a "law" to explain the range of distribution: "Parallels in depth are equivalent to parallels in latitude."[8] This mirrored Alexander Humboldt's terrestrial observations made earlier in the century that plants varied in accordance with altitude much as they did according to latitude.

While Forbes's untimely death in 1854 put an end to his own work on the subject, he had by then inspired a number of other British naturalists to take up the dredge, first in conjunction with a Dredging Committee funded by the British Association for the Advancement of Science (BAAS) and then on their own. In particular, Scottish marine zoologist C. Wyville Thomson took up the mantle. Thomson had trained in medicine at the University of Edinburgh, where Forbes, too, had studied, and where a network had formed around dredging and marine zoology.[9] He then became active with the BAAS Dredging Committee. Thomson's primary interest was zoology, so when in the mid-1860s he saw some unusual specimens dredged from the then-considered-extreme depth of 300 fathoms by Swedish father and son team Michael Sars and Georg Ossian Sars, he saw the opportunity to use international competition as a spur to encourage British science.[10] With fellow zoologist William Carpenter, he successfully convinced the Royal Society of London and the Admiralty to sponsor several summer voyages on the survey ships HMS *Lightning* and *Porcupine* off the northern coasts of Britain.[11]

These summer cruises provided the embarked naturalists—Thomson, Carpenter, and their colleague, the conchologist John Gwyn Jeffreys—the opportunity to learn and adapt techniques and technologies for sampling the bottom at ever-increasing depths. Their main tools for this were adapted from the sailors' sounding lead and further modified versions of the dredge. Sailors had long taken small specimens of bottom sediment by coating the bottom of their lead with tallow; when it hit bottom, sediment would stick, or at least leave an impression, in the tallow.[12] When naturalists desired larger samples, they adapted sounding mechanisms to capture more sediment, usually by using a weighted tube that would be driven into the sediment upon impact with the bottom, at which point the weights would detach, allowing the tube of sediment to be retrieved by the ship above.

Another sampling method, intended to capture flora and fauna but which succeeded—often entirely too well—at capturing bottom sediment, was the dredge. The naturalist's dredge had been enlarged and modified since Forbes's days but still scraped along the bottom at the end of a long line, scooping up anything in its path. When during the summer cruise on *Porcupine* the dredge often returned empty, even when there were bits of animal life stuck to the hemp line that lifted it, the ship's captain suggested adding tufts of unraveled hemp along the bottom edge; this adaptation "mopped" the bottom, sweeping up flora, fauna, and sediment alike.[13] The design worked well, especially on a rocky bottom where the dredge itself could not dig in. Using the dredge off the coast of Scotland, the embarked naturalists brought up "a bluish-white tenacious mud" mixed with the microscopic shells of Globigerina, a genus of planktonic marine foraminifera. The find was not earth-shattering, as the remains of these tiny animals had been found in abundance even by the rudimentary earlier soundings of the North Atlantic bottom.[14]

Beginning in the 1840s, American naval officer Matthew Fontaine Maury, superintendent of the U.S. Navy's Depot of Charts and Instruments, had enlisted a series of naval vessels and even commercial vessels to attempt deep soundings in the Atlantic and beyond.[15] He eventually convinced Congress and the navy to assign specific ships for the purpose. He organized three cruises between 1849 and 1852, and he worked with his lieutenants to improve the technology required to sound the deepest portions of the Atlantic and bring samples back as they did so. In fact, Lieutenant John M. Brooke, working under Maury's command at the Depot, developed the prototypical weighted sounder upon which the later British variations would be based.[16] Maury used the sounding data collected from these cruises and his other volunteer sources to create the first bathymetric chart of the North Atlantic, a map that began the transformation of the amorphous blank abyss between North American and Europe into a landscape increasingly imagined as known.[17] Over the next eight years, Maury would continuously revise this chart as new and more accurate soundings became available, slowly filling in the details in the new landscape.[18]

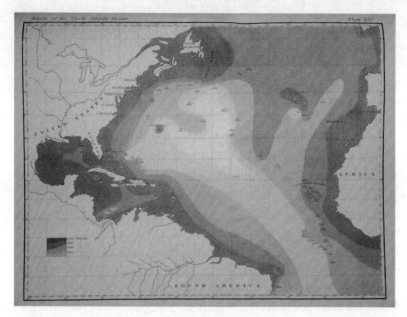

Figure 2. Matthew Fontaine Maury, "Bathymetric Chart of the Atlantic basin," Plate XIV from Explanations and Sailing Directions to Accompany the Wind and Current Charts, 5th ed. (1853).

Meanwhile, the sediment samples retrieved on these voyages, as Thomson noted later, "were eagerly sought for by naturalists and submitted to a searching microscopic examination."[19] Maury sent them first to Jacob Whitman Bailey, an American microscopist and professor at West Point who had published prolifically on microscopic fossil and freshwater organisms, as well as analyzing sediments from relatively near-shore soundings taken by officers of the U.S. Coast Survey.[20] Examining the Atlantic bottom samples, Bailey reported that with the exception of only one sounding, "the bottom of the North Atlantic Ocean . . . from the depth of about 60 fathoms, to that of more than two miles (2000 fathoms), is literally nothing but a mass of microscopic shells"—the Globigerina.[21] Their remains blanketed the bottom, but it was not clear where the Globigerina dwelled when alive. Bailey thought it likely they lived near the surface, their shells drifting down in a chalky snow once they died. German microscopist Christian Ehrenberg, on the other hand, argued that more evidence suggested they lived and died where they were found, near the bottom.[22] British naturalist George Wallich, who in 1860 talked himself into a berth as naval naturalist on HMS Bulldog's expedition to survey potential transatlantic cable routes, hoping (vainly, as it happened) to parlay the experience into a career in science, agreed. "By sinking very fine gauze nets to considerable depths," during his expedition across the North Atlantic, "I have repeatedly satisfied myself that Globigerina does not occur in the superficial strata of the ocean." Instead, "[i]ts seat of maximum development is on the deepest area of the sea-bed," though he was disappointed with his inability to find vestiges of vitality in freshly taken samples from the deep sea, as he expected had the samples been taken alive.[23]

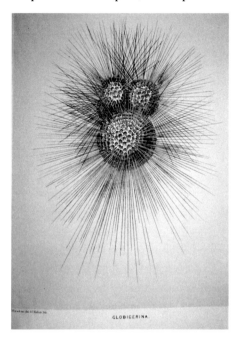

GLOBIGERINA.

Figure 3. The Challenger Reports. Vol. IX, Plate LXXVII. The Foraminifera. Globigerina. Orbulina bulloides, d'Orbigny. Image courtesy of NOAA Central Library Historical Collections.

After the *Porcupine* and *Lightning* cruises, with their own sediment samples in hand, Carpenter, Thomson, and Jeffreys could now weigh in.[24] These preliminary results convinced Carpenter and Thomson to agree with Ehrenberg and Wallich that the Foraminifera found on the bottom dwelled there. Jeffreys, on the other hand, cited reports by Samuel R. I. Owen of their appearance in near-surface collection nets in the Red Sea.[25] Owen provided a several-page list of specific species found at the surface, including their latitudes and longitudes, and he wryly concluded that he therefore "th[ought] it most probable that the Foraminifera found at the bottom were dead, or that they must have some means of again rising to the surface. To those who consider this impossible it must be left to get over the difficult ground interposed in the form of two or three miles of water, if they still consider that the bottom of the ocean is their natural habitat and the place at which they are bred."[26] Armed with these data, Jeffreys insisted fairly adamantly that the Foraminifera must be surface dwellers, recording his dissent from Thomson's and Carpenter's conclusion in a footnote to their jointly authored preliminary report.[27]

In the course of the *Challenger* expedition, Thomson was convinced to change his mind. For one thing, his *Challenger* shipmate and fellow naturalist John Murray, who had become an adherent of the surface-dwelling hypothesis early in the voyage, sampled extensively with tow-nets during the voyage, both at the surface and at relatively shallow depths between 10 and 100 fathoms. He found Globigerina "[i]n all seas, from the equator to the polar ice," and the surface fauna and bottom deposits always bore "the closest relation."[28] By the end of 1874, in a paper read before the Royal Society while he himself was still at sea, Thomson catalogued a preponderance of evidence to support his newfound agreement, including Bailey's and Owen's work, but also that of Johannes Müller, Louis Pourtalès, August Krohn, and Ernst Haeckel. (To his credit, Thomson also acknowledged his earlier "very strong opinion," which he now found "in error," and Jeffreys's early opposition.)[29]

Wherever the Foraminifera lived, Thomson's and Carpenter's exploration and interpretation of their eventual resting place launched the two zoologists into another geological and paleontological argument, this one over the so-called "continuity of the Chalk." In 1836, Ehrenberg had established through microscopic examination that the deposits of porous white limestone in Cretaceous strata in England and elsewhere—known as "the Chalk"—contained the remains of marine fossils, evidence that these layers had been laid down when the area was at the bottom of an ancient sea.[30] Now the sedimentary soundings from the Atlantic and beyond found these same creatures in the process of living, dying, and drifting into an accumulating layer at the bottom of the modern sea. This offered powerful support for Charles Lyell's uniformitarianism—the idea that the world we see today was formed by the accumulation of small changes wrought by the application of long, slow processes over an immense period of time—but Thomson took it further. This was not simply evidence of the same mechanism in operation today that had formed the Cretaceous Chalk in the past, he argued. Indeed, he claimed, "it is not only chalk which is being formed in the Atlantic, 'but *the* chalk, the chalk of the cretaceous period.'"[31] Other naturalists pushed back on the claim "that we might be regarded in a certain sense as still living in the cretaceous period." Thomson changed his wording (after all, geological periodization is "thoroughly indefinite") but maintained, with Carpenter and Jeffreys, "that the balance of probability is greatly in favour of the chalk having been uninterruptedly forming over some parts of the area" that is now the Atlantic Ocean.[32]

Figure 4. The white (Cretaceous chalk) cliffs of Dover. Photo by Gertjan van Noord. Used under Creative Commons license: https://creativecommons.org/licenses/by-nd/2.0/legalcode Source: https://www.flickr.com/photos/145907835@N07/49403089696/

When the *Porcupine* and *Lightning* cruises proved successful both in terms of results and in terms of cohesion among personnel, the naturalists were able to convince the Royal Society and the Royal Navy to jointly launch a grander project: the scientific circumnavigation of the world onboard HMS *Challenger* of Sublieutenant Swire's aforementioned complaints. From 1872 to 1876, seven "scientifics," including Thomson, would join the naval officers and crew for a three-and-a-half-year voyage studying every sea except the Arctic.[33] Historian of science Rodolfo John Alaniz and others have placed this voyage in the context of ongoing debate over Darwin's theories of evolution, noting the naturalists' hope of finding living fossils in the very deep ocean.[34] Yet when the committee established by the Royal Society to consider a scientific circumnavigation laid out its potential goals, examining the distribution of life fell fourth on a list of four, preceded by the desire "[t]o ascertain the *Physical* and *Chemical* characters of the *Deposits* everywhere in progress on the sea-bottom; and to trace, so far as may be possible, the sources of those deposits." The goal of examining life, in fact, urged investigators to do so "with especial reference to the physical and chemical conditions already referred to, and to the connection of the present with the past condition of the globe."[35]

The *Challenger* traveled 68,890 nautical miles, sampling the sea bottom at hundreds of points along the way, from the littoral to the deepest spot in the ocean (a location near the Mariana Trench now labeled "Challenger Deep" for just this reason). *Challenger* naturalists largely used the combination of tools that had been developed on the preliminary cruises. They sounded with a Baillie Sounding Machine, which had an iron tube of 2-inch diameter with holes at the top to release water as the sample replaced it. Ring-shaped weights around the tube drove the apparatus into the bottom. The weights detached in the process, and butterfly valves at the opening of the tube trapped the sediment sample, which could be hauled back to the surface.[36] The soundings were supervised by the ship's officers, who were tasked with a hydrographic mission in parallel with the ship's scientific one, mapping coastlines and potential cable routes for the Admiralty, but they worked in concert with the naturalists; the naval officers' navigational efforts were also key to the naturalists' ability to pinpoint the sources of the sediment they collected.[37] The modified naturalist's dredge, with its "hempen tangles," was retained for the longer voyage.

Based on Bailey's microscopy and their own findings on the preliminary cruises, the *Challenger* naturalists had set out expecting to find "a more or less universal chalk formation at the bottom of the ocean."[38] Yet as *Challenger* continued into deeper water, the naturalists noticed a shift from the "Globigerina ooze" they had been retrieving to a red clay with no signs of Foraminifera. The transition in sediment composition was not abrupt, they discovered, but first passed through a transitional region of "gray ooze" between about 2200 and 2600 fathoms, where "the shells gradually lose their sharpness of outline, assume a kind of 'rotten' look and a brownish color, and become more and more mixed with a fine amorphous red-brown powder, which increases steadily in proportion until the lime has almost entirely disappeared."[39] Their first thought was that this fine "red clay" was the ultimate product of the combined erosion and siltation from the coasts of the world, washed into and mixed in the great ocean. It should thus appear everywhere but was perhaps only obvious in those regions Globigerina did not inhabit. However, as time went on and evidence accumulated that the microscopic organisms lived near the surface, it also became increasingly evident that they were essentially ubiquitous.[40] The extremely fine texture of the remaining sediment in these deeper regions made it unlikely that some sort of current swept their remains away from the bottom.[41] Instead, the gradual transition—with foraminifera shells in the intermediate area showing increasing degradation—suggested a chemical reaction, perhaps "the removal, by some means or other . . . of the carbonate of lime" [calcium carbonate] which made up most of the globigerina shells.[42]

Unlike earlier expeditions, whose specimens had generally had to wait for analysis ashore, *Challenger* had well-equipped onboard laboratories.[43] The naturalists' work room, or physical laboratory, was outfitted with cupboards and drawers full of bottles and test tube racks, instrument cases, a freshwater tank and sink, and a cistern of spirit of wine, locked and secured in the overhead netting, for preserving specimens. Tools from harpoons to botanical vascula were suspended from the overhead, and a long table down the center of the room provided a convenient place to use microscopes—secured against movement at sea—in the light provided by a gunport on the port side and a skylight overhead. The chemical laboratory contained provisions for chemical analysis, including a glass-blowing forge for the creation or modification of the vessels needed to contain or test samples.[44]

When expedition chemist John Buchanan subjected a sample of Globigerina ooze to weak acid in the onboard chemical laboratory, the resulting product was a reddish mud.[45] Thomson saw this finding, too, in the light of terrestrial geology. He detailed a dredge haul full of "very well-marked red mud," in which were embedded "many of the tubes of a tube-building annelid, several of them 3 to 4 inches long, and containing the worm, a species of Myriochele, still living." Similarly, ashore one found formations, often quite thick, of "fine, smooth, homogeneous clays and schists, poor in fossils, but showing worm-tubes and tracks, and bunches of doubtful branching things, such as Oldhamia, siliceous sponges, and thin-shelled peculiar shrimps." Though usually interpreted as the product of rock disintegration, perhaps, he posited, these clays were organic in nature, just as the chalks, in this case "accumulations of the insoluble ashes of shelled creatures."[46] This had the potential to fundamentally change geological understanding. As A. S. Wilson summarized in *Scientific American*, "[I]t will appear that geologists have been in the habit of underestimating the importance of organic processes as geological agents. We will no longer be able to affirm with confidence, of a single grain of the commonest materials found on the earth's surface, that it has not at one time or other been associated with the manifestation of those mysterious forces which we call living."[47]

As the ship proceeded into deeper water, the sediment samples showed another shift, as below 3000 fathoms the red clay began to accumulate the shells of Radiolaria, a planktonic protozoa whose shells consist of silica instead of the calcium carbonate of the Globigerina. Again the transition was gradual, until eventually the red clay gave way to a siliceous "radiolarian ooze." This, too, reflected ancient geological conditions Ehrenberg

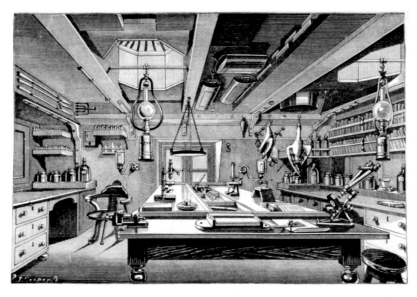

Figure 5. The Natural History work-room of the Challenger. Figure 1 in *The Voyage of the Challenger: The Atlantic*, Vol I, by c. Wyville Thomson (1878). Archival Photography by Steve Nicklas, NOS. Image courtesy of NOAA Photo Library.

had observed in Europe.[48] This alignment of depth, distance from shore, and nature of sedimentary fauna allowed the naturalists to reexamine strata ashore. They now knew what conditions in the modern ocean were producing a layer of siliceous ooze, for instance; thus, the landscape ashore that contained a siliceous stratum must once have been under those same conditions. Examining the precise mix of fossilized fauna under a microscope could provide an even closer window onto the geological past, dictating an even narrower band of conditions in which the observed layers must have formed.

Carpenter, working in London thanks to his exclusion from the voyage, nevertheless placed the bottom sediment results from *Challenger* and its predecessors in conversation with terrestrial paleontology to form arguments. In fact, he demonstrated that the link between ocean bottom sediments and terrestrial geology was now strong enough to work both directions. In the South Pacific, *Challenger* naturalists had found no less than "five absolutely distinct kinds of sea-bottom," not counting the near-shore detritus of the land.[49] The microscope remained invaluable in identifying and classifying them as a "greenish sand" found around the Agulhas current (the western boundary of the Indian Ocean) turned out to again be made up of Foraminifera.[50] Still unconvinced that these were surface dwellers, perhaps because he was left to interpret the results vicariously, Carpenter looked to the greenish sand for support for his theory—or at least for sufficient ambiguity not to accept Thomson's. Carpenter insisted that while Foraminifera might be pelagic as juveniles, they sank to the bottom as their calcareous shells thickened over the course of their lives, and there they reproduced and lived out the rest of their lives. The green sand and red clay, then, found on the bottom with no trace of their shells, would have been a "*post-mortem* deposit" of "either the green or the ochreous silicate of alumina and iron" which was changed with exposure to carbonic acid "by a metamorphic action analogous to that which changes felspar into clay." This would occur much as the "disintegration of the granite in Auvergne and of the gneiss in the alluvial plains of the Po," which Lyell had described.[51] Thomas H. Huxley, a *Challenger* enthusiast perhaps most famous for his early support of Darwin, referred to this as "the most wonderful thing" the expedition had found; the red clay was also "a great puzzle—a great mystery—how it comes there, what it arises from, whether it is, as the director [Thomson] has suggested, the ash of foraminiferæ; whether it is decomposed pumice-stone vomited out by volcanoes, and scattered over the surface, or whether, lastly, it has something to do with that meteoric dust which is being continually rained upon us from the spaces of the universe—which of these causes may be at the bottom of the phenomenon it is very hard to say; it is one of those points on which we shall have information by-and-by."[52]

Thomson's theory did not withstand further testing; chemical reaction explained the disappearance of the Globigerina, but when these creatures were captured in surface nets and subjected to the same chemical process, red clay did not result.[53] Murray then suggested that the clay was in fact the result of decomposing pumice, expelled by volcanoes and then left to drift globally until it finally sank and slowly decomposed. Under the microscope the red clay proved to contain glassy feldspar and to lack quartz, evidence to support its volcanic origin.[54]

Whatever the origin of the clay, the information was useful to understanding terrestrial geology. As *Scientific American* noted, "In studying the geology of most countries, nothing

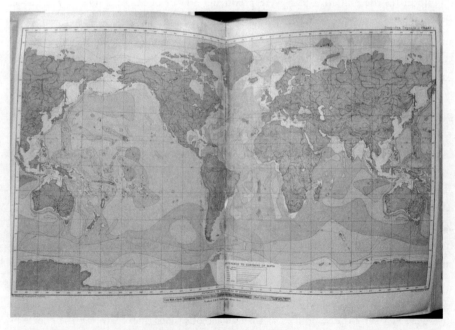

Figure 6. Deep-sea Deposits. Chart 1. From John Murray and A. F. Renard, Deep-Sea Deposits, vol. of Report of the Scientific Results of the Voyage of H.M.S. Challenger during the Years 1873–1876 (London, 1891). Image courtesy of NOAA Central Library Historical Collections.

has been more incomprehensible that the vast extent of red rocks which occur without a trace of a fossil, or with very unsatisfactory evidences of former contemporaneous life; now we know many of them to be of abyssal sea origin."[55] This American commentary, along with the continuing contributions of Carpenter and Jeffreys, who were not aboard *Challenger*, the reading of Thomson's papers in front of the Royal Society even in his absence and their republication in journals such as *Nature* and *Scientific American*, and the commentary of such scientific worthies as Huxley, suggests that Thomson's and his shipmates' efforts to use ocean sediment in geological argument worked. The speculation around geology that arose from the *Challenger* findings entered the mainstream of scientific conversation.

Over the three and a half years of the voyage, the bottom became a familiar place to the naturalists. "[W]e have met with the same phenomenon so frequently," Thomson reported by 1874, "that we were at length able to predict the nature of the bottom from the depth of the sound, with absolute certainty."[56] The various oozes and clays and their constituent parts entered the naturalists' everyday vocabulary. They were able to classify sedimentary layers as terrigenous (occurring in the littoral, in shallower water, and generally consisting of materials washed into the sea from the land), pelagic, or benthic, and they sketched them onto the contours emerging from the accompanying soundings. What emerged was a visualization, a map of the bottom as a knowable, even colorful territory—with its gray and blue and red clay, green sands, and oozes like chocolate—delineated by depth and distance from shore. The naturalists thus constructed the bottom as a site for study that they could visit virtually, though none of them could ever observe it in situ. At the same time, their comparisons with shore-based paleontology helped them understand the inhabitants of the benthic landscape as multidimensional, existing in time as well as space, and in chemistry and geology as well as biology. The bottom became a kind of time machine, a temporal laboratory for in situ study of ancient processes that had created the terrestrial geological formations that could otherwise only be interpreted through the clues left in stratigraphy and fossils.

I have elsewhere argued about the centrality of technology to the *Challenger* expedition, which refashioned a naval vessel into a new kind of vessel, using space and instruments and workshops to make authoritative claims for science done in an otherwise less-than-controlled environment.[57] When we reexamine the *Challenger* expedition through the lens of geology, it remains a very technologically contingent history, one that emphasizes not just technologies of collection but also onboard technologies of analysis—such as microscopes and chemistry setups—and the capability to modify both as needed, and technologies of representation, such as the bathymetric charts and geological maps that developed into evidence for scientific arguments.

As the *Challenger* expedition is frequently pointed to as the origins of oceanography, its naturalists' use of faunal sediment to do geological work also helps to explain the foundation of oceanography as an inherently interdisciplinary field. This interdisciplinarity is not the product of the growing complexity of modern scientific investigation, but has been present since the discipline's formation. Even as the broader structure of science was increasingly fragmenting during the nineteenth century, as natural philosophers increasingly became specialists in particular fields of research, these proto-oceanographers and their maps recognized the oceans as a place that could not be so easily subdivided, or where dividing would not necessarily lead to easier scientific conquest.

Notes

Penelope K. Hardy is assistant professor of history at the University of Wisconsin-La Crosse.

1. Swire, *The Voyage of the Challenger: A Personal Narrative of the Historic Circumnavigation of the Globe in the Years 1872–1876*, vol. 1. (London: Golden Cockerel Press, 1938), 15.

2. See, for instance, Anne-Flore Laloë, "Where is Bathybius haeckelii? The Ship as a Scientific Instrument and a Space of Science," in *Re-inventing the Ship: Science, Technology and the Maritime World, 1800–1918*, edited by Don Leggett and Richard Dunn, 113–130 (Burlington, VT: Ashgate, 2012); Eric Mills, *The Fluid Envelope of Our Planet: How the Study of Ocean Currents Became a Science* (Toronto: University of Toronto Press, 2009); Helen M. Rozwadowski, "Small World: Forging a Scientific Maritime Culture for Oceanography," *Isis* 87, no. 3 (September 1996): 409–429; Antony Adler, "The Ship as Laboratory: Making Space for Field Science at Sea," *Journal of the History of Biology* 47, no. 3 (August 2014): 333–362.

3. As Julie L. Reed's "Thinking Multidimensionally: Cherokee Boundaries Above, Below, and Beyond," in this volume, also suggests, historians should pay more attention to the multidimensionality of mapping in time, space, and beyond across cultures.

4. Edward Forbes, "On the connection between the distribution of the existing fauna and flora of the British Isles, and the geological changes which have affected their area, especially during the area of the northern drift," *Mem. Geol. Surv. U.K.* 1 (1846): 336–432. Cited in Eric Mills, "Edward Forbes, John Gwyn Jeffries, and British Dredging before the 'Challenger' Expedition," *Journal of the Society for the Bibliography of Natural History* 8, no. 4 (1978), 519.

5. Mills, "Forbes, Jeffries, and British Dredging," 514.

6. Philip F. Rehbock, "The Early Dredgers: 'Naturalizing' in British Seas, 1830–1850," *Journal of the History of Biology* 12, no. 2 (Autumn 1979), 357.

7. Mills, "Forbes, Jeffries, and British Dredging," 512.

8. Forbes, "On the Light Thrown on Geology by Submarine Researches," *The Edinburgh New Philosophical Journal: Exhibiting a View of the Progressive Discoveries and Improvements in the Sciences and the Arts* 36 (1844): 322–323.

9. Rodolfo John Alaniz has elucidated this network, among others centered on dredging practice, in his "Dredging Evolutionary Theory: The Emergence of the Deep Sea as a Transatlantic Site for Evolution, 1853–1876" (PhD dissertation, University of California, San Diego, 2014).

10. A fathom is a measurement of depth equal to 6 feet.

11. Collaborations between political entities and science expanded during the nineteenth century for a number of reasons. Certainly, scientists looked to deep government pockets for funding, as did the naturalists examined here, but they also

bolstered their burgeoning authority by encouraging governments to trust science for definitive answers to the problems of empire, which of course mapping in its various form appeared (and is still taken) to be. Naturalists involved in undersea telegraph route surveys, such as Matthew Fontaine Maury and George Wallich, below, are an example; for another see David I. Spanagel, "Putting Science to the Test: Initiating the World's Longest Unfortified Boundary," in this volume.

12. Alistair Sponsel has argued that this aspect of naval hydrographic practice was foundational to Charles Darwin's theories about the formation of coral reefs, "An Amphibious Being: How Maritime Surveying Reshaped Darwin's Approach to Natural History," *Isis* 107, no. 2 (2016): 254–281.

13. William B. Carpenter, J[ohn] Gwyn Jeffreys, and [Charles] Wyville Thomson, "Preliminary Report of the Scientific Exploration of the Deep Sea in H.M. Surveying-Vessel 'Porcupine,' during the Summer of 1869," *Proc. R. Soc.* 18 (1869): 436–437, 406.

14. William B. Carpenter, "Preliminary Report of Dredging Operations in the Seas to the North of the British Islands, Carried on in Her Majesty's Steam-Vessel 'Lightning,' by Dr. Carpenter and Dr. Wyville Thomson, Professor of Natural History at Queen's College, Belfast," *Proc. R. Soc.* 17 1868: 173.

15. While Maury is often celebrated as the "Father of Oceanography," especially in the United States, his long efforts toward the perpetuation and expansion of the institution of race-based slavery were an inextricable part of his scientific program and cannot be ignored. See Penelope K. Hardy and Helen M. Rozwadowski, "Maury for Modern Times: Navigating a Racist Legacy in Ocean Science," *Oceanography* 33, no. 3 (2020): 10–15, https://doi.org/10.5670/oceanog.2020.302.

16. George M. Brooke, *John M. Brooke: Naval Scientist and Educator* (Charlottesville: University Press of Virginia, 1980), 55–56.

17. Contours to show depth were first used on a chart of the River Merwede, part of the Rhine-Meuse-Scheldt river delta in the Netherlands, in 1728 by surveyor and cartographer Nicolaas Kruik. John Murray—*Challenger* naturalist, early oceanographer, and perhaps the first historian of the field—referred to Kruik as Cruquius, and asserted that this preceded any use of contours to show topography ashore. Murray and Johan Hjort, *The Depths of the Ocean: A General Account of the Modern Science of Oceanography Based Largely on the Scientific Researches of the Norwegian Steamer Michael Sars in the North Atlantic* (London: Macmillan, 1912): 3.

18. Maury's career in the U.S. Navy ended abruptly in 1861, when he resigned his commission and returned to his native Virginia upon that state's secession at the beginning of the American Civil War. See note 15.

19. C. Wyville Thomson, William Benjamin Carpenter, and John Gwyn Jeffreys, *The Depths of the Sea: An Account of the General Results of the Dredging Cruises of H.M. SS. 'Porcupine' and 'Lightning' during the Summers of 1868, 1869, and 1870, Under the Scientific Direction of Dr. Carpenter, F.R.S., J. Gwyn Jeffreys, F.R.S., and Dr. Wyville Thomson, F.R.S.* (Macmillan, 1873), 21.

20. Robert K. Edgar, "An Annotated Bibliography of the American Microscopist and Diatomist Jacob Whitman Bailey (1811–1857)," *Occasional Papers of the Farlow Herbarium of Cryptogamic Botany*, no. 11 (1977): 1–26; McClintock Young, "Letter from the Acting Secretary of the Treasury, communicating the report of the Superintendent of the Coast Survey, showing the progress of that work," S. exdoc. 30-6 (1847) at 25–26. The Coast Survey was superintended by Alexander Dallas Bache, whose relationship with Maury was notoriously antagonistic.

21. S[amuel] P[hillips] Lee and H. C. Elliott, *Report and Charts of the Cruise of the U.S. Brig Dolphin, Made under Direction of the Navy Department* (Washington [DC], 1854), NOTES [342]. Bailey, "Microscopical Examination of Deep Soundings from the Atlantic Ocean," *Quarterly Journal of Microscopic* Science 3 (1855): 90. Quote is from the latter.

22. Thomas Weaver, "XXXV.—On the Composition of Chalk Rocks and Chalk Marl by Invisible Organic Bodies: From the Observations of Dr. Ehrenberg," *Journal of Natural History* 7, no. 44 (1841): 296–315; Weaver, "XL.—On the Composition of Chalk Rocks and Chalk Marl by Invisible Organic Bodies: From the Observations of Dr. Ehrenberg," *Journal of Natural History* 7, no. 45 (1841): 374–398.

23. Wallich, *North Atlantic Sea-bed*, 137, 136. For Wallich's failure to thrive as a naturalist, see Rozwadowski, *Fathoming the Ocean: The Discovery and Exploration of the Deep Sea* (Cambridge, Mass.: Belknap Press, 2005), 58–61, and A. L. Rice and Harold L. Burstyn, "G. C. Wallich M.D.—megalomaniac or mis-used oceanographic genius?" *Journal of the Society for the Bibliography of Natural History* 7, no. 4 (1976): 423–450.

24. Carpenter had previously written on the subject in his *Introduction to the Study of the Foraminifera* (London, 1862), but he admitted that "[his] own studies had been restricted to a limited range of types," mostly procured by colleagues traveling in the Pacific, v. The resulting volume is more encyclopedic list than textbook.

25. Thomson, *Atlantic*, vol. 1, vii.

26. He was probably referring to the second of three of Owen's papers "On the Surface-fauna of Mid-ocean," read before the Linnean Society in London in the mid-1860s, "On the Surface-fauna of Mid-ocean: No. 2—Foraminifera," *Journal of the Linnean Society*, Zoology IX (London, 1868): 147–157. Quote is from p. 152. See also Samuel R. J. [sic] Owen, "On the Surface-fauna of Mid-ocean: No. 1—Polycystina and Allied Rhizopods," *Journal of the Linnean Society*, Zoology VIII (London, 1865): 202–205.

27. Carpenter, Jeffreys, and Thomson, "Preliminary Report of the Scientific Exploration of the Deep Sea in H.M. Surveying-Vessel 'Porcupine,' during the Summer of 1869," 443.

28. Thomson, "Preliminary Notes on the Nature of the Sea-bottom procured by the Soundings of H.M.S. 'Challenger' during her Cruise in the "Southern Sea' in the early part of the year 1874," *Proceedings of the Royal Society of London. From November 19, 1874 to June 17, 1875*, vol. XXIII (London, 1875): 32. This paper was also reproduced in two installments in "The 'Challenger' Expedition," *Nature* 11, no. 226 (3 December 1874): 95–97, and *Nature* 11, no. 227 (10 December 1874): 116–119, and in Thomson, *Atlantic*, vol. 1, vii; 199–201. Alistair Sponsel has noted Charles Darwin's somewhat

similar arguments concerning where coral polyps lived as a means toward understanding the formation of reefs, *Darwin's Evolving Identity: Adventure, Ambition, and the Sin of Speculation* (Chicago: University of Chicago Press, 2018).

29. Thomson, "Preliminary Notes on the Nature of the Sea-bottom," 33–34.

30. "Article XII: Recent Discoveries and Improvements in Science and the Arts," *The American Eclectic*, Sept. 1841: 389; Ehrenberg had also spent time at sea, in his case in the Red Sea between 1823 and 1825. Thomas Weaver, "XXXV.—On the Composition of Chalk Rocks and Chalk Marl by Invisible Organic Bodies: From the Observations of Dr. Ehrenberg," *Journal of Natural History* 7, no. 44 (1841): 305–308.

31. Thomson, Carpenter, and Jeffreys, *Depths of the Sea*, 472. Emphasis in the original.

32. Thomson, Carpenter, and Jeffreys, *Depths of the Sea*, 471–472. By 1874, Thomson referred to the calcareous deposits on the sea bottom as "the modern Chalk," "Preliminary Notes on the Nature of the Sea-bottom," 39.

33. Carpenter did not accompany them, as the committee formed to select the crew agreed with *Challenger* captain George S. Nares's suggestion that Carpenter was too old. Nares to George H. Richards, October 20, 1871; Box 9: Surveyors Letters 1871; S Papers; UK Hydrographic Office Archives, Taunton. Ironically, Carpenter would outlive Thomson, who was selected to lead the scientific staff in his stead. Neither man lived to see the completion of the entire, fifty-volume *Challenger Report*, which was instead supervised by John Murray.

34. Alaniz, "Dredging Evolutionary Theory."

35. "Report of the Committee Appointed at the Meeting of the Council Held October 26th [1871], to Consider the Scheme of a Scientific Circumnavigation Expedition," reproduced in Charles Wyville Thomson, *The Atlantic: A Preliminary Account of the General Results of the Exploring Voyage of the H.M.S. "Challenger" during the Year 1873 and the Early Part of the Year 1876*, vol. 1 (New York: Harper & Brothers, 1878), 75. Emphasis in the original.

36. Thomson, *Atlantic,* 61.

37. D. Graham Burnett has argued that the naval discipline under which shipboard hydrographic activities took place granted authority to their cartographic products, in "Hydrographic Discipline among the Navigators: Charting an 'Empire of Commerce and Science' in the Nineteenth-Century Pacific," chapter 5 in *The Imperial Map: Cartography and the Mastery of Empire*, edited by James R. Akerman, 185–259 (Chicago: University of Chicago Press, 2009). In the case of *Challenger*, the naturalists would claim this authority by association for work conducted under the otherwise chaotic conditions of their shipboard laboratories. See Hardy, "Where Science Meets the Sea: Research Vessels and the Construction of Knowledge in the Nineteenth and Twentieth Centuries" (PhD dissertation, Johns Hopkins University, 2017), 61–101.

38. J[ohn] Y[oung] Buchanan, "A Retrospective of Oceanography in the Twenty Years before 1895," *Accounts Rendered of Work Done and Things Seen* (Cambridge, United Kingdom: Cambridge University Press, 1919), 35.

39. Thomson, *Atlantic*, vol. 1, 212–213; Thomson, "Preliminary Notes on the Nature of the Sea-bottom," 39.

40. Thomson, "Preliminary Notes on the Nature of the Sea-bottom," 34.

41. Thomson, "Preliminary Notes on the Nature of the Sea-bottom," 46–47.

42. Thomson, "Preliminary Notes on the Nature of the Sea-bottom," 44.

43. The *Porcupine* had some scientific apparatus and a microscope set up in the chartroom as a temporary laboratory, Thomson, *Depths of the Sea*, 84. *Challenger's* facilities were more intentionally designed and equipped.

44. Thomson, *Atlantic*, vol. 1, 27–29.

45. Thomson, *Atlantic*, vol. 1, 215–217.

46. Thomson, "Preliminary Notes on the Nature of the Sea-bottom," 34.

47. A. S. Wilson, "New Geological Discovery," *Scientific American* 31, no. 8 (22 August 1874): 115.

48. John Murray and A. F. Renard, *Deep-Sea Deposits*, vol. of *Report of the Scientific Results of the Voyage of H.M.S. Challenger during the Years 1873–1876*, ed. C. Wyville Thomson and John Murray (London: 1891): xxi.

49. Thomson, "Preliminary Notes on the Nature of the Sea-bottom," 32.

50. Thomson, "Preliminary Notes on the Nature of the Sea-bottom," 32.

51. William B. Carpenter, "Remarks on Professor Wyville Thomson's Preliminary Notes on the Nature of the Sea-bottom procured by the Soundings of H.M.S. 'Challenger,'" *Proceedings of the Royal Society of London, From November 19, 1874 to June 17, 1875*, vol. XXIII (London, 1875): 235, 244. Italics in the original.

52. Huxley, quoted in "Dinner to the 'Challenger' Staff," *Nature* 14, no. 350 (13 July 1876): 238–239.

53. Buchanan, "Retrospective," 34.

54. Buchanan, "Retrospective," 34.

55. "The 'Challenger' Expedition," *Scientific American Supplements* 2, no. 32 (5 August 1876): 504.

56. Thomson, "Preliminary Notes on the Nature of the Sea-bottom," 39–40.

57. Hardy, "Where Science Meets the Sea," 61–101.

Elusive Henlopen, or the Cape's Role in Protracting the Boundary Dispute between Pennsylvania and Maryland

Agnès Trouillet

The Empirical Authority of the Map

On March 4, 1681, William Penn was granted his charter for Pennsylvania by King Charles II. The only boundary clearly delineated in the grant was the Delaware River, all other bounds would cause controversy with his neighbor proprietor Charles Calvert, 3rd Lord Baltimore who from the outset was suspicious of Penn's claims.[1] Both Maryland and Pennsylvania charters stipulated the 40th degree of latitude as the boundary between the two provinces, and if both proprietors agreed on this limit, there was wide discrepancy between their conceptions of the location of that meridian. William Penn was mainly concerned with being ensured control of most of the navigable part of the Delaware River as well as a crucial outlet to the ocean. Therefore, an exact measurement of the parallel was necessary to settle the matter.

William Penn would not arrive in Pennsylvania until October 1682 and left his cousin William Markham, whom he had made deputy governor of the province, to deal with his land affairs in the interim. In April 1681, Markham had gone to Maryland to deliver two letters to Lord Baltimore, the king's letter of April 2, 1681, asking him to assist Penn's agents in defining the boundaries of the two provinces and recommending him to Baltimore's neighborliness and Penn's letter requesting Baltimore to give his deputy "all the dispatch possible in the business of the bounds, that observing our just limits in that and all other things we may begin and maintain a just and friendly intercourse."[2] Several moves on the part of both proprietors would rapidly jeopardize the friendly neighborliness though.

"Observing just limits" between Pennsylvania and Maryland was required, since the exact location of the boundary would determine the extent of territory granted to each proprietor according to their charters. Boundaries were essential for circumscribing the land owned by each province, and the prospective tax revenues they meant for the proprietors, Maryland and Pennsylvania being proprietor colonies. Moreover, boundaries defined the scope of government authority of a province. European powers therefore raced to trace the colonial boundaries that allowed them to claim property, jurisdiction, and sovereignty over a territory.

When William Penn was granted his charter, several European powers had already been competing for control over the Chesapeake and the Delaware River Valley. Dutch, Swedes, Finns, and English, each attempted to lay claim on lands occupied by the local Native communities and to profit from the lucrative fur trade.[3] The Swedes developed successful relationships with the Lenni Lenape (Delaware Indians) based notably on trade and mutual exchange rather than aggressive land acquisition, which allowed both peoples to coexist rather harmoniously for several decades.[4] The Dutch and English profited from these relationships, while the Lenape were able to maintain control over their territory until the 1680s, often dictating their conditions and forging strategic alliances to avoid war, as historian Jean Soderlund has shown.[5] The first decades of Pennsylvania's settlement were rather peaceful; however, the westward expansion from the 1730s led to an open war with Maryland over the Susquehanna and all the lands west. Historian Patrick Spero has explained how colonists living in the Western and more rural parts of the province suffered repeated assaults by the Natives and perceived them rather as a threat. The back counties came to think of themselves as a vulnerable area—the "frontier"—and resented the colonial government for failing to protect them. Rebellious movements such as the Paxton Boys and the Black Boys decided to protect themselves, ignoring colonial government's sovereignty.[6] Viewing England's management of its largely autonomous Western settlement as an "imperial state" at the time gives it far too much credit, as historian S. Max Edelson observes.[7] The Crown ignored the geography of the North American continent and understood it as an empty space, royal charters using lines of latitude to mark colonies' borders and leaving colonists to make sense of these divisions locally. The lack of precision often created overlapping jurisdictions and in the 1680s, William Penn and 3rd Lord Baltimore attempted to settle the matter by taking measures on the ground.

As they visually translated measures and synthetized pages of textual descriptions, maps were used to make up for insufficiently defined charters. Since Italian artists had developed "perspective" in the 15th century, using geometric principles to imitate on a plane or curved surface the spatial relation of objects as they appear to the eye, maps were considered the most reliable way to describe geography (in the literal meaning of the word). By the 17th century, they had become the ideal instrument to represent the world. Moreover, as historian Nicholas Gliserman has written, perspective was considered as "a truth that would allow human to order and control not just images on the canvass but the physical world itself," and how the elites increasingly believed they could "control the physical environment and the people within it by acts of seeing and representing."[8] Until the mid-17th century, the English relied mostly on foreign maps, particularly from the Dutch who were the leading mapmakers in Northern Europe. Their artistic skills were extraordinary, and their cartographic knowledge was unmatched, as the Dutch merchant companies had required from navigators since the 1620s–1630s to systematically log their routes and bring back charts that professional chart-makers then translated into maps.[9] The Dutch cartographic tradition focused on coastlines and waterways, the routes used for fur trade—which explains their commercial advantage in the Chesapeake at the time, according to historian Christian J. Koot.[10] The interior of the North American continent, on the other hand, was still a geographic abstraction. As part of Charles II's, then James II's, endeavor to gather cartographic knowledge, from the mid-1670s, the Board of Trade and Plantations started sending mapmakers to the colonies and instructed colonial governors to send maps.[11] The new body of bureaucracy was also part of the Restoration effort toward order and centralization after the Civil War. A similar trend was generally observed in European powers, driven by diverse political, economic, and social changes. Nevertheless, as political scientist Jordan Branch illustrates, cartography played a central role in redefining political authority, as traditional political goals, such as territorial expansion or defense, were "redefined to fit with the cartographic ideal of rule as a linearly defined space rather than as a collection of places and jurisdictions." By the 19th century, political rule meant "exclusive and complete sovereignty over a space defined by cartographic lines."[12]

It was particularly true in the colonies, where maps provided European rulers new means for asserting political claims. Seventeenth-century North American charters as well as 18th-century disputes among colonial powers were thus structured by linear definitions of space. This led to clashing interpretations, particularly with the Natives, as the contributions on Indigenous mapping in this volume demonstrate. Julie Reed emphasizes the radically different nature of the lines used by Natives to mark out borders, essentially delineating hunting grounds and symbolizing the connections between the various nations, in fluid, amorphous delineations as opposed to the English conception of space along geometric, rectangular lines circumscribing and enclosing land. Lucas Kelley stresses antagonist conceptions, as a continent shared by the American states and Native nations for the Cherokees versus a frontier line separating two kinds of territory within the sovereign boundaries of the new United States. As he and Austin Stewart show, Natives nevertheless incorporated Western cartographic idioms, resorting to European surveying techniques and principles of international law to assert their claims.

The boundary dispute between Pennsylvania and Maryland is an interesting case study to demonstrate the importance of colonial boundaries, the role of maps in staking claims and asserting sovereignty, and the arduous task of locals trying to piece together elements of a complex mosaic (the Delaware Valley here). The conflict proved lengthy, bitter, and costly, plaguing the proprietors' families for over eight decades, one of the most long-lived border disputes in North America.[13] The financial implications were considerable since neither proprietor could collect rent for the land under dispute until it was resolved,[14] but also due to the incurred cost of legal battles. The Mason and Dixon Line that finally marked the boundary between the two colonies is probably one of the most famous today, notably as the symbolical separation between Northern and Southern states.[15] As the conference has shown, the dispute is not the only one that ran over a long period of time, nor the only conflict that was at the same time intrinsically colonial and imperial, notably because of the legal aspects that needed to be settled in the metropole.[16] It is an illuminating demonstration for the consequences of inconsistencies in grants and maps.[17] Placing the 40th parallel of latitude that marked Maryland's Northern boundary would prove challenging, yet locating Cape Henlopen, the Southern limit for the Lower Counties (present-day Delaware), would turn out equally difficult and only protract the dispute, revealing the impact of misplaced, or misnamed, landmarks.[18]

Maps were nevertheless considered the best visual evidence. Each party would produce their own maps to justify their claims, in a contest process similar to what map historian Mary Pedley has called "map wars."[19] Revisiting this dispute is therefore relevant to the field of map history that is interested in maps as sources[20] and raises the following questions: What makes a map a legitimate piece of evidence? What ensures its reliability? As much as maps pretended to be "real," "true," or "more exact," the ideal, omniscient bird's-eye view perspective they presented was impossible. No large-scale surveys had yet been conducted that would offer a coherent, whole picture of North America.[21] Given the vastness of the continent, such an enterprise would not be possible until after the Seven Years' War, notably thanks to British army engineers' skills and new scientific standards.[22] The land survey of France begun in the mid-17th century took more than sixty years to complete—and four generations of Cassinis. As Cassini III wrote, topography is "a part from geography so extensive, minute, time-consuming and costly that it cannot be conducted for a general map, but only partially and by very small counties ('*canton*')."[23] Besides, using the belfries in a county to observe angles for the triangulation process ensured its reliability, as they were fixed landmarks. By its shifty and uncertain nature, Cape Henlopen, on the other hand, would prove the exact opposite, and utterly destroy Baltimore's piece of evidence.

As astounding as was the work of cartographers and surveyors (who sometimes worked as both), given the tools these men had at their disposal in the 17th century, their instruments were not sophisticated enough. Only in the 1760s would it be possible to measure a degree of latitude with enough precision, thanks to the zenith telescope, which allowed English astronomers Mason and Dixon to finally run the line between Pennsylvania and Maryland.

Furthermore, maps are the result of selections by the numerous actors involved in their production, necessarily resulting in bias. Besides the patrons who commanded them, geographers, surveyors, and commissioners, cartographers, engravers, and printers all influenced the final object by choosing the information to include, the framing, or the ornaments. As any cartographic document, maps served diverse purposes, whether navigational, commercial, or promotional—for the majority of European maps of Northeast America up to the 1660s–1670s—or political, as tools of governance increasingly thereafter. The degree of intentionality, the production process, as well as the way they were used, all these elements must be taken into account. The power of a map resides in them, not in the object itself. As Nicholas Gliserman emphasizes,[24] the study of maps requires critical questioning, just as any kind of primary sources. One concept in particular should be questioned, that is, the concept of authority, as vested in the different actors involved, from various citizenships and trades, and in the various government officials, from the justice of the peace, solicitor, attorney general, Lord Chancellor, to the Board of Trade, the Privy Council and the Crown. Where lies the empirical authority of a map? During the conference, historian S. Max Edelson's comment on the maps used in several boundary conflicts encapsulated these concepts: "All were bids for authority to determine key places and sites, but none were independently justified as the authoritative way of seeing the world."

"This very spott Lies about twelve miles due South from the Degree of 40° North Latitude"

In the summer of 1681, as part of a promotional campaign to promote his new settlement, William Penn published a broadside sheet titled *A Brief Account of the Province of Pennsilvania in America* accompanied with a map. Titled *A Map of Some of the South and East Bounds of Pennsylvania in America Being Partly Inhabited* (Figure 1), it placed the 40th degree at a location considerably farther south than other maps, granting him 40 extra miles, although at the time Penn did not know the precise location of the parallel. Moreover, in January 1682, the Pennsylvania proprietor sent a letter to Maryland planters claiming that the Maryland counties of Cecil and Baltimore "lay within his territory and they (the planters) should pay tax to him."[25] Some residents actually refused to pay their taxes to Lord Baltimore, which understandably infuriated him, all the more so as all attempts at meeting Penn's deputy and commissioners to settle the boundary were fruitless. Having felt ill in 1681, Markham had postponed the meeting agreed for October to the spring of 1682, when he failed to appear, leading to a new rescheduling to the month of June, when Penn's deputy not only did not attend but also sent no representatives. Lord Baltimore then decided to make an observation with his commissioners, among whom Augustin Herrman found the latitude to be "39 degrees and 40-odd minutes." [26]

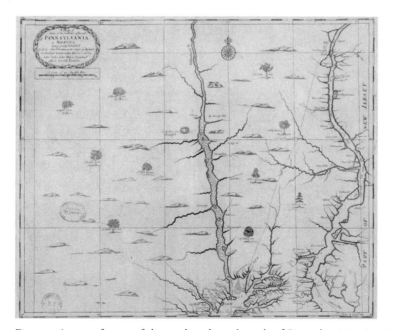

Figure 1. A map of some of the south and east bounds of Pennsylvania in America being partly inhabited, London : sold by John Thornton : by John Seller, (1681). Bibliothèque Nationale de France, Collection d'Anville. https://catalogue.bnf.fr/ark:/12148/cb406066776.

There were successive missed appointments, notably with Penn's party waiting at the head of the Delaware River when the meeting was supposed to have taken place at the head of Chesapeake Bay. Markham was reluctant to meet the Maryland proprietor, particularly as the observations taken at the head of the Chesapeake Bay by Penn's commissioner William Haige who had arrived early March 1682 actually confirmed the calculations made by Herrman: the 40th degree lay at least 40 miles farther north than Penn claimed. Unwilling to bring contradictions unsupported by evidence, Haige and Markham continued to stall until September 1682, at which point Lord Baltimore went directly to Markham's lodging in Upland (present-day Chester) and forced him to make an observation. The conclusion was unambiguous, as Baltimore pointed to him:

> S^r you know that by a Private Observation taken here yesterday, this very spott Lies about twelve miles due South from the Degree of 40° North Latitude and that therefore this plantation of Robert Wades is soe many miles within the North Bound of my Charter.[27]

Baltimore's calculations meant considerable loss for Penn. Knowing that a joint observation would place the boundary too far north, the proprietor from his arrival in the province showed the same elusiveness as his deputy, and the meetings between the two proprietors proved equally unproductive.

There was another bone of contention. In August 1682, Penn had acquired title to the Lower Counties (New Castle, Kent, and Sussex, which would become Delaware) from the king's brother, James II, Duke of York.[28] However, since he had not been granted a royal charter, his right to the area was uncertain. Besides, the territory of Delaware was included in the 1632 Maryland charter, which made Penn's claim invalid according to Lord Baltimore. Since he could not convince Penn to make a joint observation of the 40th degree of latitude, Baltimore would lay claim to the Lower Counties. Nevertheless, the Southern boundary of the Lower Delaware would prove a particularly thorny issue. Penn had received ownership of New Castle and territory "beginning twelve miles below New Castle and extending south unto Cape Henlopen."[29] Five decades later, when a momentous agreement was finally reached between the two families, the map used for the compromise would prove inaccurate, as it misplaced the Cape that was used as the landmark for the boundary, only protracting the dispute instead of settling it.

Where We See the Importance of Nomenclature

English sea captain Henry Hudson had been commissioned by the Dutch East India Company to explore North America for new trade routes. He entered the Delaware Bay in 1609 and became the first European on the Delaware River. His return to Europe triggered fierce competition between Dutch merchants and companies over the profitable fur trade with local Native communities. Dutch vessels began to make frequent visits to the Noordt River (North River, or Hudson) and the Zuydt River (South River, or Delaware[30]). In 1623, the New Netherland Company obtained a patent for the area situated between the 38th and 40th parallels that included the crucial Chesapeake Bay and Delaware Bay. As one of the major waterways of the East Coast, the Zuydt River was of particular interest to the Dutch who established their outposts along important rivers and tributaries and needed access to the interior.

Cornelius Jacobsen Mey, a captain, explorer, and fur trader, was among the private merchants who wanted to trade in the Zuydt River. Before he became a party to the New Netherland Company, Mey had explored the area situated between the 40th and 45th parallels with explorer Hendrick Christiaensen and cartographer Adriaen Block, whose map consolidated their surveys and charts from their four voyages.[31] The name *New Netherland* (*Nieuw-Nederland, Nova Belgica*, or *Novum Belgium* in Latin) appeared for the first time on one of their maps. On behalf of the Dutch West India Company, he then explored and surveyed the Delaware Bay—which had already been surveyed in 1614–1615 by explorer Cornelius Hendricksz, who sailed up to the northernmost navigable reaches of the Zuydt River in 1616. Mey ordered the construction of Fort Nassau, the first Dutch trading post in the Delaware valley, and in 1624, in command of the ship *Nieu Nederlandt*, it was he who delivered the first colonists to Governor's Island, sealing the claim to New Netherland as a province. The captain gave his own name to the Capes at the mouth of Delaware Bay, Cape May and Cape Cornelis. The name Cape May, with a slightly different spelling,[32] "remained permanently attached to the New Jersey side of the entrance, and Cape Cornelis gave way to Henlopen as the name for the cape on the Delaware side, though Captain Mey had originally applied the name Cape Henlopen to a point farther South."[33] Mey might have chosen the name Henlopen after prominent trader Thijmen Jacbosz Hinlopen, who was among his business partners on the ships *Blijde Boodschap* (*Joyful Message*) and *Beever* (*Bever*), which focused on exploration and trade with Native Indians in the Zuydt River. Located on the 38th parallel, the cape was the most Southern border of the New Netherland province, then situated between three riverine axes: the *Noortrivier* (North River, Hudson), the *Zuydtrivier* (South River, Delaware), and the *Varsche Rivier* (Fresh River, Connecticut).

Among Mey's partners was also Samuel Godyn (sometimes written Godjin or Godin), a merchant, and director of the Dutch West India Company who gave his name to Godyn's Bay (Delaware Bay) and who founded the first European settlement in Delaware, called Swanendael, on a large slip of land he bought on the Western side of Delaware Bay, on what is now Lewes Creek. Within a year though, it was entirely destroyed in what historian Jonathan Munroe has described as "the only case of a serious Indian onslaught upon Europe in the history of Delaware." The attack nevertheless dissuaded European settlers of any new plantation attempt, demonstrating how the Lenape were able to impose their conditions. The colony, although short-lived, would play a crucial role in the dispute between Pennsylvania and Maryland.

The 40th Parallel, the 12-Mile Radius Circle, and William Penn's 1681 Map of Pennsylvania

There were a host of maps that could have been used to settle the conflict over the 40th Parallel of latitude, mostly from the Dutch and the English, who had thoroughly explored this part of America septentrionalis. Captain John Smith's famous *Virginia* map, produced in 1612, was based on his explorations of the Chesapeake Bay in 1608, and of stunning geographical accuracy given the tools he had at his disposal.[34] The 1635 *Nova Belgica et Anglia Nova* map was the work of cartographer, atlas maker, and publisher Willem Janszoon Blaeu,[35] considered one of the prominent figures of Dutch cartography at the time. In 1651, Jan Jansson published the first edition of his map from the Northeastern coast of North America, titled *Belgii Novi Angliae Novae et Partis Virginiae*.[36] Produced at the peak of the Golden Age of Dutch Cartography, this fundamental prototype map of the region was a careful compilation of earlier maps by Samuel Champlain, Captain John Smith, and Willem Blaeu and was intended to promote Dutch colonization of New Netherlands. The model and nomenclature laid out by Jansson was followed by later cartographers, with no fewer than twenty-seven copies published in Holland, England, and Germany by the end of the 17th century. Nicolas Visscher, an engraver, cartographer, and publisher, issued his version of Jansson's map, titled *Novi Belgii, Novaeque Angliae nec non Partis Virginiae Tabula* (Figure 2), motivated by the recent establishment of the Dutch colony and Dutch aspirations to retain their New Netherland colony. First published in 1655, the map is known primarily from its second state issued in 1656.[37] As for the first English colonial maps, they did not appear before 1671, when "His Majesty's Cosmographer, Geographick Printer, and Master of Revels in the Kingdom of Ireland" John Ogilby published his book *America: Being the Latest and Most Accurate Description of the New World*, which included a revised version of the Jansson-Visscher map, titled *Novi Belgii, quod nunc Novi Jorck vocatur, Nova que Angliæ & partis Virginiæ: accuratissima et novissima delineatio*.[38] All these printed maps were accessible to English government institutions and officials overseeing the drafting and approval of grants. More specifically, procuring maps was one of the tasks assigned to William Blathwayt, the Secretary to the Committee of the Lords of Trade and Plantations, whose collection contained several maps relating to the Pennsylvania region, as he was in charge of the Pennsylvania matter.[39] One map in particular could have been used, the *Virginia and Maryland as it is planted and inhabited this present year 1670* by cartographer Augustine Herrman (Figure 3),[40] well known from the Calverts for whom the map was specifically produced.

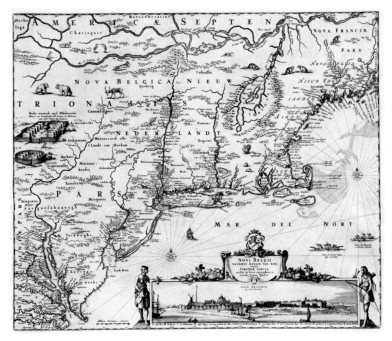

Figure 2. Nicolaes Visscher, *Novi Belgii, Novaeque Angliae nec non partis Virginiae tabula* (1655). Map. Norman B. Leventhal Map & Education Center. https://collections.leventhalmap.org/search/commonwealth:3f462s77z.

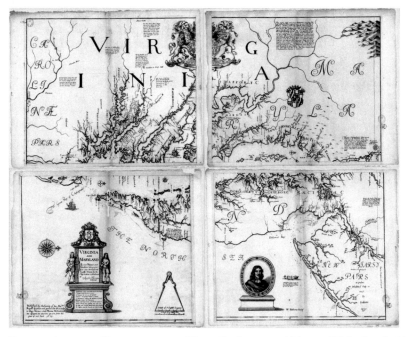

Figure 3. Augustine Herrman, 1621 or, Henry Faithorne, and Thomas Withinbrook, *Virginia and Maryland as it is planted and inhabited this present year* (London: Augustine Herrman and Thomas Withinbrook, 1673) Map, Library of Congress, www.loc.gov/item/2002623131/.

There were altogether fourteen maps dated from 1656 to 1678 that showed New Castle Town anywhere from 3 to over 30 miles south of the 40th parallel, the true distance being about 24 miles south. Of all the maps available, though, Penn did not use a single one and instead resorted to the 1681 map that had been prepared as part of the promotional campaign for his new colony, *A Map of Some of the South and East Bounds of Pennsylvania in America Being Partly Inhabited*. The first map to bear the name Pennsylvania, it conveyed a sense of order, with large available tracts of land and very sparse Native presence—in stark contrast with earlier maps of North America painstakingly describing Indian tribe names and the location of their villages.

Another notable indication in Penn's charter was the boundary as formed by a circle with a 12-miles radius from New Castle, and then west along the 40th parallel. On the 1681 map, New Castle was shown to be north of the 40th parallel, and not south. The map thus not only erroneously located the 40th parallel but also showed that the circle did not intersect the 40th parallel, which lay some 20 miles farther north. In spite of the anomaly with the latitude on the map as we have seen, Penn insisted on claiming that the 40th parallel lay at 20 miles north of New Castle.

One cannot help wondering why Penn, experienced in land dealing as he was, having acquired land in New Jersey and been involved in its partition into East and West Jersey in 1676, would use an incorrect map when more accurate maps were available. Whether intentional or not, Penn's decision allowed him to gain more land.

The Three Lower Counties, Cape Henlopen, and the 1656 Visscher Map

According to 3rd Lord Baltimore, the Lower Counties were part of his province as per the 1632 Maryland charter. However, he had never occupied the area. The Dutch had unsuccessfully established the Swanendael colony near Cape Henlopen one year before the Calverts received their charter. It was then settled by the Swedes and finally granted to the Duke of York by Charles II in 1664. The proprietor had thus no claim to Delaware, his charter granting only lands "hitherto uncultivated" by Europeans. He seemed to have ignored the presence of the Dutch or the Swedes on the Delaware until 1654, when he claimed the territory from the Swedes. After the Dutch had taken control of the area in 1659, Baltimore claimed the area once again, but the Dutch refused to cede it on the ground that their settlement predated Baltimore's charter. As for Penn, although his title was uncertain, he included the Lower Counties in his proprietorship with the Act of Union signed into law on December 8, 1682. This was notably an attempt to merge the government and ensure the legislative union of two territories.[41]

Unable to reach an agreement, the proprietors traveled to London in 1685 to have the controversy settled by the King, and on October 17, 1685, the Privy Council ruled in favor of Penn's proprietorship. Penn had demonstrated that the settlements on the west side of the Delaware Bay (the territory comprising the Lower Counties) were Dutch outposts established prior to June 20, 1632, the official date of the Maryland Charter. Penn produced evidence that on July 15, 1630, Dutch authorities had purchased from three Native headmen, certain lands "on the south side of the said Bay, called by us the Bay of the South River (Delaware), stretching, in length, from Cape Hinloop, to the mouth of the said South River, about eight large miles (three *leagues*)." [42] This invalidated Baltimore's claim to the region since the Duke of York was the English successor to the Dutch title. And on November 13, 1685, it was decreed that "the tract of land lying between the River and the Eastern Sea on the one side & Chesapeake bay on the other be divided into equal parts by a line from the latitude of Cape Hinlopen to the fortieth Degree of Northern Latitude."

William Penn would only spend two more years in his province, from 1699 to 1701. As for 3rd Lord Baltimore, he would never return to Maryland. In his absence the Protestant Revolution of 1689 overtook the colony, and the family lost its royal charter. [43] Yet the Calverts did not relinquish their claim to the Lower Counties and continued to argue from the metropole. However, 3rd Lord Baltimore's 1708 petition to the Queen to have the 1685 order set aside was dismissed, and in 1709, the Queen in Council ordered the 1685 decree to be carried into execution. And the dispute continued to poison relationships between the two families.

By 1731, the boundaries were still not clearly established. By then, the Pennsylvania proprietorship was vested in John, Thomas, and Richard Penn. But Charles Calvert, 5th Lord Baltimore, had not abandoned his family's interest in the Lower Counties. Ferdinando John Paris was an agent for the Penn family, and had been appointed by the Pennsylvania Assembly to be its London agent in 1730. He also knew Lord Baltimore and agreed to act as a mediator in the conflict. Paris organized a meeting between the proprietors in London in June 1731, where both sides produced manuscript maps of Pennsylvania, Maryland, and parts adjacent. The maps were similar and agreed on the location of Cape May at the entrance of the Delaware Bay on the Jersey side and Cape Cornelius opposite to it. About 20 miles south of Cape Cornelius was located Cape Henlopen, which determined the Southern boundary of the Lower Counties. Threatened with the cost of another legal contest, as Baltimore again petitioned the King, the Penns agreed to a private settlement. Paris drafted the compact on the points provided by Lord Baltimore, who insisted that his map, provided by one of his agents in Maryland, would be used. Baltimore's map was thus taken to the shop of engraver and mathematician John Senex, who had been Geographer to Queen Anne, to be engraved on copper, and on May 10, 1732, a momentous agreement was signed, settling a fifty-year-old dispute. As proof of Baltimore's participation in the compact, John Penn had had the agreement printed by Benjamin Franklin. Five hundred copies were produced in pamphlet form, together with the map—actually the first printed in the English colonies south of New York. It was a huge relief for the Penns that Baltimore finally voluntarily relinquished his long-standing claim to the Lower Countries. Before the end of 1732 though, in a "coup de théâtre," Baltimore refused to comply with the agreement.

Why would Baltimore try to void the agreement? It so happened that he realized that the 1656 map by Nicolaes Visscher—on which his original manuscript map was based—placed Cape Henlopen about 25 miles farther south than it really was. Paris found evidence that a Dutch captain, sailing up from the south toward Delaware Bay, had described a bold headland, but on closer view "it proved deceitful, it run away, it vanish, it disappeared," and thus called the false cape "Cape Henlopen," which in Dutch signifies Cape Run-Away, or Cape Vanishing, or Cape Disappearing—James Logan, [44] who owned two Dutch dictionaries, had furnished him this linguistic explanation. The captain might have been Cornelis Mey who entered the Delaware Bay in 1614 and named its Northern cape Mey and the Southern entrance Cornelius, as we have seen above. Paris found a corroborating account in John De Laet's *History of the New World Atlas,*[45] published in Dutch in 1625 and in Latin in 1633, where the Delaware Bay was described as follows: "This Bay has two capes or headlands, that toward the North is called Cape May & that toward the South Cape Cornelius . . . four miles (*leagues*) off of this Cape lyes another Cape, which we call Cape Hinloopen."[46] In his *History of Delaware*, Munroe explains how the name Cape Cornelis gave way to Henlopen as the name for the cape on the Delaware side, "though Captain May had originally applied the name Cape Henlopen to a point farther South, possibly Fenwick Island, which, because it was wooded, in contrast to the sand dunes on either side of it, may have looked like a cape from the sea."[47]

Whether the northward cape was named for Mey or May, the "crux of the chancery case" that would settle the dispute in 1750, as Paris pointed out, was Cape Henlopen.[48] Thus, there was no cape where Visscher's map showed Cape Henlopen to be. And Cape Henlopen was the name of the cape at the south entrance to Delaware Bay. As Baltimore rightly pointed out (with exquisitely poor timing), the problem was:

> . . . placing or describing, in his own map, Cape Hinlopen too far south, down to the sea, below Cape Cornelius; For that, as he says, there is no such thing as a cape there, but the true Cape Hinlopen, anciently and originally so called by the Dutch, and so described in their maps, was at the place we call Cape Cornelius, at the very mouth of the Delaware Bay, and, there, it was that the south bounds of the Lower Counties should have been.[49]

Penn had taken possession of the territory down to the false cape, where a mark of his ownership was placed, and granted land in this area. Paris received information on that point from James Logan, strengthened by the depositions of Sussex County farmers who knew the traditions of the Cape Henlopen area.[50]

In 1685, the Privy Council had inquired about Cape Henlopen because it was needed to define the Southern boundary for the Lower Counties. Penn must have found reasons for pushing it south, since the map he then produced happened to be the Visscher map, showing Cape Henlopen at the Southern location, thus settling the Lower Counties' Southern boundary on old Cape Henlopen—25 miles south from where the Duke of York had originally intended it. By proving that the Dutch had purchased land in the area situated between the real and the false capes in 1630, he most probably drove the Privy's decision to decree his territory to run south of the present Cape Henlopen to the false cape. The fact that he added a note on a copy of the Visscher map, stating that the map, twenty-five years old in 1681, would still be used to settle an important boundary dispute, is evidence that Penn knew about its inaccuracy.[51] By 1685 then, the area was already known as the "false" cape. Why, then, did Baltimore use the old 1656 Visscher map that incorrectly identified Cape Henlopen, when later English maps corrected the error? Why, in particular, would Baltimore not use his own Maryland cartographer's map? Herrman's map of 1673 indeed showed "Cape Hinlop" at the mouth of Delaware Bay, where it properly belonged, and made no mention of Cape Cornelius. By 1685, six other maps in agreement with Herman's had been published. Baltimore would never offer an answer, but accused the Penns of deceit and forgery, and blamed them for taking advantage of his ignorance. Unfortunately, he himself had insisted on using his version of the Visscher map.

The Penns must nevertheless have been aware of something unsatisfactory since they considered renouncing to this tract of land, situated on a territory they described as "sandy" and "very indifferent." "I think it a very great fault that so great a stress was laid on the false cape, but this is what we were advised by a very good friend on that side of the water."[52]

The Great Chancery Case, and the Senex Composite Map

In order to compel Baltimore to run the lines, Penn was advised to file a bill in chancery, another dreaded legal expense that prompted a desperate John to urge Thomas to sell land. Paris had almost found a purchaser for Pennsylvania, which would have been sold for as little as 60,000 pounds. In 1734, John Penn traveled to Pennsylvania, and in his absence, Baltimore again petitioned the King to claim the Three Lower Countries and succeeded in having a hearing scheduled before the Board of Trade. To expose Lord Baltimore's false pretense of deception, John Paris decided to produce a pamphlet containing the agreement, accompanied with a reissue of the map. The heading read "Article of Agreement etc.," and the reverse side of the last sheet bore the title "True Copies." On New Year's Day 1735, Senex printed several hundred more copies of Baltimore's map, each manually endorsed by Paris: "This is Lord Baltimore's own plan, annext to the Acts of Agreemt of 10 May 1732." Senex had produced a composite of John Smith's map of 1606, pieced out with a section covering the Delaware area and New Netherland from a Dutch map of 1650 (Figures 4 and 5). The composite map supported Baltimore's map, placing Cape Henlopen some 20 miles South of Cape Cornelius. In 1742, riots and protests erupted over the still unsettled financial disputes. The situation was so serious that the King had to order a survey to preserve peace in the colonies. From 1735 to 1743, both parties prepared to present the matter to the Chancery Court in London. To support the Penns' claim, Paris gathered considerable archival sources and produced a 116-page folio manuscript work called "The Breviate" (since it was originally 464 pages), which notably contained a further reissue of the map by Senex in 1742. In 1750, English Chancellor Lord Hardwicke ruled in favor of the Penns. Yet Frederick Calvert, who became 6th Lord Baltimore in 1751, disputed the border again.

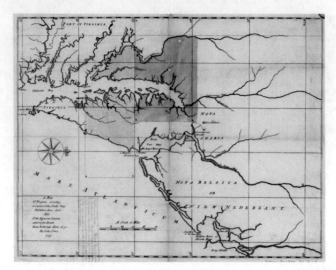

Figure 4. John Senex, -1740, George, III, King of Great Britain, Baltimore, Charles Calvert, Baron, Penn, Thomas, Penn, Richard, Penn, John, Visscher, Nicolaes, Hutchinson, Thomas (Engraver and draughtsman), and Paris, Ferdinand John, Proposed Maryland / Pennsylvania Boundary, (1735) Map, Norman B. Leventhal Map & Education Center, https://collections.leventhalmap.org/search/commonwealth:q524mt414.

Figure 5. John Senex, -1740, and Ferdinand John Paris. *Maps of the Maryland-Pennsylvania boundary used as trial exhibits in the court suit brought by the Penns against Lord Baltimore to determine the official interprovincial boundary line.* [London: s.n., ?, 1732], Map, Library of Congress, https://www.loc.gov/item/2006625071/.

Running the Line

Surveyors had already completed astonishing work on large tracts of land, like Herrman in Maryland, or Pennsylvania's first Surveyor General Thomas Holme, who laid out the capital city but also the 10,000 acres of liberty lands that surrounded it. Holme worked in difficult conditions, pressed by eager settlers, on a hostile terrain covered with dense virgin forests, and inhabited by potentially threatening Natives. Surveyors had to be out of home for weeks, and organize the logistics of expeditions composed of rodmen and other helpers, guide, bargeman, interpreter, and bodyguard. These highly experienced and practical men were able to work using rudimentary instruments like surveying chains, quadrant, and surveying compass, heavy and fragile equipment. They certainly would not have left a wooden telescope to warp in wet weather, as did the local surveyors hired by Thomas Penn in 1761. As rival teams quarreled, and local surveyors were unable to complete the work, Pennsylvania and Maryland proprietors agreed to hiring English experts, English astronomer and surveyor Charles Mason, who had been assistant at the Royal Observatory in Greenwich, and Jeremiah Dixon who had traveled around the world with him studying astronomy. These two men were able to make celestial observations and to use sophisticated tools like the zenith telescope, the only instrument then known to have sufficient accuracy to trace a parallel of latitude. They started their survey in 1763. The first step was to locate the exact starting point, 15 miles due south of Philadelphia. It was found in the middle of Mr. Alexander Bryan's plantation house, and an observation post was built in his front yard. From there, the survey moved west following the line of latitude 39 degrees, 43 minutes, and 17.6 seconds north. Axemen cleared a wide swath, and limestone markers brought from England were placed each mile to mark the way, engraved with a "P" for Pennsylvania on the north side and an "M" for Maryland on the south. Every 11 1/2 miles, the scientists would line up these posts through their telescopes and make elaborate measurements of star movement to compensate for error. All distances were measured with a 66-foot surveyor's chain. In 1766, Indian resistance forced the work to halt for a year. Negotiations allowed the surveying crew to continue until, 30 miles east of Pennsylvania's present southwest corner, they were ordered to stop for good—233 miles, 3 chains and 38 links from the starting post in Mr. Bryan's yard.[53] Mason and Dixon completed their survey in 1767, yet the engraving of a map proved complex as the Eastern part fit on a single copperplate, but the Western line was three times too long, and had to be divided in three parts and engraved on another plate. The engraved map was approved on August 27, 1768, and in November, the commissioners agreed to the certificate to be written on the plans of the Lines, finally establishing boundaries in contention since 1681 (Figure 6).

Lord Baltimore would never explain why he had produced this specific map, nor reveal the "unnamed Pennsylvania source" from whom his agent in Maryland had obtained it. The Penns tried to force Baltimore to disclose this source, but then he showed the same elusiveness as William Penn and his deputy and commissioners had demonstrated in the very first phase of the conflict. This would remain a mystery. Who could pretend to explain all the motives and intentions behind the uses of maps?

Figure 6. Charles Mason et al., *A plan of the west line or parallel of latitude, which is the boundary between the provinces of Maryland and Pensylvania: a plan of the boundary lines between the province of Maryland and the Three Lower Counties on Delaware with part of the parallel of latitude which is the boundary between the provinces of Maryland and Pennsylvania.* (Philadelphia: Robert Kennedy, 1768) Map, Library of Congress, www.loc.gov/item/84695758/.

Notes

1. Charles Calvert had been appointed deputy governor of Maryland by his father, Cecil Calvert, 2nd Lord Baltimore, and inherited Maryland when his father passed away in 1675. He then became 3rd Lord Baltimore, and Governor in his own right.

2. William Penn to Lord Baltimore, April 10, 1681, in Jean R. Soderlund, ed., R.S. & M.M. Dunn, gen. eds., *William Penn and the Founding of Pennsylvania 1680–1684: A Documentary History* (Philadelphia: University of Pennsylvania Press, 1983), 57.

3. The New Netherland colony (*Nieuw Nederland* in Dutch, *Nova Belgica* or *Novum Belgium* in Latin) was founded in 1624 and extended from New England to Virginia. The colony of New Sweden (*Nya Sverige* in Swedish, *Nova Svecia* in Latin) was settled in 1638 along the lower reaches of the Delaware River, before being annexed by the Dutch in 1655. The Dutch surrendered New Netherland to the English in 1664, contributing to the Second Anglo-Dutch War, briefly retook the area in 1673 before relinquishing it in 1674 after the Third Anglo-Dutch War.

4. The Swedish colony was able to survive notably thanks to its strategic position in a major convergence point in Native American–European trade that allowed the Swedes to become brokers in a network that involved the Lenape, the Susquehanna, the Dutch, and merchants from the English New Haven colony.

5. See Jean R. Soderlund, *Lenape Country: Delaware Valley Society Before William Penn* (Philadelphia: University of Pennsylvania Press, 2016). For the divergent Native ways in reclaiming space from the Europeans, as opposed to Natives seen as passive victims waiting for European colonizers to carve up their territory, see Juliana Barr and Edward Countryman, ed., *Contested Spaces of Early America* (Philadelphia: University of Pennsylvania Press, 2014). For the complex network of allegiances and sovereignties in the Delaware Valley, see Mark L. Thompson, *The Contest for the Delaware Valley: Allegiance, Identity, and Empire in the Seventeenth Century* (Baton Rouge: Louisiana State University Press, 2013).

6. See Patrick Spero, *Frontier Country: The Politics of War in Early Pennsylvania* (Philadelphia: University of Pennsylvania Press, 2018). According to the historian, the unrest in rural Pennsylvania, especially after the Seven Years' War played an equally significant role as the urban revolts in Eastern coastal towns in igniting the fight for independence.

7. See S. Max Edelson, *The New Map of Empire: How Britain Imagined America Before Independence* (Cambridge, Mass.: Harvard University Press, 2017).

8. Nicholas Gliserman, "Landscapes of Conflict: Cartography and Empire in Northeastern America, 1680–1713" (PhD dissertation, University of Southern California, 2016), 28.

9. The center of cartography in 17th-century Southern Europe was Portugal, whose capital Lisbon already counted six cartographic workshops in 1552. The policy of silence then imposed by the government (*Politica sigilio*) demonstrates the stakes of cartographic knowledge: Anyone circulating maps to foreign citizens or pilots who emigrated abroad were punished by the death penalty. Printing was also forbidden, which explains that most Portuguese maps were only copies (mostly nonextant today).

10. Christian J. Koot, *A Biography of a Map in Motion: Augustine Herrman's Chesapeake* (New York: New York University Press, 2017). The historian describes how the Dutch cartographic tradition emphasized fluidity and movement, suggesting a geographic imagination in sharp contrast with early English conceptions of space. Interested in demarcating property with estate surveys rather than describing the landscape as a whole, English maps emphasized small regions and their political borders, 96–97.

11. London imposed itself as the nexus for publication and circulation of maps in the 1670s, and artisans started making maps or even exclusively concentrated their trade on mapmaking, showing the growing role of maps. By then, John Sellers had become the city's leading map-seller, his shop a stone's throw away from the London Exchange, the economic, commercial, and cultural center of the metropole. See Koot, *A Biography of a Map in Motion*, 183–191.

12. Jordan Branch, *The Cartographic State: Maps, Territory and the Origins of Sovereignty* (Cambridge, United Kingdom: Cambridge University Press, 2015), 1–15, quotes in 5, 7.

13. Edwin Danson, *Drawing the Line: How Mason and Dixon Surveyed the Most Famous Border in America* (Hoboken, N.J.: Wiley-Blackwell, 2016 (2001)).

14. Although the quitrent assessed on a tract of land was calculated from the time the return of survey was completed, the money was not collected until the land was patented. For this reason, many settlers delayed completing the patenting process. After Penn's death in 1718, the difficulties of collecting quitrents continued to plague his heirs.

XVII. Rent Rolls. Pennsylvania Historical and Museum Commission, Pennsylvania State Archives. RG-17, Records of the Land Office. Series Descriptions, http://www.phmc.state.pa.us/bah/dam/rg/sd/r17sdb.htm.

15. In the antebellum period the Mason and Dixon line was regarded as the dividing line between Northern free-soil states and Southern slave states. Beyond its symbolic reach, the concept acquired concrete political meaning when the term "Mason and Dixon Line" was first used in the congressional debates leading to the 1820 Missouri Compromise.

16. William Penn and 3rd Lord Baltimore took the matter to the King in 1685. Maryland and Pennsylvania proprietors being absent from their colonies most of the time afterward, they kept arguing the case in English courts.

17. See Margaret Beck Pritchard and Henry G. Taliaferro, *Degrees of Latitude: Mapping Colonial America* (Williamsburg, Va.: Colonial Williamsburg Foundation, 2002) for the momentous consequences of locations drawn or defined in an equivocal manner, and the inaccuracy of the maps, combined with a vague or contradictory wording in grants, drafts, and charters.

18. The situation of Cape Henlopen is explained in detail later in this essay. Cape Henlopen refers to the present southeastern boundary of Delaware. The cape, now known as Cape Henlopen, is located 25 miles north at the entrance of the Delaware Bay. It was called Cape Cornelis at the time, and this imprecise nomenclature would prove the core of the matter as this essay will demonstrate.

19. Mary Pedley, "Map Wars: The Role of Maps in the Nova Scotia/Acadia Boundary Disputes of 1750," *Imago Mundi* 50 (1998): 96–104. *JSTOR*, www.jstor.org/stable/1151393.

20. See notably Martin Brückner ed., *Early American Cartographies*, Omohundro Institute of Early American History and Culture (Chapel Hill: University of North Carolina Press, 2011).

21. Edelson, *The New Map of Empire.*

22. See notably Stephen J. Hornsby, *Surveyors of Empire: Samuel Holland, J.F.W. Des Barres, and the Making of the Atlantic Neptune* (Montreal: McGill-Queen's University Press, 2016 (2011)).

23. César-François Cassini to Commissaires des États de Bretagne, 14 décembre 1784, Archives d'Ille et Villaine (C 4.924), in François de Dainville, "La carte de Cassini et son intérêt géographique," *Bulletin de l'Association de géographes français* 32, n°251–252 (May–June 1955): 138–147, https://doi.org/10.3406/bagf.1955.8014. Translation from the author.

24. Gliserman, "Landscapes of Conflict," 4.

25. William Penn to Planters in Maryland, London, September 16, 1681, in Soderlund and Dunn, *William Penn*, 79.

26. Augustine Herrman had worked for the Dutch West India Company and was a prominent trader in New Netherland. Attracted by the possibilities of developing trade exchanges with Maryland and the neighboring colonies, he had proposed the Calverts to create an "exact" map of a much-disputed region (Maryland, Virginia, Delaware, and parts of New Jersey). He was granted a large tract of land in the upper Chesapeake Bay

as compensation for the cost of creating the map and became one of the most successful tobacco traders in Maryland.

27. Archives of Maryland 17: 156, 159, in Irma Corcoran, *Thomas Holme: 1624–1695: Surveyor General of Pennsylvania*, Memoirs of the American Philosophical Society (Philadelphia: American Philosophical Society, 1992), 100.

The report of the meeting was written by Baltimore's secretary. Robert Wade had settled his residence in 1675 on the tract that had been known as Prinzdorp, the residence of the Swedish Governor Printz, head of New Sweden from 1643 to 1653. Wade's residence was known for being the dwelling where Penn was first entertained upon his landing in Upland, on October 29, 1682.

28. Charles II had issued a charter for the lower counties to his brother, who had planned to give his chartered rights to William Penn, but the Lords of Trade forbade the Duke of York to transfer the title to Penn until the dispute with Baltimore was settled.

29. John Moll's Account of the Surrender of the Three Lower Counties to William Penn, 1682, in Soderlund and Dunn, *William Penn*, 186.

On August 24, 1682, the Duke of York conveyed the area to William Penn in two deeds. The first deed transferred ownership of New Castle and a 12-mile circle surrounding the town, and the second deeded the territory below the 12-mile circle, or present-day Kent and Sussex counties. New Castle had been the regional capital under Dutch authority (New Amstel). As the largest town in the region and the first port of call for vessels arriving from Europe by the time Penn obtained his charter, its position was key.

30. The Delaware Bay was named in 1610 for Lord de la Warr, the governor of Virginia. The English then applied the name to the bay, the river, and finally the land on the Western shore.

31. The Miriam and Ira D. Wallach Division of Art, Prints and Photographs: Print Collection, The New York Public Library. "The figurative map of Adriaen Block," New York Public Library Digital Collections, 1614, http://digitalcollections.nypl.org/items/510d47d9-7bf7-a3d9-e040-e00a18064a99.

32. It might have been named after his cousin, the then more famous sailor Jan Cornelisz May, who led several expeditions to explore the Northwest passage.

33. Jonathan A. Munroe, *History of Delaware* (Cranbury, N.J.: Associated University Press, 2006), 17.

34. John Smith and William Hole, *Virginia* (London, 1624) Map, Library of Congress, https://www.loc.gov/item/99446115/.

The contributions of the Native communities to Smith's understanding of the geography of the region played a significant role in the overall accuracy of his work. His map is invaluable due to firsthand knowledge of the Chesapeake Indians and the locations of their villages and served as the prototype for the geography of the area for more than fifty years.

35. Willem Janszoon Blaeu, *Nova Belgica et Anglia Nova* (Amsterdam: Joan Blaeu, ?, 1635) Map, Library of Congress, https://www.loc.gov/item/2017585968/.

In this promotional map, Blaeu depicted potential sources of colonial wealth by inserting images of flora and animals with valuable pelts.

36. Jan Jansson, *Belgii novi, angliæ novæ, et partis Virginiæ: novissima delineatio* (Amsterdam: J. Jansson, 1651) Map, *Norman B. Leventhal Map & Education Center*, https://collections.leventhalmap.org/search/commonwealth:3f462s73v.

Jan Jansson, the son of a mapmaker and publisher, married into a leading Dutch publishing house, and was instrumental in the rivalry between the two principal publishing houses that brought Dutch mapmaking to its prominence. Unlike many maps of the time, his shows virtually all known European settlements.

37. Visscher copied much of Jansson's original map but inserted several decorative details.

38. John Ogilby, *Novi Belgii, quod nunc Novi Jorck vocatur, Novæ que Angliæ & partis Virginiæ: accuratissima et novissima delineatio* (London: Ogilby, ?, 1670) Map, Library of Congress, www.loc.gov/item/78695384/.

Ogilby published the atlas *Britannia* in 1675, a major achievement in early English cartography which enjoyed several reissues. It showed 2519 miles of road in 100 strip maps, a technique widely adopted in the 18th century.

39. The collection of maps is now called the *Blathwayt Atlas*. The original is at the John Carter Brown Library in Providence. See Jeannette D. Black, *The Blathwayt Atlas: Volume I The Maps, Volume II Commentary* (Providence, R.I.: Brown University Press, 1970–1975).

40. Herrman's map was the most complete map of the region by the 1670s. When asked by the Board of Trade to submit a map of his colony, Lord Baltimore praised Herrman's map for its delineation of Maryland's borders that made up for the imprecise 1632 Maryland charter. However, as historian C. Koot has explained, Herrman was influenced by the Dutch cartographic tradition, which emphasized waterways. His map delineated the water routes Herrman himself used in his efforts to develop a nexus of trade between the colonies, as opposed to the boundaries between them. By enlarging the frame to include the Delaware Bay and much of New Jersey, he linked the colonies "visually—as economically—but also highlighted the water's continuity throughout the Delmarva peninsula, rendering the borders between the colonies irrelevant." Koot, *A Biography of a Map in Motion*, 96–98, quote in 98.

41. Gary Nash's primeval works have illuminated the different factions vying for legislative power and political representation, as well as the conflicts taking place along religious, class, and ethnic lines in an otherwise rather peaceful province. Conflicts were recurrent with Swedes, Dutch, and English settlers, understandably reluctant to see the center of commercial activities and political power move from New Castle to Philadelphia. Members of the two assemblies clashed so frequently that Penn had to agree to two legislative entities. Officially separation was pronounced in 1704, yet 1701 was

the last year the assemblies sat together, after which Delawareans met in New Castle, and Pennsylvanians continued to meet in Philadelphia. Inherent to this conflict was the religious diversity of Delawareans, who were predominantly non-Quaker. While it was a concession from Penn, the legislative separation only reinforced Quaker control over the province.

The Three Lower Counties were a region in the province of Pennsylvania, not a separate colony, and were supervised by the same governor as the rest of the province. This status was maintained until Independence in 1776.

42. Cadwalader Collections, Penn Agency, Coates List 59. Quoted in Nicholas B. Wainwright, "Tale of a Runaway Cape. The Penn–Baltimore Agreement of 1732," *The Pennsylvania Magazine of History and Biography* 87, no. 3 (July 1963): 280.

43. In 1708, Charles Calvert unsuccessfully petitioned the King to reinstate the family's charter. His son Benedict understood that the question of religion was the main obstacle to the restoration of his family title and converted to Anglicanism in 1713, much to the dismay of his father, who died in February 1715. As soon as he became 4th Lord Baltimore, Benedict petitioned King George I; however, he died only two months later. His son, Charles Calvert, 5th Lord Baltimore, had to swear publicly that he was a Protestant and would embrace the Anglican faith for the King to restore the Maryland title to his family.

44. James Logan came to Pennsylvania in 1699 as William Penn's Secretary. He was one of the most involved actors in the Province affairs—serving as member of the provincial council, mayor of Philadelphia from 1722, then the colony's chief justice from 1731 to 1739—but also in land policy, as commissioner of property, receiver general, then in charge of most land dealing from 1712, while being the most prominent proprietary officeholder in the colony.

45. John de Laet (1581–1649) was a famous Dutch cartographer. He published the *History of the New World Atlas* in 1640 and was the first to print maps with the names *Manhattan, New Amsterdam,* and *Massachusetts* on them.

46. The Plaintiffs Case, 2. Penn v. Baltimore, Depositions (Philadelphia), I, 152–153; Cadwalader Collection, Penn Agency, Coates List 25. Quoted in Wainwright, "Tale of a Runaway Cape," 279.

47. Munroe, *History of Delaware,* 17.

48. The Great Chancery case referred to *Penn v. Baltimore.*

49. The Plaintiffs Case, 2, 7. Penn v. Baltimore, Depositions (Philadelphia), I, 152–153.

Quoted in Wainwright, "Tale of a Runaway Cape," 276.

50. Deposition of William Waples of Sussex County, Penn v. Baltimore, Depositions (Philadelphia), I, 152–153. Quoted in Wainwright, "Tale of a Runaway Cape," 279.

51. "The Map by which the privy Council 1685 Settled the the (*sic*) Bounds between the Lord Baltimore & I, & Maryland & Pennsylvania & territorys or annexed Countys. W.P."

Quoted in Wainwright, "Tale of a Runaway Cape," 282.

52. John Penn to Thomas Penn, Mar. 4, 1733/4, Penn Papers, Correspondence of the Penn Family (1732–1767), 21.

See Nicolas B. Wainwright's interesting theory about James Logan being responsible for advising the Penns. As Secretary to William Penn, Logan had been told by him where the Privy Council intended the Southern boundary of the Three Lower Countries to be. Wainwright, "Tale of a Runaway Cape," 263.

53. Mason and Dixon to their commissioners, October 10, 1767. Quoted in Danson, *Drawing the Lines*, 179.

William Darby's *A Map of the State of Louisiana* and the Extension of American Sovereignty over the "Neutral Ground" in the Louisiana –Texas Borderland, 1806–1819

Jackson Pearson

WILLIAM DARBY BELIEVED HIS due place in history had passed him by. In 1854, the aged surveyor and writer had spent the past fifteen years working as a clerk at the National Land Office. From his desk job in Washington, D.C., he sat far removed from the Western frontiers he had surveyed and written about frequently since the year 1805. As his finances tightened, Darby harbored feelings of resentment that his important role as the original surveyor of the Louisiana–Texas borderline lay forgotten and credited to another, more famous mapmaker, John Melish. He believed that Melish had both profited from his physical labors in the remote Louisiana–Texas borderland and stolen his credit as the knowledgeable expert on the western boundary of Louisiana. On April 19, 1854, the United States Senate passed a bill for the relief of the aged Darby. The bill stipulated that Congress pay the former surveyor the sum of fifteen hundred dollars as compensation for his labor and materials used in surveying and mapping Louisiana in the 1810s. Finally, the forgotten surveyor received government recognition that his labors provided the cartographic reference point for the southwestern border in the Transcontinental Treaty of 1819.[1]

Darby's belated recognition raises the question, how did his *Map of the State of Louisiana with Part of the Mississippi Territory* and its accompanying *Geographical Description of the State of Louisiana* influence American ambitions and reflect local realities in the contested Louisiana–Texas borderland? John Melish published the map and geographical treatise in April 1816. The combined materials provided valuable insights detailing the uncharted southwestern frontier of the United States. The map (Figure 1) illustrated the results of the first surveys of the Sabine River, Calcasieu River, and western portion of Louisiana. Intriguingly, the map did not depict the existence of the infamous "Neutral Ground" (Figure 2), which had existed between Louisiana and Texas since 1806. Rather it incorporated this disputed region within the boundaries of the state of Louisiana as defined in its bill of annexation. William Darby's physical survey and subsequently published map represented the extension of American authority over the disputed region between

155

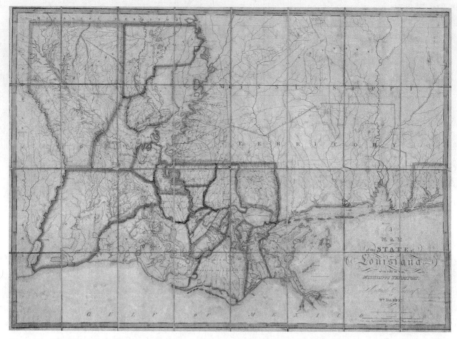

Figure 1. William Darby's *A Map of the State of Louisiana with Parts of the Mississippi Territory* (Philadelphia: Published by John Melish, 1816). Image Courtesy of David Rumsey Map Collection, David Rumsey Map Center, Stanford Libraries. Access at www.davidrumsey.com.

Louisiana and Texas. The map and survey served as another cog in the larger process of American expansion orchestrated by American officials on the nation's periphery. Thus, the Transcontinental Treaty of 1819 affirmed the incorporation of a region already annexed by the United States.[2]

Darby's map and *Geographical Description* have received scholarly attention from both literary and geography specialists. J. Gerald Kennedy's biographical account of William Darby represents the most complete analysis of Darby's literary treatises of the American frontier between the 1810s and 1840s. Several geographical studies have analyzed the accuracy of Darby's map in terms of mathematical and scientific exactitude. Gay Gomez highlights that his map played an important role in populating blank spaces of previous maps. Ralph Ehrenberg argues that Darby's map served as the standard cartographic production of Louisiana during the 1810s and 1820s. Most recently, John Evans and Jim Tiller assert that Darby's map remained the most accurate cartographic illustration of the state until the twentieth century. However, the map did more than just depict survey measurements.[3]

Darby's map provides a platform to evaluate cartography and anticipatory empire as defined by J.B. Harley. Harley asserts that maps intersect historical events with geopolitical and social processes. *A Map of the State of Louisiana* illustrates the extension of American sovereignty over a contested region. Therefore, it manifests processes of annexation. The map also revealed the commercial ambition of its author. Martin Brückner argues that maps needed to perform geopolitical, scientific, and commercial functions for success

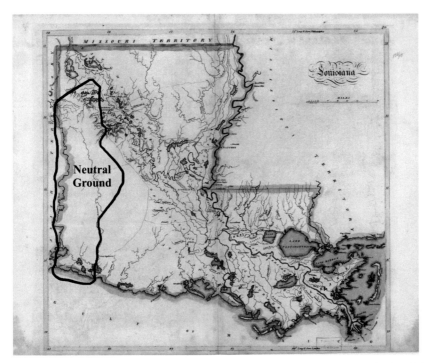

Figure 2. This is an edited version of Matthew Carey, "Louisiana" from *General Atlas of the World and Quarters* (Philadelphia: Published by Matthew Carey, 1814). *LOC.* https://www.loc.gov/item/2002624016/. Image courtesy of Library of Congress, Geography and Map Division, Louisiana: European Explorations and the Louisiana Purchase. The author has edited the image to illustrate the Neutral Ground. This map provides an excellent example of the lack of cartographic knowledge of the western and northern regions of Louisiana prior to William Darby's map of Louisiana.[8]

in the Early Republic. The publication of the map during the extended negotiations to define the Louisiana Purchase enhanced its appeal, since it provided scientific knowledge about a distant and obscure region. The map also fit within the larger realm of Jeffersonian Manifest Destiny as defined by Frank L. Owsley, Jr., and Gene Allen Smith. The map visualized the desires of American officials bent on projecting American authority further into the southwestern borderlands. Peter Kastor and Cameron Strang argue that the collection and publication of scientific knowledge aided the extension of national sovereignty by enhancing claims to a region. Darby's physical labor and subsequent publications provided scientific reinforcement for the American annexation of the Neutral Ground despite the lack of an international treaty allowing it to do so.[4]

The geopolitical context in which William Darby conducted his surveys of Louisiana and Subsequently published his map represents one facet thus far overlooked in the historical literature. This context is precisely what makes Darby's survey and map relevant for its manifestation of American ambitions in the Louisiana–Texas borderland. The Louisiana Purchase in 1803 created a geopolitical storm in the western territories. Spain and the United States each sought to define the exact territorial boundaries included in the purchase in the most advantageous manner possible. In turn, the Louisiana–Texas region witnessed the development of an acute struggle to define international borderlines. Both Thomas Jefferson and William Darby agreed that the Louisiana Purchase included all the territory between the Río Grande del Norte and the Perdido River. In contrast, Spain asserted that the purchase included only the region between the Mississippi and Mermantau Rivers. These conflicting claims sparked tensions as American and Spanish officials sought to enforce presumed boundaries in the contested region.[5]

Beginning as early as 1804, runaway slaves, Indian diplomacy, and military patrols generated constant tensions between American officials in Louisiana and Spanish officials in Texas. These issues intensified in February 1806, when American forces under Captain Edward Turner expelled Spanish forces from the old mission at Los Adaes. The American patrol ushered the Spanish force back across the Sabine River. The next flashpoint occurred in the summer of 1806 when an American scientific expedition under the leadership of Thomas Freeman and Peter Custis attempted to ascend the Red River to its source. The Freeman–Custis Expedition aimed to fulfill scientific and diplomatic goals of acquiring knowledge on the region and creating amicable ties with Native American tribes in the Southern Plains. Thus, the Freeman–Custis Expedition represented a multifaceted affront to Spanish sovereignty, as it would reinforce American claims of possession through the accruement of scientific knowledge and diplomacy. In July 1806, a large Spanish force under the command of Lt. Col. Simón de Herrera stopped the expedition at present-day Spanish Bluff, Texas, before it could accomplish its goals.[6]

When the expedition returned to Natchitoches, word quickly traveled to New Orleans where Gov. William C. C. Claiborne organized a military response. By late August 1806, Claiborne arrived in Natchitoches, where he gathered a combined force of territorial militia and army regulars. Conflict seemed inevitable as these forces eagerly anticipated the arrival of their military commander, General James Wilkinson. General Wilkinson, the famed double agent, belatedly arrived just as tensions cooled in October 1806. Even though Spanish forces had withdrawn across the Sabine River, the general still conducted a show of force through a march to the river. Lt. Col. Simón de Herrera promised to resist any attempt by Wilkinson's force to cross the waterway. Both officers desired to avoid overt hostilities. After one day of negotiations, they concluded the "Neutral Ground Agreement" on November 5, 1806 (Figure 2). The agreement declared the region between the Sabine River and Arroyo Hondo as outside the sovereignty of either nation-state pending an international treaty. Samuel Davenport later provided a more thorough definition that defined the Neutral Ground as the territory between the Sabine River in the west and the Calcasieu River, Arroyo Hondo, and Bayou Pierre in the east.[7]

The Neutral Ground Agreement of 1806 established a demilitarized zone outside the control of either Spain or the United States. Both nations agreed to send military forces into the disputed Neutral Ground only in the form of joint Spanish and American patrols. This temporary diplomatic solution de-escalated tensions in the Louisiana–Texas borderland. Though the agreement averted open hostilities between Spain and the United States, both nations continued efforts to manipulate any future boundary agreement to its favor. The context in which Darby's map manifested American expansion over the Neutral Ground emerges from this geopolitical competition to define the boundaries of the Louisiana Purchase amid the Neutral Ground Agreement. Local actors now seized the initiative to determine the course of American ambitions in the region.[9]

In 1805, William Darby arrived in Opelousas of the Orleans Territory with hopes of putting his past financial failings behind him. Darby had recently accepted employment as a surveyor for the Government Land Office located in Opelousas. During his employment, the surveyor completed hundreds of surveys largely centered in the Atchafalaya Basin and St. Landry Parish. His job planted the idea for a new business undertaking, a map of the Orleans Territory based on survey data of the entire region. At the time, Barthélémy Lafon's *Carte générale du territoire d'Orléans comprenant aussi la Floride Occidentale et une portion du territoire du Mississippi* represented the only map of any reputable value. This map revealed a stunning dearth of knowledge regarding the western and northern reaches of the Orleans Territory. Lafon cleverly utilized his cartouche to disguise his lack of knowledge on the western limits of the state (Figure 3). Darby began working on the project in 1808 by compiling notes gathered during his employment at the Land Office. The surveyor completed the first extensive surveys of the Atchafalaya Basin, Attakapas Parish, and Opelousas Parish during his term of employment. These surveys and Lafon's previous surveys of New Orleans provided the foundation for Darby's new project.[10]

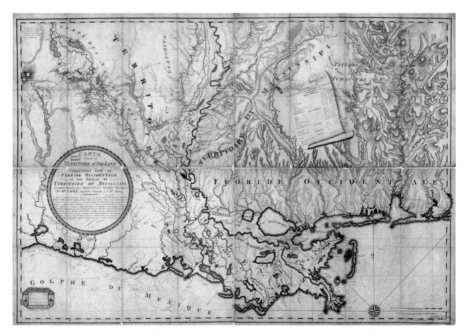

Figure 3. Barthélémy Lafon and Charles Picquet, *Carte générale du territoire d'Orléans comprenant aussi la Floride Occidentale et une portion du territoire du Mississippi* (Paris: Charles Picquet, 1806). LOC. https://www.loc.gov/item/2003623380. Image courtesy of Library of Congress, Geography and Map Division, Louisiana: European Explorations and the Louisiana Purchase.

His duties at the Land Office meant that Darby could not complete surveys of other regions that he needed to complete his map. Therefore, he resigned his commission in 1811. He then planned survey expeditions of the northern and western portions of the Orleans Territory. In the fall of 1811, Darby commenced his first tour to document the northern region from Natchitoches to Fort Miro to the Mississippi River. This first expedition examined territory excluded from the territorial disputes between Spain and the United States. It also set the standard for Darby's operating procedures. He compiled extensive notes on the region's fauna, climate, topography, settlements, roads, waterways, and other interesting or relevant information. He completed some survey measurements to detail the region, but he did not have to survey the entire northern boundary as an 1806 survey expedition had already completed these measurements. Lastly, he compiled his data into an accessible treatise for the consumption of prospective consumers. Darby concluded his survey in January 1812 after four months of travel. Simultaneous to this expedition, the Orleans Territory applied for statehood in the United States. The proposed state constitution proclaimed the Sabine River from its mouth to the 32nd parallel then along a meridian line to the 33rd parallel as the state's western border. The proposed boundary extended American claims over the disputed Neutral Ground without any mention of the Herrera–Wilkinson Agreement negotiated five years earlier.[11]

As Congress processed Louisiana's application for statehood, Governor Claiborne manipulated a series of events in the Neutral Ground to extend American sovereignty to the Sabine River. After its inception in 1806, nefarious characters exploited the Neutral Ground and its geopolitical murkiness. The region developed an unsavory reputation for violence and lawlessness as illicit characters sought refuge within its boundaries. The escalation of the Napoleonic Wars with France's invasion of Spain and Padre Hidalgo's rebellion in New Spain generated further turmoil in the region. These developments forced Spanish officials in Texas to look toward American markets for supplies. Spanish trade caravans soon routinely carried an average of fifteen to twenty thousand dollars' worth of silver pesos to exchange for goods in Natchitoches. General Walter Overton estimated that the trade between American Natchitoches and Spanish Texas was worth an annual total of three hundred thousand dollars by 1812. The lucrative trade attracted bandits who preyed on Spanish trade caravans during the return trip across the Neutral Ground. In January 1812, merchants in Natchitoches filed a petition urging American authorities to take action to preserve the commerce. Gov. Claiborne directed civil and military officials to exercise jurisdiction to the Sabine River. Thus, the first phase of American annexation began. American officers planned an expedition to expel the bandits from the region. Initially, the officers planned a joint Spanish–American patrol, but American officers pushed ahead without Spanish assistance as stipulated in the 1806 agreement. The patrol arrested nine individuals. During the corresponding trial in territorial court, the defendants argued that no state possessed sovereignty in the Neutral Ground as per the agreement between James Wilkinson and Simón de Herrera. They argued that no government or laws applied to the Neutral Ground. Despite their legal arguments, the court convicted two of the accused bandits. These convictions symbolized the extension of judicial authority to the Sabine River. This episode served as another assertion of American sovereignty over the nefarious region.[12]

Simultaneous to these events, Darby planned his second expedition for the fall months in 1812. A month before he began his travels, circumstances again changed in the Louisiana–Texas borderland. A filibuster operation under Mexican revolutionary Bernardo Gutierrez de Lara and former American military officer Augustus Magee invaded Spanish Texas. The Magee–Gutierrez Expedition began on August 9, 1812, with robust support from many Louisiana citizens. The expedition achieved initial success, and it created a short-lived Texas Republic in the spring of 1813. The expedition resulted in two significant developments. First, it temporarily dismantled Spanish authority in Texas; Spain no longer possessed the physical ability to dispute American territorial ambitions. Second, Claiborne utilized the expedition to annex Bayou Pierre, the only remaining Spanish settlement east of the Sabine River. Claiborne and the state legislature approved the annexation of Bayou Pierre on August 25, 1812. The legislature quickly appointed Marcel de Soto, the Spanish Indian Agent at Bayou Pierre, as a justice of the peace in Natchitoches Parish. This government action completed the extension of American civil authority to the Sabine.[13]

These developments provide context for Darby's second survey as a scientific and cartographic supplement for American sovereignty over the Neutral Ground. Due to the turmoil in New Spain, Spanish officials stood unable to oppose any expedition on the Sabine. Darby began his western expedition in September 1812. Dr. John Sibley, the American Indian Agent in Natchitoches, hosted Darby during his stay at the town. The two men shared similar visions of American expansion in the Louisiana–Texas Borderland. Sibley agreed with Jefferson and Darby's view that the Río Grande del Norte represented the most natural boundary for the United States. He provided Darby with guides, tools, and supplies to help the surveyor navigate the region and compute his measurements. Therefore, while it was not nationally sanctioned support, a local American official did provide material support to Darby; thus, he generated a government interest in its outcome.[14]

William Darby and his party departed Natchitoches in late September 1812. The group consisted of Darby, Wallace, and two unnamed men. Wallace worked as a guide, hunter, and translator for the expedition. He seems to have had a working relationship with Dr. Sibley at the Natchitoches Indian Agency, which led to his employ on the expedition. The group traveled along the trail from Natchitoches to Bayou Pierre. Darby specifically yearned to include Bayou Pierre due to its recent annexation. Bayou Pierre lay approximately 50 miles north by northwest of Natchitoches, just west of the Great Raft that impeded the Red River. The expedition visited the plantations of Manuel Prudhomme and Marcel de Soto, the newly appointed justice of the peace in Natchitoches Parish. Darby collected data based on observations and conversations with those he visited and encountered along his route. The data Darby gathered enhanced American knowledge of the region, and it reinforced American claims of sovereignty.

The group departed Bayou Pierre in the latter part of October. The party then visited Wallace's home north of the western bend of the river. Thence, they traveled southward to the river. The party finally arrived at the river in early November 1812. The date of arrival suggests that the party traveled at a leisurely pace, as it took the group over one month to travel approximately 120 miles.[15]

Darby spent three days traversing swamps in his search for the Sabine's intersection with the 32nd parallel. He speculated, "from all appearances which he could discover—except, for a few Indian traces, no other marks of the human race were visible—he was the first individual who ever reached that spot with any civilized object in view." Darby marked the boundary point by inscribing trees between the Sabine and a lake to its north. Geographers Jim Tiller and John Evans assert that Darby's point of intersection, while 3 miles east of the present corner, served as the most accurate placement of the corner until the twentieth century. At this point, Wallace sent word of the trip's progress back to Sibley. Sibley misinterpreted Darby's intentions, as he believed that Darby planned to survey the meridian line from the Sabine River north to the 33rd parallel. He incorrectly assumed that the line excluded the Nandaco and Caddo villages from American territory. Under this misunderstanding, Sibley proposed that Congress alter the Northwestern limits of the state to include these villages. The geopolitical implications of Darby's map now revealed the vested interest that American officials placed in its outcome. The final cartographic product held the potential to transform American geopolitical realities in this contested borderland.[16]

Darby descended the Sabine River with Wallace and two other companions. During the group's journey, they completed the first survey of the river's course. The group provided invaluable descriptions of the landscape, river's course, ferries, villages, and the coastline. William Darby boasted of his excellent health during the trip even though he survived for weeks on a diet of fish and venison. After arriving at the mouth of the Sabine in December 1812, the surveyor reflected that "no prospect can be more awfully solitary, than that from the mouth of the Sabine." The lonely shores revealed a land uninhabited by the civilized society to which the surveyor yearned to return. He concluded his survey expedition by ascending the Calcasieu River before traveling to his home in Opelousas. Again, the group completed the first surveys of this waterway. His extensive notes on the prairies, waterways, and bottomlands provided invaluable information for officials determined to consolidate control over the region. Darby arrived back to his home in mid-January 1813. Thus, his final survey expedition ended.[17]

The expedition surveyed a land seemingly far removed from civilized society. The knowledge gained of the region aimed to correct this. Darby's actions bolstered American hopes for the rapid legal settlement of the region. His treatise and surveys now supported American scientific and cartographic authority to the Sabine River. It should be noted that a diverse support network helped the expedition achieve success. Rather than simply an Anglo American success story, French Creoles (Marcel de Soto and Manuel Prudhomme), Native Americans (including Wallace, Yatasees, Alabamas,

Coushattas, Caddos, and Choctaws), Anglo-Americans (including Samuel Davenport, John Sibley, and Edward Livingston), and other unmentioned persons enabled William Darby to gather data and complete astronomical observations for his map. The final map reveals the assistance of these various actors, as Darby included their villages and homes in his final product. This inclusion demonstrates their essential role in Darby's success and that numerous actors helped design Darby's map.

With his surveys completed, Darby prepared his notes for publication. He eyed publication with one of the premier American mapmakers in Philadelphia. Philadelphia not only represented the hub of American cartography but also meant a return to Darby's home state of Pennsylvania. The untimely outbreak of hostilities in the War of 1812 and subsequent British operations in the Gulf region delayed his publication plans. The surveyor ultimately served as a topographical engineer for Andrew Jackson in the New Orleans campaign. American operations enabled him to conduct additional surveys of the Louisiana and Mississippi coastlines. Through his service, he shared his map and treatise with high-ranking American officials. His work clearly impressed them, as he received letters of endorsement from notable figures, such as Andrew Jackson, Edmund Gaines, and William Claiborne. Jackson declared that he had no doubts that Darby's map "was more correct than any which had been published of that country." These letters are particularly revealing, as they illustrate that Darby's map appeased the territorial ambitions of American officials.[18]

The surveyor finally departed for Philadelphia in May 1815, never to return to Louisiana. Upon arriving in Philadelphia, he quickly reached an agreement with John Melish for the publication of his map and its accompanying geographical description of Louisiana. His project hit shelves in April 1816. The treatise sold for twelve dollars, a significant sum for the time. Darby's depiction of the Sabine River and western boundary of Louisiana reveals important insights into the region. His efforts filled in the blank spaces of previous maps. Figures 2 and 3 illustrate the previous lack of cartographic knowledge, as Lafon's map included a large cartouche to disguise the lack of detail in the western quadrant of the map and Carey's map left the western portion blank other than an estimate of the Calcasieu River's course. The inclusion of Indian villages, homes of influential individuals, roads, ferries, topographical information, and waterways reflected the accruement of detailed information related to the Louisiana–Texas borderland. When taken together, the map and geographical description provided a strengthened American claim of sovereignty through access to reliable publicly available information about the southwestern border.[19]

Another aspect that invokes the extension of American sovereignty is the colored boundaries. The colors used to define parish boundaries provide an artistic cohesiveness to American sovereignty. John Melish and his publishers undoubtedly added the color boundaries on top of Darby's parish boundaries. Still, the use of color presents neat divisions of power. They provide a vivid illustration of civil and judicial jurisdiction and its supposed outer limits. Thus, the map presents an orderly and coherent image of the Neutral Ground as rightfully attached to the United States. It effectively conceals the chaotic history of expansion and existence of the disputed Neutral Ground. The map fragments in Figures 4 and 5 illustrate how Darby's map provided a cartographic illustration of anticipatory empire that illustrated American expansion and expanded knowledge of the region that reinforced American conceptions of authority over the Neutral Ground.[20]

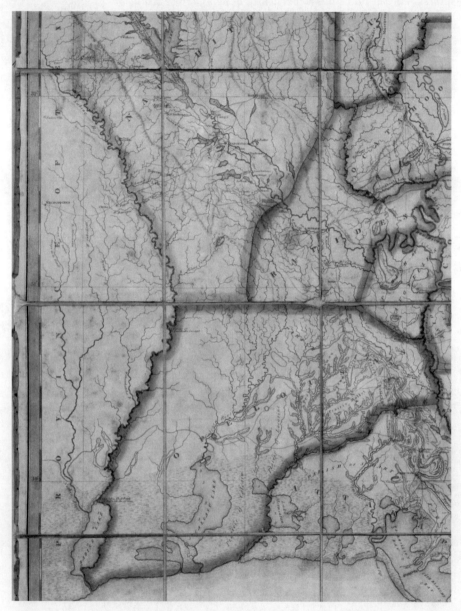

Figure 4. Section illustrating the incorporation of the Neutral Ground in William Darby, *A Map of the State of Louisiana with parts of the Mississippi Territory* (Philadelphia: Published by John Melish, 1816). Image courtesy of David Rumsey Map Collection, David Rumsey Map Center, Stanford Libraries. Access at www.davidrumsey.com. The section shows an expansive interpretation of Natchitoches and St. Landry Parishes whose jurisdictions extended to the Sabine River.

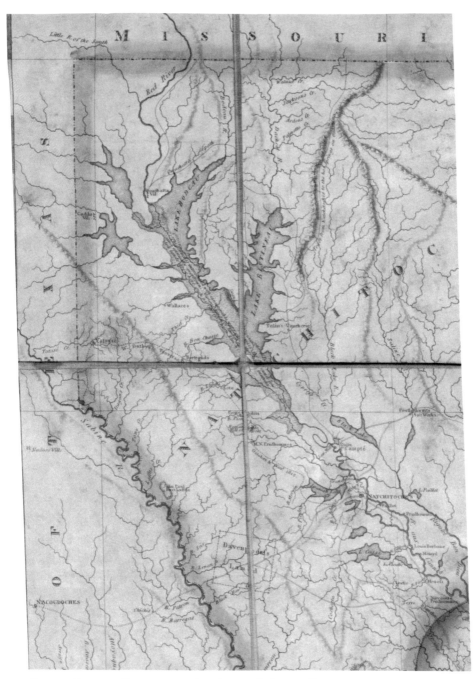

Figure 5. Fragment illustrating Natchitoches Parish from William Darby's *A Map of the State of Louisiana with Part of the Mississippi Territory* (Philadelphia: John Melish, 1816). Image courtesy of David Rumsey Map Collection, David Rumsey Map Center, Stanford Libraries. Access at www. davidrumsey.com. This fragment includes the homes of Wallace, Prudhomme, and de Soto. It also notes the placement of Native American villages that Darby visited during his expedition.

The details provided in the preceding map fragments display a region not devoid of people, as other maps had done. Darby's inclusion of details offers the perception that the region contained more than empty wilderness. Homes and villages within the map provide glimpses of communal order while also highlighting which areas prospective settlers might find available. He included homes of influential settlers, such as Manuel Prudhomme, Marcel de Soto, and Samuel Davenport's La Nana land grant. The map even marked the house of his guide, Wallace. Darby's map also noted the location of Native American tribes in the region. As Juliana Barr has argued, his inclusion of villages hints at their continued influence in the region. It also underscores that consistent trade and exchange allowed Americans to acquire knowledge of spaces inhabited by these tribes. Thus, his map illuminated a complex and populated scene at the periphery of American influence.[21]

Unbeknownst to him, Darby's survey competed with a simultaneous historical cartography project undertaken by Fray José Antonio Pichardo. Spanish Commandant-General of the Interior Provinces Nemesio Salcedo appointed the friar to his task in 1807. Pichardo's project aimed to legitimize Spanish territorial claims in the region and affirm Spanish possession of Eastern Texas and Western Louisiana. The friar mined provincial records in Nacogdoches and San Antonio de Bexar that contained land and mission records dating back to the Spanish founding of Los Adaes in 1717. Pichardo utilized these archival records as the sole source for his cartographic project, as he never completed physical surveys for his map. Rather, he relied on individual travel accounts to chart distances between locales. In his conclusion, he asserted that Spain held rightful claim to a borderline running from the mouth of the Mermantau River on the Gulf of Mexico to the Arroyo Hondo, then northwesterly along Bayou Pierre to the former Spanish outpost of the same name, before running in a lengthy northeasterly direction to the mouth of the Missouri River. In 1812, Pichardo sent his map and corresponding treatise to Nemesio Salcedo, who forwarded it to royal officials. The treatise and map serve as an excellent counterpoint to Darby's map. Pichardo never visited any of the areas he depicted, and his map remained hidden in the hands of select Spanish imperial officials rather than being made publicly available. He computed latitudinal and longitudinal coordinates in addition to distances between locations based on data compiled from dated travel accounts. This process contrasts Darby's action of physically surveying the boundaries of his map. Darby computed astronomical readings at specific locations to pinpoint latitudinal and longitudinal coordinates. Thus, Darby's physical toil and individual initiative reflected physical processes that counter Pichardo's historical archive that emphasized original settlement and exploration as the basis for sovereignty.[22]

The cartographic influence of Darby's map appears apparent when compared to Pichardo's. The public proliferation and its subsequent incorporation by other mapmakers and publishers such as John Melish and Henry Tanner increased Darby's influence far beyond the map's sales numbers. Interestingly, disputes quickly emerged between author and publisher when Darby discovered that Melish incorporated his cartographic image of Louisiana within his own larger map of the United States and geographic atlas beginning in 1816. Darby expressed dismay that Melish failed to award credit to the surveyor for his contribution. In fact, Melish compiled information from various sources without acknowledging the true authors. Historian Martin Brückner highlights that Melish did this for every map he produced. A comparison of maps produced in 1813 and 1816 reveals Darby's cartographic influence on Melish's image of Louisiana. In 1813, Melish's *A Map of the Southern Section of the United States* depicted an elongated northwestern border of Louisiana that jutted far to the west of the actual border. This elongated section created a distorted image of Louisiana that greatly increased the land area of the region between the Sabine and Red Rivers in the northwest section of the state. In contrast, Melish's *A Map of the United States of America: With Contiguous British and Spanish Possessions*, published in 1816, displayed an altered cartographic image of Louisiana that directly mimicked Darby's map. (Refer to Figures 1 and 6 to see Darby's Louisiana and Melish's later incorporation of it.) In Figure 6, Melish's 1816 map clearly replicates Darby's image of Louisiana, and it remained Melish's standard for the state in every subsequent map production. In response, Darby proudly boasted that he was the only person capable of creating an accurate map of the region, since he was the only individual with actual survey notes of it. Darby soon showed his dissatisfaction by publishing a second edition of *A Geographical Description of Louisiana* and its accompanying *A Map of the State of Louisiana* in 1817 with Jacob Olmstead in New York instead of John Melish. Most subsequent maps followed Melish's lead and simply incorporated Darby's cartographic image of Louisiana into their own maps.[23]

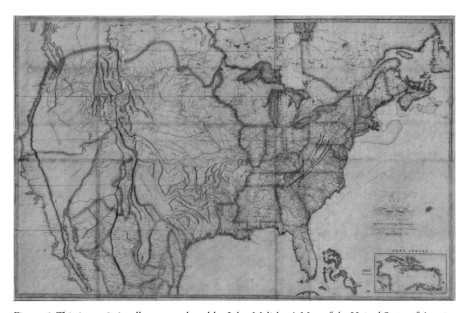

Figure 6. This is an 1816 wall map produced by John Melish, *A Map of the United States of America: With Contiguous British and Spanish Possessions* (Philadelphia: John Melish, 1816). LOC. https://www. loc.gov/item/96686672/. Image courtesy of Library of Congress, Geographic and Maps Division, Louisiana: European Exploration and Louisiana Purchase. Compare this image of Louisiana to Darby's image of Louisiana in Figure 1 to see the cartographic standardization of Louisiana.

Developments in 1818 and 1819 raised Darby's ire regarding Melish's incorporation of his southwestern survey into his own maps. According to cartographic historian Walter Ristow, Secretary of State John Quincy Adams and Spanish minister Luis de Onís y González-Vara utilized an 1818 edition of Melish's *A Map of the United States of America: With Contiguous British and Spanish Possessions* as the cartographic reference for their discussions on western borderlines in the winter months of 1818–1819 (see Figure 6). Onís viewed the map and mused that American officials must have sanctioned the map to further their territorial ambitions as its boundaries incorporated large areas of Spanish territory. He argued that Louisiana's boundary should be at the Arroyo Hondo, not the Sabine River, let alone the Rio Grande del Norte as the Neutral Ground Agreement still held accord in the minds of Spanish officials. Onís's view illuminated his ignorance of the physical actions and geopolitical processes that American officials had already utilized to exercise authority to the Sabine River. In contrast to his Spanish counterpart, Adams believed the map to be a reliable cartographic image. The Melish map informed geopolitical orientations of the two diplomats, as it provided visual reference point for an area that neither man had seen with his own eyes. Ultimately, the two men utilized Darby's southwestern borderline when they finalized the Transcontinental Treaty of 1819, as it established the Sabine River as the boundary between the two nations. In fact, the line followed the precise boundaries as laid out in Louisiana's 1812 Constitution and as surveyed by Darby himself.[24]

William Darby's survey and publication symbolized the physical actions and processes undergirding American expansionism. When Darby completed his surveys and notes for his subsequent publications, the 1810 census placed the total population of Natchitoches and St. Landry parishes at approximately eight thousand persons. Darby's western border survey coincided with the commodification and increased settlement of lands in western Louisiana. Indeed, Darby's publication date in 1816 coincided with significant western movement into present-day Alabama, Mississippi, Louisiana, and Arkansas territories. By 1820, the population in western Louisiana more than doubled to nearly twenty thousand persons. In a confidential report to Spanish ministers, Arséné Latour and Jean Lafitte "drew the conclusion that such an increase of the population is . . . a terrible weapon in the hands of the American government, threatening the future peace of the western possessions of the Spanish crown in the New World." Thus, *A Map of the State of Louisiana* illustrated geopolitical and social processes that firmly attached the contested region to the American government through population growth.[25]

With neither a treaty nor a military campaign, American officials annexed the Neutral Ground long before international authorities deemed it appropriate. William Darby's *A Map of the State of Louisiana* culminated the process of annexing the Neutral Ground. The fact that negotiators recognized Melish's 1818 map as the authority on the Louisiana–Texas border underscored the geopolitical authority that Darby's survey and map provided for American officials. It provided American diplomats with a firm claim to authority over the Neutral Ground that reflected local processes of American annexation. The conviction of bandits, annexation of Bayou Pierre, and appointment of former Spanish officials represented the assertion of American civil and legislative sovereignty. Darby's map represented the cartographic culmination of these processes. These processes did not rely on international treaty; rather local individuals shaped the region in a manner more conducive to their ambitions. It also highlights why Spanish officials readily accepted the Sabine River as the boundary between Louisiana and Texas.[26]

When Congress approved the bill of relief for the aged Darby, they unwittingly acknowledged the power of local, physical action in providing the foundation for international diplomacy. Through the remainder of his life, Darby witnessed the development of the American West for three decades after Spanish and American diplomats verified his borderline as the true divider between the American Louisiana and Spanish Texas. He even witnessed the annexation of Texas into the United States. This annexation completed what he, Thomas Jefferson, Dr. John Sibley, and many other American officials believed to be the rightful limits of the Louisiana Purchase. Most importantly, the physical actions of men like Darby are often forgotten in lieu of the high-level political and diplomatic negotiations. These men of action played an essential role in drawing the borderlines found on imperial maps.

Notes

The author is a PhD Student at Texas Christian University in Fort Worth, Texas.

1. John Melish's *Map of the United States, 1818*, is cited as the map that negotiators utilized when deciding the Spanish–American boundary in 1819. See *Daily National Intelligencer*, 11 March 1819. Washington, D.C. *19th Century U.S. Newspapers*. Web. Accessed 28 Aug. 2019. Walter Ristow determined that Melish's 1818 edition influenced diplomats during negotiations related to the Transcontinental Treaty of 1819. See Walter Ristow, *A la Carte: Selected Papers on Maps and Atlases* (Washington D.C.: Library of Congress, 1972), 162–170. The Senate approved the bill in April, but Darby did not receive the funds until August of that year. Bill no. 340, Senate, 33rd Congress, 1st Session, S 342. 19 April 1854. https://memory.loc.gov/cgi-bin/ampage?collId=llsb&fileName=033/ llsb033.db&recNum=1110. For a biographical account of William Darby, see J. Gerald Kennedy, *The Astonished Traveler: William Darby, Frontier Geographer and Man of Letters* (Baton Rouge: Louisiana State University Press, 1981): 4–128. Darby was born in 1775 in Western Pennsylvania. He published approximately two hundred tracts regarding western territory and expansion. Two stand out above the rest, his *Geographical Description of the State of Louisiana, the Southern Part of the Mississippi Territory, and Territory of Alabama; Together with a Map from Actual Survey and Observation* (Philadelphia: John Melish, 1816) and *Emigrant's Guide to the Western and Southwestern States and Territories* (New York: Kirk & Mercein, 1818). Darby died a mere two months after receiving his bill of relief in October 1854. See William Darby to Col. Abraham Wooley, 30 November 1849. *Edward A. Parson's Collection*, microfilm reel 2. Briscoe Center for American History. Austin, TX. Hereafter, cited as *EAP*; and Kennedy, *Astonished Traveler*, 1–4.

2. See William Darby to Col. Abraham Wooley, 30 November 1849. *EAP*, reel 2. Briscoe Center for American History. Austin, TX; see Figure 1 for William Darby's *Map of the State of Louisiana with Part of the Mississippi Territory*. Darby's geographical description of the state of Louisiana accompanied his map. Darby, *Geographical Description*. The Neutral Ground formed part of present-day western Louisiana, roughly the region between the Sabine and Calcasieu Rivers. For the Neutral Ground, see Figure 2 on page 7.

3. Kennedy, *The Astonished Traveler*, xi–xii, 4–8; Ralph E. Ehrenberg, "'Forming a General Geographic Idea of a Country': Mapping Louisiana from 1803 to 1820," in *Charting Louisiana: 500 Years of Maps*. Edited by Alfred E. Lemmon, John T. Magill, and Jason R. Wiese. Foreword by Mary Louise Christovich (New Orleans: Historic New Orleans Collection, 2003): 123–161; Gay M. Gomez, "Describing Louisiana: The Contribution of William Darby," *Louisiana History: Journal of the Louisiana Historical Association* 34, no. 1 (Winter 1993): 87–105. Hereafter, *Louisiana History: Journal of the Louisiana Historical Association* will be cited as *LHJ*. http://www.jstor.org/stable/4233001; and Jim Tiller and John P. Evans, *Evolution of the Texas–Louisiana Boundary: In Search of the Elusive Corner* (Dallas: Southern Methodist University Press, 2016): xv–xvi, 5–25.

4. See J. B. Harley, *The Nature of Maps: Essays in the History of Cartography*. Edited by Paul Laxton (Baltimore: Johns Hopkins Press, 2001): 46–57; Martin Brückner, *The Social Life of Maps in America, 1750–1860* (Chapel Hill: University of North Carolina Press, 2017): 3–10. For more information on Jeffersonian Manifest Destiny and American expansion in the Gulf South from 1800 to 1821, see Frank L. Owsley, Jr., and Gene Allen Smith, *Filibusters and Expansionists: Jeffersonian Manifest Destiny, 1800–1821* (Tuscaloosa: University of Alabama Press, 1997): 1–6. For more on the role of frontier individuals increasing natural knowledge, see Peter Kastor, *William Clark's World: Describing American in an Age of Unknowns* (New Haven, Conn.: Yale University Press, 2011), 1–4. For the collection of data as means to expand sovereignty, see Cameron Strang, *Frontiers of Science: Imperialism and Natural Knowledge in the Gulf South Borderlands, 1500–1850* (Chapel Hill: Omohundro Institute and University of North Carolina Press, 2017), 7–10.

5. For more information relative to Louisiana Purchase and American possession, see Alexander DeConde, *This Affair of Louisiana* (New York: Charles Scribner's Sons, 1976): 209–240. For William Darby and Thomas Jefferson's perspectives relative to the boundaries of Louisiana, see Darby, *Geographical Description*, 28–29; William Darby to Thomas Jefferson, 12 June 1817. *LOC*. Manuscript/Mixed Media. https://www.loc.gov/item/mtjbib022888/; and Thomas Jefferson to William Darby, 22 June 1817. *LOC*. Mixed Media/ Manuscript. https://www.loc.gov/item/mtjbib022907/. For Spanish claims in the region, see José Antonio Pichardo, *Pichardo's Treatise on the Limits of Louisiana and Texas*. Vols. 1–4, Edited by Charles A. Hackett (Austin: University of Texas Press, 1931).

6. For information relative to tensions in the Louisiana–Texas borderland, see John Sibley Report, 30 September 1805. *Library of Congress*. Mixed Media/Manuscript. https://www.loc.gov/item/mtjbib015167/; and Edward Turner to William Claiborne, 30 July 1804, 31 March 1805; William Claiborne to Gov. Salcedo, 1 October 1807. *TPO*, IX, 764–765. For more information on the Freeman–Custis Expedition, see Henry Dearborn

to Thomas Jefferson, 31 August 1806; and for the most comprehensive analysis of the expedition, see Dan Flores, *Jefferson & Southwestern Exploration: The Freeman & Custis Accounts of the Red River Expedition of 1806* (Norman: University of Oklahoma Press, 1984).

7. For tensions preceding the Neutral Ground Agreement, see William Claiborne to Secretary of War, 29 March 1806. *TPO*, IX, 618; William Claiborne to Thomas Jefferson, 12 November 1806. *TPO*, IX, 686–687; and Flores, *Southwestern Exploration*, 1–87. For Wilkinson's march to the Sabine and course of negotiations with the Spanish officers, see *United States Orderly Book*, 22 October–9 November 1806, Mss. 2663, Louisiana and Lower Mississippi Valley Collections, LSU Libraries, Baton Rouge, La. For analysis of the negotiation itself, see Jack D.L. Holmes, "Showdown on the Sabine: General James Wilkinson vs. Lieutenant-Colonel Simón de Herrera," *Louisiana Studies* 3 (1964): 46–76. For the most comprehensive analysis of the Neutral Ground, see J. Villasaña Haggard, "The Neutral Ground Between Texas and Louisiana, 1806–1821," *Louisiana Historical Quarterly* 28, no. 4 (October 1945): 1018–1129. Deposition of Samuel Davenport on 1 Nov. 1824, in "Claims to Land between the Río Hondo and Sabine Rivers, in Louisiana," *American State Papers: Public Lands*, IV, 90. Hereafter cited as *ASPPL*.

8. Another article detailing the Neutral Ground utilizes Carey's map to illustrate the Neutral Ground. However, the dimensions in the other image do not align with the description provided by Samuel Davenport. The edits used in this image adhere more closely to Davenport's description of the limits of the Neutral Ground. For the other image, see J. Edward Townes, "The Neutral Strip." https://64parishes.org/entry/the-neutral-strip.

9. Scholars highlight that diplomats capitalized on the turmoil caused by Americans in the frontier, but they underemphasize government support and tacit approval of such actions. For examples of scholars focused on the diplomatic negotiations at the international level, see Philip Brooks, *Diplomacy and the Borderland: The Adams–Onís Treaty of 1819* (Berkeley: University of California Press, 1939), v–vi; J.C.A. Stagg, *Borderlines in Borderlands: James Madison and the Spanish–American Frontier, 1776–1821* (New Haven, Conn.: Yale University Press, 2009), 134–209; and William Weeks, *John Quincy Adams and American Global Empire* (Lexington: University of Kentucky Press, 1992), 1–84, 127–175. Other scholars have emphasized the role of individuals in fulfilling the American ideology of expansion; see Owsley and Smith, *Filibusters*, 1–6, 32–60.

10. For more on Darby's early life and career before arriving in Opelousas, see Kennedy, *Astonished Traveler*, 10–35. Darby stated that Lafon's map possessed real merit for its measurements related to the New Orleans region. See Darby, *Geographical Descriptions*, iv. For more on Darby's intentions, see William Darby to Col. Wooley Abraham, 30 November 1849. *EAP*, and Kennedy, *Astonished Traveler*, 10–35. For more information on and analysis of Lafon's map, see Ehrenberg, "Mapping Louisiana," 124–126, and Gomez, "William Darby," 90.

11. For more details on Darby's survey of 1811–1812, see William Darby to Col. Wooley Abraham, 30 November 1849. *EAP*. Reel 2. Austin, TX. For details and

examples of the data gathered by Darby during this expedition, see Darby, *Geographical Description*, 2nd ed., 28–50; Ehrenberg, "Mapping Louisiana," 134–135; and Gomez, "William Darby," 92. For the submission of Louisiana's Constitution for Statehood, see Julien Poydras to the President, 28 January 1812. *TPO*, 998. For the boundaries outlined in the proposed constitution, see *1812 Constitution of the State of Louisiana*, 30 January 1812. Records of the U.S. Senate, RG 46. Web access on 5 September 2019. https://www.archives.gov/legislative/features/louisiana-statehood/louisiana-constitution.html.

12. As early as 1808, local citizens in Natchitoches petitioned that the Embargo be lifted to facilitate trade with Texas. See John Sibley to Henry Dearborn, 12 October 1808. *Library of Congress*. Mixed Media/Manuscript. https://www.loc.gov/item/mtjbib019158/. For an estimation of the value of the trade, see Walter Overton to Zebulon Pike, 6 March 1812. *TPO*, IX, 1003–1004. For the merchant memorial complaining of bandit attacks, see Merchant Memorial to Governor Claiborne, 4 January 1812. *TPO*, IX, 976–978; John Carr to William Claiborne, 7 January 1812. *TPO*, IX, 975–976; William Claiborne to Wade Hampton, 20 January 1812. *Official Letter books of W.C.C. Claiborne, 1801–1816*, vols. 1–6. Edited by Dunbar Rowland (Jackson, MS: State Department of Archives and History, 1917), VI, 34–36; and William Claiborne to John Carr, 20 January 1812. *Letterbooks*, VI, 36–37. For Pike's patrol, see William Claiborne to John Carr, 16 February 1812. *Letterbooks*, VI, 56–57; Wade Hampton to Zebulon Pike, 6 February 1812. *TPO*, IX 998–1000; and John Sibley to Amos Stoddard, 2 April 1812. *Sibley Collection*. Mary E. Amber Archives, Lindenwood College, St. Charles, MO. For details on the trial, see William Claiborne to James Monroe, 21 May 1812. *Letterbooks,* VI. 103–105; and Samuel Davenport to Bernardo Montero, 6 May 1812. *Bexar Archives*, Microfilm Reel 51. Briscoe Center for American History, University of Texas at Austin. Austin, TX. For an account of the Spanish perspective of these episodes, see Haggard, "Neutral Ground," 1070–1098.

13. For information relative to the Magee-Gutierrez Expedition, see Thomas Linnard to John Mason, 15 August 1812 and 18 August 1812. *LBNSFF*. Reel T1029. Julia Kathryn Garret, *Green Flag Over Texas: A Story of the Last Years of Spain in Texas* (Dallas: Cordova Press, 1939); Harris Gaylord Warren, *The Sword Was Their Passport: A History of American Filibustering in the Mexican Revolution* (Baton Rouge: Louisiana State University Press, 1943), 22–74; Owsley and Smith, *Filibusters and Expansionists*, 32–60; and Ed Bradley, *We Never Retreat: Filibustering Expeditions into Spanish Texas, 1812–1822* (College Station: Texas A&M University Press, 2015), 39–90. For the annexation of Bayou Pierre, see William Claiborne Proclamation to the Louisiana Senate and House of Representatives, 25 August 1812. *Letterbooks*, VI, 167–168. For the appointment of Marcel de Soto, see William Claiborne to John Sibley, 16 November 1812. *Letterbooks*, VI, 200.

14. For more information on John Sibley hosting Darby, see John Sibley to William Eustis, 28 November 1812. Garrett, "Dr. John Sibley," 417–418. For Sibley's aid to Darby, see Darby, "Letter to the Editors," *National Intelligencer*, 13 May 1836 (Washington, D.C.).

15. Wallace's full name is lost to the historical record. Darby and Sibley refer to him only as Wallace. For information on Darby's party and progress, see William Darby, "Letter to the Editor," *National Intelligencer*, 13 May 1836 (Washington, D.C.). For Darby's visit to Natchitoches, see John Sibley to William Eustis, 28 November 1812. Garrett, "Dr. John Sibley," 417–418. For Darby's visit to Bayou Pierre and his route, see Darby, *Emigrant's Guide*, 85. For more information on the party's route and data collection, see Gomez, "William Darby," 92–93; and Evans and Tiller, *Elusive Corner*, 13–17.

16. Quotation from William Darby, "Letter to the Editors," *National Intelligencer*, 13 May 1836 (Washington, D.C.); William Darby to Abraham Wooley, 30 November 1849. *EAP*. For descriptions of Darby's accuracy, see Gomez, "William Darby," 92–93; and Evans and Tiller, *Elusive Corner*, xv–xvi, 8–9, 13–17. For Sibley's convictions, see Letter from John Sibley to William Eustis, 28 November 1812, in Julia Kathryn Garrett, ed., "Dr. John Sibley and the Louisiana–Texas Frontier, 1803–1814," *Southwestern Historical Quarterly* 49, no. 3 (January 1946): 417–418.

17. A Spanish expedition under the Marqués de Caso Calvo had surveyed the mouth of the river in 1805, but it did not ascend the river further than a few leagues. See Jack Holmes, "Marques Caso Calvo, Nicolas DeFiniels, and the 1805 Spanish Expedition through East Texas and Louisiana," *Southwestern Historical Quarterly* 69, no. 3 (January 1966): 324–339; and Jack Jackson, *Shooting the Sun: Cartographic Results of Military Activities in Texas, 1689–1829*. Vols. 1–2 (Austin: Book Club of Texas, 1998), II, 336–337. For Darby's notes on the region, see Darby, *Geographical Description*, 21–25; William Darby to Col. Abraham Wooley, 30 November 1849. *EAP*.

18. For Philadelphia's centrality to American cartography, see Brückner, *Social Life of Maps*, 51–52. For duties at New Orleans, see Kennedy, *Astonished Traveler*, 35–45. For the letters of endorsement, see William Darby to Col. Abraham Wooley, 30 November 1849. *EAP*. They are listed in Darby, *Geographical Description*, 333–337. For the quotation, see Darby, *Geographical Description*, 333–334.

19. For Darby's travels to Philadelphia and publication, see Kennedy, *Astonished Traveler*, 46–57. For a sales advertisement, see *Evening Post*, 6 August 1816 (New York City, NY). Website database, Newspapers.com. Accessed 1 September 2019. For Lafon's map, refer to Figure 3. See Figures 1, 4, and 5 for visual representations of Darby's added details. Ehrenberg, "Mapping Louisiana," 134–135; Gomez, "William Darby," 94–100. Refer to Figures 1 and 4 for an example of the color differentiations. Darby, *Map of the State of Louisiana*, DRMC.

20. For a discussion of colored boundaries and divisions of power, see Mark Monmonier, *How to Lie with Maps* (Chicago: University of Chicago Press, 1996), 163–173. Darby chose to represent only parish boundaries for the simplicity rather than add judicial or military districts on top of the parish boundaries. Darby, *Geographical Descriptions*, 47–49. Darby's inclusions of physical topography and environmental aspects provide detail in the previously blank quadrants of earlier maps. For greater analysis of the environment he surveyed, see Darby, *Geographical Descriptions*, 97–252; and Gomez, "William Darby," 94–100.

21. Darby, *Map of the State of Louisiana, DRMC*; Tiller and Evans, *Elusive Corner*, 13–17; Gomez, "William Darby," 94–100; Juliana Barr, "Geographies of Power: Mapping Indian Borders in the 'Borderlands' of the Early Southwest," *William and Mary Historical Quarterly* 68, no. 1 (January 2011), 5–10. For more detailed studies on the Caddoan tribes, see Cecile Elkins Carter, *Caddo Indians: Where We Come From* (Norman: University of Oklahoma Press, 1995); David La Vere, *The Caddo Chiefdoms: Caddo Economics and Politics, 700–1835* (Lincoln: University of Nebraska Press, 1998); and F. Todd Smith, *The Caddo Indians: Tribes at the Convergence of Empires, 1542–1854* (College Station: Texas A&M University Press, 1995).

22. For further discussions on the use of archives and historical cartography, refer to another article in this book, Derek O'Leary, "Archival Lines, Historical Practice, and the Atlantic Geopolitics behind the 1842 Webster–Ashburton Treaty." Pichardo believed that the discussion should be entirely historical; therefore, he never conducted a physical survey. Interestingly, Pichardo believed that rivers served as the natural limiters of sovereignty, yet he did not identify a river as a natural border. He instead pointed to the Arroyo Hondo, a deep stream or creek, before following survey line based on longitude and latitude that cut across rivers. See Pichardo, *Pichardo's Treatise*, I, 42–45; III, 111–113, 128–150, 451–461; IV, 119–126, 253–297, 395–476. For further analysis of Pichardo and other Spanish cartographers, see Jack Jackson, *Shooting the Sun*, II, 308–380. For Darby's objective and a poetic description of the landscape of the Sabine River, see Darby, *Geographic Description*, 21–26; and Kennedy, *Astonished Traveler*, 42. For Darby's precise measurements and distances, see Darby, *Emigrant's Guide*, 44–50, 85.

23. For Darby's complaints about Melish, see William Darby to Col. Abraham Wooley, 30 November 1849. *EAP*; and *National Intelligencer*, 13 May 1836. For Melish's compilation of various sources, see Brückner, *Social Life of Maps*, 65–81. For the changes in Melish's maps, see John Melish, *A Map of the Southern Section of the United States Including the Floridas and the Bahamas Showing the Seat of War in that Department* (Philadelphia: John Melish, 1813) and John Melish, *A Map of the United States of America: With Contiguous British and Spanish Possessions* (Philadelphia: John Melish, 1816). Ehrenberg, "Mapping Louisiana," 134–135. For Darby's boasts, see *National Intelligencer*, 13 May 1836. For Darby's second edition, see William Darby, *A Geographical Description of Louisiana*. 2nd ed. (New York: Jacob Olmstead, 1817). Darby's image was incorporated most prominently by Melish and Henry Schneck Tanner.

24. See *Daily National Intelligencer*, 11 March 1819. Washington, D.C. *19th Century U.S. Newspapers*. Web. Accessed 28 August 2019. Walter Ristow determined that one of Melish's 1818 editions influenced diplomats during negotiations related to the Transcontinental Treaty of 1819. See Walter Ristow, *A la Carte: Selected Papers on Maps and Atlases* (Washington, D.C.: Library of Congress, 1972), 162–170. For more on Onís's perspective during negotiations, see Brooks, *Diplomacy and the Borderland*, 142–144. For John Quincy Adams, perception of the map, see John Quincy Adams to George William Erving, 20 April 1818 in *The Writings of John Quincy Adams*, Volume VI, Edited by Worthington C. Ford (New York: McMillan Company, 1916), 306–310; John Quincy

Adams to Don Luis de Onis, 31 October 1818. *Ibid.*, 455–462; and John Quincy Adams entry for 3 February 1819 in *John Quincy Adams: Diaries, 1779–1821*. Edited by David Waldstreicher (New York: The Library of America, 2017), 468–472.

25. For census data, see https://www.census.gov/content/dam/Census/library/working-papers/2002/demo/POP-twps0056.pdf. Online resource. For Latour's report, see Edwin H. Carpenter, Jr., "Latour's Report on Spanish–American Relations in the Southwest," *Louisiana Historical Quarterly* 30, no. 3 (July 1947): 715–748. For this quotation, see *Ibid.*, 730.

26. William Darby to Col. Abraham Wooley, 30 November 1849. *EAP*. Reel 2. For more information on the Transcontinental Treaty of 1819, see Phillip Brooks, *Diplomacy and the Borderland: The Adams–Onís Treaty of 1819* (Berkeley: University of California Press, 1939), v–vi, 1–7, 142–170; William Earl Weeks, *John Quincy Adams and American Global Empire* (Lexington: University of Kentucky Press, 1992), 150–169; and J.C.A. Stagg, *Borderlines in Borderlands: James Madison and the Spanish-American Frontier, 1776–1821* (New Haven, Conn.: Yale University Press, 2009), 169–209. William Darby to Col. Abraham Wooley, 30 November 1849. *EAP*.

Archival Lines, Historical Practice, and the Atlantic Geopolitics behind the 1842 Webster–Ashburton Treaty

Derek Kane O'Leary

American Citizen, American Historian

In the second mammoth tome of *The Life of Jared Sparks* (1893), historian Herbert Baxter Adams commended the role that Sparks had played a half-century earlier in the 1842 Webster–Ashburton Treaty. Then a Harvard professor (and later its president), Sparks was the most influential gatherer and editor of the nation's historical records before the Civil War. In 1842, the new Conservative government in Britain dispatched its envoy, Alexander Baring, or Lord Ashburton, to Washington, D.C., where he and U.S. Secretary of State Daniel Webster negotiated a constellation of issues lingering from the 1783 Treaty of Paris. Sparks had just concluded a European tour spent easing open the gates to state archives in England and France. There, he had sought material for his long-envisioned history of the American Revolution. He would never publish the project, but by extracting archival evidence that bore on Webster and Ashburton's negotiations, he awkwardly wrote himself into a belated epilogue to the Revolution.

In 1842, Webster and Ashburton hoped to quell the tensions irking British–American relations on far fringes of the Atlantic. Many in the U.S. and Britain feared that these augured war. "A train was laid in America," Lord Brougham, a leading British antislavery advocate and polymath, later shuddered in Parliament:

> . . . if any mischance had happened to peace in Europe . . . one spark of that fire which then would have broken out in the old world, borne across the ocean, would have kindled the train thus ready laid to explode, extended the flame to America, and involved the new world as well as the old in endless war.[1]

The most flammable cabin in this train seemed the disputed border between New Brunswick and Maine. The region was so poorly known and described by American and British commissioners in Article II of the 1783 Treaty of Paris that decades of surveys and transatlantic debate had failed to determine the exact international boundary. As in the "neutral ground" along the Louisiana–Texas border early in the nineteenth century explored by Jackson Pearson in his essay in this volume, the Northeast Boundary was a poorly mapped zone of modest worth, disputed between two empires and those local actors who hoped to exploit "its geopolitical murkiness." Lord Brougham may have been carried away by his own metaphor: U.S. and British geostrategic and commercial interests were largely in harmony during these years, and low-stakes woodland warfare between the two empires would have imperiled this. Yet, as the Aroostook War stoked violence across this borderland in 1838 and 1839, the resurgence of militant Anglophobia in Maine and declarations of support from numerous states seemed to threaten that the old British–American contest for North America could indeed reignite war.[2]

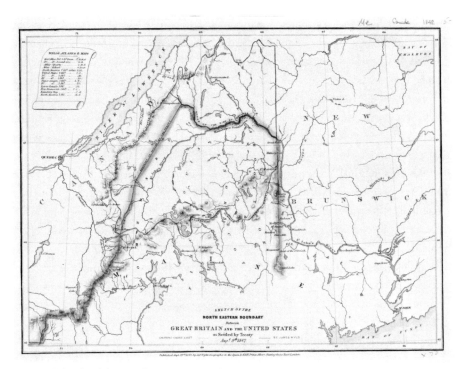

Figure 1. "Sketch of the North Eastern Boundary Between Great Britain and the United States as Settled by Treaty, August 8, 1842." By James Wyld. The southernmost line marks the boundary claimed by Great Britain; the northernmost marks the boundary claimed by the U.S., and the boundary between them is that settled by the treaty. Image provided by the Osher Map Library and Smith Center for Cartographic Education.

In 1842, on the eve of negotiations, Sparks divulged to Webster what seemed a crucial piece of evidence toward determining the boundary: a December 1782 letter by Benjamin Franklin to French Foreign Minister le Comte de Vergennes. It alluded to a copy of the well-known 1755 map of North America by John Mitchell—one of the central maps in the *Mapping a Nation* exhibition at the American Philosophical Society (2019–2020)—on which Franklin had traced in red ink the boundary between colonial New Brunswick and the U.S. as the Treaty of Paris negotiators conceived it. In 1841, Lewis Cass, the U.S. minister to France, had helped Sparks gain access to the French foreign affairs archives, where he intended to peruse eighteenth-century diplomatic correspondence for his account of the American Revolution. In his search through the archives, Sparks was assisted by Alexis de Tocqueville, whom he knew from the Frenchman's famous tour of the U.S., and fellow historian François Guizot, who admired Sparks's twelve-volume compilation *The Writings of George Washington* and had just ascended to Minister of Foreign Affairs. When Sparks encountered the Franklin letter, he urged the French archivists to locate the red-lined map among the nearly 60,000 in their archive—soon they found it, he told Webster.[3]

In revealing this to Webster, Sparks was ostensibly skittish about transgressing the line between historical research and geopolitics. To the state keepers of archives in both Britain and France, Sparks and the U.S. diplomats who advocated on his behalf had claimed that he was pursuing a strictly literary project that would illuminate American history but not bear on current affairs. In the previous decade, preeminent German historian Leopold von Ranke had begun to establish the archive as "the most important site for the production of historical knowledge." In his peregrination through Austria, Prussia, and Italy, Ranke confronted the resistance of administrators to scholarly research of documents preserved for the stake of policy-making—indeed to the very notion that historical and politically sensitive documents could be neatly separated.[4] The principle of the scholar's right to access archival materials in other nation-states remained contested, and Sparks knew that the privilege of American historians to do research abroad was at stake when he entered British and French archives. Sparks nonetheless crossed the line between historical inquiry and current affairs when he assured Webster that the Franklin letter and red-lined map established the true New Brunswick–Maine boundary according to the Treaty of Paris. However, Sparks warned, "it would seem to afford conclusive evidence" *against* the American boundary claim, placing Maine's northern border well south of the St. John River, rather than to its north, where Mainers wanted it.

Webster perceived the potential that this evidence might herd Maine to the negotiating table, moderate the state's unyielding land claims, and enable the elusive border agreement. Webster dispatched Sparks to share this inconvenient counterevidence with the Maine government in Augusta, along with the blunt message that if Maine did not accept a compromise boundary now, Britain might find and array such cartographic proof against its claim in some future arbitration. By the summer of 1842, Webster and Sparks had succeeded in urging Maine to send a delegation to Washington, D.C., where they softened their position. Webster again deployed this and a related map he had acquired in order to push the final treaty through Congress in August. When this behind-the-scenes gambit became public knowledge in Britain, it was thrashed by some in the press and inflamed parliamentary debate. Looking back at the episode a half-century later, however, Herbert Baxter Adams absolved Sparks as both an upright citizen and a disinterested scholar. "Mr. Sparks felt it his duty, as an American citizen and as a student of history, to communicate this discovery . . . even though the map was apparently adverse to our territorial claims."[5] In fact, Sparks was caught betwixt the two identities, civic and intellectual.

Historians since Adams have studied the decades of dizzying claims and counterclaims to this wooded and watery terrain that ricocheted across the Atlantic from the Treaty of Paris to the lasting compromise of Webster–Ashburton.[6] In contrast to the joint Anglo-American boundary commission to the Great Lakes stipulated by the 1814 Treaty of Ghent, evaluated by David Spanagel in "Putting Science to the Test" in this volume, the joint commission to the Northeast Boundary (1816–1822) broke down in disagreement, and the U.S. rejected the subsequent international arbitration proposal from the Dutch King William I in 1831.[7] By 1842, the boundary dispute had spurred a massive international research project. Year by year its archive accumulated, spanning from colonial documents and maps to the most sophisticated contemporary surveying techniques. American negotiators were mired in the morass of land surveys, maps, conflicting interests, and proposals that had pooled around it.

Although many in Maine and others across the U.S. rallied for war, most interested Americans were eager to cut this Gordian Knot. The Treaty in swift fashion resolved the U.S.–Canada boundary from the Northeast across the Great Lakes while deferring or skirting other clashes concerning American sovereignty and property around the Atlantic. Reconstructing the negotiations, studies of the Webster–Ashburton Treaty have hardly missed the influential cameo appearance during the negotiations of Franklin's red-lined map. Typically, they trace and evaluate Webster's use of it to manipulate Maine's governor and commissioners, query whether Lord Ashburton was privy to this ploy, and observe the fallout after the map's existence went public during the Senate's ratification.[8]

The rest of this paper pivots from the border and those diplomatic machinations to the unexamined Atlantic archival context where Sparks encountered this map. With a six-decade delay after the Treaty of Paris, Webster–Ashburton resolved the slipshod boundary set by Article II. Sparks, meanwhile, was enmeshed in another of 1783's unresolved stipulations: Article VII, which stated that the King "shall also order and cause all archives, records, deeds, and papers belonging to any of the said states, or their citizens, which in the course of the war may have fallen into the hands of his officers, to be forthwith restored and delivered to the proper states and persons to whom they belong." Sparks did not claim access to British records under this article or, it seems, find much in British archives that bore on the boundary dispute. But in its shadow he raised the question of where a nation's historical papers belonged and who should have access to them during a period when the boundaries both of these nation-states and of the inchoate discipline of history were not fully defined. In ferrying a copy of the red-lined map from the historical realm of the archive to the present of the Northeast Boundary dispute, Sparks revealed his own anxiety about what it meant to be an American historian within this context.

Walking Archival and National Lines

When Jared Sparks alighted in England for archival research in 1840, the British government lacked a policy for regulating access by foreigners to state records offices. Since the 1820s, American agents sent by different states and U.S. ministers to Britain had petitioned the British government to acquire, copy, or view manuscripts bearing on colonial American history. They met scattered success in this, but were generally fended off. Often, the materials were deemed potentially injurious to British pride or politically sensitive (to open disputes like the Northeast Boundary question).

For instance, in 1838, U.S. minister Andrew Stevenson called repeatedly on British Foreign Secretary Lord Palmerston to let Georgia's historical agent review and copy its colonial papers. These appeals languished through the summer and fall. Responding to Foreign Secretary Lord Palmerston's consternation about Stevenson's repeated request, an official in the Colonial Office reasoned that those records contained "confidential communications written in periods of great difficulty and impending danger." As a result, "there may be many things which it would be improper to publish, and the publication of which might not only be painful to individuals, but might, under existing circumstances, be prejudicial to the interests of Great Britain."[9] In other cases, such as John Romeyn Brodhead's archival mission on behalf of New York in the early 1840s, the archival gatekeepers simply denied the principle international archival access. In the State Papers Office, George William Featherstonhaugh sniffed, "I do not see the advantage of permitting foreigners to publish from our Archives, what would seem to be more properly the privilege of British men of letters."[10]

If access were even granted, it was unclear which of the three British secretaries of state (Colonial, Home, or Foreign) should authorize it, the grounds on which access could be allowed, and how foreigners could physically interact with archived materials. Once the Colonial Office resigned responsibility over the question to Palmerston and the Foreign Office, in late 1838 Stevenson finally received word, four months after his initial request, that Georgia's agent could "inspect and make extracts" from a list of documents ranging from 1735 to 1775, which was well shy of Georgia's request for copies of papers up to the Treaty of Paris. In order to sequester documents that might bear on the boundary dispute, Palmerston responded to Stevenson's requests by limiting to materials before "the commencement of the Disturbances in America."[11] This separated the safely historical, on one side, from the potentially political, on the other. If slow and uncertain, this response revealed the formulation of a British policy that acknowledged the right of foreigners to access archival material but sought to patrol the porous boundary between history and current affairs.

The New Brunswick–Maine boundary was one of the few boundaries in North America that the sprawling American empire had not obliterated. As the Aroostook War smoldered along it from 1838 into 1839, British disquiet that Americans might exhume evidence in favor of Maine's claims only hardened. In late 1839, Stevenson wrote again to the Foreign Office, this time on behalf of the young Massachusetts theologian and historian, George Ellis, who was researching colonial American history. "[A]greeably to the 7th Article of the Treaty of 1783," Stevenson wrote to Palmerston, the American government requested "certain Public Records, of the Councils of Massachusetts, from the year 1765–1775, inclusive."[12] The request halted on the eve of the American Revolution, where the Foreign Office had placed the documentary firewall. Yet, Massachusetts's claim for the original documents, mediated through the State Department in accordance with the Treaty of Paris, suggested an emergent American belief that their scholarly access to British archives was justified by their belonging to a nation-state. If the U.S. had already proven itself "treaty-worthy," such claims to foreign archives by Americans raised the ongoing question of what such treaties made Americans worthy of.[13]

Amid these repeated requests, a British administrative procedure for managing American access to state papers coalesced. Palmerston approved Ellis's request to survey catalogues of relevant materials in the State Paper Office, where Ellis was allowed to note those he wished copied. Then, these selections were vetted by Palmerston at the Foreign Office, who either approved or denied copies on a manuscript by manuscript basis.[14] With the Boundary dispute at a tipping point, however, Palmerston erred toward caution and distrust. For instance, some of the colonial Council records sought by Massachusetts were uncovered in three volumes in the Board of Trade archive in early 1840. They were shuttled to the Foreign Office for Palmerston to determine whether Ellis could copy them. Palmerston stalled and, despite approval of officials in the Home Department and State Papers Office, ultimately denied the Americans' request.[15] Stevenson soon received word that contrary to the British government's original response, these records were "part of a Series of Historical Papers of considerable interest commencing as far back as the year 1736; which were forwarded from time to time by the Governor of Massachusetts for the Archives of the British government; and it is conceived that these Volumes, therefore, ought not to be separated from the series to which they belong."[16] Notoriously critical of the U.S., Palmerston offered this dubious defense of maintaining the collection's integrity rather than abiding by the terms of the Treaty of Paris. Waffling on whether to grant access to claims made in the name of historical inquiry and the Treaty of 1783 or to insulate evidence that might vitiate British claims in the Boundary dispute, Palmerston showed that the British administration remained unsure about the principle of international archival access.

Sensing this, Sparks in the autumn of 1840 tried to circumvent Palmerston's wary eye. He initially won the approval of Lord Phillips in the Home Department to peruse five volumes of pre-revolutionary records. This put Palmerston markedly ill at ease when he found out. He soon asserted his new policy to approve or deny all requests to view and make transcriptions of state papers on a document by document basis.[17] Meanwhile, other papers transferred to the State Papers Office, which was then consolidating eighteenth-century colonial papers, were marked as simply off-limits to foreigners.[18] In theory, the Foreign Office recognized the Americans' right to claim or copy these papers, whether due to the 1783 treaty or an ideal of liberal exchange among nation-states. However, in practice, these American requests were scrutinized, their chronological and thematic scope restrained, and the process of transcription closely censored.

Against such suspicions and amid mounting British–American geopolitical anxiety, Sparks introduced a stronger justification for archival access into these conversations. In the autumn of 1841, the former Massachusetts governor and fellow New England man of letters Edward Everett was confirmed as the U.S. minister to Britain. He was championed by his old friend, Secretary of State Webster, and just barely overcame Southern senators' opposition to his antislavery reputation.[19] Both Sparks and Everett were avid scholars of their nation's history and believed in an open Atlantic circulation of historical documents. "I am persuaded that there is nothing in [the records] of a historical nature," Sparks leveled against the objections of the British Foreign Office, "that can be deemed in the least degree objectionable." Rather, he ventured, these documents were "of such a character as to set the motives of conduct of the great actors in public events of that period in a much more favorable light than could possibly be done without the use of them."[20] Though compiling records of the pivotal event in his nation's history, he proposed that his "sincere aim at truth through whatever channel it may be found" was of equal importance to both the U.S. and Britain. In Paris during the winter of 1841, Sparks similarly assured Francois Guizot of the strictly historical quality of his research into France's diplomatic correspondence concerning the American Revolution. De Tocqueville interpreted between Sparks and the chief archivist, French historian Francois Mignet, who charmed Sparks with his "liberal view" of the project.[21]

Once in residence, Everett mingled eagerly with the literati and political elite of London, among whom he echoed Sparks's justification. When not busy allaying Southerners' concerns by protesting the search of American ships by British antislaving patrols, Everett advocated for American access to British archives. Access to state records, he argued in letter after letter to the new Foreign Secretary, Lord Aberdeen, represented a universal value that transcended the narrow interests of any nation. A statesman's decision to open his nation's archives to foreigners demonstrated his liberality, the highest virtue in Everett's eyes. Sparks and Everett argued, moreover, that such policy could only do justice to British history and reflect its current enlightened policy. This became the strongest and most influential articulation of Americans'—and, by extension, all foreigners'—right to see and copy historical documents in foreign archives. Whereas Stevenson had requested a privilege, Everett and Sparks implied that Americans had a right of access to archival materials across sovereign lines according to the principle of liberal intellectual exchange among nation-states. Everett was more successful than any previous American spokesman in making this case. During his tenure, however, Aberdeen struggled to convince Everett of the importance of another cause of universal concern that depended on British–American cooperation across their respective national lines: the eradication of the Atlantic slave trade.

Even when Sparks viewed and received copies of archival papers on the terms set by Palmerston, the British archival gatekeepers remained anxious. And rightfully so. To the Foreign Office in 1841, the presence of Sparks in the archive still appeared like "fishing among the British Records for Documents which may by some ingenious perversion be converted by the Americans into grounds for the support of their pretensions."[22] Over the preceding decade, the New York Historical Society and Massachusetts Historical Society had indeed been scoured for documents that might bolster U.S. claims in the Northeast Boundary dispute. Although such private learned institutions were often sustained by transnational intellectual networks and espoused the disinterested pursuit of knowledge, they also supported national geopolitical interests. The interest of Sparks and Everett in the British state archives was in part an extension of their own research in American repositories.[23]

Everett hoped for definitive proof of the U.S. claim in the British records, a task made much easier under the new government of Prime Minister Sir Robert Peel, who was eager to move beyond Palmerston's contentious policies and improve relations with the U.S.[24] (Turning to the Pacific Northwest land dispute with Britain in the mid-1840s, Everett would also mobilize the American representatives in Madrid and Paris—Washington Irving and Lorenzo Draper—to seek precedents for American claims lodged in those national archives.[25]) During his archival research in France and England, Sparks had likewise imagined that some vital proof of the true boundary line lay abandoned, somewhere, among the papers. Whether related to the Northeast Boundary dispute or not, Sparks likely abused his access to colonial volumes in the State Papers Office. After his departure for the U.S. in the spring of 1841, Featherstonhaugh, furious, wrote to Palmerston that, "a most important Document of considerable bulk presenting of course proportionate difficulties against a furtive transcription of it, has been cut out of the Book" from which Sparks had requested transcriptions. "Mr. Sparks," Featherstonhaugh accused, "meanwhile, has betaken himself with his spoils, across the Atlantic."[26]

Sparks certainly kept an eye peeled in the British archives for materials related to the Northeast Boundary dispute, but it was in France in early 1841 that he encountered what he first perceived as a smoking gun: Franklin's red-lined map. However, only as news about Lord Ashburton's commission to negotiate with Webster became known in 1843 did Sparks contact Webster with this finding and his interpretation of it. In doing so, he breached the line that he and Everett had worked to delineate between the historical record for disinterested international scholars, on one side, and the records for self-interested national policy-makers, on the other.

Making and Unmaking Cartographic Meaning

From the revelation by Sparks of the red-lined map in 1842 to the transatlantic dispute that emerged over the tactical use of it by Webster in 1843, Sparks and others manipulated the meaning of Franklin's red-lined map. In doing so, Sparks in particular waded through the uncertainty of international archival research and his own cognitive dissonance around it. He had gained access to British and French archives by insisting that his project was a historical and literary undertaking: their archives would enable him to write a history that did more justice to their respective policies and statesmen during the Revolution than was typically done, and their gesture of archival openness would attest to their liberal support of this literary project. In itself, the claim that a nation-state's construction of its distinctive historical narrative could harmonize with the cosmopolitan ideal of a disinterested exchange of manuscripts was fraught. It became more so when Sparks used this very access to plumb the British archives for evidence in support of America's territorial claims, however unsuccessfully, and then ferried copies of sensitive material from the French archives to the U.S. Secretary of State.

Upon learning of the map's alleged existence in early 1841, Sparks was quick to convince himself of its stakes: "It would be an extremely important document at this time, as it would show in the most positive manner the meaning of the commissioners, and put to rest the dispute between England and the United States respecting the northeastern boundary."[27] Other than the red line along the border, there was no indication on the map subsequently furnished by the French archivists that it pertained to Franklin's letter. Sparks nonetheless assumed that it did and then copied that line onto a blank map. The following year, the copied map in hand, Sparks convinced Webster of the map's authenticity and conclusiveness in determining the boundary. Surveying the current stalemate, Sparks observed to Webster that British "appeals to history and ancient records leave us, at last, in a wilderness of conjecture." By contrast, Sparks insisted that Franklin's map cut through this wilderness. To Webster, he argued, "it would be difficult to explain the circumstances of its agreeing so perfectly with his description, and of its being preserved in the place where it would naturally be deposited by Count de Vergennes."[28] The American historian saw the map that he wished to see.

Within the vast, international archival project that the Northeast Boundary dispute had become by that point, this stray document became a double-edged sword— or rather, paper that could cut on both edges. Back in Massachusetts in the spring of 1842, Sparks met with Webster. The secretary used the president's secret-service fund to send Sparks on his special mission to Augusta with the red-lined map, as well as a corroborating map from the Prussian General Friedrich von Steuben, which Webster had recently obtained.[29] Sparks aimed to impress upon Maine's Governor John Fairfield the urgency of sending commissioners to endorse the negotiations. According to Sparks, upon viewing the maps Fairfield "saw at once their bearing, and seemed to view them as worthy of deep consideration."[30] The uncovering and use of these maps reflected another example of Austin Stewart's observation in his essay on Cherokee–U.S. diplomacy in this volume that surveying and mapping can be "ambivalent tools of power," available for use toward different ends. When the Senate debated the treaty later that summer, Webster again slipped Sparks's own letter, the maps, and the copied 1782 Franklin letter into the proceedings. The Senate Foreign Affairs Committee received these materials, and its chairman, Virginia Senator William Rives, presented them in session and expounded on their risky implications, which helped usher the treaty toward ratification. Sparks's letter to Webster and the diplomatic use Webster had made of the red-lined map soon circulated in the press, becoming public knowledge in both the U.S. and Britain.

In contrast to Spark's initial reading of it, for both Maine's commissioners and the Senate the significance of the red-lined map shifted from whether or not these documents were authentic and definitive to how they would be perceived by an international audience. The map lost, in this sense, some of the historical value that Sparks coated it with. Rives and most Americans were content with the outcome of negotiations and relieved that these maps had not undermined American claims. Responding to their revelation in the senate, South Carolina Senator John Calhoun concluded that no resolution could win out that derived strictly from an interpretation of the 1783 Treaty of Paris or any cartographic or documentary evidence meant to sustain it. Only a compromise, or "conventional," decision could resolve the issue for good. Calhoun doubted that this new evidence proved anything.

However, to reject the treaty, he reasoned, would likely lead to international arbitration, in which Sparks's findings and "farther research into the public archives of Europe might bring to light some embarrassing (even though apocryphal) document, to throw a new shade of plausible doubt on the clearness of our title."[31] Speaking to the Senate, Calhoun wished to have his cake and eat it too, settling the dispute by compromise while maintaining the validity of the American claim. He also wanted to save a slice for Sparks, "the learned and distinguished gentleman," who came across the document "while pursuing his laborious and intelligent researches connected with the history of our own country." Sparks, as Calhoun put it, had aided his country in the negotiations and undertaken his historical research without transgressing a line between the two; the archival documents uncovered by Sparks, it seemed, could have one meaning in the diplomatic realm and another in his "laborious and intelligent researches." Unlike the claims made by Sparks and Everett in Britain, Calhoun did not see Sparks's service to his country's geopolitical interests and his intellectual inquiry as mutual exclusive acts.

Despite this reasoning, when the use of the red-lined map went public, the authority of the treaty, the character of American diplomacy, and the principle of Americans' access to British archives were all cast in doubt for British critics. In addition to the vociferous critiques in the British press, George William Featherstonhaugh published a major account of the boundary dispute in 1843. Featherstonhaugh, who was the U.S. government's first geologist in the 1830s prior to returning to administrative work in London, had also assisted in Ashburton's negotiations. Upon learning of the Senate's debate on the treaty, he assured readers that the red-lined map, although hard to authenticate, corresponded exactly with the findings of Britain's most recent survey of the boundary in 1840 and to other "ancient maps" of the boundary, all of which American negotiators had dismissed as evidence. On these grounds, he reached the opposite conclusion to Rives and Calhoun about the map and indicted Webster's furtive use of it. In his published account of the Webster–Ashburton Treaty, he argued:

> There being no room, therefore, to doubt its authenticity, we are unavoidably brought to a conviction that whilst the highest functionaries of the American Government were dealing with lord Ashburton with a seeming integrity, they were, in fact, deceiving him; and that whilst they were pledging the faith of their Government for a perfect conviction of the justice of their claim to the territory which was in dispute, they had the highest evidence in their possession which the nature of the case admitted of, that the United States never had the slightest shadow of right to any part of the territory . . ..[32]

This and other denunciations of American diplomacy and integrity, including a debate roused in Parliament by Lord Palmerston, reverberated back across the Atlantic.

To counter these arguments, the Americans who had been most engaged in the boundary dispute pivoted, now denying that the red-lined map held "the highest evidence." Addressing an enthusiastic crowd gathered in New York University's chapel that spring, Albert Gallatin similarly hoped to deactivate "an incident of so little real importance as the discovery of a certain Map."[33] Through minute analysis of extant maps of the boundary, Gallatin asserted that Franklin's alleged production of the red-lined map was implausible and that Maine's original claim to far more territory than the compromise allotted was in fact just. This assertion reflected Gallatin's half-century commitment to enabling and justifying the continental expansion of the American republic, which George Gallwey analyzes in his essay, "Albert Gallatin, Mapping Old and New Empires in the Early United States" in this volume. Ultimately, however, Gallatin put aside his concern with proving "an abstract right" to the disputed zone, concluding that peace was more important than a boundary "settled according to strict justice"—that is, based on historical evidence.[34]

Following Gallatin's speech, the wildly popular Webster at once diminished the significance of the red-lined map and mocked the British objections to his own use of it. "Every office in Washington was ransacked" for evidence in the boundary question, he explained, and the map was just one of those innumerable documents considered during negotiations. "I must confess," he announced to the crowd's laughter, "that I did not think it a very urgent duty on my part to go to Lord Ashburton and tell him that I had found a bit of doubtful evidence in Paris, out of which he perhaps might make something to the prejudice of our claims, and from which he could set up higher claims for himself, or obscure the whole matter still further!"[35] Following Rives and Calhoun, Webster and others sought to depict the map's meaning as a political and diplomatic tool, rather than as a document that bore authentic information. In this way, they detached the authority of their geopolitical settlement from the authority of historical documents: both the copious materials pertaining to the boundary dispute and those summoned by Sparks from the French archives. Whereas Americans had spent decades attempting to use historical evidence to authenticate their geopolitical claim, once the treaty was ratified, they negated the relevance of historical records in determining the boundary.

In tandem, Sparks also hoped to disentangle the historical archive and himself from transatlantic politics. Following the negotiations, he remained particularly anxious about Americans' access to foreign archives and his own international reputation as a historian.[36] In early 1843, Sparks wrote to U.S. minister Everett in London for help repairing his reputation with Lord Aberdeen. Sparks fretted about the chilly reception in London of fellow historian James Savage, the Massachusetts Historical Society president then scouring England for genealogical records linked to New England families. The wariness that Savage had encountered at British archives troubled Sparks, "not because there is the least foundation for it, but because a suspicion of this kind cannot easily be removed."[37] Sparks was "extremely desirous to remove an impression so injurious to my motives and character," but also to salvage Americans' relationship with British records offices. To dispel this, he insisted to Everett—who surely knew otherwise—that during his own historical research in British offices he never intentionally or inadvertently wandered into the boundary dispute.

Meanwhile, Sparks also reframed the red-lined map. Whereas just a year previously he had infused it with meaning when he presented it to Webster, in early 1843 he tried to dismantle its historical authenticity and relevance for the boundary question. To Everett, he wrote, "leave the map to stand on its only foundation, that of conjectural authenticity, and their clamors [in British press] are without point. As to the map itself, it contains no memorandum, writing, or mark of any sort, from which it can be inferred that it was ever in the hands of Franklin." None of these red flags shook his confidence a year prior. Sparks soon published a forceful essay in the *North American Review*, through which he hoped to reclaim the narrative of the boundary negotiations and his own part in it. "The answer is most conclusively in the negative," he asserted there, that negotiators could have reached any agreement about what the original treaty meant based on historical evidence.[38] On "the unattractive controversy about maps," he concluded that no definitive answer about the red-lined map's authenticity was possible. But he defended Webster's nondisclosure of it, for to have shared the maps with Lord Ashburton during negotiations "might have done infinite mischief," perhaps "stirring up and embroiling all the old difficulties, with a worse prospect than ever for the future." Thus, Sparks the historian joined American politicians in diluting the map of its historical meaning. In doing so, he also occluded his own role in instrumentalizing it toward geopolitical ends.

Across the Atlantic, despite Palmerston's protests against "the Ashburton surrender" in the popular press and Parliament, many were inclined to agree with Sparks's position and mollify British–American relations.[39] Lord Brougham discredited the tenuous link between Franklin's letter and the map, believing that, "it is by no means upon evidence as that, so doubtful, and unexplained, and surrounded with so many suspicions" that nations could place their negotiations.[40] Lord Thomas Babington Macaulay, who would author the five-volume *History of England* (1848), added that conflict with the U.S. "would unite with all the horrors of foreign war many of the peculiar enormities of civil conflict."[41] He suggested that the British and Americans were bound by a kinship that transcended geopolitical interests. On both sides of the British–American Atlantic, politicians were simply eager to move beyond this and the other issues that most rankled their deepening commercial, strategic, and cultural alliance.

Beyond the Northeast and, soon Northwest, boundary questions, Sparks also looked forward to closer intellectual ties between the U.S. and Britain, including the movement of American researchers through British archives such as George Bancroft, who would author the major history of the Revolution that Sparks never produced. In Europe, Sparks had pushed the principle that archival access across sovereign boundaries was a laudable, enlightened, and mutually beneficial policy. To the extent that the physical boundary between the U.S. and British Canada remained undefined, so did the lines imagined between historical and political documents, foreign researchers and sovereign interests. The historicization and de-historicization of the red-lined map by Sparks showed the confusion around these questions. He nonetheless nudged forward the principle and practice of historical research across borders. As the U.S.–Canada border was established, American access to British records became less fraught. A month after Bancroft settled into Everett's former post as the U.S. minister in London in 1846, he received word from Lord Palmerston—once again the Secretary of State for Foreign Affairs—that he could review all American papers in the State Papers Office up to the Treaty of Paris.[42]

Coda: Webster–Ashburton's Many Atlantic Lines

In terms not of access to archival materials or the sovereignty over arable land, timber, and access to waterways, the Webster–Ashburton Treaty addressed another question of the lines separating British and American interests in the Atlantic world that lingered from the unresolved articles of the Treaty of Paris. Studies of the treaty focus overwhelmingly on the Northeast Boundary. But in terms of human welfare and suffering, the most consequential outcome related to American vessels linked with the Atlantic slave trade and British naval opposition to it; indeed, many American and British observers perceived this as the crucial question addressed by Webster and Ashburton. The same Treaty of Paris article that called for the return of American archives and other papers also stipulated the withdrawal of British forces without "carrying away any Negroes or other property of the American inhabitants." Six decades later, the Webster–Ashburton Treaty again addressed the loss of American property in enslaved people, including the case of the *Creole*, whose captives had overtaken the ship and been liberated in the British Bahamas in 1841. For years, prominent Americans such as Edward Everett in Britain and Lewis Cass in France had stridently objected to Britain's search of ships flying the American flag and suspected of slaving while undermining Britain's effort to lead an international coalition against it.

Although the Webster–Ashburton treaty clearly delineated the Maine–New Brunswick border, it so vaguely defined the new antislave trade policy that the Tyler administration could interpret it in direct contrast to how Sir Robert Peel's ministry read the document. In his celebratory 1842 address to Congress, President Tyler made clear that American commercial freedom from British naval interference was the core of the treaty and a victory for American sovereignty at sea: "The immediate effect of the treaty upon ourselves will be felt in the security afforded to mercantile enterprise, which, no longer apprehensive of interruption, adventures its speculations in the most distant seas, and, freighted with the diversified productions of every land, returns to bless our own. There is nothing in the treaty which in the slightest degree compromises the honor or dignity of either nation."[43]

Northerners, Sparks included, shared this suspicion of British power in the Atlantic and praised the treaty for resisting it. Henry Wheaton, the leading antebellum scholar of international law, penned vehement support of Webster–Ashburton's resistance to the right of search in his *History of the Law of Nations in Europe and America* (1845).[44] Writing to Wheaton in March 1843, Sparks asked for some legal insight for a follow-up article to his discussion of the Northeast Boundary negotiation in the *North American Review*, in which he would critique the British policy of searching American vessels suspected of slaving. Questioning the motives behind the Quintuple Treaty of 1841, in which Russia, Austria, and Prussia agreed to cooperate with Britain's policy, Sparks sneered that, "since the days of the Crusades, no nation has been known to measure its policy by a refined philanthropy at the expense of its interests."[45] Until the Civil War, the treaty and such responses enabled a derisory American antislaving squadron in West African waters, the hamstringing of international cooperation to halt the trade, and mounting American involvement in it prior to the Civil War.

In the Webster–Ashburton Treaty, these many lingering lines intersected: geographical, archival, proprietary—as well as Americans' desires to demarcate, traverse, or reaffirm them. Whereas the U.S.–Canada line would be settled by the end of that decade and the clash over British searches of American ships by the Civil War, the archival line between professional and national identities that Sparks struggled to navigate would remain undefined.

Notes

Dr. O'Leary received his Ph.D. in the History Department at UC Berkeley in 2020. He is a Postdoctoral Teaching Fellow in the History Department at the University of South Carolina, as of the 2021–2022 academic year. He is working on a book project about the Atlantic context in which nineteenth-century U.S. archives and historical narratives were built.

1. "Lord Brougham's speech upon the Ashburton treaty: delivered in the House of Lords on Friday, 7th April, 1843" (London: J. Ridgway, 1843), 10.

2. Howard Jones, "Anglophobia and the Aroostook War," *The New England Quarterly*, vol. 48, no. 4 (December, 1975), 527–529.

3. Jared Sparks to Daniel Webster, 15 February 1842, MS 147G, Jared Sparks Papers, Houghton Library, Harvard University.

4. Kasper Risbjerg Eskildsen, "Leopold Ranke's Archival Turn: Location and Evidence in Modern Historiography," *Modern Intellectual History*, vol. 5, no. 3 (2008): 425–453.

5. Herbert Baxter Adams, *The Life and Writings of Jared Sparks*, vol. II (Boston: Houghton, Mifflin and Company, 1893), 394.

6. The best recent analysis is provided by John P.D. Dunbabin, "'Red Lines on Maps' Revisited: The Role of Maps in Negotiating and Defending the 1842 Webster–Ashburton Treaty," *Imago Mundi*, vol. 63, no. 1 (2011): 39–61.

7. Richard W. Hale, Jr., "The Forgotten Maine Boundary Commission," in *Proceedings of the Massachusetts Historical Society*, ed. Marjorie F. Gutheim (Boston: Massachusetts Historical Society, 1959), 147–155.

8. Book-length treatments of the Webster–Ashburton Treaty include Howard Jones, *To the Webster–Ashburton Treaty: A Study in Anglo-American Relations, 1783–1843* (Chapel Hill: University of North Carolina Press, 1977) and Francis M. Carroll, *A Good and Wise Measure: The Search for the Canadian–American Boundary, 1783–1842* (Toronto: University Press of Toronto, 2001).

9. Lord Glendy to Lord Palmerston, 3 September 1838, FO83 222, State Papers Office records, Kew, United Kingdom.

10. Featherstonhaugh to Backhouse, 27 March 1841, FO83 222. I discuss Brodhead's experience at much more length in "New Netherlands, Archival Deficiency, and Contesting New York History in the Antebellum U.S." *Dutch Crossing*, vol. 43, no. 3 (2019): 252–269.

11. Lord Palmerston to Lord Glendy, 10 September 1838, FO83 222.

12. Andrew Stevenson to Lord Palmerston, 17 December 1839, FO83 222. When prompted by the Foreign Office to look into the matter, the State Papers Office claimed not to find the sought records, noting that it had only correspondence between the

British Secretaries of State and governors of Massachusetts for those years, with some council documents interspersed. Henry Hobhouse to John Backhouse, 26 December 1839, FO83 222.

13. The term refers to Eliga Gould's influential book *Among the Powers of the Earth: The American Revolution and the Making of a New World Empire* (Cambridge, Mass.: Harvard University Press, 2012).

14. Stevenson to J. Backhouse, 28 March 1839, FO83 222.

15. Lord Palmerston to Andrew Stevenson, 7 March 1840, and Andrew Stevenson to Lord Palmerston, 11 April 1840, FO83 222.

16. Lord Palmerston to Andrew Stevenson, 26 February 1841, FO83 222.

17. Hobhouse to Backhouse, 30 November 1840, and Backhouse to Hobhouse, 20 March 1841, FO83 222.

18. Backhouse to Hobhouse, 19 November 1840, FO83 222. Colonial papers from both North America and the Caribbean were being transferred from the Board of Trade archives to the State Papers Office in the early 1840s, under the Foreign Office's direction. Lord Aberdeen to Hobhouse, 30 March 1842, FO83 223.

19. John O. Geiger, "A Scholar Meets John Bull: Edward Everett as United States Minister to England, 1841–1845," *The New England Quarterly*, vol. 49, no. 4 (December, 1976): 577–595.

20. Jared Sparks to Backhouse, 5 September 1840, FO83 222.

21. Jared Sparks Journal, 18 December 1840, MS 141J, Jared Sparks Papers.

22. W. Phillips to Backhouse, 15 July 1841, FO83 222.

23. As late as the summer of 1842, he insisted to Webster that he believed cartographic proof of the U.S.'s most ambitious claims lay in the British archives. Edward Everett to Daniel Webster, 16 June 1842, Edward Everett Papers, Massachusetts Historical Society (MHS).

24. John O. Geiger, "A Scholar Meets John Bull: Edward Everett as United States Minister to England, 1841–1845," *The New England Quarterly*, vol. 49, no. 4 (December, 1976): 577–595; George L. Bernstein, "Special Relationship and Appeasement: Liberal Policy Towards America in the Age of Palmerston," *The Historical Journal*, vol. 41, no. 3 (1998): 725–750.

25. Writing to Irving that fall, he stressed, "If by a judicious application in the proper quarter at Madrid, we could procure a copy of all the documents brought forward by Spain in 1790 in her controversy with England about Nootka, it might very materially aid us as now representing the rights of Spain in that quarter. You will perceive the great delicacy of the investigation and if you think it prudent to undertake it, you will know how to put it in the most promising train. The sooner it is commenced the better. We have not an hour to lose." Edward Everett to Washington Irving, 31 November 1843, Edward Everett Papers, MHS.

26. Featherstonhaugh to Lord Palmerston, 6 April 1841, FO83 222.

27. Adams, *Life of Jared Sparks*, vol. II, 392.

28. Jared Sparks to Daniel Webster, 15 February 1842, reprinted in Adams, *Life of Jared Sparks*, 355–359.

29. Howard Jones and Donald A. Rakestraw, *Prologue to Manifest Destiny: Anglo-American Relations the 1840s* (Wilmington, Del.: SR Books:, 1997), 114–115.

30. Dunbabin, "'Red Lines on Maps,'" 45.

31. "Speech of Mr. Calhoun, of South Carolina, in Senate, August, 1842, on the Treaty of Washington," 3 (1842), accessed at https://catalog.hathitrust.org/Record/100267154.

32. George William Featherstonhaugh, *Observations upon the Treaty of Washington, signed August 9, 1842 with the treaty annexed, together with a map, to illustrate the boundary line as established by the treaty between Her Majesty's colonies of New Brunswick and Canada and the United States of America* (London, 1843), 100–103.

33. Albert Gallatin, *A Memoir of the North-Eastern Boundary* (New York: NYHS, 1843), 5. Gallatin had been open to a compromise agreement as early as the 1831 international arbitration by William I of the Netherlands. John P.D. Dunbabin, "The 1831 Dutch Arbitration of the Canadian–American Boundary Dispute: Another View," *The New England Quarterly*, vol. 75, no. 4 (December, 2002): 622–646.

34. Gallatin, *Memoir*, 52.

35. Gallatin, *Memoir*, 67.

36. In the 1850s, his professional reputation would take a considerable hit when Lord Mahon, a leading British historian, and Sparks engaged in a heated, publicized dispute in the press about Sparks's bowdlerizing of George Washington's correspondence in the 12-volume *Writings of George Washington* (1834–1837).

37. Jared Sparks to Edward Everett, 30 January 1843, reprinted in Adams, *Life of Jared Sparks*, 405–406.

38. Jared Sparks, *The Treaty of Washington* (Boston, 1843), published in *The North American Review* vol. LVI, 460–468.

39. Evelyn Ashley, ed., *The Life and Correspondence of Henry John Temple, Viscount Palmerston* (London, 1879), 423.

40. Henry Brougham, "Lord Brougham's speech upon the Ashburton treaty: delivered in the House of Lords on Friday, 7th April, 1843" (London: J. Ridgway, 1843), 44. British attempts to locate the original red-lined map that Sparks had copied turned up only D'Anville maps with red lines diverging significantly from that described by Sparks, only heightening doubt that Franklin's map existed or could furnish proof of anything (Dunbabin, 55).

41. Thomas Babington Macaulay, *Miscellanies*, vol. I (Boston: Houghton, Mifflin and Company, 1900), 348.

42. Lord Palmerston to George Bancroft, 24 December 1846, Box 16, George Bancroft Papers, Ms. N-1795, MHS.

43. For more context of U.S. resistance to international antislave trade cooperation, see Don E. Fehrenbacher, *The Slaveholding Republic: An Account of the United States Government's Relations to Slavery* (Oxford, United Kingdom: Oxford University Press, 2002), 157–178.

44. Henry Wheaton, *History of the Law of Nations in Europe and America: From the Earliest Times to the Treaty of Washington, 1842* (New York, 1845), 585–699.

45. Jared Sparks to Henry Wheaton, 29 March 1843, reprinted in Adams, *Life of Jared Sparks*, vol. II, 415.

Putting Science to the Test

Initiating the World's Longest
Unfortified Boundary

David I. Spanagel

A SPIRIT OF OPTIMISM permeated early nineteenth-century appeals to scientific expertise in many fields. Perhaps this impulse derived from the Enlightenment dream of science's promise to provide rational solutions to all categories of material, social, and political difficulty. The problem of unstable or indefensible territorial boundaries loomed as one promising domain for scientific intervention. North America provided an early test; three different wars had erupted across the boundary that defined the limits of Britain's colonial possessions there between 1754 and 1814. At the end of that third war, British and American negotiators of the Treaty of Ghent in 1814 decided to invest their trust in a novel approach premised on jointly redefining that boundary in a manner that might somehow put a stop to the repeated hostilities. Alongside the military men from each country, each side would also appoint savants who were acquainted with astronomy, geology, and mineralogy. Together, these men would negotiate hydrography (the study of seas, lakes, and rivers and in particular the measurement of water movement). This paper examines scientific contributions to that Joint Boundary Commission charged under the Sixth and Seventh Articles of the Treaty of Ghent (to survey and delineate an international boundary throughout the Great Lakes). This Commission employed American soldier-mineralogist Major Joseph Delafield, British surveyor-astronomer David Thompson, and British surgeon-geologist Dr. John Jeremiah Bigsby, whose collaborations hinted at science's potential to transform the diplomatic challenge of establishing a peaceful, stable frontier between nations.[1]

Maps: Tools that Distort Nature

Early twenty-first-century scholars understand the complexity of territorial boundary disputes as being just the external manifestations of a tangled series of interrelated cultural, economic, historical, political, ideological, and environmental tensions.[2] Two centuries ago, boundary problems were considered to be simpler in nature, if complicated in practice. Four competing technical traditions vied to inform and address the security needs of modern nation-states. In order of historical longevity and perceived relevance at the time, they were: (1) the art of *politics* (an artful blending of ancient wisdom with modern expressions of diplomacy, commerce, morality, and social criticism); (2) theory of *natural law* (and its implications for jurisprudence in international law); (3) navigational and surveying applications of the *exact sciences* (astronomy, geometry, and geodesy); and (4) geographical *earth science* investigations (geology, topography, and hydrography).[3] By the dawn of the nineteenth century, all four of these increasingly disciplined modes of human knowledge emerged as potential ways to augment or secure national power in a global arena.

Among the domains of natural science expertise, the exact sciences initially seemed more salient as Great Britain and the United States sought new ways to settle their differences more amicably after the War of 1812. Land surveyors, armed with rudimentary instruments based on astronomical means of determining precise terrestrial locations, inscribed and demarcated the abstract (otherwise invisible) Cartesian lines of latitude and longitude upon the uneven and poorly mapped surfaces of the interior of the North American continent.[4] These efforts would be essential for expansion of white settlement across the Great Lakes region and the exercise of sovereign control over the prairie lands that stretched beyond. Given the insistence and frequency with which state-sponsored violence had erupted in the Great Lakes, one wonders just how much the Treaty of Ghent negotiators expected of its Boundary Commissioners.[5]

The proposed demilitarization of an unprecedentedly extensive international boundary between quarrelsome Canadians and Americans was a very tall order. Initially, Britain's representatives were instructed to be very forceful, demanding, for example, the establishment of a buffer state for Great Lakes Native American peoples to be carved out of parts of the state of Ohio and the Michigan Territory. News of battlefield victories for each side took months to cross the ocean, however, so the diplomats finally settled on a curious solution to their lag-time predicament. Though the Americans who launched the War of 1812 had cherished conquest of additional Canadian territory, worsening economic conditions due to suppressed trade, not to mention damaging British military incursions into the nation's capital itself, induced President Madison and his embattled administration to signal to the American treaty negotiators that an end to fighting could be negotiated on the basis of restoring a territorial *status quo ante bellum*. In the absence of a string of military victories, Americans were prepared instead to entrust the terms of a lasting peace, and any subsequent alterations of the previous boundaries, on a collaborative process of diplomacy informed by the natural sciences. Intriguingly, 1814's Treaty of Ghent articles authorized a series of joint international boundary commissions to be formed over the coming decade to examine and redefine each portion of the boundary from the shore of the Atlantic Ocean to the Lake of Woods, deep in the heart of the continent.

Since maps had helped contribute to the problem of North American boundary confusion, new improved maps were considered essential to its solution. We should recall just how crudely eighteenth-century maps had represented the significant natural features of the North American continent. Negotiators meeting half a world away (in Paris, to end both the Seven Years War in 1763 and the American Revolution in 1783) were forced to rely upon diagrams that contained barely any accurate information with respect to the locations of most of the landmarks that the appointed diplomats even had names to designate. The comparative challenges of administering 1783 Treaty of Paris language west of the Great Lakes proved ultimately to be physically impossible. Negotiators in Paris relied upon John Mitchell's 1755 map (see Figure 1), which, unfortunately, obscured the relative location of the headwaters of the Mississippi River beneath an inset of the Hudson's Bay region of northern Canada. Their invalid assumptions about the northerly reach of that river were doubtless rooted in geographical errors perpetuated by maps that derived from French cartographer Guillaume de L'Isle's 1722 map (see Figure 2). Thus, the late-eighteenth-century diplomats supposed that a line running due west from the northwestern corner of the Lake of the Woods would hit the Mississippi River, so that was how they described the United States' northwesternmost point in the Treaty of Paris.

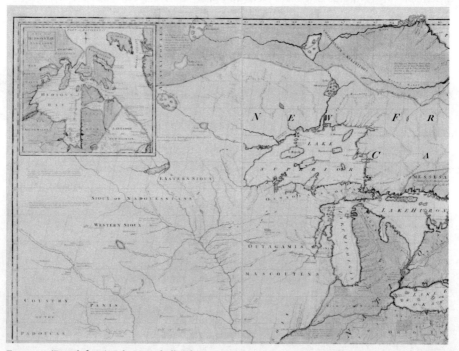

Figure 1. (Detail from) John Mitchell, Thomas Kitchin, and Andrew Millar. *A map of the British and French dominions in North America, with the roads, distances, limits, and extent of the settlements, humbly inscribed to the Right Honourable the Earl of Halifax, and the other Right Honourable the Lords Commissioners for Trade & Plantations.* [London: Millar, 1755] Map. https://www.loc.gov/item/74693173/

White explorers would not clearly identify the fabled source of the headwaters of this great interior waterway until native tribesmen finally escorted Henry Schoolcraft to the place that he dubbed Lake Itasca (a cleverly abbreviated truncation of the Latin for true head: *veritas caput*) in 1832.[6] Decades before that long-awaited "discovery," however, rumors that the Mississippi River began well to the south of the supposed latitude referent had induced diplomats to recommend the matter of the western extension of the Canadian–U.S. boundary to a process of international arbitration. This proposal was included in the Jay Treaty of 1794.

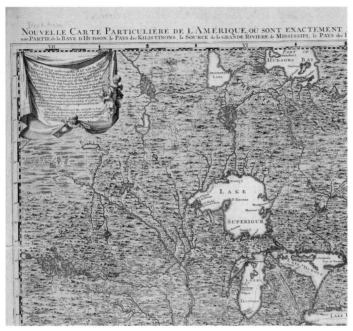

Figure 2. Henry Popple's appropriation of Guillaume de L'Isle's 1722 map *Nouvelle carte particulière de l'Amérique où sont exactement marquées une partie de la baye d'Hudson le pays des Kilostinons, la source de la grande riviere de Mississipi, le pays des Illinois &c.* Reproduced in Guillaume de L'Isle, *Atlas nouveau contenant toutes les parties du monde.* Amsterdam: Covens & Mortier, ca. 1742. Vol. 9, Plate no. 41. http://quod.lib.umich.edu/c/clark1ic/x-003011281/39015091185879

Tensions again began to rise between the United States and Great Britain when the Jay Treaty expired a decade later, under Thomas Jefferson's Republican administration. Some British fortifications in the upper Mississippi valley remained occupied, and Canadian fur enterprises were active in adjacent territories, obviously violating Treaty of Paris language. Using allies recruited among the Native American tribes, upon whose lands both of the governments were continually encroaching, a series of proxy wars flared up during the buildup to the War of 1812. And so it was after that inconclusive and messy struggle sputtered on for a few years that the Treaty of Ghent once again referred persistent boundary questions across the North American continent to a series of jointly administered international investigative commissions.

As historian of cartography Denis Wood puts it: "Maps do work."[7] With the rise of the modern nation-state, maps shifted from being mere artistic and imaginative representations of space to becoming important tools capable of influencing social behavior and exercising political control over territory. But even when maps do accurately represent relative positions of locations with reference to the four cardinal directions, they still necessarily distort and simplify. Reality is messy, changeable, and confusing, particularly when it comes to the idealizations of natural features. Mountain ranges rarely form unbroken chains of well-aligned peaks. Seashores continually change (even the diurnal movements associated with tides can radically transform the outline of a coast). Lakes grow and shrink over time. Rivers occupy complicated channels (never the simple curves drawn on a map) and migrate in their courses with notorious unpredictability.[8]

Amid these challenges, the Boundary Commission had to perform two acts of inscription. One was visceral: The commissioners would tread upon the land itself, recording observations, taking measurements, and erecting physical monuments or markers where feasible to indicate key landmarks for their interpretation of what treaty language might reasonably translate to on the ground. The other form of inscription was more abstract: Written reports and maps would officially define the boundaries through that territory henceforth.

Nature, in turn, would also do a considerable amount of work on the surveying parties during the visceral phase of inscription. Echoes of the commissioners' travails through difficult terrain would register significantly on the maps they created to designate where the boundary should lie thenceforward. Ultimately, the Commissioners established a new legal basis for delimiting territorial and natural resource claims for all subsequent political entities inhabiting that region of North America (both existing states, like Ohio, New York, and the British colonies of Upper and Lower Canada, and other units yet to be organized, such as Michigan, Wisconsin, Minnesota, Ontario, and Quebec). The resulting maps also did unprecedented work to constrain the freedom and sovereignty of Indigenous peoples in North America, whose movements and options had previously remained remarkably fluid, despite the steady influx of European and American immigrant populations into the Great Lakes region over the preceding 150 years.

Assembling the Scientific Team

The demilitarization of the Great Lakes after the War of 1812 would be accompanied by a remarkably comprehensive hydrographic and geological analysis of the physical geography of the borderlands that had inadequately separated British and American territories in North America for nearly half a century. Appointees to each of the Joint Boundary Commission teams were therefore selected with care, anticipating that each member would be called upon to muster feats of technical prowess, physical endurance, and diplomatic sensitivity in the course of his duties.[9] Each country would appoint a Commissioner, an Agent, a Secretary, and an Astronomer to work together to oversee and manage the joint effort to accurately map and fairly demarcate divisions of land and water between the two former adversarial powers.[10] Initially, Britain chose John Ogilvy to serve as its Commissioner. Ogilvy had spent time among both the Canadian and Indian settlements throughout the Great Lakes region, and British Foreign Minister Lord Castlereagh trusted that Ogilvy understood the views and interests of the respective nations. The Americans appointed Peter Buell Porter as their Commissioner; he had been a prominent Republican War Hawk Congressman from western New York in the heady lead-up to the 1812 outbreak of hostilities. Porter also served as the U.S. Army Assistant Quartermaster during the war and had prior relevant survey expedition experience gained while a member of New York State's exploratory Erie Canal Commission in 1810.[11]

This scientific survey expedition, deemed at the time to be essential to the permanent demilitarization of the Great Lakes, inadvertently also launched a comprehensive geological investigation of the region. Dr. John Jeremiah Bigsby, who belonged to the British Army's medical staff stationed in Canada, was appointed in 1820 to succeed Stephen Sewall as Secretary for the Boundary Commission. Major Joseph Delafield served as Agent for the American Commission. Though both men were avid amateur naturalists, neither was selected because of his natural history acumen.[12] Delafield's field experience as a soldier and skilled leader in the New York State Militia was what had recommended him. Bigsby's appointment, however, followed only after having to deal with field conditions that had been poorly understood at the outset of the work. Sewall had resigned after the particularly dreadful summer of 1819, when at the upper (southwest) end of Lake Erie, sickness took the life of British Commissioner Ogilvy and disabled the entire American Commission: "Scarcely a man escaped either ague or bilious remittent fever under severe forms."[13] To replace Ogilvy, Lord Castlereagh tapped Anthony Barclay, who had served as Secretary to the Joint Boundary Commission which had determined the offshore boundary between Maine and New Brunswick in 1817.[14] Bigsby thus brought needed medical expertise so work could proceed more smoothly the following spring.[15]

Bigsby's geological curiosity thrived during extensive journeys with astronomer David Thompson (see Figure 3) and his team of surveyors, soldiers, and voyageurs. Altogether, they formed a crew of about three dozen men. Over the next four years, Bigsby documented and described much of the terrain and physical geography of the Great Lakes. During the summers of 1820, 1821, and 1822, Bigsby collected geological observations all around the shores of Lakes Erie and Huron; 1823 brought the surveying team to the northern shore of Lake Superior and up the waterways along the Grand Portage leading northwest to the Lake of the Woods (with Delafield and Bigsby interacting and journeying together over some stretches, but sometimes investigating alternative river channels).[16] Bigsby was fascinated by the enormous scope, and the hints of northerly bedrock origins, of the widely scattered erratic boulders and other debris that we now attribute to repeated episodes of continental glaciation.[17]

Figure 3. Charles William Jefferies, *David Thompson taking an astronomical observation*. Pen and black ink over pencil sur wove paper.   https://www.bac-lac.gc.ca/eng/CollectionSearch/Pages/ record.aspx?app=FonAndCol&IdNumber=2900259   Image courtesy of Library and Archives Canada (Bibliothèque et Archives Canada). Accession Number 1972-026 X PIC 01406.

Boundary determination work certainly presented earth scientists like Bigsby and Delafield rich opportunities. In the spirit of international scientific cooperation, Bigsby's geological discoveries were publicized among British colleagues back in London, as well as being featured in numerous articles in the *American Journal of Science*. Characteristic of popular contemporary theories of catastrophic flooding, Bigsby inferred from observations gathered throughout the region evidence of a tumultuously violent geological past:

> I am inclined to the opinion that an enormous body of water has rushed over these countries (a "debacle") swept from distant lands, the colossal fragments of rock so frequent in the Lake; and formed the breaches called the [Manitouline] detours; perhaps at the same time when the passages of the Hudson and Shenandoah were opened, and the heights of Quebec, and the marshes of Montreal were covered with the ruins of annihilated mountains.[18]

Delafield, for his part, took advantage of the Commission's journey into the continental interior as an extraordinary opportunity to amass an unmatched collection of North American minerals. These precious specimens helped him obtain membership in prestigious international scientific societies and the presidency of New York's Lyceum of Natural History from 1827 to 1866.

Case Study: Resolving the Neebish Channel Maze

As fascinating as geological investigation and mineralogical collecting may have been for Bigsby and Delafield, respectively, the task of erecting a fair and stable division of territory required other kinds of knowledge and judiciousness. Bigsby recounted how the Commission encountered myriad difficulties:

> The want of any established precedents in international law was a good deal felt. They would have greatly facilitated discussion. The words used by the treaty-makers, whose topographical knowledge was limited, were sometimes vague. For example, it was uncertain whether the term 'water-communication,' employed in the treaty, had a commercial or geographical signification. The Commissioners decided on the latter, as being the most useful.
>
> . . . The distribution of the very numerous and often fertile islands caused great labour in soundings, measurements, and valuations. The islands which were unequally divided by the boundary-line were usually given to that party which became entitled to the largest share, compensation being made in some other part of the frontier, as contiguous as possible. The inconvenience of two nationalities on one small island was not to be endured.[19]

The Commission's linguistic decision to interpret "water-communication" geographically rather than commercially forced them to perform a hydrographic analysis of where the preponderance of water was flowing whenever multiple channels separated islands in a river or lake. According to one international law historian, "The greatest difficulty of the partition [of the Great Lakes] was caused in the section up-stream [of] the Neebish Falls."[20] Despite the apparent simplicity of tracing a "mid-water" line, the tangle of islands and waterways at the entrance to Lake Huron posed extremely complicated navigational and hydrographical issues (see Figure 4). Bigsby's narrative reveals a struggle to assess which route constituted the "main" channel between the Lakes, and then to make a fair assignment of lands:

> Narrow as this strait is, it contains eighteen islets—those nearest the main partaking of its forbidden character; sometimes being divided from each other by mural rents, only a few feet across. As the islets approach St. Joseph they lower, and have marshy coves. The current is inconstant—sometimes strong . . ..

> This second or upper group of rapids and narrows forms the outlet of Lake George. This lake is eighteen miles long by five in average breadth. Its west side is formed by Sugar or George Island, which, twenty miles long, stretches from the Straits of St. Mary to within a mile of St. Joseph. It is fertile. But narrow. A shallow water, a mile broad, intervenes between the main on the west and Sugar Island. At its foot, on the south, we have Nibish Island, squeezed in between the main and St. Joseph.[21]

Based on their findings, the Commissioners awarded Sugar Island (shown as "St. George's Island" in Figure 4) to the United States. Land values then had to be

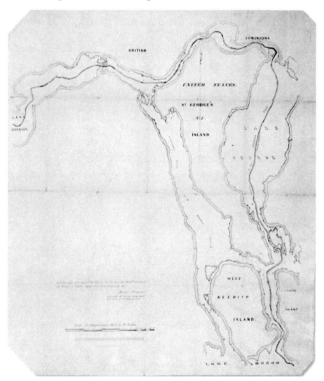

Figure 4. David Thompson. *A True Copy of a Copy of the Map of the Survey under the 6th Article of the Treaty of Ghent, signed by the Commissioners & c. & c., David Thompson, Astronomer & Surveyor.* G. Matthews Lith., Montreal, [ca. 1826]. Image courtesy of Archives of Ontario Cartographic Records Collection, Reference Code: B-40-03, AO 3697.

calculated to enable compensation to British Canada elsewhere.[22] They kept track of the net impact of territorial reassignments to ensure the overall fairness of the impact on both nations. Both sides needed to persuade their home governments to ratify the whole package. In this regard, the Neebish channel compromise is surprising. Not yet widely settled by whites, these strategic locations nevertheless hosted important sites of commerce with Great Lakes Native peoples (see Figure 5 for Bigsby's sketch of a view looking northwest from St. Joseph's Island, which includes a small trading post building). Great Britain had already surrendered its fortifications at Mackinac Island at the mouth of Lake Michigan at the close of hostilities in 1815 and relocated to a newly constructed fort on Drummond Island. The Commission's decision to also award Drummond Island (which lay to east and south of St. Joseph's Island) to the United States meant yet another fort abandonment and removal in the same neighborhood by the British. Americans had been far less understanding in 1818 about their fort at Rouses Point, New York, which Article V Boundary Commission astronomer Johann Ludwig Tiarks had found illegally placed just a few yards north of the 45th parallel latitude on Quebec soil.

Figure 5. John Jeremiah Bigsby. *View N. W. from I. St. Joseph, Lake Huron*. Undated pen and ink drawing. Image courtesy of Library and Archives Canada, 1939-447-116. Available online MIKAN no. 2837945

Conclusion: Did Anyone Suppose Science Made Peaceful Boundaries?

When Dr. Bigsby packed up his bags and went home to London in 1827, nobody could have predicted the tremendous long-term success of most of his Commission's accomplishments. The U.S.–Canadian border has since become the longest unfortified boundary in the world and appears on its face to validate the confidence that Enlightenment thinkers invested in both mathematicians and earth scientists to help establish rational, peaceful borders. The work performed by Boundary Commission scientists in the Great Lakes did indeed offer a tantalizing shred of positive evidence on behalf of technical geographical solution approach to establishing peaceful borders. But we must also remember that Bigsby's hydrographic contributions were made relevant only by virtue of the interpretation that his Commissioners assigned to the vague Treaty of 1783 language. Assigning meaning to the definition of "middle of a watercourse" was the key step that allowed for geographical expertise to come into play. Where diplomats had specified geometrical rather than natural landmarks, the Boundary Commission relied upon astronomical and mathematical determinations, which Bigsby argued were even harder to resolve than the myriad challenges of threading a boundary through the Neebish channels.[23]

Interestingly, the English geologist John Finch (who also happened to be chemist Joseph Priestley's grandson) did take great inspiration from Bigsby's achievements; indeed, he went on to extrapolate from them a quite grand Enlightenment-style theory of rational boundary design. In his popular 1833 book of *Travels in the United States and Canada*, Finch presented these ideas in an Appendix entitled "Essay on the Natural Boundaries of Empires." Here, Finch advised that small streams form better boundaries than do large rivers and that oceans provide the most enviable borderlines, but he allowed that large lakes and mountain ranges may serve almost as well to effectively keep the peace between nations that understand and respect these natural barriers. Finch illustrated this generalization by pointing to the North American lakes, and claiming that they (already by 1833) clearly formed a good natural boundary between the United States and Canada.[24]

Alternatively, of course, we all know that Thomas Jefferson's idealized mode of inscribing a rectangular grid of latitude and longitude lines across the continent was already designating the bounds of American townships throughout the trans-Appalachian west. This more abstract mathematical/astronomical technique for territorial boundary definition would certainly undergo its own dramatic tests in the decades to come, both in reifying the 49th parallel of latitude as a means of separating the western extensions of Canada and the United States and in being implicated in various European powers' negotiations to carve up and colonize Africa and the Middle East later in the nineteenth century. John Finch would have objected vigorously to this application of science to diplomacy. As he insisted in his 1833 essay: "Something more is necessary to restrain the ambition of man than a mere artificial line, even though it was ornamented with flowers. Some powerful obstacle is required to control the love of conquest and the love of plunder, which the human race, in their collective capacity, possess."[25] Finch's argument proceeded, with direct relation to examples he took from the North American context: "The most clear, the best defined, the most regular parallelogrametrical Empire, ever made my the hand of a skilful [*sic*] mathematician, is not so likely to retain its boundary entire, as an Empire with irregular but strongly marked limits, formed by the rude hand of Nature." Finch concluded: "For all these reasons, in making future treaties of peace, or in fixing the boundaries of those Semi-Sovereign States called into existence by the fiat of American Congress, not the mathematician, but the geographer, or the individual who has the greatest knowledge of the country in dispute, should be consulted."[26]

As it happened, however, Finch's ultimate preference for and confidence in natural boundaries was not uniformly rewarded in practice. Peaceful settlement of the Maine–New Brunswick–Quebec portion of the U.S.–Canada boundary would continue to elude both negotiators and scientific investigators for at least another decade, precisely because the 1783 Treaty of Paris had invoked a "line of highlands" that could not actually be found on the ground. This stretch of the international boundary was not even finding resolution through the innovative auspices of the Joint Boundary Commissions. In 1827, President John Quincy Adams appealed to the good offices of King William I of the Netherlands, who agreed to review the competing national claims and offer a compromise. Setting aside the findings of the deadlocked scientific delegations, the Dutch ruler proposed an arbitrary line dividing the disputed territory as follows: 7,908 acres going to Maine and 4,119 acres to Canada. Local political leaders in New England were so vocal in their displeasure about this compromise that Adams's successor Andrew Jackson was forced to scuttle the solution, even though he privately considered it to be both reasonable and attractive.[27] Eruptions of boundary violence in 1838 and 1839 (the so-called "Aroostook War") triggered renewed efforts to find a solution, both by competing teams of geological experts (who could not agree on the same "highlands" boundary line) and ultimately by teams of top-level diplomats who settled the matter finally through some old-fashioned horse-trading without such careful regard for the scientific details of physical geography.[28]

Unlike his sanguine countryman and colleague John Finch, John Bigsby had never supposed that even the best, most scientifically accurate boundary work could actually prevent an army from transgressing a designated frontier. From early in his sojourn to North America, when first exposed to the brutal consequences of the recent war's toll near Niagara, Bigsby noted that only "true religion" could prevent warfare along any frontier.[29] Even as late as 1850, when Bigsby published his lengthy memoir, he reported that there was yet very little hope among Canadians that the Great Lakes had seen the last of an invading American force. They had just witnessed how aggressive Yankees recently wrested a massive territory away from Mexico (land now comprising the states of California, Nevada, Arizona, Utah, and portions of New Mexico, Colorado, and Wyoming). Contemporary Canadians did not assume that the Webster–Ashburton Treaty of 1842 and the Oregon Compromise of 1846 actually guaranteed stable peace, especially with such recent proof of the apparently inexhaustible American appetite for empire. In 1849, Bigsby found himself in a heated political conversation with a leading French-Canadian politician. M. de Rouville Pothier framed his plea for Quebeçois political rights by alluding to the persistent invasion threat from the south:

> It is only prudent to do what is right by Canadians, for their country is in the grasp of the United States at any moment; contingents from the four nearest states would take it irrevocably in one campaign. You will remember that it has become the fashion among American Presidents to signalize [sic] their four years' reign by some distinguished acquisition. Neither principle nor their true interests will stop an excitable people like the Americans, with an ambitious politician at their head.[30]

Despite these lingering and quite valid anxieties, the history of the demilitarized Great Lakes region would ultimately fulfill the hopes invested in the innovative gamble that the Ghent Treaty had set forth back in 1814. Those diplomats asked scientifically informed boundary commission teams to explore and jointly agree upon where to draw line segments upon a new map crossing the eastern half of the North American continent. Serious invasion attempts into or from the United States and Canada did diminish to zero. Although nobody had clearly anticipated what depth and breadth of natural knowledge expertise would be required, contingencies in the choice of participants and in the political decisions made on the ground enabled a positive "test" result to come from the Great Lakes experiment of science and diplomacy. The larger prospects envisioned by John Finch and others who might draw hopeful lessons from this misleadingly successful outcome, however, would have to be tested elsewhere around the world as various techniques for boundary definition have proliferated, with no universal recipe for peaceful coexistence yet being consistently attributable to the scientific expertise of boundary makers.

Notes

1. Valuable histories of the International Boundary Survey include D.W. Thomas, *Men and Meridians: The History of Surveying and Mapping in Canada* (3 vols.), Ottawa, 1966–1969; William E. Lass, *Minnesota's Boundary with Canada: Its Evolution Since 1783* (St. Paul, Minn., 1980); and Francis M. Carroll, *A Good and Wise Measure: The Search for the Canadian–American Boundary*, 1783–1842 (Toronto, 2001). This paper emphasizes primary source testimony from Bigsby's field scientist perspective: J.J. Bigsby, *The Shoe and the Canoe* (2 vols.) (London, 1850).

2. See, for example, Étienne Balibar's essay "What Is a Border?" in É. Balibar, *Politics and the Other Scene* (London, 2001): 76–79; J. Painter, "Cartographic Anxiety and the Search for Regionality" in *Environment and Planning A* 40 (2008): 342–361; P. Banerjee, *Borders, Histories, Existences: Gender and Beyond* (New Delhi, 2010); Sandro Mezzadra and Brett Neilson's discussion of "borderzones" in S. Mezzadra and B. Neilson, *Border as Method, Or, the Multiplication of Labor* (Durham, N.C., 2013): 235–242; and Omer Bartov and Eric D. Weitz's introduction to *Shatterzone of Empires: Coexistence and Violence in the German, Hapsburg, Russian, and Ottoman Borderlands,* O. Bartov and E.D. Weitz, eds. (Bloomington, Ind., 2013): 1–20.

3. Peter Gay laid out in his classic essay a nicely comprehensive account of the shared attitudes and distinctive Enlightenment political philosophies articulated by intellectuals ranging from Locke and Voltaire to Bentham, Condorcet, Diderot, Helvetius, Hume, Kant, Montesquieu, Rousseau, and Smith. P. Gay, "The Enlightenment in the History of Political Theory," *Political Science Quarterly* 69 (1954): 374–389.

4. For a rich contextual discussion of René Descartes' ideas about geometry and its impact on Enlightenment science and political theory, see S. Elden, *The Birth of Territory* (Chicago, 2013): 290–298.

5. These diplomats included, for Britain's Regency government, the Admiral Gambier, Parliamentary Secretary for War, and for the Colonies, Henry Goulbourn and William Adams, a Doctor of Civil Law. The American negotiators included prominent intellects such as future President John Quincy Adams, the Princeton-educated Federalist former Delaware Senator James A. Bayard, and the Swiss-born Jeffersonian mastermind

of internal improvements and former Secretary of the Treasury Albert Gallatin. George Gallwey provides a nuanced portrait of this last figure's importance in "Albert Gallatin: Mapping Old and New Empires in the Early United States" in this volume.

6. H.R. Schoolcraft, *Narrative of an expedition through the upper Mississippi to Itasca Lake, the actual source of this river; embracing an exploratory trip through the St. Croix and Burntwood (or Broule) Rivers, in 1832* (New York, 1834).

7. D. Wood, *Rethinking the Power of Maps* (New York, 2010): 1.

8. During his geological survey expedition in upper Canada the year before he was appointed to the Boundary Commission, Bigsby described his descent along the River des François, portraying a course so ill defined as to make it an object lesson for why rivers should *not* be designated as useful or stable for boundary marking: ". . . it is a very peculiar river. It less resembles a single stream than a bundle of watercourses flowing, with frequent inosculations, among lengthened ridges of rocks. The utterly barren and naked shores seldom present continuous lines bounding a compact body of water, but are commonly excavated into deepened narrow bays, obscured by high walls of rock and stunted pines. It is seventy-five miles long. Its breadth is exceedingly various, sometimes swelling into a broad lake for miles, and crowded with islands." Bigsby, *Shoe and Canoe,* vol. I: 168.

9. Bigsby described the initial commission meeting in May 1823 in Kingston, for example, as follows: "We were engaged for several days in general conferences, verifying accounts, examining the beautiful maps, which (2½ inches to the geographical mile) had been completed during the past winter, and in laying down instructions for the service of the coming summer. These things done, the Commissioners dispatched the working party already enumerated on their long journey of 1400 miles. Until the month of November they were to lose sight of civilised life." Bigsby, *Shoe and Canoe,* vol. II: 55–56.

10. "All this stretch of country had to be mapped accurately, as a standing official document in evidence—a work which includes minute surveys by astronomical observation, and by triangulation, various measurements, &c., and the construction of numerous maps on a large scale in quadruplicate,—a copy for each Government and each Commissioner." Bigsby, *Shoe and Canoe,* vol. I: 249.

11. For more on Peter B. Porter as a "War Hawk" U.S. Congressman on the eve of the War of 1812, see A. Taylor, *The Civil War of 1812: American Citizens, British Subjects, Irish Rebels, and Indian Allies* (New York, 2010): 128–137. For Porter's participation in the search for a feasible Erie Canal route, see D.I. Spanagel, *DeWitt Clinton and Amos Eaton: Geology and Power in Early New York* (Baltimore, 2014): 86–87.

12. Delafield was a keen collector of rocks, minerals, and curious fossil petrifactions. Delafield's geological observations and expedition journals from the boundary commission years were later edited and privately published by Robert McNutt McElroy and Thomas Riggs under the title *The Unfortified Boundary: A Diary of the First Survey of the Canadian Boundary from St. Regis to the Lake of the Woods, by Major Joseph Delafield, American Agent*

under Articles VI and VII of the Treaty of Ghent (source: University of California library; private publisher, 1943).

Bigsby also started out by collecting fossils and butterflies, but his geological work done while participating in the Boundary Commission eventually gained him an international reputation as an expert on what later came to be known as North America's Silurian fossils, in accordance with Roderick Murchison's system of nomenclature. See J.J. Bigsby, *Thesaurus Siliricus: The Flora and Fauna of the Silurian Period* (London, 1868).

13. "The whole American party, General Porter (the Commissioner) included, caught one or another of these diseases among the marshes of the Miami River, or at Point Pelé in Lake Erie. Not one of them died; but many had narrow escapes, and few recovered until the succeeding spring. Mr. Ogilvy, the British Commissioner, was taken ill on the 12th of September, 1819, on Boisblanc Island, in the River Détroit, and ten days after he died in the contiguous village of Amherstburgh . . .. Mr. David Thompson, the British astronomer . . . fell sick early in the same September, at first with extreme weakness, and then with high fever and delirium." Weakened by the illness, Sewall died the following year. Bigsby, *Shoe and Canoe,* vol. I: 250–251.

14. "Mr. Barclay was selected with particular felicity, if fitness for office be determined by personal character, by great diligence, ability, and firmness of purpose, and by a large acquaintance with its duties, acquired as secretary to a similar Commission . . ., he of all men was enabled, by previous education and quiet amenity of manner, to cope with the eager and exacting temper of American diplomatists, and to make good the right thing." Bigsby, *Shoe and Canoe,* vol. I: 253. For details on the Treaty of Ghent Article IV Commission's membership and its decision to award three islands in Passamaquoddy Bay to the United States but the rest (including the Isle of Grand Manan) to Great Britain, see T. Donaldson, *The Public Domain: Its History, with Statistics . . .* (Washington, D.C., 1881): 4.

15. "As the Commission had again to work in Lake Erie, and the sickly regions on the way to Lake Huron, it was resolved to place a medical man in the office of secretary, then vacant by the resignation of Mr. Stephen Sewall; and I was appointed." Incidentally, Bigsby already knew Delafield from an encounter while on a geological tour of Upper Canada in 1819. Bigsby, *Shoe and Canoe,* vol. I: 252.

16. "In the summer of 1823, my esteemed friend Col. Delafield [footnote indicates Delafield later become Commandant at the West Point Military Academy], the American agent of the Boundary Commission, the two astronomers, with their staff and myself, were directed to proceed to the Lake of the Woods, for the purpose of surveying it, and Rainy Lake, another very large body of water. The ground to be passed over on the way thither, was mostly new to me." Bigsby, *Shoe and Canoe,* vol. II: 36.

17. Even at the furthest reach of the journey, while seeking the elusive northwest "corner" of the Lake of the Woods, Bigsby observed: "erratic blocks of great size; one of which, perched upon a granite mound (seventeen miles from Lapluie), must have weighed fifty tons. They line the coast in inconvenient numbers; for, as far as Driftwood Point, there is some difficulty in getting near dry land." Bigsby, *Shoe and Canoe,* vol. II: 295.

18. J.J. Bigsby, "Geological and Mineralogical Observations on the North-West Portion of Lake Huron," *American Journal of Science* 3 (1821): 255. Keep in mind that Bigsby's speculations here preceded the time when geologists anywhere had yet promoted an Ice Age theory. For more on the origins and timing of the emergence of the glacial hypothesis, see J. and K. Imbrie, *Ice Ages: Solving the Mystery* (Cambridge, Mass.: 1979): 21–28; and for a description of prevailing diluvial explanations among Bigsby's American contemporaries, see Spanagel: 20–22.

19. Bigsby, *Shoe and Canoe,* vol. I: 246–247.

20. J.H.W. Verzijl, *International Law in Historical Perspective*, vol. 3 (Leiden, 1970): 589.

21. Bigsby, *The Shoe and the Canoe*, vol. II: 119–120.

22. "With correct maps, soundings, and information as to the agricultural or public value of the islands, there is no difficulty in determining the boundary line, or in giving for such determination a satisfactory reason." Bigsby, *The Shoe and the Canoe*, vol. II: 165–166.

23. Bigsby's claim about which challenge posed the greater technical difficulty derived from the mathematical and surveying dilemmas Thompson and the commission encountered trying to designate the "corner" of a nonconvex lake shore. William Lass notes that diplomatic discussions through 1826 and 1827 linked those two hotly disputed items (where to locate the northwest corner of the Lake of the Woods, and which nation was awarded Sugar Island in the Neebish Channel), so ultimately technical solutions still fed into diplomatic trade-offs. Lass: 50–62.

24. J. Finch, "Essay on the Natural Boundaries of Empires," in *Travels in the United States and Canada* (London, 1833): 358.

25. Finch: 397.

26. Finch: 401.

27. See A. McEwen, "Introduction," *In Search of the Highlands—Mapping the Canada–Maine Boundary, 1839: The Journals of Featherstonhaugh and Mudge, August to November, 1839* (Fredericton, N.B., 1988): 10; and H. Jones, *To the Webster–Ashburton Treaty: A Study in Anglo-American Relations, 1783–1843* (Chapel Hill, N.C., 1977): 133.

28. This negotiation produced the Webster–Ashburton Treaty of 1842. For a detailed analysis of the circumstances and events that yielded this outcome, see D. O'Leary's "Archival Lines, Historical Pratice, and the Atlantic Geopolitics behind the 1842 Webster–Ashburton Treaty" in this volume.

29. Bigsby, *Shoe and Canoe,* vol. II: 20.

30. Bigsby's footnote to this remark characterized one of Gen. Winfield Scott's presidential campaign statements as being tantamount to calling for the annexation of all of Canada. Bigsby, *Shoe and Canoe,* vol. I: 207n. For an excellent synthetic historical analysis of the territorial expansion of the United States, with detailed explanations of each of the contingencies and alternative possibilities seriously entertained in those instances when Americans negotiated for or forcefully acquired additional territory, see W. Nugent, *Habits of Empire: A History of American Expansion* (New York, 2008).

Mapping Inequality, Resistance, and Solutions in Early National Philadelphia

Billy G. Smith

I wander thro' each charter'd street,
Near where the charter'd Thames does flow.
And mark in every face I meet
Marks of weakness, marks of woe.
In every cry of every Man,
In every Infants cry of fear,
In every voice: in every ban,
The mind-forg'd manacles I hear

—William Blake, *Songs of Innocence and Experience* (1794)

TWO AND A QUARTER centuries ago, the radical British poet William Blake suggested that strolling around a city, looking and listening closely to its residents, was one of the best ways of learning about it, especially if the *flâneurs* could overcome the blinders that afflict us all. Inspired both by Blake's idea and by the original conference call for papers that emphasized using historical maps to measure inequalities in the past, I have recreated a brief walking tour of Philadelphia in 1794. The journey promises to help us better to understand the nation's new capital both from the personal standpoint of two women—Martha Washington and the enslaved Ona Judge—and from a modern scholarly perspective.[1]

This essay explores inequalities based on race, gender, class, and epidemics, all of which not only were visible to eighteenth-century people but also are directly relevant to our own times. Admirably, many Americans, optimistic about the new nation, worked to resolve problems in a way that might inspire us in our own cynical era, which is characterized by political and social turmoil amid a pandemic. Many Philadelphians, both Black and white, actively opposed slavery during the 1790s, just as many Americans today are reexamining their own racial prejudices and behavior. Philadelphians also endured terrible epidemics, like the dilemma our current world faces with the pandemic of COVID-19. During the 1793 epidemic, Black residents saved the nation's capital, risking (and sometimes losing) their own lives to serve as nurses and caretakers. Their commitment is comparable to the heroic efforts of health care workers during our current pandemic. Although they made mistakes, early Americans did not fear acting to improve their communities and their country. Hopefully, we can do the same.

The use of an extraordinarily detailed historical map of the city created by John Hills in 1796 in combination with the computer technology of ArcGIS enabled our team of researchers to create numerous accurate maps of various characteristics of the city. Hills's masterpiece (see Figure 1), *The Plan of the City of Philadelphia and its Environs*, is the work of a mature surveyor and drafter, one of the most talented ones in early North America. Trained in London and Woolrich, England, Hills served in the British military in the mid-Atlantic during the Revolutionary War, creating dozens of manuscript maps of the region to assist officers in planning for battles. He remained in America after the war, living and working as a mapmaker and surveyor, primarily in New York and Philadelphia. Offering his services to George Washington in 1796 to survey the Northwest Territory, Hills boasted of his "long practical experience which I have had from a continual devotion of my time to this business [mapmaking] for upwards of twenty-five years past." Hills did not obtain that job, though he lived and prospered in Philadelphia for the next two decades.[2]

Figure 1. John Hills, *This plan of the city of Philadelphia and its environs (showing the improved parts) (1797)*. Nat Archives: https://www.loc.gov/item/2007625050

A landmark of early American urban cartography, Hills's map includes outlines of most buildings, indications of wooded and swampy areas, relief hachures, and an index to points of interest such as churches, markets, and federal buildings. Essential to our team's modern mapping project were the names and locations of numerous streets, alleys, lanes, and courts, as well as the many wharves along the Delaware River. All these details took Hills a half dozen years to complete. Seeking subscribers, in 1790 he initially advertised his intention to produce an "Accurate Survey" of the city. The cost was two dollars, half in advance and half on delivery of the map. (For comparison, Philadelphia male laborers typically earned one dollar per day). In the Spring of 1797, Hills advertised that the map was finished and was being engraved in London, to be ready in the Fall for subscribers to obtain. New purchasers would pay five dollars for a colored map or three dollars for one not colored. Hills subsequently bought more than a hundred newspaper advertisements to sell the map during the next thirteen months.[3]

While Hills's map was vital to our modern mapping project, we also required information from other sources that exist in abundance for early national Philadelphia. Two censuses, several tax lists, a dozen city directories, and computer-searchable newspapers record names, occupations, street addresses, taxable wealth, ownership of slaves, the composition of each household, and the like. These sources, however, skew toward recording primarily white male householders. To find, locate, and map everyone else, including women, African Americans, and poorer people, required an enormous amount of time and energy. We undertook computer searches in contemporary newspapers, scoured censuses to find women and non-white men who headed households, searched for slaves inscribed in tax lists, compared the varied information contained in numerous city directories, and used databases of runaway slaves from newspaper advertisements. In the process, we were able to recover tens of thousands of people largely silenced by both maps and other historical records. We are proud to, literally, put many overlooked people back on the map.[4]

Coming from different classes, races, and positions of power, Ona Judge and Martha Washington saw the city and its peoples from vastly different standpoints. Their differing perspectives may help us shed some of the "mind-forged manacles" noted by William Blake as we accompany them on their hypothetical walk. Ona ("Oney") Judge was born to her mixed-race mother Betty at Mt. Vernon, the plantation of George and Martha Washington, most likely in 1773. Martha ordered Ona, aged ten, into the mansion as a playmate for her granddaughter and, eventually, as a personal servant. When George became president, they moved their household, including Ona (who had no choice), first to New York City in 1789 and then to Philadelphia in the 1790s as the seat of the federal government shifted from one city to the other. Ona served at Martha's pleasure, helping her wash, dress, fix her hair daily, and perform a host of other tasks. She often sat with Martha as she sewed, one of Martha's favorite activities. Ona became an expert seamstress, out of necessity rather than pleasure.[5]

Born into a Virginia plantation family that enslaved hundreds of people, Martha Washington quickly grew accustomed to bound people performing work for her. She belonged to the American elite for her entire life. When her first husband died, Martha became a rich young widow with five plantations and 300 enslaved women, men, and children. Her property vastly increased the wealth of George Washington (himself already a slave owner) when they married in 1759. As wife of the president, Martha entertained other elite women regularly in Philadelphia, assigning the labor of preparation and serving to the nine slaves brought from Mt. Vernon along with hired and indentured white servants.[6]

Ona and Martha will be our guides on a hypothetical eight-block trip from the president's house at 190 High (now Market) Street to the new nation's most famous museum (see Figure 2).[7] July 17, 1794, was probably another ordinary rainy day to Martha.[8] Ona, although not taught anything about religion while enslaved by the Washingtons, still likely knew that on that day Absalom Jones and other Blacks opened the African Church of Philadelphia (later renamed the African Episcopal Church of St. Thomas), one of the

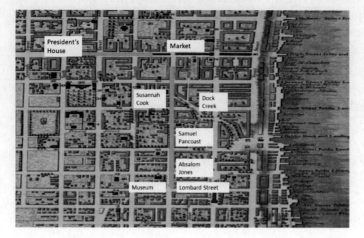

Figure 2. Ona and Martha's Walk.

first such congregations in the new nation. It was a sign of pride among the emerging free Black community, who now numbered 5,000, in the city.[9]

Both befitting her status and to avoid the muck in the streets, Martha rode the eight blocks to the museum in a small carriage driven by a servant or slave and with "postillion Joe" (as George called him) perched on the back of the coach to serve as Martha's footman. When the federal government moved to Philadelphia during the 1790s, the number of carriages of affluent people mushroomed, growing so numerous that they created crowded, dangerous roads. In response, during the 1790s the newly incorporated city passed a series of laws to control the chaotic traffic. They included the first requirement in America to drive on the *right* rather than the traditional *left* side of the street, part of the new nation's many attempts to distinguish itself from Great Britain. Meanwhile, Martha assumed that Ona would walk behind the carriage.[10]

A few blocks east along Market Street, Ona and Martha passed the shop of Michael Roberts, ironmonger, where John Hills's map would be sold in a few more years. Roberts's shop was on the edge of the most impressive bazaar in North America. Stretching from Front to Fourth Street, three brick halls, open on the sides and roofed on top, occupied the middle of the street. Slaughtering beef, veal, poultry, and chickens in the New Shambles Hall, butchers made this market, according to one French visitor, "only second to that of London-hall" in its display of animal flesh. Shooing away flies, Ona stepped over small mounds of animal entrails left by butchers from the previous market day.[11]

Since July 17 was Tuesday, the day before Wednesday markets, in the evening church bells would attract people from both the city and the countryside to dances held in the halls. Farmers rolled into town, according to the same French visitor, "in great covered wagons, loaded with all manner of provender, bringing with them rations for themselves and feed for their horses—for they sleep in their wagons." These nights were busy times not only for tavernkeepers but also for constables and prostitutes. Streetwalkers congregated at the west end of the market, very near to where Ona and Martha arrived. Constables often arrested sex workers in this area; six months after their journey, constables detained Margaret Britton for "skulking about Country Wagons in Market Street at a late Hour of the Night." Britton straightforwardly acknowledged her purpose: "she wished to have carnal Intercourse with [farmers] to get money." Just a few years earlier, Ona and Martha might have witnessed public whippings and prisoners exhibited in stocks in the middle of the market. According to one grateful vendor, the large crowds gathered to see the spectacles allowed him to increase the price for eggs and butter.[12]

On Wednesdays and Saturdays, the market attracted one of the most heterogeneous collections of people in the Western World. The Quaker open-mindedness regarding religious freedom that characterized Philadelphia from its founding had encouraged a varied group of immigrants. Ona consequently heard a medley of tongues, not just different dialects of English but also German, Dutch, French, Spanish, Portuguese, and Gaelic, as well as a smattering of African and Native American words and languages. Philadelphia was among the most multicultural cities in the Western World.[13]

As Ona walked, she took care to avoid the droppings left by animals wandering the streets. Unlike antiseptic modern cities, animals roamed without restrictions: Pigs, chickens, cows, goats, dogs, and cats all scavenged in the rubbish in the streets. Horses were ubiquitous; perhaps 2,000 of them clip-clopped on the cobblestone streets in downtown Philadelphia, carrying people and pulling carriages, carts, and drays. Residents tethered them in front of houses, in backyards, in empty lots, and in private and public stables.

Turning South on Third Street and walking a block past Chestnut, they entered a neighborhood where many widows resided. Susannah Cook, a widow and washerwoman, lived here, struggling mightily to earn enough income to keep her family intact. Ona did not know Cook, but she surely recognized the struggles of impoverished women, both white and Black, in a sexist society that limited jobs and restricted pay for females. When a severe yellow fever epidemic scythed through the city in 1793, Cook lost her husband and a son. Nearby Dock Creek, filled with yellow-fever-carrying mosquitoes, condemned Cook's neighborhood to extremely high mortality (see Figure 3). In this area and others along the northern docks where mosquitoes proliferated, as many as two-thirds of the population died in a three-month span.

Figure 3. Yellow Fever Deaths 1793.

After the epidemic, thousands of widows desperately sought ways to earn a living. Many turned to washing clothes, taking in boarders, or working as domestic servants. After her husband's death, Cook began to scrub clothes in a washtub behind her house to support her two surviving children. She also hosted boarders, providing them shelter and meals. The physically demanding work perhaps contributed to the deterioration in her health, or maybe she just could not cover expenses regardless of how hard she worked. She died in the almshouse eight years later, after the Guardians of the Poor forcibly indentured her children. Tellingly, after 1793, admissions of women to the almshouse, workhouse, and jail increased considerably. Like Cook, women without husbands could quickly slide into fatal poverty.[14]

Martha was little aware of women like Cook, just as she usually paid scant personal attention to slaves or servants unless they displeased her. However, Martha was close friends with two prominent women who lived in nearby mansions—Ann Bingham and Elizabeth Powel. Married to very rich men, both were well known in Philadelphia upper-class society, both attended some of the weekly Friday soirees hosted by Martha at the president's house, and Martha likewise had been a frequent visitor at their homes. Ona would have recognized them in that capacity, as women she served during the parties and to whom she had been respectful—always a requirement of slaves regardless of their own personal feelings.[15]

Elizabeth was also widowed by the yellow fever epidemic, although she remained quite wealthy from the inheritance of her husband's estate, as he was a wealthy merchant and former mayor of the city. She never endued the financial disasters suffered by Cook. The Washingtons had invited Elizabeth and her husband Samuel to escape the 1793 epidemic by visiting them in Mount Vernon. The Powels declined the invitation, and Samuel succumbed to the fever. Besides hosting frequent salons for affluent women, Elizabeth was unusually outspoken about politics. She had an "uncommon command of Language," according to her sister, and her "ideas flow with rapidity." She belonged to a generation of women inspired by the Revolution to challenge societal restrictions and improve the possibilities, especially in terms of education, for their gender.[16]

Elizabeth was a confidant of and even offered political advice to George Washington, urging him not to resign from the presidency after his first term; it apparently had an impact on his thinking. She likewise hosted delegates to the 1787 Constitutional Convention and asked Benjamin Franklin at the conclusion of the convention about the character of the new government, whether it was a monarchy or a republic. "A republic," Franklin purported replied, "if you can keep it." That might well serve as a caution for our own perilous times.[17]

Class as well as gender differences were starkly evident in this neighborhood. The contrasting size of structures occupied by Cook and Ann Bingham (at 122 South Third Street, next door to Elizabeth Powel's mansion) mirrored the growing economic inequality in the city and new nation.[18] Cook's two-story frame house, typical of many working-class homes in Philadelphia, measured approximately 18 feet × 18 feet; the lot was only slightly larger than the house. At 100 feet × 60 feet, Bingham's property dominated most of a city block. The lot was even bigger (292 feet × 396 feet), and it contained fruit trees, a garden with 500 exotic plants, an icehouse, milk house, and stables. The differences in the two properties were seemingly inescapable to anyone traveling on Third Street, although an elite woman like Martha may have worn blinders in this regard.[19]

The widening economic chasm dividing the classes is apparent in the intensification of residential segregation throughout the city (see Figure 4). Merchants and wealthy shop owners coveted locations both on eastern Market Street and along the wharves to be near the center of economic action. Rapid population growth added to the enormous pressure that the new federal government put on available housing, and the creation of new offices drove up the value of land, the cost of houses, and rent in the center of the city. Like gentrification in our own times, counting houses, elite shops, and new government offices displaced a good many lower-class residents. In the heart of the city, as one newspaper essayist lamented, "you can scarcely add ornament, without the loss of accommodation of two houses to the mechanic or laborer, which measure bears exceedingly hard on them." Meanwhile, laborers moved to the fringes of the city as well as the "suburbs" of Southwark and the Northern Liberties during the 1790s. By 1801, after the federal government moved to Washington, D.C., few laborers lived anywhere in the center city because of exorbitant real estate prices. The laborers joined a good many working-class people sharing wooden houses and tenements on the city's perimeter.[20]

Figure 4. Households of Laborers and Merchants 1801.

As Ona and Martha continued south to Union Street, they passed the home of Samuel Pancoast, a white Quaker, master carpenter, and one of the elected officers of the Pennsylvania Abolition Society. As an "inspector" of the Society, Pancoast knew many African Americans, both slave and free, since he routinely visited Black neighborhoods and the jail where suspected runaways and recalcitrant slaves were incarcerated. Ona admired the activities of the first abolition society in America, founded in 1775 and well known by African Americans in the city. The Society fought both to end racial thralldom and to assist impoverished free Black people. Men like Pancoast, as well as African American communities, both enslaved and free, sometimes provided shelter for refugees fleeing their masters in the new nation, establishing Philadelphia as a vital haven for free Blacks during the ensuing decades.[21]

Martha disliked, likely even despised, the Abolition Society because it disrupted her life, threatened her enormous wealth in slaves, and struggled for human rights for people who she doubted were entirely human. The Society played a significant role in passing Pennsylvania emancipation laws in 1780 and 1788, the first in the nation. In addition to gradually freeing slaves, those laws forbade out-of-state owners from keeping their slaves in the state for more than six months. After that time, the enslaved had a right to claim their freedom, and many did so with the legal assistance of the Abolition Society.[22]

When Martha and George moved to Philadelphia with their slaves, George instructed his secretary, Tobias Lear, to evade the 1788 law by rotating their slaves out of the state, if only briefly, before each six-month deadline. He wanted to keep this rotation strategy secret as well as to involve Martha in the conspiracy. "I wish to have it accomplished under pretext that may deceive both them [his slaves] and the public," George wrote to his personal secretary, "and none I think would so effectually do this, as Mrs. Washington coming to Virginia [from Philadelphia] next month." During the six years they lived in Philadelphia, the Washingtons routinely sent their enslaved people back to Mount Vernon or to other destinations outside Pennsylvania. At other times, as on May 17, 1791, Martha visited nearby Trenton, New Jersey, for only a day or two, most likely taking Ona and other slaves with her to prevent their legal claim to freedom.[23]

George and Martha feared that the lure of liberty might affect their bondspeople. "The idea of freedom," George admitted, "might be too great a temptation for them to resist. At any rate it might, if they conceived they had a right to it, make them insolent in a State of Slavery."[24] Simultaneously, the Washingtons did not credit their own enslaved people nor the city's free African American community with the intelligence or knowledge to understand Martha and George's subterfuge. They were entirely wrong. Because of their racist misconceptions about their slaves, they would be stunned when Ona claimed her freedom by taking flight while living in Philadelphia.

Continuing south across Pine Street, Ona and Martha passed the house of Absalom Jones, an organizer and leader of the newly emerging community of free and enslaved Blacks in Philadelphia. He was a major moving force in constructing and opening the African Church of Philadelphia, becoming the rector of that church. The first sermon was preached on July 17, 1794—the day that Ona walked by his house. Along with Richard Allen, William Gray, Anne Saville, and others, Jones worked tirelessly to construct institutions to improve the lives of the mushrooming population of Black Philadelphians. They established the Free African Society, created mutual-aid organizations, founded churches, and cared for sick people, both white and Black, during the 1793 epidemic.[25]

Philadelphia served as a special draw for African Americans from the nearby regions as well as from the southern states. Their numbers tripled between 1790 and 1800, growing from 2,150 (about 5 percent of the city's population) to 6,436 (approximately 9 percent). Most Black migrants had freed themselves, either legally or illegally. Some earned their liberty by serving in the Continental army or navy during the American Revolution. Others, like Jones and Allen, after laboring and saving for years, purchased their own and their family's freedom from their masters. Many others ran away.[26]

Slaves in Philadelphia and the surrounding environs devised clever, if somewhat perilous strategies to liberate themselves. They used the state's gradual emancipation laws as leverage. As the moral and legal power of slave owners in Pennsylvania declined after the Revolution, some bondspeople seized the initiative and challenged their masters by refusing to obey them. With fewer lawful disciplinary options (like whipping or selling slaves out of state), frustrated owners more frequently paid to incarcerate recalcitrant enslaved people. Between 1793 and 1797, whites imprisoned nearly 700 enslaved humans in the Philadelphia jail. Incarcerated slaves thus comprised one-third of the 2,000 slaves in the state at the time.[27]

Even the Washingtons' power over servants stretched thin in their own household. Two weeks before Ona and Martha journeyed around the city, the steward of the presidential household confined Wilhelmina Tyser, likely a white indentured servant, to the workhouse for "being frequently Drunk, neglecting her duty, and otherwise misbehaving." A month later, the steward appeared at the workhouse and, "by desire of the President," jailed his servant Martin Cline for two weeks for the same offenses. The challenge by servants to George and Martha's power surely was not lost on enslaved people.[28]

Through similar resistance strategies, many of the enslaved forced their owners to negotiate freedom contracts, often drawn up by the Pennsylvania Abolition Society. By agreeing to serve their master faithfully as an indentured servant for a specific number of years, slaves would afterward gain their liberty. As a result of these actions by the enslaved, the number of Philadelphians held in bondage declined to only fifty-five by 1800, although the gradual emancipation laws had freed almost none of them.[29]

Computer-generated maps help us understand the contours and experiences of the free and enslaved Black community in the city. The institution of racial bondage, ironically, created a racially integrated city in 1790, as evident in the maps showing residences (Figure 5). Slave owners and their 1,805 bondspeople spread almost evenly across the nation's capital, with a slightly heavier concentration of them south of Market Street. While this geographic pattern brought Black and white people into frequent contact, it may have done little to ease racial tensions, especially among whites who refused to see African Americans as equal. Still, as Gary B. Nash found, racial attitudes seemingly softened somewhat during the 1790s, and African Americans, both unfree and free, may have become more confident in dealing with whites. Few of the enslaved lived in separate quarters (as did the nine bound people brought to Philadelphia by the Washingtons), since only a handful of the city's masters possessed more than three slaves. Most of the enslaved found space in stables, attics, or basements, or occupied small, out-of-the-way rooms in their owner's home. A few resided in all-Black households, enjoying somewhat more freedom away from the constant supervision of their racist enslavers.[30]

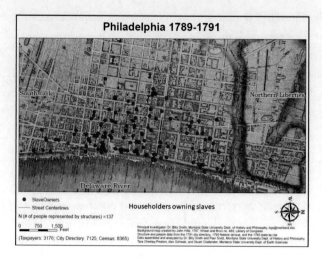

Figure 5. Slaves and Slaveowners, 1789–1791.

Free Black Philadelphians congregated primarily in two areas of the city (Figure 6). A few blocks north of Martha and George's house, a sympathetic white Quaker was willing to rent housing to them in a working-class neighborhood. Most Black people lived in alleys and small side streets. Another group settled along South Sixth Street, creating what would become a central neighborhood for Black Philadelphians. When Jones opened the African Church in 1794 at South Fifth and Adelphi Streets, they selected a spot in the middle of where most free Black householders lived. The church became the center of African American life in this neighborhood and throughout the city.[31]

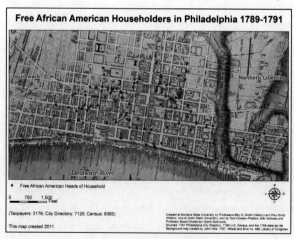

Figure 6. Free Black Householders, 1789–1791.

Many free African Americans found lodging in large all-Black households containing between six and fifteen people. These households lined South Fifth Street in 1790 and, a decade later, South Seventh and Eighth Streets as well. Free African Americans probably preferred to live in groups, partly to save money, but also for self-protection as well as to shield fugitive slaves. Tellingly, these houses were located near where several major roads entered the city. Escapees from the South and the West often used these routes to freedom, and they could hide, quickly, in Black households near the roads. Not surprisingly, since they wanted to hide runaways from slave catchers and the gaze of white people, the inhabitants of these households often refused to provide their names or other information to white census takers in 1800. Census takers thus listed almost all of the householders simply as "Blacks," which was unusual in other parts of the city.[32]

As Ona and Martha neared the museum, they may have had yellow fever on their mind. Only a year previously, the disease had attacked the city. Would it return? The 1793 epidemic was one of the most important events in the new nation, as we can appreciate today as the world endures another pandemic. It appalled many Americans who were optimistic about the future of the country. The mortality was ghastly, but the inhumanity on display, as fearful family members abandoned sick relatives, was equally horrifying. In addition, this epidemic was just the beginning. For the next dozen years, yellow fever epidemics recurred, sweeping up and down the East Coast, destroying the lives of thousands of people in every major American port city.

However, it was also a time of some optimism, when Philadelphians, especially African Americans, jeopardized and often forfeited their lives to save the nation's capital city. Computer-generated maps (see Figures 3 and 6) help us analyze the event more deeply and to evaluate both the praise and the racist criticism leveled at the city's Black community.

It started in late July 1793 in a brothel near a pier in the northern part of the city. Two mariners, mostly likely from the ship *Hankey* or one of the other vessels that had arrived a few days earlier from the West Indies, had rented a room at the "disorderly house." A violent fever quickly killed one of the sailors. An English boarder in the house shivered with an elevated temperature, vomited a black substance, and died a few days later. Mrs. Parkinson, an Irish lodger (perhaps a prostitute), suffered with sunken eyes, jaundiced skin, and blood trickling from her nose and mouth for a week before she expired. Both brothel owners died, as did the second mariner and several next-door neighbors.[33]

All these fatalities in such a brief time attracted the attention of Dr. Benjamin Rush, the most distinguished physician in the new nation. (He also was a neighbor of Elizabeth Powel and Susanna Cook, both discussed previously.) After visiting a few ailing folks along the docks, he announced in late August that yellow fever now stalked the city's streets. During the next three months, the disease killed more than 5,000 people—one out of every ten Philadelphia residents. Not until the late nineteenth century did physicians understand that infected *Aedes aegypti* mosquitoes were the source of all this human misery.[34]

Philadelphians fled in panic. George and Martha bolted to Mount Vernon on September 10, taking Ona with them—likely pleasing Ona, as she was able to visit her family. "So great was the general terror," the newspaper printer Mathew Carey noted, "that for some weeks, carts, wagons, coaches, and [riding] chairs, were almost constantly transporting families and furniture to the country in every direction." At least one-third of the city's inhabitants abandoned their homes. Thomas Jefferson and virtually every other prominent federal leader numbered among the refugees from Philadelphia. State and city officials likewise joined the flight. Government at all levels ceased to function. By mid-September, Mayor Matthew Clarkson was the sole elected city administrator remaining in the city.[35]

In desperation, Clarkson appealed directly to the ordinary citizens of Philadelphia to help. The most pressing needs were nurses to care for the sick, cartmen to haul away bodies piling up in the streets and houses, and gravediggers to bury the bodies. However, everybody feared these duties were too dangerous, since they involved direct contact with the supposed sources of infection.

Even though they were the most despised and disadvantaged residents solely for the color of their skin, Black Philadelphians shouldered the moral responsibility of aiding their neighbors. After a banquet celebrating the roof-raising of the first free Black church in North America, members of the congregation learned about the mayor's plea for help. In conjunction with the Free African Society—an organization founded in 1787 that emphasized self-determination by choosing the name "African"—they volunteered their services. Two clergymen, Absalom Jones and Richard Allen, assumed leadership. When they visited City Hall, the mayor responded enthusiastically to their proposal. He even agreed to free Black prisoners in the Walnut Street Jail—most of them confined for fleeing or resisting racial bondage—if they would help rescue the city.[36]

Jones and Allen, along with William Grey, another leader of the Free African Society, placed ads in newspapers announcing that Black Philadelphians stood ready to care for the sick and collect and bury the dead. Members of the church and the Free African Society "set out to see where we could be useful." In groups of two, they walked the streets every day, stopping to see who needed help. For the next several months, African Americans, both free and enslaved, cared for the stricken, carted the ill to the hospital and the dead to the cemetery, organized workers to dig graves, and interred the dead. They also acted as constables by patrolling the streets, guarding abandoned properties, apprehending looters, and keeping order amid chaos. For the first time in its history, Black people wielded enormous public authority in the United States.[37]

During the epidemic, Black Philadelphians were comparable to the much-admired health care workers who treat COVID-19 patients in our own time, risking their own well-being. Jones, Allen, Grey, and others worked tenaciously themselves while supervising a large group of others willing to help. They visited and cared for patients of Dr. Rush, who himself treated more than one hundred sick people a day. Moreover, since hydration is one of the keys to the survival of yellow-fever patients, nurses saved numerous lives.[38]

Black volunteers likewise helped transform the Bush Hill estate (owned by a wealthy lawyer) from a private mansion into a hospital. When authorities first assumed control of the building, it served primarily as a warehouse for sick people on their way to the grave. Lacking beds, medical supplies, food, blankets, doctors, and nurses, it quickly became known as a den of death. Many of the ill refused to go to the hospital during the early weeks of the epidemic, preferring to take their chances at home.[39]

As Black laborers and draymen steadily carted supplies and water to Bush Hill, Anne Saville, a member of the Free African Society, took over the nursing responsibilities, not only caring for individual patients but also organizing the staff, both Blacks and whites. Under her direction, the hospital changed within weeks from "a great human slaughterhouse," according to the supervising doctor, to an institution where most patients survived the disease.[40]

During their duties, volunteers encountered horrifying scenes. They discovered hundreds of corpses alone in homes, reported Jones and Allen, "many of whose friends and relations had left them, died unseen, and unassisted." Some lay "on the floor, without any appearance of their having had even a drink of water for their relief; others were lying on a bed with their clothes on, as if they had come in fatigued, and lain down to rest; some appeared, as if they had fallen dead on the floor, from the positions we found them in."[41]

The encounters with orphans were particularly heartrending. "We found a parent dead and none but little innocent babes to be seen, whose ignorance led them to think their parent was asleep. On account of their situation, and their little prattle, we have been so wounded and our feelings so hurt, that we almost concluded to withdraw from our undertaking." Fear of catching the disease kept white neighbors and kin from offering help, sometimes to the extent that it gave the "appearance of barbarity." When possible, the humanitarian patrols "picked up little children that were wandering they knew not where, and took them to the orphan house."[42]

As they exposed themselves to the disease by going into homes around the city, especially those near the Delaware River, where the infection was most intense, many African Americans began to sicken and die. Dr. Rush had assured them that yellow fever "passes by persons of your color." However, except for those few who had immunity from growing up in tropical West Africa and contracting the disease during childhood, Black Philadelphians possessed no biological resistance to yellow fever. To draw attention to the sacrifice of the African American community, Allen and Jones cited the increase in burials: "In 1792, there were 67 of our color buried, and in 1793 it amounted to 305; thus the burials among us have increased more than fourfold." They concluded that just "as many colored people died in proportion as others."[43]

Mapping the residents of the city during the 1790s confirms Allen and Jones's contention about the unusually high mortality endured by Black Philadelphians. Figure 3 records higher and lower concentrations of deaths caused by the disease. In darker red areas, along the northern wharves and in a crooked line along Dock Creek, between 20 and 67 percent of the residents died. In the middle and western portions of the city, however, deaths were much fewer. The reason for this disparity was the range of the mosquitoes that spread the virus. The *Aedes aegypti* fly fewer than 100 yards in their lifetime, meaning that after they were introduced along the wharves by newly arriving ships, they fed primarily on people living within a few blocks of the Delaware River. However, as is evident in Figure 6, most free African American householders congregated in the middle or western edge of the city, the safest neighborhoods suffering the least mortality during the epidemic. As Black people volunteered to nurse and bury infected victims of the disease, however, they walked the streets near the wharves and Dock Creek, exposing themselves disproportionately to the diminutive denizens of death. Their higher mortality almost surely resulted from their selfless commitment to the greater good.

After the epidemic, many white people praised Black Philadelphians' invaluable service to the city. Both Mayor Clarkson and Dr. Rush commended African Americans for their work. Other white citizens agreed. As Isaac Heston noted appreciatively, "I don't know what the people would do if it was not for the Negroes, as they are the Principal nurses."[44]

Racism would devise its own interpretation, however. In his popular instant history of the epidemic, the prominent printer Mathew Carey accused Black nurses and gravediggers of extorting money for their services. In virtually all epidemics throughout the previous century, caretakers had drawn criticism for ineptitude, thievery, and neglect of their patients. This attack was different, however, since it was racially based. Black leaders were appalled to see their community excoriated in one of their finest hours. Moreover, if this was the reaction to their heroic sacrifices, then what hope did they have for gaining acceptance and some measure of equality from the larger white community?[45]

An outraged Allen and Jones responded to Carey's censure, writing a remarkable pamphlet, *A Narrative of the Proceedings of the Black People, during the Late Awful Calamity in Philadelphia in the Year 1793*. The document provided an extraordinary eyewitness report of the conduct of one of the earliest free Black communities. Even more important, it also publicly articulated the anger of many Black people not only toward Carey but also toward the wider institution of slavery. These feelings had never previously found their way into print in early America.

Since Carey's account praised Jones and Allen by name, the two ministers might easily have decided not to reply to his criticism of other African Americans. Their heated response indicates that they identified deeply with their community, believed that they needed to defend its reputation, and desired to establish an African American voice independent of the control of whites. Carey's critique also required a response because it undermined arguments that the behavior of Blacks during the epidemic demonstrated their rights to equality and full citizenship.

The epidemic thus provided the first platform for Black Americans to critique slavery in a public forum. Jones and Allen pointed out that slaves were not content with their lot, contrary to what many whites believed. Were "we to attempt to plead with our masters, it would be deemed insolence," the authors explained. "We do not wish to make you angry, but excite your attention to consider, how hateful slavery is in the sight of that God, who hath destroyed kings and princes, for their oppression of the poor slaves." Jones and Allen also warned whites of the danger inherent in keeping people in bondage. North American slaves, like their contemporary counterparts in St. Domingue, might rebel and slay their owners.[46]

Jones and Allen also addressed other African Americans. As Christian ministers, the authors exhorted slaves to take solace in religion and to love their masters regardless of their misdeeds. Individuals in bondage, they urged, should try to convince their owners to grant them an opportunity to gain freedom. The two ministers, along with thousands of other enslaved persons, had achieved their liberty through self-purchase or individual manumission during the earlier decade. They advocated the same avenue for others.[47]

Regardless of Carey's criticism, the laudable behavior of African Americans during the 1793 epidemic helped soften the racial attitudes of many white Philadelphians during the 1790s. "We have been beholden to the poor; to the despised Blacks, for nurses to attend the sick," read the report of the Committee to Alleviate Suffering, "as if Providence were determined to convince us that they are equally the objects of His care, with ourselves."[48]

Still, the larger society ultimately refused to embrace Blacks as either citizens or equals. Carey's original criticism, coupled with the obvious fact that Blacks did *not* enjoy a special immunity to yellow fever, discouraged many African Americans from attending the sick in subsequent epidemics in the city during the next decade. As discouraged Black people withdrew from the fight against the disease, the city's mortality rose even higher during some subsequent outbreaks.

Martha and Ona arrived at their destination at the museum of Charles Willson Peale at South Third Street and Lombard. Martha knew Peale, who painted her and her husband several times along with numerous prominent figures in the late eighteenth century. His Philadelphia museum, founded in 1784, evolved from Peale's display in his house of his paintings and miniatures of revolutionary war heroes. Peale, a representative of the Enlightenment, gradually added other artifacts from nature and from other cultures, hoping the gallery would help "instruct the mind and sow the seeds of Virtue" in the new nation. When the two women arrived, Peale was in the process of moving his museum to the American Philosophical Society next to the Pennsylvania State House (now Independence Hall). The museum would remain popular and stay open for another half century.[49]

Peale sired seventeen children by three wives. Some of the boys became famous painters, thereby creating the preeminent artistic family in America in the early nineteenth century. Daughters, of course, were highly discouraged from becoming or not permitted to become artists, regardless of their talent. As were slaves. Peale had a complex relationship with slavery and with African Americans. While voting for the 1780 Pennsylvania Gradual Emancipation Act, he still owned slaves. Like his friend Thomas Jefferson, Peale opposed slavery primarily because of the harmful impact on white people, since it supposedly made masters lazy and took jobs away from poorer whites. Peale seems to have been unconcerned with how slavery severely damaged the lives of slaves themselves.[50]

In 1786, for unclear reasons, Peale freed a mixed-race slave couple, Lucy and Scarborough, whom he had owned for a decade. However, he continued to enslave their young son Moses Williams, which undoubtedly troubled his parents greatly. Peale did not free Moses until he reached age twenty-seven, only one year before the law dictated. Had Martha paid the museum's entrance fee for Ona, they would have seen fourteen-year-old Williams tending the items in the museum. He was a budding artist and, had he been white or a son of Peale, he may have become another famous painter. Without that advantage, Williams became an expert at cutting out paper profiles of visitors to the museum for a small fee. Making thousands of silhouettes working at the museum for decades after gaining his freedom, he was able to earn a modest living in the early decades of the nineteenth century.[51]

In 1787, Peale designed and engraved *The Accident in Lombard Street* as an advertisement for his museum. Peale's combination residence and gallery is evident on the southwest corner on the left of the image (see Figure 7). This is one of the first paintings in early America of African Americans participating in an ordinary daily event. The Black chimney sweeps at the forefront laugh at the white girl who accidentally dropped a pie as she brought it home from the bakery. Subsequently, Peale and his son Rembrandt painted the Reverends Absalom Jones and Richard Allen and an ex-slave, Yarrow Mamout, in a very respectful fashion. Making a handful of African Americans the subject of their paintings was quite unusual for white artists at the time.[52]

Figure 7. Charles Willson Peale, *The accident in Lombard Street Philadelphia*. Nat Archives; https://www.loc.gov/pictures/item/93508047/

The *Accident in Lombard Street* also portrays the block of houses west of Peale's museum, another rarity at this early date. Modern mapping techniques combined with traditional research allowed my team of scholars to identify the people who lived in those structures. The householders in the block were ethnically diverse, much like the rest of the city. Blacks were increasingly moving into the area as Jones and Allen established churches nearby. In 1794, five Black Philadelphians, including Catherine Smith, lived together in a house across the street from the museum and a few doors west. A few years earlier, a newspaper advertisement for a runaway slave accused Smith of harboring a fugitive, her own son, Cuff. He initially fled his Philadelphia owner in 1790. A constable apprehended and incarcerated him on January 1, 1791, and then kept him in the workhouse for a month until he was claimed by his master. Cuff fled for freedom several more times before landing in jail once again in May 1791. However, this time he renamed himself Henry, a common practice among Blacks when they claimed their liberty and created a new identity. Negotiating with his master while in the workhouse, Henry was able to bargain successfully for a contract as a bound servant for a set number of years of faithful service, after which he would become free. As noted previously, this was a relatively common experience at the end of the eighteenth century in Pennsylvania and other northern states, as slaves brought an end to slavery much more quickly than state legislatures had directed.[53]

While the Washingtons "were packing up to go to Virginia," Ona told an abolitionist newspaper interviewer fifty years later, "I was packing to go, I didn't know where; for I knew that if I went back to Virginia, I should never get my liberty." On May 21, 1796, about twenty-two months after our fictional walk, Ona took decisive action to declare her freedom. She simply walked out the door while the Washingtons "were eating dinner."[54] It was a bold, calculated move, an absolute refusal to spend the rest of her life in bondage. The odds of failure were significant for all runaways and for their families and friends left vulnerable to vindictiveness from angry masters. Anyone who helped them also faced stiff penalties. Ona's case was even more extreme; she had the audacity to challenge the most powerful man in the nation.

We can only admire her courage, her planning, and the assistance provided by members of the city's African American community. "I had friends among the colored people of Philadelphia," Ona said, and "had my things carried there beforehand."[55] She spent several weeks concealed by her friends in the city, and then was helped on board the *Nancy*, perhaps by a Black mariner or dockworker, just before the ship weighed anchor for Portsmouth, New Hampshire. Overheard conversations as she served in the presidential household may have shaped her choice of destination. Black sailors in Philadelphia likewise knew that Portsmouth had a vibrant free African American community, among whom she might be able to establish a new life and to avoid capture by the slave catchers Washington would send after her.[56]

Frederick Kitt, the steward of the president's house, paid for an advertisement in the newspaper:

Absconded from the household of the President of the United States, ONEY JUDGE, a light mulatto girl, much freckled, with very Black eyes and bushy hair. She is of middle stature, slender, and delicately formed, about 20 years of age . . .. As there was no suspicion of her going off, nor no provocation to do so, it is not easy to conjecture whither she has gone, or fully, what her design is . . .. Ten dollars will be paid to any person who will bring her home.[57]

Neither Martha nor George could shed William Blake's "mind-forg'd manacles" noted at the beginning of this essay. They thought that Ona had "no provocation," and they could not understand "her design." Completely blind to Ona's desire for freedom, they raged at "the ingratitude of the girl, who was brought up & treated more like a child than a servant." They seethed at all the "ungrateful" and "inhuman" fugitives who defied their authority. Martha captured the indignation felt by many other masters seeking runaways: "the Blacks are so bad in their nature that they have not the least gratitude for the kindness that may be shewed them." George stated his feelings succinctly: "I abominate" runaway slaves.[58]

The Washingtons discovered Ona's whereabouts and pursued her relentlessly. They sent slave catchers and intermediaries (some of them government agents) to bargain for her voluntary return or, if that failed, to use more forceful methods. If she would return, the Washingtons assured her through his friend, then "she could be freed on their decease."

Ona demurred, saying she would return to Mount Vernon (in part to be near her family), but only if she gained her freedom immediately. "To enter into such a compromise with *her*," the furious ex-President replied, "is totally inadmissible." Like many masters, George pursued Ona for as long as he lived.[59]

After talking with Ona, one negotiator conveyed that "a thirst for complete freedom . . .. had been her only motive for absconding." Ona proclaimed that she would rather suffer death than return to slavery. In her final reply to the Washingtons, she stated it simply: "I am free now and choose to remain so."[60]

Ona married John Staines, a mariner, had three children, struggled with poverty, since working as a seamstress and domestic servant paid little, and lived a long *free* life in Portsmouth and environs, dying in 1848. The Washingtons sent agents to apprehend her for years, until George's death. With her own good judgment and the help of sympathetic people, both Black and white, she evaded every one of them.[61]

During the 1790s, the United States faced numerous inequalities as well as terrible epidemics, much like our own times. Slavery was the preeminent "inequality" of the day, and it would grow ever more important during the next seven decades. Admirably, many Philadelphians challenged the system of racial bondage, perhaps echoed in the Black Lives Matter movement today. Ona endangered her life for freedom. The Pennsylvania Abolition Society worked with members of the Black community to combat slavery and racism and to assist fugitives from slavery. Meanwhile, Absalom Jones, Richard Allen, Anne Saville, Benjamin Rush, and many other ordinary people endangered themselves to save patients afflicted with yellow fever. Gender inequality continued, of course, but a few women like Elizabeth Powel broke norms by speaking out about revolutionary ideals and against racial bondage. Other women, like Ona Judge, took control of their own lives. While they did not solve the problems of their era, they acted, improved the lives of numerous Americans, and set foundations on which future generations might build a more equal society. It serves as a lesson for our own times.

Notes

1. William Blake, *Songs of Innocence and Experience* (London, 1794). I thank Professor Michelle Maskiell, a fellow historian, for her valuable help with this essay.

2. "To George Washington from John Hills, 26 February 1796," *Founders Online*, National Archives, https://founders.archives.gov/documents/Washington/05-19-02-0402. Information about Hills is from computer searches of Philadelphia newspapers as well as from "To Alexander Hamilton from James McHenry, 6 June 1798," *Founders Online*, National Archives, https://founders.archives.gov/documents/Hamilton/01-21-02-0273. See also Adam E. Zielinski, "Rediscovering British Surveyor John Hills," *Journal of the American Revolution*, Volume 2018, https://allthingsliberty.com/2018/12/rediscovering-british-surveyor-john-hills/.

3. An advertisement seeking subscribers first appeared in the *Federal Gazette*, March 3, 1790; the completed map was first advertised in *Claypoole's American Daily Advertiser*, April 22, 1797. Subsequent advertisements selling the map appeared in a host

of newspapers published in Philadelphia. On the wages of laborers, see Billy G. Smith, *The "Lower Sort": Philadelphia's Laboring People, 1750–1800* (Ithaca: Cornell University Press, 1990), chapter 4.

4. A team of scholars led by Dr. Paul Sivitz and me computerized information from a host of city directories, tax lists, censuses, and newspapers from early national Philadelphia. We coordinated with a team of Geographic Information Systems (GIS) specialists, led by Professor Stuart Challender, to create computerized maps of the city using the 1796 map by John Hills as the base. A detailed description of the sources and methods using GIS technology in this essay is available at http://mappinghistoricphiladelphia.org/appendix-to-flaneur.html. We have made our datasets available to share at https://repository.upenn.edu.

5. Most of the information about Ona Judge in this essay is gleaned from the marvelous book by Erica Armstrong Dunbar, *Never Caught: The Washingtons' Relentless Pursuit of Their Runaway Slave, Ona Judge* (New York: Simon and Schuster, 2017). Judge was a *dower* slave who belonged to Martha's Custis family rather than to George Washington, but he would be responsible for reimbursing the estate if Ona escaped.

6. The literature on Martha Washington is vast. A starting point for the Washingtons and slavery is Henry Wiencek, *An Imperfect God: George Washington, His Slaves, and the Creation of America* (New York: Farrar, Straus and Giroux, 2003), 327–332. See also Helen Bryan, *Martha Washington: First Lady of Liberty* (New York: Wiley, 2002).

7. Ona and Martha's excursion, though imaginary, may well have occurred while the two women lived in the city. Martha and George visited the museum on more than one occasion, and it was a popular destination for Philadelphians who could afford the entrance fee. At least once, Martha had given Ona money to attend the circus, and she may have been willing to buy a museum ticket for Ona. Regardless, Martha surely wanted her personal servant to attend to her needs (Dunbar, *Never Caught*). While the walk through the city taken by Ona and Martha is hypothetical, the people and places all draw on primary and secondary sources. To avoid making the prose even more burdensome than it is in this essay, I have intentionally used assertive language to describe their journey.

8. In her extensive journal, Elizabeth Drinker noted that it rained on July 17, 1794; Henry D. Biddle, ed., *Excerpts from the Diary of Elizabeth Drinker* (Philadelphia, 1889), 232.

9. On the Black community and the founding of the churches, see Gary B. Nash, *Forging Freedom: The Formation of Philadelphia's Black Community, 1720–1840* (Cambridge, Mass.: Harvard University Press, 1991); and Richard S. Newman, *Freedom's Prophet: Bishop Richard Allen, the A.M.E. Church and the Black Founding Fathers* (New York: NYU Press, 2008).

10. George Washington referred to Joe (Richardson) as "postillion Joe." When Joe's wife and their children gained their freedom after Washington's death, the family took the last name Richardson. Edward Lawler, Jr., "Joe (Richardson)," *The President's House in Philadelphia*, https://www.ushistory.org/presidentshouse/slaves/joe.php. Driving regulations are in John C. Lowber, *Ordinances of the Corporation of the City of Philadelphia* (Philadelphia, 1812), 123–124.

11. John Hills noted that Roberts sold the map; *Claypoole's American Daily Advertiser*, April 22, 1797. Roberts also appears in the 1795 city directory; Edmund Hogan, *The Prospect of Philadelphia* (Philadelphia: Bailey, 1795). Quotes from *Moreau de St. Mery's American Journey, 1793–1798*, ed. and trans. Kenneth Roberts and Anna M. Roberts (Garden City, N.Y.: Doubleday, 1947), 25.

12. Roberts and Roberts, *St. Mery's American Journey*, 112. Britton appeared in the Vagrancy Docket, January 16, 1794, Philadelphia City Archives. Public punishments are described in Negley K. Teeters, *The Cradle of the Penitentiary: The Walnut Street Jail at Philadelphia* (Philadelphia: n.p., 1955).

13. Billy G. Smith and Paul Sivitz, "Identifying and Mapping Ethnicity in Philadelphia in the Early Republic," *Pennsylvania Magazine of History & Biography*, 140: no. 3 (October 2016), 393–411.

14. Susanna Cook's life is reconstructed from a host of city records; see Smith, *The "Lower Sort,"* 27–39. On the growth of the incarcerated population, see Simon Newman and Billy G. Smith, "Incarcerated Innocents: Inmates, Conditions, and Survival Strategies in Philadelphia's Almshouse and Workhouse," in Richard Bell and Michele Tartar, eds., *Buried Lives: Incarcerated in America* (Athens, Ga.: University of Georgia Press, 2012), 60–84.

15. Bryan, *Martha Washington*, 281–285, 312–316.

16. David W. Maxey, "A Portrait of Elizabeth Willing Powel (1743–1830)," *Transactions of the American Philosophical Society*, 94: no. 4 (2006), quotes on 29–30.

17. Maxey, "Portrait of Elizabeth Willing Powel," 30.

18. Although the names of many streets remain the same today, house numbers in early national Philadelphia were considerably different than in the present. Structures were numbered consecutively across streets, meaning that 115 High Street was on one corner and across the street was 117 High Street. Philadelphia did not establish a modern system of numbering by block (100, 200, etc.) until the nineteenth century.

19. The federal tax lists of 1798 record the size of property and structures in early national Philadelphia; Wilbur J. McElwain, Ed., *United States Direct Tax of 1798: Tax List for the City of Philadelphia* (Bowie, Md.: Heritage, 1999).

20. Other historians have detected, incorrectly from my perspective, a lack of residential and class differentiation. See, for example, Dale Upton, *Another City: Urban Life and Urban Spaces in the New American Republic* (New Haven, Conn.: Yale University Press, 2008); Stuart M. Blumin, *The Emergence of the Middle Class: Social Experience in the American City, 1760–1900* (Cambridge, United Kingdom: Cambridge University Press, 1989).

21. Pancoast's election is recorded in *The Philadelphia Gazette & Universal Daily Advertiser*, March 12, 1795. On the Abolition Society, see Nash, *Forging Freedom*; Newman, *Freedom's Prophet*.

22. Paul J. Polgar, *Standard-Bearers of Equality: America's First Abolition Movement* (Chapel Hill, N.C.: University of North Carolina Press, 2019).

23. Fritz Hirschfeld, *George Washington and Slavery: A Documentary Portrayal* (Columbia, Mo.: University of Missouri Press, 1997), 187–188. Quote from the letter

"From George Washington to Tobias Lear, 12 April 1791," *Founders Online,* National Archives, https://founders.archives.gov/documents/Washington/05-08-02-0062. Martha's visit to Trenton is noted at "Timeline of Martha Washington," https://www.mountvernon.org/george-washington/martha-washington/timeline.

24. "From George Washington to Tobias Lear, 12 April 1791," *Founders Online,* National Archives, https://founders.archives.gov/documents/Washington/05-08-02-0062.

25. Emma J. Lapsansky-Werner, "Teamed up with the PAS: Images of Black Philadelphians," *Pennsylvania Legacies,* 5: no. 2 (November 2005), 11–15.

26. Newman, *Freedom's Prophet.* On runaways in Pennsylvania and New Jersey, see Billy G. Smith and Richard Wojtowicz, *Blacks Who Stole Themselves: Advertisements for Runaways in the Pennsylvania Gazette, 1728–1790* (Philadelphia: University of Pennsylvania Press, 1989).

27. On the negotiations for freedom, see Newman and Smith, "Incarcerated Innocents."

28. Vagrancy Docket, July 2 and August 6, 1794, Philadelphia City Archives.

29. Polgar, *Standard-Bearers of Equality*; Gary B. Nash and Jean R. Soderlund, *Freedom by Degrees: Emancipation in Pennsylvania and its Aftermath* (New York: Oxford University Press, 1991). *Also* see Box 4A: Manumissions, Indentures and Other Legal Papers, Papers of the Pennsylvania Abolition Society, Historical Society of Pennsylvania.

30. Nash, *Forging Freedom*; Smith, *Lower Sort,* chapter 7.

31. Nash, *Forging Freedom,* 130–131.

32. The information here is based on my detailed analysis of the 1790 and 1800 censuses, as described at http://mappinghistoricphiladelphia.org/appendix-to-flaneur.html.

33. Contemporaries agreed on the neighborhood where the epidemic began, even as they disagreed about its cause; see the city's official report, *An Account of the Rise, Progress, and Termination of the Malignant Fever Lately Prevalent in Philadelphia* (Philadelphia, 1794); Mathew Carey, *A Short Account of the Malignant Fever, Lately Prevalent in Philadelphia* (Philadelphia: Carey, 1794). Also see Billy G. Smith, *Ship of Death: A Voyage that Changed the Atlantic World* (New Haven, Conn.: Yale University Press, 2013), chapters 8 and 9.

34. Benjamin Rush, *An Account of the Bilious Remitting Yellow Fever, as it Appeared in the City of Philadelphia, in the Year 1793* (Philadelphia: Dobson, 1794), 8–11.

35. Mathew Carey, *A Desultory Account of the Yellow Fever, Prevalent in Philadelphia, and of the Present State of the City* (Philadelphia: Carey, October 16, 1793), 2, 5, 27.

36 Phillip Lapsansky, "'Abigail, a Negress': The Role and the Legacy of African Americans in the Yellow Fever Epidemic," in *'A Melancholy Scene of Devastation': The Public Response to the 1793 Philadelphia Yellow Fever Epidemic,* eds. J. Worth Estes and Billy G. Smith (Philadelphia: Science History Publications, 1997), 61–65.

37. Nash, *Forging Freedom,* 122; Absalom Jones and Richard Allen, *A Narrative of the Proceedings of the Black People, During the Late Awful Calamity in Philadelphia in the Year 1793* (Philadelphia: William W. Woodward, 1794), 18.

38. Smith, *Ship of Death,* chapter 9.

39. Smith, *Ship of Death.*

40. On Anne Saville, see the first-hand account by Dr. Jean Devèze, *An Enquiry into, and Observations upon the Causes and Effects of the Epidemic Disease, which Raged in Philadelphia from the Month of August till Towards the Middle of December, 1793* (Philadelphia, 1794), 54–56.

41. Jones and Allen, *Narrative of the Proceedings*, 18.

42. Jones and Allen, *Narrative of the Proceedings*, 19–20.

43. Jones and Allen, *Narrative of the Proceedings*, 16.

44. Edwin B. Bronner, ed., "Letter from a Yellow Fever Victim: Philadelphia, 1793," *Pennsylvania Magazine of History and Biography* 86 (1962), 206.

45. Carey, *A Desultory Account*, 41. A subsequent account of the 1797 epidemic also demeaned black conduct; Richard Folwell, *Short History of the Yellow Fever, that Broke Out in the City of Philadelphia, in July, 1797* (Philadelphia: Folwell, 1797), 34.

46. Jones and Allen, *A Narrative of the Proceedings*, 24–25.

47. Nash, *Forging Freedom,* 174–175; Nash and Soderlund, *Freedom by Degrees,* 131–132, 180.

48. *Minutes of the Proceedings of the Committee . . . to Alleviate the Sufferings of the Afflicted with the Malignant Fever Prevalent in the City and its Vicinity* (Philadelphia: Aiken & Son, 1794).

49. Karie Diethorn, "Peale's Philadelphia Museum," *The Encyclopedia of Greater Philadelphia*, https://philadelphiaencyclopedia.org/archive/peales-philadelphia-museum.

50. Nash, *Forging Freedom*, 85–86.

51. Gwendolyn DuBois Shaw, "'Moses Williams, Cutter of Profiles': Silhouettes and African American Identity in the Early Republic," *Proceedings of the American Philosophical Society*, 149: no. 1 (March 2005), 24–27.

52. The images are accessible at https://librarycompany.org/blackfounders/section5.htm.

53. The story and residential location of Catherine and Henry Smith is recreated from the following sources: an advertisement for a runaway slave in the *Pennsylvania Packet,* December 14, 1790; entries in the Vagrancy Docket, Philadelphia City Archives, for Cuff on January 1, 1791 and for Henry on May 28, 1791; and Clement Biddle, *The Philadelphia Directory 1791* (Philadelphia, 1791). On Black people changing their names to match new identities, see Nash, *Forging Freedom,* 79–88.

54. *The Granite Freeman, Concord, New Hampshire* (May 22, 1845), reprinted at https://www.ushistory.org/presidentshouse/slaves/oneyinterview.php.

55. *Ibid.*

56. The mother of the president's secretary (who was antislavery) became good friends with Martha Washington and visited her often in Philadelphia. She likely talked about her hometown.

57. *The Philadelphia Gazette & Universal Daily Advertiser*, May 24, 1796.

58. "From George Washington to John Francis Mercer, 6 November 1786," *Founders Online,* National Archives, https://founders.archives.gov/documents/

Washington/04-04-02-0302; and "From George Washington to Oliver Wolcott, Jr., 1 September 1796," *Founders Online,* National Archives, https://founders.archives.gov/documents/Washington/99-01-02-00910. Martha Washington as quoted in Wiencek, *An Imperfect God,* 326–332.

    59. As quoted in Wiencek, *An Imperfect God,* 327–328, 334.

    60. Wiencek, *An Imperfect God,* 332–334.

    61. On Ona's life as a free person, see Dunbar, *Never Caught.*

Index

Note: Page numbers followed "*f*" indicate figures.